# STORM
# WORLD

ALSO BY
**CHRIS MOONEY**

*The Republican War on Science*

# CHRIS MOONEY

# STORM WORLD

## HURRICANES, POLITICS, AND THE BATTLE OVER GLOBAL WARMING

HARCOURT, INC.
Orlando   Austin   New York   San Diego   Toronto   London

www.HarcourtBooks.com

Library of Congress Cataloging-in-Publication Data
Mooney, Chris (Chris C.)
Storm world: hurricanes, politics, and the battle over
global warming/[Chris Mooney].—1st ed.
p. cm.
Includes bibliographical references and index.
1. Hurricanes. 2. Hurricanes—Social aspects.
3. Global warming—Political aspects. 4. Climatology. I. Title.
QC944.M66 2007
363.738'74—dc22 2007009742
ISBN 978-0-15-101287-9

Text set in Adobe Garamond
Designed by Linda Lockowitz

Printed in the United States of America

First edition
A C E G I K J H F D B

# CONTENTS

PART III

# STORM WORLD

"Meteorology has ever been an apple of contention, as if the violent commotions of the atmosphere induced a sympathetic effect on the minds of those who have attempted to study them."

—Smithsonian secretary Joseph Henry, U.S. Patent Office, *Annual Report, Agricultural,* 1858

# 6229 Memphis Street

On the day after Christmas 2005, four months after Hurricane Katrina swamped it with polluted water, the neighborhood of Lakeview, New Orleans, showed only the faintest signs of life. Piles of debris sat on each curbside, loose dogs roamed the streets, and the vegetation everywhere was dead. The houses remained almost entirely uninhabited. Some were now hollow shells, gutted by work crews; others still sported interiors that looked as though they had been ransacked by the Creature from the Black Lagoon—collapsed floors, stinking refrigerators, disintegrating piles of paper, and huge tapestries of mold on the walls.

My mother's house was one of these. A tree had crashed across the backyard, knocking down a flimsy fence. A sewing machine protruded from beneath a pile of boards. On the side of the house rescue crews had painted a red mark; beneath it had lain the carcass of Mewls, a feral cat my mother had been feeding. Inside, a clock still ticked and the smoke alarm let out occasional bleeps. The floors were spongy, especially in the hallway, which had become a graveyard of congealing paper after a bookcase collapsed. Everything was caked with mud and grime. "Substantially damaged" is how the city bureaucrats, with their knack for understatement, described it.

Yet despite countless scenes like this, many residents of Lakeview had vowed to return and rebuild their neighborhood. They had grown up in this safe, conservative Catholic community, and couldn't imagine living anywhere else. Outside one battered church a sign read, "Behold, I am making all things new"—and that's just what these New Orleanians planned to do. "ReNew Orleans" reads the popular T-shirt in town, capturing a passionate sense of devotion to the city and its restoration.

That devotion came across journalistically on Christmas Day 2005—the day before my mother, sister, and I ventured into Lakeview to see the destruction first-hand—when the local *Times-Picayune* ran a front-page feature article entitled "What Will New Orleans Look Like Five Years From Now?" Starry-eyed plans for light rail, raised houses, and new green spaces were described, but my eyes lingered on a sentence dropped in toward the end: "Surrounding it all is a dependable Category 3 levee system...." That hardly sounded like planning for the worst-case scenario. Katrina was a mid-range Category 3 storm on the Saffir-Simpson hurricane scale\*, with maximum sustained winds estimated at about 120 miles per hour, when it made its final landfall near the Louisiana-Mississippi border. Winds experienced in New Orleans weren't even at Category 3 strength, since the storm didn't hit the city directly. It *missed.*

Knowing this, I worried in late 2005 that those charged with rebuilding New Orleans might be paying inadequate attention to the possibility of an even worse hurricane disaster at some point in the future. Not only could a stronger storm come in any season. Considerable, if hotly disputed, evidence suggests we may be entering a world in which, thanks to human-induced global warming, the average hurricane itself becomes more powerful and deadly. The threat to New Orleans—and to other vulnerable coastal cities like Miami, Tampa Bay, Houston, Charleston, Providence, New York, and even possibly San Diego—could be steadily rising, along with the sea levels that further amplify hurricane risks.

Out of that sense of concern—which grew more seasoned and nuanced as I traveled to scientific conferences and learned more about hurricanes—arose this book. You might think of it as a homegrown New Orleans science writer's idiosyncratic way of coping. Certainly it is no polemic, no work of alarmism. At least as I write these words in late 2006, our scientific understanding of the hurricane–climate rela-

---

\*See Appendix I.

tionship remains too incomplete to justify such an approach. Instead, as I examined this ongoing debate through the lens of my own concern, I saw staring back at me the story of how a largely unsuspecting group of scientists had been drawn by politics, the media, the weather, and the history of meteorology itself into a situation of tense conflict more typical of political operatives and opposition researchers (although the scientists by and large acquitted themselves more admirably).

Still, this book was inspired by thoughts of my family and friends who lived or who are still living in New Orleans, and is dedicated to them. So, for that matter, was an article I published on May 23, 2005—some hundred days before Katrina formed southeast of the Bahamas—entitled "Thinking Big About Hurricanes: It's Time to Get Serious About Saving New Orleans." But while the piece ricocheted around the Internet after Katrina, it went largely unnoticed at the time of its publication, like many similar calls of warning.

That's all past, though; those remaining in my hometown must consider their future, rather than what might once have been done. I only hope that when they do so they will include global warming as part of the picture—precisely *because of* the considerable scientific uncertainty about just how severe its consequences will be.

At the outset, let me offer a critical point of clarification: *Global warming did not cause Hurricane Katrina, or any other weather disaster.* Or to put it more precisely, we just can't say scientifically that global warming either does or does not "cause" individual weather events. Why? As the climate-scientist writers of RealClimate.org, the leading global-warming blog, observed after Katrina:

> We only have one Earth, and it will follow only one of an infinite number of possible weather sequences. It is impossible to know whether or not this event would have taken place if we had not increased the concentration of greenhouse gases in the atmosphere as much as we have. Weather events will always result from a combination of deterministic factors (including greenhouse gas forcing or slow natural climate cycles) and stochastic factors (pure chance).

To explain the difference between weather and climate, RealClimate.org used the analogy of rolling a die: You never know what's going to come up on any given roll, but over time and across many rolls, you can get a very good sense of the odds (and thus, whether or not the die is loaded).

With this caveat out of the way, we can get to the central issue: whether global warming will strengthen or otherwise change hurricanes in general, even if it can't explain the absolute existence, attributes, or behavior of any single one of them. To determine the answer, scientists have to consider what they think they know about hurricanes and why they intensify; pore over the statistics they've compiled on global hurricanes, summed across the various ocean basins where these storms occur; and then determine whether their theory aligns with the data.

There the debate commences. Resolving it on a purely scientific level would be challenging enough to begin with. And that's without the media klieg lights, the brazen political acts of scientific suppression, and the storms slamming the coasts.

# INTRODUCTION

# "The Party Line"

The worst Atlantic hurricane season on record still hadn't ended when the American Geophysical Union held its fall meeting in San Francisco in December 2005. Twelve thousand scientists packed themselves into the Moscone Center, the city's space-age mall of a conference facility, for lectures on topics such as the massive 2004 Sumatra-Andaman earthquake and the tsunami that it generated, and data beamed from NASA's Mars rovers and the Cassini spacecraft. Many of the presentations were being given on the center's upper levels, and security guards had to police the towering escalators just to prevent overcrowding.

MIT hurricane theorist Kerry Emanuel arrived on this scene riding a swell of fame that few researchers ever experience. A short man with striking blue-green eyes and a slightly surprised smile, Emanuel had just seen his latest work featured in a *Time* magazine cover story and would soon find it rated (along with the work of several colleagues) the top science story of the year by *Discover.* He was averaging five to ten media calls per week. Later, he would be named one of the hundred "Most Influential People of 2006," once again by *Time.* At the American Geophysical Union meeting, Emanuel had been slated to speak following another of *Time*'s most influential: NASA's James Hansen, the nation's best-known climate scientist and the man sometimes dubbed the "father" of global warming.

The science presented at the average American Geophysical Union meeting features a heavy helping of catastrophe. Tornadoes, volcanoes, earthquakes, tsunamis—the proceedings offer a subject roster that Hollywood disaster-movie directors would appreciate. But that December, the cause of destruction at the front of everyone's mind was the strongest and deadliest storm on Earth, a meteorological monstrosity capable of churning out as much power as all the world's electricity generators combined: the tropical cyclone, typhoon, or, as we call it in the United States, the hurricane.

Katrina had wiped out New Orleans just a few months earlier.

On the day of Emanuel's talk—Tuesday, December 6—Hurricane Epsilon whirled on in the North Atlantic some 600 miles southwest of the Azores. The aimless cyclone had already executed a full loop, completely reversing its original westward trajectory, and now began a southwest turn. Epsilon wasn't a particularly strong storm—its maximum sustained winds* peaked at around 85 miles per hour—and it never seriously threatened land. But it was stubborn. Moreover, Epsilon had the distinction of being only the sixth hurricane ever recorded as occurring in the Atlantic during the month of December, as well as the twenty-seventh storm of a seemingly never-ending season—so never-ending, in fact, that forecasters had resorted to Greek letters after pre-assigned storm names—like Katrina, Rita, Wilma— ran out.

At the National Hurricane Center in Miami—a steel-reinforced concrete bunker of a building on the campus of Florida International University that was built to withstand Category 5 hurricanes and whose roof bristles with dishes and antennae—the experts awaited Epsilon's demise. With it, they hoped, would come the official end to the devastating 2005 season, and more than a few sighs of relief.

Traditionally, the hurricane season in the Atlantic basin—which comprises the North Atlantic, the Caribbean Sea, and the Gulf of Mexico—begins on June 1 and ends on November 30. In 2005, however, nature had already toppled such bookends. And now, despite days of

---

*"Maximum sustained winds" are defined as the highest one-minute wind at a height of ten meters (33 feet) from the surface. In a hurricane over water, for obvious reasons, this quantity is more often inferred or estimated than directly measured.

forecasts predicting steady weakening, Epsilon had held on to hurricane strength and even put on a few small bursts of intensification.

"I HAVE RUN OUT OF THINGS TO SAY...AND THIS ONE WILL BE SHORT," wrote Cuban-born forecaster Lixion Avila in an exasperated 4:00 A.M. discussion of the storm's progress, written in the all-caps and heavily elliptical style that remains the standard for weather communiqués.

"EPSILON APPEARS TO STILL BE A HURRICANE...BUT JUST BARELY," wrote forecaster Richard Knabb six hours later.

"THE END IS IN SIGHT," echoed forecaster James Franklin at 10 that evening. "IT REALLY REALLY IS."

By the time Epsilon finally died down—having been for five days a hurricane, a December record—Kerry Emanuel had generated a tempest of his own in San Francisco. Speaking before a crowd of hundreds in one of the largest of the Moscone Center's high-ceilinged conference rooms, the normally cautious and apolitical scientist fired a shot straight at the bosses of government forecasters like Avila, Knabb, and Franklin.

Earlier in the day, the audience had heard the wiry Midwestern climatologist James Hansen warn that global warming could cause the disintegration of the Greenland and West Antarctic ice sheets, triggering rises in sea level sufficient to inundate many of the globe's heavily inhabited coastal areas. After a break, Emanuel launched into a seemingly typical scientific talk, constructed out of PowerPoint images rather than paragraphs. He flashed slides demonstrating that although global tropical cyclone numbers do not show any obvious trend up or down—averaging about eighty to ninety per year in the world's six regularly active ocean basins—storms in the Atlantic and the Northwest Pacific had grown stronger and longer lasting over the past several decades, closely tracking a trend of rising temperatures at the surface of the oceans.

To explain this phenomenon, Emanuel then introduced a series of equations. These probably meant little to the nonscientists in the audience, but to specialists capable of reading the equations as if they were sentences, the message was clear: Increasing hurricane strength is linked to human enhancement of the greenhouse effect.

The Earth's atmosphere contains certain gases, such as carbon dioxide and water vapor, that have a very important property: They absorb infrared or "longwave" radiation and also emit it in all directions. As a result, these gases play a crucial role in regulating the flux of energy to and from the planet. Even as the sun's rays heat the Earth's surface, the Earth also emits radiation in the infrared part of the spectrum, with a longer wavelength than that of visible light. The "greenhouse gases" then absorb some of that outgoing heat radiation (which might otherwise escape into space), warm up, and emit more radiation back down toward the lower atmosphere and the Earth's surface. In the process, these gases keep our planet much warmer than it would be if it lacked an atmosphere.

Through industrial processes such as smokestack and tailpipe emissions, humans have been steadily increasing the concentration of carbon dioxide and other greenhouse gases in the atmosphere. As a result, we've caused additional warming of the Earth's surface, lower atmosphere, and oceans—and that's where hurricanes come into the picture. Since these storms draw their power from the energy stored in tropical ocean waters, warmer seas should (everything else being equal) make them stronger.

This hypothesis—that hurricanes would intensify in a warmer world—had been around at least since 1987, published in that year by Emanuel himself. Theoretically based predictions, however, don't hit you in the gut like hard data. And by 2005, Emanuel was going beyond such predictions. He was saying, it's actually happening.

Anyone could see Emanuel's findings had potentially enormous implications. When they strike land, and especially when they strike places where people live, strong hurricanes cause dramatically more destruction than weak ones. Hurricane damage doesn't simply increase linearly with increasing wind speed; rather, it goes up much more steeply, in part because damaged structures (for example, the roof torn off a house) become missiles flung into other structures. It has been estimated that a land-falling Category 4 or 5 hurricane, with maximum sustained winds greater than 131 miles per hour, causes 64 times as much destruction as a Category 1 storm (winds from 74 to 95 mph) and 256 times as much as a mere tropical storm (winds up to and including 73 mph). Emanuel was telling his audience that we're helping transform more and more hurricanes into monstrous city-smashers. If true, the discovery would rank as one of the most dramatic manifestations yet of human-caused global warming—and perhaps the most terrifying.

Emanuel's scientific message was breathtaking enough, but he took it farther. He showed a slide featuring a statement from the man who was then director of the National Hurricane Center, Max Mayfield, asserting that the dramatic upswing in Atlantic hurricane activity since the year 1995 sprang from "natural fluctuations" and was "not enhanced substantially by global warming." This Emanuel somewhat derisively dubbed the "party line" of the Bush administration's National Oceanic and Atmospheric Administration (NOAA), a branch of the Department of Commerce that includes the hurricane center as well as numerous other scientific and forecasting branches, ranging from the National Climatic Data Center to the National Marine Fisheries Service.

In his next slide, Emanuel juxtaposed the NOAA "party line" with a statement he attributed to an unnamed agency scientist: "I have been told not to speak with reporters about the connection between global warming and hurricanes without prior permission from NOAA management." According to Emanuel, the unidentified scientist worked at the Geophysical Fluid Dynamics Laboratory (GFDL) in Princeton, New Jersey, a hub for research on climate change employing sophisticated computer models of the atmosphere and the oceans. On the one hand, scientists at GFDL have pioneered a cutting-edge hurricane model that the forecasters in Miami rely heavily upon in their day-to-day storm tracking. But GFDL researchers have also taken a much longer view, producing a series of studies similarly suggesting that global warming will increase the strength of the average hurricane over the course of the twenty-first century.

Some in the audience had heard stories about NOAA stifling the ability of its scientists to speak freely to the media about hurricanes and global warming, or about global warming in general. They had also seen an agency publication claim a "consensus" among its hurricane specialists on this question, asserting that they accepted what Emanuel had defined as the "party line." So the audience was primed for what came next. Emanuel, almost in passing, stated his opinion that NOAA really ought to stop censoring its scientists. It was antithetical to science (which thrives on the open exchange of ideas). It had to stop.

The statement was political, but it wasn't delivered in a mode of political oratory. Emanuel didn't bang his fist on the podium, much less raise it. That's not his style. He simply resumed his presentation, neatly bracketing his political remark with hard science.

Nevertheless, Emanuel's brief suspension of scientific etiquette had struck a chord. The room erupted with applause.

If Emanuel had issued a verbal challenge to the government's hurricane forecasting community, the Atlantic would soon issue yet another meteorological one.

In his final dispatch on Epsilon, Lixion Avila had declared, "I HOPE THIS IS THE END OF THE LONG LASTING 2005 HURRICANE SEASON." It wasn't. Several weeks later, the ocean and atmosphere served up Tropical Storm Zeta, noteworthy not for its strength but for its timing. The storm formed in the central Atlantic some 675 miles northwest of the Cape Verde Islands on December 30, fully a month after the season's official endpoint. "ALTHOUGH THE ATMOSPHERE SEEMS TO WANT TO DEVELOP TROPICAL STORMS AD NAUSEAM," quipped forecaster James Franklin when Zeta appeared, "THE CALENDAR WILL SHORTLY PUT AN END TO THE USE OF THE GREEK ALPHABET TO NAME THEM."

The calendar did not put an end to Zeta, however. Like Epsilon, the storm didn't die when it was supposed to. Zeta never became a hurricane, but it clung tenaciously to life. Frustrating and confounding forecasts, the storm stayed organized until January 6, 2006, in the process shattering a few last seasonal hurricane records. In his farewell to the storm and the 2005 season—during which he and his fellow storm-trackers had collectively put in hundreds of overtime hours—forecaster Stacy Stewart expressed his amazement and exhaustion alike:

I SUPPOSE IT IS ONLY FITTING THAT THE RECORD-BREAKING 2005 ATLANTIC HURRICANE SEASON ENDS WITH A RECORD BREAKING STORM. TODAY... ZETA SURPASSED 1954 ALICE #2 AS THE LONGEST-LIVED TROPICAL CYCLONE TO FORM IN DECEMBER AND CROSS OVER INTO THE NEXT YEAR. ZETA WAS ALSO THE LONGEST-LIVED JANUARY TROPICAL CYCLONE. IN ADDITION...ZETA RESULTED IN THE 2005 SEASON HAVING THE LARGEST ACCUMULATED CYCLONE ENERGY...OR ACE...SURPASSING THE 1950 SEASON. SO...UNTIL THE 2006 SEASON BEGINS... UNLESS ZETA SOMEHOW MAKES AN UNLIKELY MIRACLE COMEBACK...THIS IS THE NATIONAL HURRICANE CENTER SIGNING OFF FOR 2005...FINALLY.

It was, at long last, the end of a staggering hurricane year. And it was a beginning: the launch of a full-scale scientific and political battle over the relationship between hurricanes and global warming that would bring out the best, and occasionally the worst, in two groups of researchers whose areas of expertise overlap so much that they might be considered siblings—climate scientists on the one hand, and hurricane and weather forecasters on the other.

This is their story, first set in its historical context and then told as it unfolded across the dramatic hurricane years of 2004, 2005, and 2006. It's a narrative of scientific understanding developing in real time, in all of its inevitable messiness, under immense political pressure and in the full glare of media scrutiny. Scientists, like hurricanes, do extraordinary things at high wind speeds. Such conflicts may bring out their human side, but also inspire their very best work.

To grasp the roots of the present dispute, however, we must first glance back to the great "American Storm Controversy" of the nineteenth century, which featured a divide between scientists similar in many respects to the one that exists today. And we must visit the heroic post–World War II storm-flying era of hurricane research, when the mentors of the scientists embroiled in the current hurricane–global warming argument conducted their most important studies. This history reveals how longstanding personal and methodological schisms among meteorologists have, like a hurricane's steering currents, helped guide us to the present moment—and how they explain, at least as much as present-day political alignments, why the hurricane–climate debate became so charged and even, at times, venomous.

Scientists disagree constantly, of course. That's not news. But rarely has there been quite as much on the line. If we're really making the deadliest storms on Earth still deadlier, it will represent one of humanity's all-time greatest foot-shooting episodes. Short of a collapse of the Greenland or West Antarctic ice sheets, it's hard to imagine many hypothesized manifestations of global warming more likely to shock the public, or to generate a call to action. The 1992 United Nations Framework Convention on Climate Change announced the goal of preventing "dangerous anthropogenic interference with the climate system," and while the term "dangerous" was never explicitly defined, surely increasing the intensity of the average hurricane would fit the bill.

With stakes such as these—and with special interests on both sides eager to spin the latest science to their advantage—the circulation of ideas in the hurricane–global warming argument could easily attain gale force. Add to this an administration that has shown a strong tendency to suppress or twist inconvenient scientific information pertaining to global warming; a historically rooted and methodologically grounded rivalry between two groups of scientists studying the same meteorological phenomenon from very different vantage points; and a towering figure of American hurricane science, William Gray of Colorado State University, who rejects entirely the notion that humans have been causing substantial global warming, and whose students hold positions of great scientific influence; and you have the makings of the perfect hurricane.

# PART I

# WARMING AND STORMING

"[This] seems to be a rule in our science:
*progress is impeded by want of meteorological knowledge
on the part of the theoreticians and by a too poor
mathematical training of weather-men.*"

—Swedish meteorologist Tor Bergeron,
"Methods in Scientific Weather Analysis and Forecasting," 1959

# 1 • Chimneys and Whirlpools

Communities and nations, and especially their ships and navies, have been ravaged by hurricanes from time immemorial. The ancient Mayans, who dubbed their storm god *hunraken,* wisely built their cities inland from the coasts. The thirteenth-century Japanese blessed the *kamikaze* ("divine wind") for not once but twice wiping out the invading fleets of Mongol ruler Kublai Khan. In 1502, during his fourth and final voyage to the New World, the fleet of Christopher Columbus weathered a hurricane while docked at the island of Hispaniola in the Caribbean Sea.

Yet beyond scattered accounts from mariners who had lived through storms they described as whirlwinds—and ancient images from Caribbean civilizations, whose iconic depictions of the storm god featured counterclockwise spirals—hurricanes remained almost entirely mysterious up through the eighteenth century. It wasn't until 1743 that Benjamin Franklin first conceived of storms in general as collectives of wind and clouds traveling together over large areas, an insight that may well mark the beginning of modern meteorology.

In the early nineteenth century, scientific understanding finally began to penetrate the storm vortices that form over tropical oceans. Yet even then, researchers did not always see their work as an attempt to explain the nature of one particular type of storm rather than that of all storms (or at least the majority of them). An accurate meteorological taxonomy of large-scale cyclonic storm systems*—one that distinguished the warm-core cyclones of the tropics from the more massive cold-core or "extra-tropical" cyclones of the middle and higher latitudes,

---

*See also Appendix II, "Cyclone Typology."

which frequently dump snow rather than torrential rain and whose energy derives from the clash of warm tropical and cold polar air along a front—only arrived later.

In part because of this vagueness about the central object of study; in part because meteorology itself, and the massive data-gathering needed to support it, had not yet become fully established and institutionalized; and in part because modern standards governing scientific debate and disputation did not yet exist; the so-called American Storm Controversy of the nineteenth century raged on for decades. The squabble had its origins in a simple set of observations taken following a devastating hurricane. By the end, it had grown into an international conflict implicating the very nature of science, as the debate's two chief disputants split over whether storm studies should be rooted in the careful collection of data and observations or in theory-based deduction from the laws of physics.

The divide between these two approaches to conducting research—as the British physicist Ernest Rutherford famously put it, "All science is either physics or stamp collecting"—has long dogged meteorology. It reemerges at the heart of the current conflict over the relationship between hurricanes and global warming, a debate in which longtime hurricane specialist William Gray, who trained as a traditional map-reading weather forecaster, holds out for data-driven approaches even as his more mathematically inclined critics, like Emanuel, apply data as well as theory, equations, and computer models to the problem. In Rutherford's admittedly biased (and overly crude) classification scheme, Gray would be the stamp collector, Emanuel the physicist.

In the nineteenth century just as today, then, meteorologists who adopted different styles of research often arrived at different conclusions. The American Storm Controversy thus prefigured today's battle over hurricanes and climate, as well as shaping the development of knowledge about hurricanes more generally. As we'll see, the controversy's resolution shows that scientific debates, whether over the influence of global warming on hurricanes or simply over the nature of storms, can be settled by the discovery of new data, the development of new theories, or some combination of both.

The American storm saga began in 1831 when William Redfield, an amateur and self-taught weather researcher who ran a steamboat business and dabbled in a variety of scientific pursuits on the side, published a very important study in the *American Journal of Science and Arts*. The work presented a range of evidence suggesting that storms, and especially hurricanes, are giant rotating bodies whose winds move much more rapidly around the storm center than the storm itself moves over land or water.

The central data that Redfield used to substantiate this view came from his own experience, ten years earlier, of the devastation left behind by the great Norfolk and Long Island Hurricane of 1821, which delivered a direct hit to New York City. Even at low tide, the storm flooded the Battery and overflowed wharves, and then proceeded to rampage across New England. Shortly after it passed by, Redfield took a journey by foot through the countryside and examined a large number of trees that had been felled by it. Amid the destruction, he detected a pattern. Trees in the northwestern part of Connecticut and nearby Massachusetts had been "prostrated *towards the south-east*" by winds blowing hard from the northwest, Redfield observed; yet in central Connecticut, the winds at the same time seemed to have blown in the opposite direction, toward the northwest, and "fruit trees, corn, &c." had fallen in this direction. How could two locations within the same state have experienced such different winds? Redfield saw only one solution: "*This storm,*" he wrote, "*was exhibited in the form of a great whirlwind.*"

With this discovery, Redfield launched an influential career of storm research that culminated when he became the first president of the American Association for the Advancement of Science in 1848. Throughout that career, Redfield hewed to a strict empiricist methodology—or at least so he claimed. He collected a large array of data on storms from ship's logs and their captains, from eyewitnesses who'd been present when storms made landfall, and from other sources. When it came to theorizing, however, Redfield aligned himself with the seventeenth-century English thinker Francis Bacon, who had described science as an "inductive" process of reasoning in which open-minded investigators painstakingly gather observations about the natural world and only then seek to generalize from them, rather than beginning with a commitment to any particular theory or interpretation.

Scientists' rhetoric about methodology can diverge from their actual practices, however, and Redfield did in fact have a "theory" about the origins of hurricanes and other rotary storms, such as tornadoes. He considered these phenomena the atmospheric equivalent of water in a pot being stirred, meaning that whirlwinds and whirl*pools* were very similar phenomena in his mind. "The analogy between the tides and currents of the ocean, and of the atmosphere, is perhaps sufficient for our argument," Redfield wrote. In turn, Redfield ascribed the behavior of atmospheric tides to "mechanical gravitation." His theoretical account wasn't particularly convincing, however, and later, one of his own supporters faulted him for violating his principles by advancing it.

The strength of Redfield's argument lay in his data. He soon attracted a group of allies who supported and tried to extend his interpretation of storms, both by gathering together more observations and by applying them practically to ensure safe navigation for ships at sea. Redfield's work had a considerable influence on British researcher William Reid, who experienced a deadly hurricane in Barbados in 1831 and later confirmed the rotational nature of storms with much additional data, and on Henry Piddington, a former ship commander and president of Marine Courts of Enquiry in Calcutta, India. Piddington coined the term *cyclone* (meaning "coil of a snake") and published a book for sailors detailing what he called the "Law of Storms," which provided tips on how to steer your vessel clear of a hurricane's most powerful winds.

In the Northern Hemisphere, hurricane winds whirl in a counter-clockwise direction; in the Southern Hemisphere it's the opposite. Redfield, Piddington, and their supporters didn't understand the true reason for this (that would come later), but they recognized the value of such knowledge for safe navigation. In the Northern Hemisphere, whichever direction a hurricane is heading its right front quadrant will be the most dangerous for a ship, since the winds in this quadrant will have the storm's own forward momentum behind them. In the Southern Hemisphere, the reverse is the case. Piddington therefore counseled ship's captains to determine the direction in which a storm was moving and steer for its weakest quadrant.

For much like the work of today's Miami-based hurricane forecasters, the Redfield-Reid-Piddington school of storm studies had a strongly practical orientation. The research focused on protecting mariners from having their masts torn off by shrieking hurricane winds, and their ships engulfed by massive hurricane waves. This was not so much about scientific theory as it was about saving lives. In his 1848 book, Piddington even announced his intention to write in what he called "the familiar terms of common sailor-language," eschewing "more scientific forms of expression."

Yet even as some navigators began putting Redfield's findings about rotating storms into practice, James Pollard Espy, the so-called "Storm King," denounced them as sheer bunkum. A theorist and popularizer who in 1842 became the de facto national meteorologist with the U.S. War Department and later worked at the Smithsonian Institution, Espy had been influenced by the English chemist John Dalton, who experimented with the properties of gases and derived the first modern atomic theory. This background led him to a very different view of storms from Redfield's. Espy highlighted the key role of what we now call "latent heat" in storm development, and then used this insight to forge a theory with a strong thermodynamic emphasis, one that placed phase changes of molecules of water (most centrally, evaporation and condensation) at its very center.

Today, the concept of "latent" or hidden heat seems almost intuitive. In the process of evaporation, heat drawn from the environment allows energized molecules of water to escape from their liquid phase. A commonly used analogy is that of getting out of a swimming pool or the shower. As water evaporates from your skin you feel a chill, because heat is being pulled into the air and away from your body. The heat has now taken the form of "latent heat" and become locked within the molecules of water vapor. It will be released again into the air as "sensible heat"—heat you can actually feel—when the vapor condenses back into liquid water.

Espy combined this notion of latent heat release (or as he called it, "latent caloric") with the atmospheric process of convection—the transfer of heat upward by rising currents of air—and used it to explain the formation of clouds and rain. When the sun heats the Earth's surface, warm air rises, carrying heat as well as water vapor aloft. Indeed, the more water vapor the air contains, the more buoyant it becomes, and thus the more likely it is to rise in the first place.

As the air rises through the atmosphere, it experiences a drop in pressure as the cumulative weight of air molecules from above diminishes—the same thing that happens as you ascend a mountain. So the air expands and cools. When it cools sufficiently, the water vapor that it contains begins to condense into droplets of water or change into ice crystals, which organize into clouds. In the process, latent heat gets

Formation of cumulus clouds as envisioned by James Espy in his book *The Philosophy of Storms* (Boston, 1841).

released, once again becoming sensible heat and thus further enhancing the ascent of warm, moist air. Soon a thunderstorm may emerge.

With this account, Espy articulated several key principles underlying the behavior of thunderstorms and, therefore, of hurricanes (which are gigantic rotating groups of thunderclouds). And he made a major step toward transforming meteorology from a purely observational science, dominated by diarists and data collectors like Redfield, into one that sought to establish universal theories based upon the behavior of heat and gases. If Redfield envisioned storms as analogous to whirlpools, you could say Espy viewed them as more akin to chimneys. And he applied his ideas about latent heat and convection to all storms in all situations, further asserting that storm winds rush straight inward, from all directions, to a central point or region where air pressure is lowest. This led him to dismiss entirely Redfield's arguments about rotating winds. For Espy, all storms were the same, and his theory captured them perfectly.

Given this position, it was probably inevitable that Espy would get drawn into a spat with Redfield over the nature of storms. Their conflict began in the mid-1830s and soon degenerated into personal attacks and accusations of underhanded data manipulation. Writing in 1835, Espy described Redfield's views as "so anomalous and inconsistent with received theories, that I hesitate to put entire confidence in them, and shall continue to doubt, until I have the most certain evidence of the facts." In a bile-filled 1839 rebuttal, Redfield countered, "I did not anticipate so complete an evasion of all the distinguishing points at issue, and so barren an effort at confusing and mystifying the most distinct phenomena of this storm, as is manifested in [Espy's] present examination." Espy, Redfield charged (in typically Baconian language), labored under the "bias of a preconceived hypothesis."

Ultimately the highly public conflict between these two scientists, amplified by the participation of a third scientist, the volatile Robert Hare (who thought Espy and Redfield were both wrong, and ascribed storm formation to electricity), resonated overseas. British scientists sided with Redfield, the French with Espy. The battle helped spur the growth of American meteorology, as the Smithsonian Institution set up a national network of weather observers, as well as a smaller network situated along newly established telegraph lines, to help resolve it. For many years, however, the dispute dragged on, its participants refusing to concede any ground.

Perhaps the most memorable commentary on the controversy came from Joseph Henry, the first secretary of the Smithsonian, who observed that "meteorology has ever been an apple of contention, as if the violent commotions of the atmosphere induced a sympathetic effect on the minds of those who have attempted to study them." Henry suspected future researchers would see that both Espy and Redfield had grasped a part of the truth, and that's precisely what happened. We now know Redfield was correct to describe many storms (especially hurricanes and tornadoes) as whirlwinds. The theory of atmospheric tides that he invoked to explain his observations, on the other hand, had little to recommend it. Espy's basic theory, involving convection and the release of latent heat caused by the condensation of water vapor higher in the atmosphere, was much more sound. But he applied it too broadly and let it lead him down the wrong path with respect to the behavior of storm winds. His "centripetal" theory—that all winds blow straight inward in a storm—has died a merciful death.

The squabbling between Redfield and Espy seems to have prevented each from appreciating the other's insight. But the conflict turned as much on methodology as personalities. Redfield was a "data" guy, a perceptive observer who'd seen a pattern in the arrangement of winds and fallen trees and extrapolated from there. Espy also gathered data, pushed for the formation of weather observation systems, and experimented with the properties of gases on a small scale. But ultimately he was a theoretician who sought the grandest of generalizations—to explain storms based on the behavior of the tiny molecules that comprise them.

The struggle over these two disparate views of how to conduct research was further aggravated by the contrast between Redfield's status as a scientific amateur and Espy's popularity and institutional support. As Espy became increasingly sought after as a lecturer on storms, Redfield looked on with jealousy and resentment. Matters came to a head in 1849 when Espy, in his official capacity, submitted a report to the Navy Department that debunked the rotational theory of storms. Redfield objected that it was inappropriate for the navy to lend the "official endorsement by government" to Espy's theory. He also added that the navy's behavior was downright dangerous: Espy's mistaken understanding of storms could pose deadly risks to mariners who might come in contact with them. Redfield's complaint parallels more recent protestations (from those such as Kerry Emanuel) that in 2005, amidst unprecedented storm destruction, the National Oceanic and Atmospheric Administration inappropriately took sides on the question of whether hurricanes had been amplified by global warming.

As they battled for scientific primacy, Espy and Redfield sought more data, more observations, to advance their respective positions. To fully resolve the issue, however, both empirical and theoretical approaches, bringing to bear as many disparate elements of the scientific tool kit as possible, would be needed.

On the "data" side, the Yale-trained, Ohio-based meteorologist Elias Loomis, another Baconian in his scientific outlook, made an early stab at settling the budding storm controversy. First Loomis tried to do so by intensively studying an individual winter storm system; he later turned to statistical studies of large groups of storms. Loomis saw the importance of taking many simultaneous observations of a single storm from different locations, so as to discern its full scale and direction of movement. In the course of his research he published an early example of what is now known as a synoptic chart or weather map, drawing simple lines (known as isobars and isotherms) to connect regions with similar measurements for air pressure and temperature, accompanied by arrows for wind direction and shading to denote different forms of precipitation. Loomis thus helped set the stage both for the modern, systematic collection of meteorological observations and for the use of these observations in map-based weather forecasting by scientists like William Gray (a synoptically trained forecaster and another meteorological empiricist in the Redfield-Loomis tradition).

By its very nature, the synoptical approach allows forecasters to favor the practical over the theoretical. One can learn to use a weather map without mastering all of the physical equations that govern the atmosphere—in fact, the lack of such mastery may even be an asset. As George Bliss, a meteorologist with the U.S. Weather Bureau, put it in 1917:

> In order to excel in the profession one must possess a special faculty for intuitively and quickly weighing the forces indicated on the weather map and calculating the result. This special faculty is developed by long and continued study and association with the maps, rather than by a profound study of atmospheric physics.

Loomis helped set this tradition in motion. It would require another Espy-style theoretician, however, to resolve the storm controversy's central point of contention.

In character, William Ferrel seems to have been a rather shy man, much more so than either Espy or Redfield. Born in rural Pennsylvania and working as a schoolteacher in Tennessee when he made his key breakthrough, Ferrel excelled at mathematics. Studying the works of Isaac Newton and the Frenchman Pierre-Simon Laplace (famous for his work on celestial mechanics), Ferrel began to take an interest in meteorology. Before long he had managed to explain how the Earth's rotation—from west to east, or counterclockwise if you're looking down on the planet from above the North Pole—influences not only the general circulation of the atmosphere, but also the rotational shape of storms. Ferrel has been described as the first true "dynamical meteorologist": a scientist who successfully reduced the behavior of the atmosphere to the laws of physics, and thus, to equations.

A French scientist, Gaspard-Gustave de Coriolis, had noted in 1835 that because of the planet's rotation, objects in motion are subject to a certain "force"*—now known as the Coriolis force—that deflects their trajectory. Coriolis did not discuss atmospheric motions, however, and his work wasn't widely known until much later. But Fer-

---

*The Coriolis "force" is merely an apparent force in that it is dependent upon one's frame of reference. It is observed while situated on the rotating Earth.

rel recognized that the Earth's rotation deflects winds "to the right in the northern hemisphere, and to the left in the southern," as he put it. That includes the winds of hurricanes as well as those of extra-tropical cyclones (like most other scientists of the time, Ferrel did not draw firm distinctions between these two storm species).

Picture a hurricane in the Northern Hemisphere, its winds flowing inward toward a central region of low pressure, which has been created by the rising of warm air. Without the Coriolis force, the winds would blow straight into the storm's center along a gradient from higher to lower pressure, perfectly conforming to Espy's theory. But the winds don't do that. Instead they deflect to the right due to the Earth's rotation, just as an apple core thrown from the window of a car driving counterclockwise around a traffic circle will also veer to the right as it travels through the air (from the perspective of someone riding in the car, anyway; as viewed by someone suspended in the air above, the core would appear to follow a straight trajectory).

In effect, the hurricane's winds experience an array of different forces upon them: a pull inward due to the gradient in pressure, a deflection to the right due to the rotation of the Earth, and a centrifugal acceleration outward. (These forces are nearly in what scientists call "gradient balance," although that balance is upset slightly by friction from the sea surface.) Because of the combination of the different forces, winds in Northern Hemisphere hurricanes spiral counterclockwise around a calm area (the "eye") in the storm center. In the Southern Hemisphere, it's the opposite: Winds rush inward due to a differential in pressure but also get deflected to the *left*, and the combination of forces acting upon them results in a clockwise spiral.

To help conceptualize why cyclonic rotation reverses at the equator, you can perform a simple experiment. Sit at a table across from a friend and roll a cylindrical object, like a soda can, across the table from your left to your right (your friend's right to left). You will perceive a clockwise rotation, but your friend will perceive a counterclockwise one. It's the same with the planet Earth—although contrary to popular misconceptions, the Coriolis force does *not* determine which direction water spirals when a toilet flushes or a sink drains. The Earth's rotation certainly influences the trajectories of winds, ocean currents, and airline flights, but at the tiny scale of a kitchen or bathroom, the Coriolis force is too minuscule to have a significant effect.

Ferrel recognized that the rotating Earth explains not only why cyclonic storms rotate in different directions in different hemispheres, but also why they never form at or very near to the equator (much less cross it and reverse their rotation). At the equator, the Coriolis force equals zero, making it the only place on Earth where Espy's theory actually holds true—where winds *do* rush straight inward toward low-pressure regions without being deflected. And so Ferrel finally explained why Redfield had been right about the rotational nature of storms, despite Espy's powerful theory—which Ferrel himself endorsed in a modified form and helped to develop further in later years—about convection and the release of latent heat. Ferrel had resolved the American Storm Controversy, and provided a dramatic new perspective on the nature of rotary storms such as hurricanes.

Scientists wedded to pet theories they've spent a lifetime developing and defending can have a hard time changing their minds, however. The novelist Arthur C. Clarke captured this inertia in what he called his "First Law": "When a distinguished but elderly scientist states that something is possible he is almost certainly right. When he states that something is impossible, he is very probably wrong." That aptly describes the aging James Espy, who late in life reviewed and criticized one of Ferrel's early works, and who clung to his centripetal winds theory to the end. "His views were positive and his conclusions absolute, and so was the expression of them," one of Espy's contemporaries remarked after his death in 1860. "He was not prone to examine and re-examine premises and conclusions, but considered what had once been passed upon by his judgment as finally settled."

William Redfield died in 1857 without ever knowing of Ferrel's work.

"In my beginning is my end," T. S. Eliot wrote. Something similar could be said of meteorology. The American Storm Controversy had been fueled by personal and methodological tensions that find many parallels in today's hurricane–climate debate. One can hear echoes of Redfield and Loomis in Colorado State University's empiricist and global warming skeptic William Gray, and detect further similarities between Espy, Ferrel, and Kerry Emanuel. The empirical and theoretical (or "dynamicist") camps in meteorology had already become well defined and begun to diverge well over a century ago.

More knowledge would have to accumulate, however, before scientists could conceivably clash over hurricanes and global warming. The greenhouse effect itself had hardly been conceived of. And despite nineteenth-century insights into the nature of hurricanes by empiricists and theoreticians alike, huge gaps in understanding persisted. Well into the twentieth century, in fact, many commentators still thought of hurricanes as meteorological midgets whose storm column extended no more than a few kilometers from the sea surface up into the air. By contrast, it's now known that hurricanes can extend up through the entire weather-containing layer of the atmosphere, known as the troposphere. The strongest can stretch past the tropopause (the troposphere's top layer) and into the lower part of the Earth's stratosphere, reaching heights of ten miles or more.

Modern hurricane science took a long time to get organized for many reasons. One was the general misapplication of Espy's "thermal theory of cyclones": It was most centrally used to explain not hurricanes but wintry extra-tropical cyclones, which are far more common than hurricanes over the landmass of the United States and especially Europe, and whose strongest winds occur many miles up in the atmosphere rather than near the Earth's surface. This general failure to distinguish between types of cyclones severely hobbled the "thermal" or convective theory and set the stage for its decline after the nineteenth century, as scientists increasingly doubted that latent heat release could explain extra-tropical cyclone dynamics.

During World War I, a meteorologist named Vilhelm Bjerknes gathered together a talented group of young scientists in Norway to form what came to be known as the Bergen School of meteorology. The Bergen scientists pioneered the alternative "polar front" theory of cyclones, attributing winter storms to the interaction of cold and warm air masses along fronts: In their view, the temperature contrast itself was the source of their power. "Cyclones," concluded two young Bergen scientists in a famous 1921 paper, "may be said to be links in the interchange of air between the polar regions and the equatorial zone." Extra-tropical cyclones also feature the release of latent heat, as cold air drives warmer air aloft (triggering condensation), but it's not the primary source of their power. The ideas of Espy, Ferrel, and the other thermodynamic storm theorists were thus found inadequate to explain extra-tropical storms even as most meteorologists focused their attention and energies upon them.

Logistical and practical factors also contributed to the neglect of hurricane science. Instead of forming over land, these storms form over remote tropical oceans where scientific observations were scarce throughout the nineteenth century and well into the twentieth. The hurricane that strikes a populated area is a relatively rare occurrence; before the availability of radar and satellite observations, it's likely that many hurricanes that never made landfall were never observed at all (during a time when "observation" often meant little more than being encountered by a seagoing vessel that managed to stay afloat and tell the tale). So it's no surprise that most meteorologists paid more attention to observing and analyzing daily weather than to studying distant extremes.

Finally, the nineteenth-century understanding of hurricanes didn't translate very well into an ability to predict their behavior or to respond to it (except, perhaps, among the mariners who grasped Piddington's "Law of Storms"). That became tragically clear right at the turn of the century, when a powerful hurricane obliterated Galveston, Texas, killing more than eight thousand people (who appear to have gone unwarned) with a fifteen-foot storm surge. Present-day analyses suggest the storm may have intensified just before landfall, which would have dramatically increased its destructive impact. Either way, the Galveston strike remains the deadliest natural disaster in American history. Before it sustained a direct hit from the 1900 hurricane— which was likely a Category 4 storm on the modern-day Saffir-

Simpson scale—Galveston had been a thriving port city. It has never fully recovered.

Galveston proved the need for a much better scientific under-standing of hurricanes. World War II, which led to a dramatic buildup of the institution of meteorological science, helped supply it. The war, and the new technologies that sprang from it, greatly accelerated scientific study of weather, the atmosphere, and the oceans. Hurri-canes and typhoons became less mysterious and easier to track and predict. But the new discoveries did not lead to a seamless merger be-tween empirically oriented meteorologists and more theoretical ones. Instead, the war and postwar era gave scientists of both broad persua-sions better tools for studying storms: radar, satellites, balloon-borne measuring devices, and even storm-flying airplanes for the empiricists and complicated computer simulations for the math-whiz theoreti-cians (who also relied upon the influx of new data to gear up, or "ini-tialize," their computer models).

The two most longstanding disputants in the hurricane–global warming conflagration—Gray and Emanuel—were themselves trained by two scientists who stood at the forefronts of these two trajectories of research. Gray's "major professor," as he puts it, was the empiricist Herbert Riehl—"Herbie," as friends and colleagues called him—who is now widely recognized as the founder of the field of tropical meteo-rology. Emanuel, meanwhile, studied under theoretician and computer-modeling pioneer Jule Gregory Charney in the late 1970s at MIT. In fact, during the 1950s and 1960s, Riehl and Charney themselves pro-posed divergent interpretations of hurricanes.

Riehl and Charney did not fight over their theories with anything approaching the hostility exhibited in the earlier American Storm Controversy—or, for that matter, the animosity sometimes exhibited by the global warming–hurricane combatants of today. Neither was an absolutist about methodology. Yet the contrasting interpretations of hurricanes that they advanced were deeply grounded in different approaches to scientific research. Riehl's understanding—the "heat engine" theory—grew out of his empirical investigations, including a large number of research flights into hurricanes. Charney's theory—referred to as "Conditional Instability of the Second Kind," or CISK—was unmistakably the product of a meteorological theoretician.

Riehl and Charney both also brought us closer to entertaining the possibility that hurricanes might grow stronger because of global warming. Riehl's description of hurricanes as "heat engines" envisioned them as reliant upon ocean heat as their central power source—and in a warmer world, ocean heat is bound to increase. Charney, meanwhile, studied and supported the possibility that human beings might cause global climate change, including a warming of the world's oceans, through relentless industrial emissions of carbon dioxide and other greenhouse gases. This leading advocate of the use of computer simulations to predict short-range weather also pronounced that long-range global climate models, commonly referred to as GCMs, were essentially sound in their basic findings. These are the models used today to project how emissions of carbon dioxide and other greenhouse gases will change global climate, and their results suggest that the planetary experiment we're now undertaking could leave us with a radically different Earth in the space of less than a century.

# 2 • Of Heat Engines...

T
he rain was torrential," Herbie Riehl would later recall, as the
U.S. Navy reconnaissance plane penetrated a tropical depression to the south of Guam on August 29, 1947. In the Northwest Pacific ocean basin, which produces the most intense tropical
cyclones on Earth, this storm's winds of 30 to 35 miles per hour were
hardly remarkable. But in the context of Riehl's current research they
didn't have to be. The thirty-two-year-old hurricane scientist—a German expatriate who liked to smoke cigars and play bridge and climb
mountains, and who was sometimes a bit hard to get along with—
had traveled to Guam along with several other University of Chicago
meteorologists seeking to unravel the process by which typhoons
form. This weak depression would teach Riehl a great deal about just
how knotty and complex that problem truly is.

In the opinion of the naval aerologist on board the plane, who'd
flown into many past Pacific storms, the rainfall in the depression
seemed just as intense as what's found in a full-blown typhoon. So
Riehl expected such a storm to spin up shortly. But nothing happened, and the depression slowly meandered westward, unchanged, all
the way to the China Sea.

Riehl had witnessed an enigma that confronts every hurricane
forecaster. Not every storm with the apparent potential to do so grows
into a hurricane or typhoon, and not even the best forecasters can
always predict which will and which won't. To Riehl, the experience of
flying into this weak but very rainy depression had an important implication: "Condensation energy alone cannot create intense tropical
storms," he wrote. Instead, the release of latent heat, leading to clouds
and rainfall, constituted a "necessary, but not sufficient, condition for

both inception and growth" of tropical cyclones. It was just one of many important insights to arise from Riehl's eagerness to fly onboard midcentury military planes and survey hurricanes from the inside.

"I desired very much to do something," Riehl would later comment of his storm-flying ventures, "which produced a bit of life in an otherwise perhaps rather dreary research environment." He still felt the same way in 1960, at age forty-five, and was incensed when the navy made him get a physical before allowing him to go on his final flight, admonishing him that "at your age you're supposed to sit behind a desk and not up in front on airplanes."

Riehl epitomized a group of scientists who, for reasons having as much to do with the national interest as basic curiosity, began to unravel the mysteries of the tropics. Born in Munich in 1915 to a Jewish mother and a German father, he'd emigrated to the United States in 1933 as Hitler rose to power. Not long after receiving his master's degree in meteorology from New York University in 1942, Riehl joined his new country's war effort against his old one. In 1943, the U.S. Army Air Corps (later the Air Force) teamed up with the University of Chicago to establish an Institute of Tropical Meteorology at the University of Puerto Rico, and Riehl moved down as part of the team. He became head of the institute a few years later, commuting back and forth between the Midwest and the Caribbean even though he hadn't officially earned his Ph.D. yet.

The U.S. military's sudden interest in tropical meteorology reflected a strategic necessity. There was a war on, much of it set in the Pacific theater, where new meteorological risks confronted U.S. military forces. The point became painfully apparent in late 1944, when three U.S. destroyers under the command of Admiral William F. "Bull" Halsey were sunk by a powerful December typhoon in the Pacific ocean, and 790 of the Third Fleet's sailors perished beneath the waves.

And so World War II and its aftermath gave meteorology a tremendous boost in the United States. At a time when aviation was far more vulnerable to weather conditions than today, the war effort needed forecasts, and obligingly, the University of Chicago and four other

American universities (MIT, UCLA, Caltech, and New York University) trained an entire generation of weather experts. Many of these scientists then traveled to the tropics and found themselves in an entirely new world. Inspired by the discoveries of the Bergen School, early twentieth-century meteorologists had focused most of their energies on understanding the cyclonic storms that occur over the middle and higher latitudes. In the Pacific, however, a large number of relatively unschooled forecasters confronted a very different problem—predicting cyclones in a place where the Norwegian theory of "fronts" didn't apply. They had catching up to do, and they had to do it quickly.

Riehl led the way, both through his research in the U.S. tropical territories of Puerto Rico and Guam and through the University of Chicago's training program for military meteorologists. He served as mentor to a large number of newly minted tropical scientists, many of whom took Riehl's courses at the University of Chicago and, once it had been written, studied from his foundational 1954 textbook, *Tropical Meteorology*. In the process, Riehl helped establish two key traditions in hurricane science: storm-flying as a means of getting data, and empiricism as a broad means of learning about tropical weather. Both would be carried forward by William Gray, one of Riehl's most distinguished students (and surely the most famous of them).

Riehl was more than a mentor, however. Working closely with his onetime student Joanne Malkus (later Joanne Simpson), he helped to develop the basic thermodynamic understanding of hurricanes that's accepted today. And not unlike Redfield or Loomis, Riehl built up this edifice from a vast reservoir of scientific data. In the words of Richard Anthes, a hurricane specialist who is president of the University Corporation for Atmospheric Research in Boulder, Colorado, in the 1950s and early 1960s Riehl and Malkus led an "observational assault on the mysteries of the tropics."

That's not to say that Riehl couldn't transform an equation; he certainly could. But he was first and foremost an observational scientist. When *Science* magazine glowingly reviewed *Tropical Meteorology*, the writer observed: "The over-all treatment is empirical or synoptic rather than dynamic; the mathematics is simple and unobtrusive."

The foundation for Riehl's advances centrally lay in the unprecedented compilation of hurricane data that the war and postwar era made possible.

One data source was the balloon-borne "radiosonde," which allowed for vastly improved measurements of the upper atmosphere. As they float up into the air, radiosondes provide readings of temperature, pressure, and relative humidity at different elevations. Later, Riehl also drew upon measurements from "rawinsondes," a special type of radiosonde that can be tracked using radio or radar, thus allowing for measurements of the direction and strength of upper-level winds. Such devices gave scientists a three-dimensional glimpse of the structure of the atmosphere at any given place or point in time. World War II spurred the establishment of radiosonde and rawinsonde networks, and scientists like Riehl first made sense of the new data.

Cobbling together radiosonde measurements taken over San Juan, Swan Island in the western Caribbean, and other locations in the tropics, Riehl took a major step forward in our understanding of hurricane formation. In 1945 he published a pioneering report on the meteorological perturbations now known as African easterly waves—or as Riehl then called them, "waves in the easterlies." These aren't the sort of waves that surfers catch; they undulate in the fluid of the atmosphere rather than the fluid of the oceans. Preceded by a drop in sealevel air pressure and often followed by intense thunderstorm clusters, the waves originate over sub-Saharan Africa and ripple through the tropical atmosphere from east to west, passing by once or twice per week at 10 to 15 miles per hour during the summer season in the Atlantic. Sometimes, for reasons that remain poorly understood, a wave can spark the development of a closed air circulation—the first step in the growth of a hurricane.

Riehl's radiosonde studies of tropical waves pushed him toward another important insight. Hurricanes don't just spring into existence spontaneously. Rather, these most destructive of storms always develop "within preexisting disturbances," such as easterly waves. It was the earliest of many data-induced revelations that would emerge from Riehl's research career.

In addition to radiosondes, Riehl and other mid-century hurricane scientists drew upon a glut of other newly available observational tools. Radar, a wartime technology quickly converted to civilian use, greatly expanded knowledge of hurricanes. The first radar images of these storms—showing their unmistakable spiraling outer rain bands—were taken in the 1940s, and by the 1950s, the groundwork had been laid for establishing a national weather radar network in the United States. Then in 1960, the first weather satellite was launched into space, so that before long scientists peering down into hurricane eyes as glimpsed from above could see the storms peering right back at them. By the 1970s, satellite imagery, combined with cloud-pattern recognition techniques, meant even hurricanes never penetrated by aircraft or seen on radar could be detected and described. No longer would a devastating storm go entirely unnoticed until landfall, or be observed only by ships that had the misfortune of coming near it.

But perhaps the most significant of the new postwar data-gathering technologies, and one of the techniques most exploited by Riehl, was the use of instrument-equipped aircraft that could take scientists straight into the heart of hurricanes. No other data-gathering technique could rival these storm flights. They allowed for targeted forays into specific regions, at specific elevations, and at different points in a storm's life cycle. And they provided a life-transforming experience to boot.

The first deliberate hurricane flight took place during the war, in 1943. Despite occasional crashes in the early years, they quickly became common. While it would be suicide to maneuver a ship into such a storm, flying into them isn't particularly dangerous so long as you stay away from the sea surface, know how to navigate using instruments rather than the naked eye, and have a strong stomach.

Originally hurricane flights were conducted by the military and used strictly for forecasting, but soon scientists started hitching rides on board and occasionally even got their own research expeditions. Robert Simpson, a colleague of Riehl's who would later direct the

National Hurricane Research Lab and the National Hurricane Center (the Saffir-Simpson scale is named after him), was among the first to exploit this opportunity. One notable mission, involving several 1947 flights into the Great Atlantic Hurricane, allowed Simpson to observe the anticyclonic (or clockwise) rotation of the storm's upper outflow levels, where spiraling winds reversed direction. Meanwhile, following a 1951 flight into Typhoon Marge in the Pacific—the most intense storm ever penetrated at the time, with a central pressure of 895 millibars* or 26.42 inches as measured from the aircraft (the average at sea level is about 1,013 millibars or 29.92 inches)—Simpson wrote of his experience in the eye of the storm:

> Around us was an awesome display. Marge's eye was a clear space 40 miles in diameter surrounded by a coliseum of clouds whose walls on one side rose vertically and on the other were banked like galleries in a great opera house. The upper rim, about 35,000 feet high, was rounded off smoothly against a background of blue sky. Below us was a floor of smooth clouds rising to a dome 8,000 feet above sea level in the center. There were breaks in it which gave us glimpses of the surface of the ocean. In the vortex around the eye the sea was a scene of unimaginably violent, churning water.

Soon even journalists started flying on hurricane-hunting missions. In 1954, legendary newsman Edward R. Murrow rode on board a B-29 out of Bermuda as it set out to penetrate Hurricane Edna, later broadcasting stunning footage from inside the storm. As Murrow put it: "In the eye of a hurricane, you learn things other than of a scientific nature. You feel the puniness of man and his works. If a true definition of humility is ever written, it might well be written in the eye of a hurricane."

As these passages show, the perception of hurricanes, by scientists as well as the public, would be forever altered by the opportunity to safely experience them from the inside. Suddenly being an observa-

---

*See note on units of measurement in Appendix I.

tionally inclined hurricane researcher like Riehl or Simpson meant regularly going on adventurous, quasi-military missions. Like North Pole or Arctic exploration, hurricane research became romantic, dangerous, and heroic, and those who flew into storms justifiably came to view themselves as possessed of special insights by virtue of their unique experiences. The research also became well funded: In August 1956, specialized flights began after elected representatives created the National Hurricane Research Project (NHRP). As is often the case in hurricane science, the dollars followed the destruction: In 1954, hurricanes Carol, Edna, and Hazel had pummeled the U.S.'s eastern coastline in quick succession.

Much like the 1821 storm that Redfield studied, Hurricane Carol struck Long Island with 100-mile-per-hour winds on August 31 and then swept through New England. Hurricane Edna followed eleven days later, cutting across Cape Cod and making landfall along the eastern coast of Maine in the midst of transitioning into an extra-tropical cyclone, as northward traveling hurricanes sometimes do.* Both storms also brushed the Outer Banks of North Carolina. But on October 15 the year's most devastating storm, Hazel—which had already killed hundreds in Haiti through landslides and flooding— made a full landfall at the South Carolina–North Carolina border at Category 4 strength. Along the Carolinas the storm surge reached 18 feet; "every pier in a distance of 170 miles of coastline was demolished and whole lines of beach homes literally disappeared," noted a report from the time. Still considered the worst hurricane in North Carolina history, Hazel blew north over land so quickly that it delivered hurricane-force winds to Washington, D.C., and, after undergoing another extra-tropical transition, killed 81 people in Toronto from massive flooding. No wonder Hazel helped kick off a new era in hurricane research. It didn't hurt that North Carolina saw three more destructive hurricane landfalls (Connie, Diane, and Ione) in 1955.

As the dean of tropical meteorology, Riehl was angered not to be named director of the newly launched National Hurricane Research

---

*For more details, see Appendix II, "Cyclone Typology."

Project. Whatever his scientific strengths, apparently he wasn't a good enough politician. In fact, Riehl was almost as well known for his abrasive personality as for his scientific influence. Offered a variety of more subordinate roles with the NHRP, he rejected all of them and refused to participate—a stance that, had it continued, would have been a severe blow to the project. Later, however, Riehl came around and flew on a large number of NHRP hurricane flights as they traced their standard "cloverleaf" paths through any Atlantic storm within range, allowing Riehl and his fellow scientists to gather unprecedented observations.

Riehl also passed the storm-flying experience on to his students. In 1958, he took a young William Gray down to the NHRP's headquarters in West Palm Beach, Florida, and got him on board two B-50 flights into Hurricane Helene, a Category 4 storm at its peak. Helene looked as if it might threaten Charleston, South Carolina, and later skirted the North Carolina coast, but ultimately its path recurved and it remained at sea. Flying into the storm, the scientists bent the rules a little. "Riehl talked the pilot into staying down at 1,500 feet when we had 120 knot winds"—almost 140 miles per hour—Gray remembers. "You were supposed to go up to 5,000 if you had winds above hurricane force." If a hurricane's strongest winds could be found at the lower altitude, so could great data. Not surprisingly, the experience piqued Gray's interest in hurricanes.

"He used to ask me as a graduate student, what makes a hurricane form?" Gray recalls of Riehl.

Storm flights allowed scientists like Riehl to do with tropical cyclones what Loomis had done with mid-latitude storms: Take a wide range of observations of the same storm and analyze the picture that emerged. In general, Riehl's mode of science relied heavily upon data-gathering, though it didn't end there. "He wasn't entirely an observationalist, I wasn't entirely an observationalist," remembers Riehl's frequent co-author Joanne Malkus. Rather, data-gathering gradually merged with theory.

First, either Riehl or another storm-flying scientist—not Malkus, because at first women weren't allowed on the research flights—would take a range of measurements inside hurricanes. Then came attempts to create storm models that could explain at least some of the observations successfully. The messiest part was gathering the data: Not all storms were equally approachable by aircraft; not all storm regions could be equally accessed (the "boundary layer" between air and sea was pretty strictly off-limits, for obvious reasons); and instrument failures sometimes wrecked the best-planned missions. But over time, the approach led to considerable progress.

Perhaps Riehl's most significant contribution to hurricane science lay in his discovery of the thermodynamic nature of these storms. Once again, this "theory" grew out of his observational approach. It has also stood the test of time and, despite having been largely eclipsed for several decades, prevails today.

In the late 1940s and early 1950s, Riehl and a small group of other scientists identified the key characteristic of hurricanes that would subsequently inspire concerns that global warming might intensify them—namely, that a hurricane's central energy source lay in the evaporation of warm seawater, a process that releases heat from the ocean up into the air. This discovery was related to, and yet represented a great advance over, the previous thermal theory of cyclones espoused by Espy, Ferrel, and their followers. That theory credited latent heat with the central role in driving a cyclone, whether extra-tropical or otherwise. Riehl and his scientific compatriots also understood the importance of the release of latent heat from condensation in rising currents of moist air. But they recognized that for hurricanes, this meant little except in the context of a deep reservoir of energy delivered by the sun to the tropics and stored in tropical oceans.

In a sense, it all went back to Riehl's 1947 experience inside the very rainy Pacific depression that never intensified into a typhoon, which had cautioned him not to ascribe everything important about hurricanes to condensation. It's trivially true that clouds require moisture to form. But the towering cumulonimbus clouds and powerful winds of hurricanes could not exist without an ocean heat source, and that's what makes them unique—and so dangerous.

The emphasis on ocean heat began with a seminal 1948 paper, in which the Finnish scientist Erik Palmén—who spent time at the University of Chicago—compiled data suggesting that hurricanes formed only in regions where temperatures at the sea surface exceeded 26 or 27 degrees Celsius (about 80 degrees Fahrenheit). In other words, these storms form in the warmest parts of the ocean during the warmest seasons of the year. Thanks to Palmén's paper, scientists now knew of the importance of easterly waves and had identified two further conditions for hurricane formation in a particular region. First, due to the Coriolis force, the area had to be north or south of (but not too close to) the equator. Second, the region apparently had to have sea-surface temperatures that exceeded the threshold of 26 or 27 degrees Celsius during at least part of the year (although hurricanes can move out of such regions once formed).

Before long, Riehl and a scientist still working in Germany, Ernst Kleinschmidt, expanded upon Palmén's emphasis on ocean heat. In a 1950 paper drawing on a glut of upper-air observations from the previous decade, Riehl described the hurricane as a "heat engine": a thermodynamic system that converts heat energy into mechanical energy (the ability to do work or, in the case of hurricanes, lift air and drive winds) by processing it from an area of high heat to one of lower heat. For hurricanes the central heat reservoir is the warm tropical ocean, and its energy gets transferred up into the atmosphere through the processes of evaporation and condensation, which first store heat in the air and then release it. Finally, energy not used to power the storm gets released in the hurricane's outflow region, high in the freezing upper troposphere (or lower stratosphere), as a kind of exhaust stream. "Atmospheric machines do not differ in principle from the machines known in physics and engineering," Riehl wrote in *Tropical Meteorology*. Later he continued with the same metaphor: "If the machinery is faulty, a hurricane will no more form than a man-made machine will run."

Thanks to Riehl's heat-engine theory, we can now give a much fuller picture of how hurricanes work, merging the important but incomplete discoveries of men like Redfield, Espy, and Ferrel with knowledge gained during and after World War II. It's important to understand the basic mechanisms driving these storms to see why global climate change could intensify or otherwise change them. By making this intuition more plausible, Riehl's work provided an early eddy that would swirl into the modern hurricane–global warming debate.

As air flows into a hurricane—moving toward a central low pressure region and spiraling due to the Earth's rotation—it draws up water vapor from the evaporating sea surface. This vapor contains energy in the form of latent heat. The air also takes up warmth from the ocean, a factor that turns out to be very important. As the air spirals inward near the surface, it experiences a pressure drop, which (according to very basic physics) should cause it to expand and its temperature to decrease. Yet "*such decreases never occur,*" wrote Riehl in 1950. Instead, "rapid transfer of heat from ocean to atmosphere" helps to keep the air warm. This means the inflowing air cannot disrupt the hurricane by cooling it off. The air is, however, slowed down by friction as it drags along the sea surface—a central constraint upon the intensity that hurricanes can achieve.

Before long, the warm, humid, and buoyant air converges near the storm center, where it begins to rise rapidly upward. (Rising also occurs in the hurricane rainbands, threads of cloud organized in spiral arrays farther from the storm center.) The ring-shaped eye wall of the hurricane is, in essence, an air elevator, sloping slightly outward with height, whose lifts are thick towers of cumulonimbus clouds. The air never reaches the storm center because it is rotating, thanks to the Coriolis force. That's why hurricanes can have calm eyes, where air is slowly sinking, surrounded by eye walls in which air is rushing upward, winds are howling, and torrents of rain fall almost horizontally—a phenomenon that would surely have mystified Espy, with his centripetal theory of winds.

As the air rises in the hurricane eye wall, it cools, and eventually the water vapor it contains condenses into clouds or rain. As this occurs, the once-latent heat gets released back into the atmosphere as sensible heat, warming the air further. Eventually, the air will be expelled at the top of the hurricane, miles above the Earth's surface, in anticyclonic outflow jets that spiral clockwise in the Northern Hemisphere. Here in this exhaust region, the ejected air joins cooler upper-atmospheric winds and travels many miles away, radiating some of its remaining heat to space.

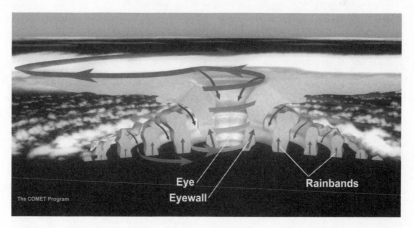

Image of a hurricane's heat engine in cross section. *Image credit: NOAA.*

At any time, however, more air is being pulled into the hurricane at lower levels, and with it more heat. And in an intensifying hurricane, air gets pulled in, and rotates, faster and faster. That's why scientists measure hurricane strength by estimating the storm's maximum sustained wind speed and minimum sea level pressure (hurricanes create the most dramatic pressure falls ever recorded at the Earth's surface). As pressure decreases due to rising heated air, winds spiral inward more quickly. The winds also blow harder as the radius of spiral rotation shrinks toward the center of the storm due to a law of physics known as the "conservation of angular momentum"—the same reason that figure skaters twirl faster when they tuck in their arms.

The storm's powerful winds, in turn, dramatically roil the ocean, generating gigantic waves and then lopping off their tops, sending sheets of sea spray through the air. Through processes not yet completely understood (and difficult to study), sea-spray effects at high wind speeds apparently create more evaporation, leading to still more heat being carried into the center of the storm. The state of the ocean in a full-fledged hurricane—the final sight of many an unfortunate sailor—must be terrifying to behold. As Riehl put it in his textbook: "It is hard to say where the ocean ends and where the atmosphere begins!"

If not disturbed by other environmental factors, a hurricane will continue to strengthen as long as its central energy source, the warm ocean, can sustain it. It's simple thermodynamics. If the storm turns over land, it will quickly weaken, having lost its power source. If it veers over a patch of cooler water—perhaps stirred up from the ocean depths by a previous hurricane—it will also weaken. Finally, hurricanes weaken themselves by mixing the ocean and drawing up cool water from below. Should a hurricane plow over a deep layer of warm water, however, it can rapidly intensify to Category 4 or 5 strength. One of the most dramatic cases was 2005's Hurricane Wilma, which had the lowest central pressure—882 millibars, or 26.05 inches—of any known Atlantic hurricane. Wilma strengthened from a mere tropical storm into a Category 5 monster in just twenty-four hours before slamming the Yucatán and, later, southern Florida.

As we'll see, many environmental factors besides ocean heat also influence hurricane strength and regions of formation. But by the 1950s, the essential linkage between hurricanes and heat—specifically ocean temperatures—had been clearly established. Riehl could describe these storms as being "sensitive to slight temperature and moisture variations." He could even suggest—and did—that given reliable measurements of tropical sea surface temperatures, it ought to be possible to predict seasonal hurricane activity in advance. All of this strongly foreshadows not only future forecasting schemes, but the present-day global warming–hurricane debate.

More generally, thanks to the work of Riehl and his colleagues, it became possible to say, for the first time, that scientists on some level actually *understood* how hurricanes amass their deadly power. The "observational assault on the mysteries of the tropics" had borne fruit—and Riehl's student, William Gray, would carry it still further.

# 3 • ... and Computer Models

At the time when Riehl conducted his most important research, understanding hurricanes constituted a major national priority. The 1950s and 1960s continued a very active Atlantic hurricane era that began in 1926. Just a few of the more notable storms to affect the United States during this period included the San Felipe/Okeechobee Hurricane of 1928 (which killed 1,500 people in Puerto Rico and several thousand more during an inland storm surge in southern Florida), the Great New England Hurricane of 1938 (which killed hundreds and flooded Providence, Rhode Island, under twenty feet of water), 1965's Hurricane Betsy (which hit New Orleans as a Category 3 storm and led to the creation of the levee system that failed in Hurricane Katrina), and finally, 1969's Camille—one of only three storms in recorded history to strike the United States at full Category 5 intensity.

Camille's maximum surface winds over the Gulf of Mexico were estimated to have exceeded 200 miles per hour; the day before landfall, a reconnaissance aircraft measured the storm's minimum central pressure at 905 millibars (26.73 inches). Retrospective analyses suggest Camille's relentless intensification is explainable only if the storm tracked straight up the Loop Current, a deep pulse of warm water that circles through the Gulf at varying locations and intensities in different times of the year. The storm blitzed the Mississippi coast just before midnight on August 17, killing 150 people and propelling a storm surge of well over twenty feet at Pass Christian. "The old antebellum residences, which had stood in grandeur along the Mississippi coastline from Pass Christian to Biloxi and had withstood the ravages of many hurricanes for more than a hundred years, had been totally or substantially destroyed, with few exceptions," wrote then National Hurricane Center director Robert Simpson. In the Pass Christian area, "houses had been swept entirely off their foundations and splintered into unrecognizable small pieces, characteristic of the wind damage ordinarily associated with major tornadoes." Camille then blew inland and dumped rain measured in feet, not inches, over Virginia's Blue Ridge Mountains, causing flash flooding and landslides that led to more than 150 additional deaths.

In the context of such destruction, society depended heavily upon scientists like Simpson and Riehl, who flew into these killer storms to study and track them. Yet even during an active hurricane era, tropical meteorology remained outside the meteorological mainstream. "It was not that popular, even at the University of Chicago," remembers Riehl student T. N. Krishnamurti, now a meteorologist at Florida State University. "It was a side issue. Most people were still worried about North American weather."

And not just weather itself. Even as Riehl and colleagues flew into storms, most meteorologists were moving in a different direction, one rooted much more deeply in theory and mathematics than data-gathering. They aimed to reformulate weather forecasting on the basis of the laws of physics, which in turn required understanding the large-scale dynamics of the atmosphere—the central equations governing its fluid flow. These "dynamical meteorologists" sought to simplify the equations so that they could be plugged into early computers and used to predict weather. They weren't conducting aircraft reconnaissance; they were far too busy writing code.

The theoreticians who provided the greatest insights into dynamical meteorology became the central leaders of the field, the scientists everyone else admired and wanted to follow. Perhaps the most distinguished of them all was Jule Gregory Charney, who would become one of the most famous meteorologists of the twentieth century and chair the meteorology department at MIT. Not only did Charney train today's central hurricane–climate theorist, Kerry Emanuel, but he

also helped to found the tradition of weather and climate modeling—
now centered, among other places, at Princeton's Geophysical Fluid
Dynamics Laboratory, a branch of NOAA—that has bolstered concerns about the effect of global warming on hurricanes and about
global warming in general.

Despite dramatic differences in immediate posthumous stature,
Charney's early career overlaps with Riehl's. He grew up in Los Angeles and showed a strong mathematical aptitude, teaching himself calculus as a teenager. Then he attended UCLA, another major early hub
of American meteorology. Soon Charney, like Riehl, found himself
giving military meteorologists a crash course in synoptic forecasting
techniques. Ironically, Charney loathed the drudgery of drawing isobars on charts. For a mathematically inclined thinker like himself,
such exercises were a "chore" and a "total waste of time." Weather map
analysis was the only UCLA meteorology course in which he didn't
get an A, and he would later describe the map-based extrapolation
techniques of synoptic meteorology as far too subjective in nature—
an art, perhaps, but not a science. But during wartime everything
hinged upon the immediate and the practical, so Charney pitched in.

After the war, however, Charney demonstrated what mathematical tools—and a theoretical style of thinking that stripped complex
problems down to their essential components—could do for his field.
For his doctoral thesis, he ambitiously set out to solve what he called
the *"haute problème* of meteorology"—the longstanding question of
how extra-tropical cyclones (not hurricanes) originate. The thesis developed, mathematically, a tremendously influential concept now referred to as "baroclinic instability," which explains the origins of
extra-tropical cyclones on a rotating planet by showing how the westerly winds of the mid-latitudes become a "seat of constant instability"
due to their increasing speed with altitude and the temperature differences to their north and south. The latter arise inevitably from the
planet's differential heating by the sun: The equatorial regions receive
much more solar energy than the poles. The huge cyclonic eddies of
the mid-latitudes are thus the atmosphere's way of mixing together air

of different temperatures and redistributing heat pole-ward. That means they're critically locked in to the climate system—indeed, fundamental to it.

In this early work, Charney maintained meteorology's selective emphasis on extra-tropical (specifically North American and European) weather. The bias was embedded in the very analysis of baroclinic instability. In his unending quest to pare down meteorological problems to their core elements, Charney privileged dynamic over thermodynamic thinking in his famous thesis and deliberately ignored latent heat release from condensation. No scientist concerned with the tropics could have safely made a similar simplification—but most meteorologists were not so concerned, and baroclinic instability quickly became a dominant paradigm.

Charney's explanation of baroclinic instability helped usher in the age of numerical weather prediction or numerical modeling, in which computers—today they are invariably supercomputers—forecast future weather and climate states by starting with observations from nature and then solving the equations governing motion (which include the Coriolis force), conservation of energy, the behavior of gases including water vapor, and other fundamental attributes of the atmosphere (or, in "coupled" models, the ocean-atmosphere system). Numerical models essentially divide the atmosphere up into different sections or cells of a grid, and then solve the relevant equations for each section, as well as calculating how the different parts relate to each other. The higher the model's "resolution," the more sections there will be and thus the more calculations, which means that more computer power is necessary to run the model.

There's a long history to the notion that if scientists had perfect knowledge of the state of the atmosphere and the equations governing it, they could predict weather and climate far into the future. In 1904 the Norwegian Vilhelm Bjerknes proposed precisely this idea: Get together enough observations about the atmosphere's initial state, and then solve all the equations to get a forecast. It was a bold new vision for meteorology, one that would, if realized, make the field a much more direct extension of physics. Meteorology, Bjerknes wrote, would become an "exact science." But in the early 1900s that was merely a distant dream. Another scientist, Lewis Fry Richardson, had devised a similar plan and spent six weeks trying to calculate six hours of weather over Europe, only to come out with a result that was dramatically off base. Still, the hope of calculating the weather remained alive. Finally in the early 1950s, two scientists more than any others made it happen: Charney and the mathematician and computing pioneer John von Neumann, both based at Princeton's Institute for Advanced Study at the time.

In 1946 von Neumann had issued a proposal to launch an "investigation of the theory of dynamic meteorology in order to make it accessible to high-speed, electronic, digital, automatic computing, of a type which is beginning to be available and which is likely to be increasingly available in the future." Von Neumann had the vision, but Charney's participation in the project was crucial. With his genius for reducing the atmosphere's behavior to its most essential processes, he set to work extending the process of dynamic simplification that he had begun in his baroclinic instability paper, filtering out factors, such as fast-moving sound and gravity waves, that were less essential to forecasting the weather. Ultimately, Charney honed his equations down enough to be used in early computers. And so in 1950 the team of Princeton scientists traveled to Maryland to run the first numerical weather prediction using the famous ENIAC (short for Electronic Numerical Integrator and Computer), a hulking machine that used punch cards, malfunctioned frequently, and had vastly less processing power than today's PCs. The era of numerical modeling had begun, and it would transform meteorology forever, making purely data-driven forms of research and forecasting a thing of the past.

During the heady days of the 1950s, some speculated that it might be possible to perfectly predict weather years into the future. But the modelers would soon be humbled by the 1961 discovery of chaos, or the so-called "butterfly effect," by Edward Lorenz, Charney's colleague at MIT. There's a limit to how accurate future weather prediction can be, Lorenz realized, because tiny differences in a model's initial description of the state of the atmosphere can have a large impact on the forecast. As a consequence, it would never be possible to reliably predict the weather beyond about a week or two at most. Weather predictions within this range, however, have become increasingly accurate over time, as computers have grown more powerful and the equations contained in the models more comprehensive.

In the late 1950s, scientists began attempting to use numerical models to track the paths of hurricanes. It would not be until the 1990s, however, that the hurricane model run by NOAA's Geophysical Fluid Dynamics Laboratory could show more accuracy when it came to projecting storm paths than statistical models, which employed a variety of techniques including comparing a present storm to previous historical cases so as to determine the best analogue, and then using that analogue as the basis for the forecast. This was a significant breakthrough: Scientists' dynamic understanding of hurricanes, based upon equations and executed through a computer, now provided the best means of forecasting where they will go.

Today, when you're watching the Weather Channel during hurricane season, the familiar white cone projecting where a storm may travel within the next seventy-two hours is based upon the combined outputs from a variety of dynamical forecasting models (plus the judgments of National Hurricane Center experts who analyze those model outputs). This is known as an "ensemble" forecast. When forecasters employ multiple models to track the same hurricane, they get a far better sense of the range of possibilities for where it might end up— and accordingly, for which areas should be evacuated.

To Charney, computer modeling represented a grand merger of theory and observation. It used equations to explain the behavior of the atmosphere as well as hard data to determine what values to plug into those equations. As Charney wrote in a 1972 essay: "When a computer simulation successfully synthesizes a number of theoretically-predicted phenomena and is in accord with reality, it validates both itself and the theories—just as the birth of a child who resembles a paternal grandfather legitimizes both itself and its father." In other words, models must be tested against reality, and judged by that standard.

Charney noted in the same essay, however, that in the absence of a complete theoretical understanding, models themselves become the source of experiments: Vary the equations or other aspects of the model, plug the data back in, and see how much closer to reality you can get. But from the perspective of some scientific empiricists, this seemed an ungrounded and even suspicious way of doing things. "Tuning" the models to make them line up better with observations sounded like rigging the game.

Charney envisioned a variety of other uses for computer models. They could be used to study phenomena on different time scales, from short-range weather to long-range climate, as well as on different spatial scales—from the general circulation of the atmosphere down to individual types of storms, such as hurricanes. In fact, a decade or so after unleashing numerical weather prediction upon the world, Charney sought to carry his simplifying approach over into hurricane science, which had theoretical aspects of its own but had fundamentally been driven by the influx of new data from radar, upper-air measurements, and storm-flying. The resultant clash between different views of storms, while less contentious than the earlier American Storm Controversy, has many parallels to it and continued to create friction among meteorologists into the 1990s.

As for so many other scientists, Charney's interest in hurricanes arose from direct experience—not in the air in his case, but on the ground. In 1954 he spent the summer as an associate lecturer at the Woods Hole Oceanographic Institution in Cape Cod, Massachusetts. It was the same summer that hurricanes Carol and Edna bore down on New England. Both storms gave the Woods Hole area, which is wedged between Buzzard's Bay and the Nantucket Sound at the southwest corner of the Cape, a thrashing. "A tree fell on our car, electricity was shut off, and I was very impressed by Hurricane Carol," Charney later recalled. He directly attributed his later work on hurricanes to this experience: "I think, in my life, there have always been incidents which sort of set me off on something." Later, Charney traveled down to Florida to visit with the scientists involved in the National Hurricane Research Project.

Charney's heavily mathematical theory of how tropical cyclones originate—known as "Conditional Instability of the Second Kind," or CISK—was first published in a 1964 paper entitled "On the Growth of the Hurricane Depression," coauthored by the Norwegian dynamicist Arnt Eliassen, who had also worked on the Princeton meteorology project. Another dynamicist based at New York University named Vic Ooyama had influential early discussions with the two and later came up with his own version of what's sometimes called CISK, but has criticized Charney's account.

CISK sought to solve a problem that had arisen during early failed attempts to simulate hurricane formation in simple mathematical models. The theoreticians behind these studies postulated a state of "conditional instability"*—in other words, an atmosphere very conducive to convection and thus thunderstorm formation because it cooled steadily with elevation. Because air will rise as long as it remains warmer than its surroundings, such a vertical structure will encourage convective updrafts and the release of latent heat in clouds. And sure enough, in response to the unstable atmosphere, the simple models produced clouds and thunderstorms. But these were merely the building blocks of hurricanes, not hurricanes themselves.

So CISK sought to explain why the tropical atmosphere sometimes releases energy through the large-scale phenomenon of a hurricane, rather than simply through a random assortment of smaller individual thunderstorms. In other words, CISK sought to account for the *organization* of thunderclouds into hurricanes. Charney and Eliassen also postulated an unstable atmosphere but added a twist: a positive-feedback relationship between the release of latent heat and

---

*The original and well-established theory of conditional instability, which is taught in every meteorological textbook, might be termed conditional instability of the *first* kind; Charney's theory of CISK was therefore conditional instability of the *second* kind.

rising air in clouds, leading to ever lower surface air pressure, and still more low-level inflowing air, delivering up moisture through frictional processes at the sea surface. As their paper put it: "The cumulus- and cyclone-scale motions are thus to be regarded as cooperating rather than as competing—the clouds supplying latent heat energy to the cyclone, and the cyclone supplying the fuel, in the form of moisture, to the clouds." It has been observed that in placing latent heat so close to the center of the story, CISK echoes Espy's old thermal theory.

CISK was a sensation—a highly theoretical account of hurricanes for a theoretical and modeling era. It quickly crowded out Riehl's heat-engine theory. Attached to the image and reputation of Charney, CISK brought hurricanes to the attention of the dynamicist mainstream of meteorology. Although now considered flawed, it proved influential for a very long time, prompting a great deal of follow-on work and many permutations of the original Charney-Eliassen account (some arguably mislabeled as CISKs of various sorts). "There are fashions in science, and that was a fashion," recalls University of Oklahoma meteorologist Doug Lilly, a skeptic of CISK who supported a "heat engine" revival in the 1980s.

CISK had a number of key problems, many of which sprang from the attempt, so characteristic of Charney, to strip hurricanes down to mathematical essentials rather than study them in their full-blown reality. As in his doctoral thesis, Charney went searching for a mathematical type of instability to explain hurricanes—and he thought he had found it in an unstable atmosphere. Yet in the tropics, any temporary instability generated by the sun's heating of the oceans is quickly released through the formation of clouds and thunderstorms, which lift heat upward and tend to restore stability. This made sense: Riehl had learned many years earlier that tropical cyclones need an independent disturbance, such as an easterly wave, to get churning. Typical thunderstorm formation alone cannot do it, no matter how favorable the atmosphere is to convection and no matter how impressive the thunderstorms of the tropics may become.

Moreover, there was a problem with the way CISK treated the ocean. According to Charney and Eliassen, spiraling winds supply energy to the storm through "frictional convergence": Rough seas near the storm center slow down the incoming winds, causing them to converge inward toward that center rather than circling it. In such a situation air gets forced upward, carrying water vapor higher so that it can condense and release latent heat—thereby lifting more air, decreasing central pressure, and pulling in still more spiraling winds at low levels. The sea surface figured in the CISK account, but only by providing an environment in which the air at the boundary between sea and sky was suffused with moisture ready to be driven aloft. Yet for simplicity's sake, the original version of CISK explicitly ignored the importance of fluxes of warmth from the ocean, and generally deemphasized the ocean energy source.

From the 1960s until the 1980s, when it began to fall out of favor, CISK thus distracted attention away from the concept of hurricanes as ocean-driven "heat engines." In fairness, the theory also prompted a great deal of thinking—wrong ideas can be productive in that way. But CISK has also been characterized as a "setback" for the field, and has incited finger-pointing over who was responsible. "Don't bury me in the grave of CISK with Charney," Vic Ooyama, who protests his inclusion among traditional CISK adherents, has written. Apparently, Riehl also argued with Charney over CISK in the 1970s. The two scientists had great respect for one another, but here they diverged. By then, however, CISK was well on its way to becoming yet another dominant paradigm.

By eclipsing Riehl's heat-engine approach and sending hurricane science off on a bit of a tangent, CISK may have helped delay concern about the influence of global warming upon hurricanes. If he's truly guilty of this, though, Charney more than atoned with another theoretical and modeling foray—this time into climate science itself. Just like his student Emanuel, Charney combined hurricane and climate research among his many interests. Indeed, Charney played a central

role in evaluating whether we ought to trust global climate models—
the same models that predict dramatic changes from a doubling of
atmospheric carbon dioxide concentrations and that are roundly dismissed by global warming skeptics even today.

Like the study of hurricanes, the trajectory of research that would
eventually grow into modern climate science began in the nineteenth
century. In mid-century the Irish scientist John Tyndall first discovered
the greenhouse effect; by the early 1900s the Swede Svante Arrhenius
had calculated that doubling carbon dioxide concentrations in the
atmosphere could trigger a dramatic increase in global temperature,
warming the Earth by 4 degrees Celsius. But like hurricane research,
climate science developed unevenly until the period following World
War II. At that point, the two fields were set on a collision course, with
the ultimate impact timed for the present moment.

Data gathering helped drive the new concern about climate
change. In the 1950s, following decades of rising temperatures between 1910 and 1945, the U.S. Weather Bureau provided funding to
begin definitive measurements of atmospheric carbon dioxide at the
Mauna Loa Observatory in Hawaii. The scientist responsible was
Charles David Keeling of the Scripps Institution of Oceanography,
and his "Keeling Curve," showing ever-rising concentrations over
time, has become one of the canonical images of human-caused
global warming. Concerns were also spurred, however, by theory and
modeling. In 1955, once again at Princeton's Institute for Advanced
Study, Norman Phillips created the first simple but workable simulation of the Earth's atmosphere. It was called a "general circulation
model," or GCM. Before long, scientists would use this type of
model to predict the effects of the increasing atmospheric carbon
dioxide concentrations tracked by Keeling. Indeed, today "GCM"
more frequently refers to "global climate model" than to "general circulation model."

With the support of Charney and von Neumann, Phillips's work
became institutionalized through the General Circulation Research
Section of the U.S. Weather Bureau in Washington, D.C., headed by
Princeton project scientist Joseph Smagorinsky, another pioneer of

the data-theory scientific hybrid that is modeling. The General Circulation Research Section later changed its name to the Geophysical Fluid Dynamics Laboratory and moved back to Princeton, where modeling had originated, in 1968. Beginning in the 1960s, GFDL modeler Syukuro ("Suki") Manabe published several breakthrough papers with his collaborators detailing their attempts to simulate the workings of the atmosphere. Manabe headed up one prominent climate-modeling group; James Hansen, at the NASA Goddard Institute for Space Studies in New York City, led the other. Their and other models would gradually get faster, better at representing all three dimensions of the atmosphere, more highly resolved, and coupled to models attempting to simulate the behavior of the oceans. Most important, the different teams began to hone in on a key measurement: the so-called climate sensitivity, or the amount of globally averaged warming expected for a doubling of atmospheric concentrations of carbon dioxide. By the late 1970s Manabe's group had calculated a sensitivity of roughly 2 degrees Celsius, while Hansen's group got 4 degrees.

When viewed in context of the later hurricane–climate debate, one particularly intriguing result emerged from these early modeling studies. In a 1970 paper on GCM simulations of the tropics, Manabe and colleagues noted that disturbances similar to tropical cyclones appeared in the model, with low central pressures and warm core structures. Many of the computerized storms developed in the same regions of the globe where real hurricanes form, although others developed over land. In general, the modeled storms were unrealistically large and far weaker than real hurricanes. But scientists like Manabe suspected these discrepancies sprang from the fact that the GCM, with its very coarse resolution, simply could not capture the details of such small-scale phenomena as the hurricane eye, eye wall, or spiral rainbands. Manabe and his fellow scientists did not try to see what happened to the modeled storms if they doubled the carbon dioxide concentrations—not yet. But they had come up with a way of studying hurricanes radically different from the approach of the empiricists, who would heavily criticize them for it in later years.

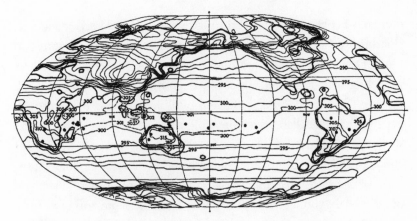

Figure from Manabe's 1970 study, showing the formation locations
for Southern Hemisphere tropical cyclone analogues (the black dots)
in an early global model.

It was around this time that Charney, the godfather of numerical
modeling, got involved in climate science. By then he occupied an en-
dowed chair and had recently stepped down from heading MIT's meteorology department. He was the establishment. Shortly before his
death from cancer in 1981, Charney chaired a highly influential 1979
National Academy of Sciences panel charged with evaluating the
models showing a substantial rise in global temperatures should atmospheric concentrations of carbon dioxide continue to increase. The
Charney Report, as it came to be called, had been requested by President Carter's science adviser Frank Press and was the first of many
studies from the hallowed National Academies to address the possibility of human-induced global warming. It carefully examined whether
any strong reasons existed for calling into question the latest projections of substantial warming for doubled $CO_2$ concentrations, but
couldn't find any. Instead, Charney's group noted that while several
positive feedbacks seemed likely to increase the amount of warming—
for example, the melting of reflective snow and ice, which would lead
to more absorption of solar radiation by the Earth's surface, which
would lead to more melting of snow and ice—no negative feedbacks
seemed capable of significantly offsetting that warming.

The "most important and obvious" positive feedback identified in the Charney report involved atmospheric water vapor. Due to a physical law known as the Clausius-Clapeyron equation, the amount of moisture that can be carried by the air increases along a steeply sloping curve as temperature rises. This means an atmosphere containing more carbon dioxide will also contain more evaporated water, another greenhouse gas sure to cause additional warming by absorbing and emitting still more infrared radiation.

Due in part to the magnitude of the water vapor feedback, Charney and his fellow panelists proclaimed that the two leading climate models of the time—those of Manabe and Hansen—were more or less reliable. Combining their most recent estimates, the Charney Report therefore concluded that the climate sensitivity for a doubling of $CO_2$ concentrations lay in the range of 1.5 to 4.5 degrees Celsius, with the most likely value falling smack in the middle: 3 degrees Celsius. That's roughly in line with Arrhenius's calculations made almost a century earlier. It's also extremely similar to the range—2 to 4.5 degrees Celsius, with a "best estimate" of 3 degrees—offered in 2007 by the Intergovernmental Panel on Climate Change, a United Nations body created to inform policymakers about the state of knowledge about global warming and its impacts, and today considered the gold standard of climate science.

At the time of the Charney Report in 1979, global warming had not yet become the battleground that it is today. The politicization of climate science and climate policy during the late 1980s and 1990s occurred for reasons that will be discussed later. But if we seek to understand why so many of today's hurricane specialists, as well as members of the broader hurricane preparedness and response community, became so skeptical of global warming and its effect on the storms in which they specialize, at least one of those reasons hinges upon a single very influential personality.

During the 1970s and 1980s, the Atlantic basin went into a relative lull period for hurricanes—especially "major" storms of Category

3 strength or higher—and interest in studying them correspondingly declined, at least in the United States. There were plenty of other exciting areas of disaster research—including, increasingly, climate change. But throughout this lull, one of the few American scientists who stuck with intensive hurricane research was Riehl's student William Gray. At Colorado State University, Gray was training a formidable team of students of his own. Some hailed from nations such as China and Australia, which also have to deal with tropical cyclones regularly. For all who were up for it, part of Gray's training regimen involved taking a flight into a hurricane. And part of it involved learning his empirical approach to meteorology.

In his research, Gray applied a data-crunching methodology to further elucidate the structure of hurricanes and uncover a wide range of factors associated with their formation. Much more than Riehl, he distrusted research reliant on complicated equations. Despite his skepticism of modeling, however, Gray excelled at detecting patterns in nature, much as Redfield had, long before him. Over the years, Gray's work made him a widely recognized leader of American and global hurricane science. After unveiling the first Atlantic seasonal hurricane-forecasting system in 1984, he became a hurricane superstar and a darling of the media. But he had absolutely no use for the notion of global warming, much less the idea that it might seriously affect the storms he'd spent a lifetime studying. And he had no problem saying so—loudly and often.

# 4 • "Lay That Matrix Down"

Bill Gray has a song he sometimes sings about computer modelers. He made it up, and seems quite proud of it. The song is mischievously funny, like Gray is. And it's deeply old-fashioned—again, like Gray.

It's a parody of "Pistol Packin' Mama," first recorded by Al Dexter in 1942 but also sung by Bing Crosby and Frank Sinatra. The original lyrics go like this:

> *Lay that pistol down, Babe.*
> *Lay that pistol down.*
> *Pistol packin' mama*
> *Lay that pistol down.*

Gray's version goes:

> *Lay that matrix down, Babe.*
> *Lay that matrix down.*
> *Equation-pushin' mama*
> *Lay that matrix down.*

Gray half sang and half recited "Equation-Pushin' Mama" for me on a cloudy Sunday in February 2006, as he drove me back to his home from his office at Colorado State University after a long interview. Gray's office was an empiricist's office: Nothing high-tech, just maps on the walls and, on a whiteboard, the results from years of competitions between Gray and his students to see who had produced the most skillful seasonal hurricane forecast for the Atlantic. It looked like most years, Gray had been victorious.

As we drove, Gray explained that although he rejects the idea that there's a strong human component to the recent global warming trend, he's no right-winger. "I don't drive a pick-up, I don't go to church, and I don't listen to Rush Limbaugh," he said. He even offered that he accepts the theory of evolution. In fact, Gray pronounced Charles Darwin one of the greatest scientists ever, in part because *The Origin of Species* wasn't reliant upon complex equations. Darwin, an empiricist to the core and another fan of Francis Bacon's inductive methods of reasoning, had built up his theory from decades of carefully compiled data—much like the work that Gray had done on hurricanes.

The analogy between biology and meteorology was unexpected, but Gray seemed pleased with it. After once again labeling his scientific rivals "equation pushers," he looked over at me, almost winking, and said: "You see how I get myself in trouble."

Five hours earlier, I'd pulled my rental car up to Gray's one-story blue house in Fort Collins, unsure what to expect from an encounter with the nation's most famous hurricane-scientist-turned-global-warming-debunker. To prepare, I'd read a number of nearly interchangeable profiles of Gray in newspapers from over the years. The story was usually the same: big tall guy with a stutter (it's most pronounced when he tries to say "hurricane"), might have been a ballplayer but for a busted knee. Got into meteorology instead, flew into a storm in 1958, started forecasting. Drives the same beat-up old car (actually he's since gotten a new one), has worked in the same office for over thirty years. And then in the late 1980s, Gray started predicting an uptick in Atlantic hurricane activity after the two-decade lull period. In 1995 he correctly forecast a near-record year, thereby becoming the number-one celebrity of American hurricane science. The disasters we've seen recently? Gray knew they were coming.

That's Gray the living legend, the man applauded by large crowds each spring at the National Hurricane Conference and Florida Governor's Hurricane Conference, where he ritually releases his forecast in advance of the coming season. But not all the profiles noted Gray's increasingly controversial role as a leading "skeptic"* of human-caused global warming who has stood before the U.S. Senate to debunk the theory—as well as (it goes without saying) the notion that global warming is changing hurricanes.

The man who opened the door to greet me didn't seem like an environmentalist's nemesis. Gray stands a towering six foot five, but somehow he isn't overwhelming, perhaps because age has stooped him a little (he's seventy-seven) or perhaps because he's gotten used to leaning over to talk to shorter people. My first impression when we met was of a kindly, elderly man. Gray wore drab brown pants and a brown sweater that day, his thin white hair combed back. He lives alone; his children have left and his wife, Nancy, the former mayor of Fort Collins (and a Democrat), died suddenly several years ago of cancer.

The famous hurricane scientist invited me into his kitchen and offered me coffee, only to discover he lacked sugar. So he pulled open a drawer filled with powdered sugar and used that. Later, when Gray told me he was devoting his remaining energies to debunking global warming, I could tell which aspects of life had been receiving less attention.

After spending much of the day with Gray—he talked on and on, an attribute I would notice again during his public speeches—it became obvious how he could have mentored a generation of influential hurricane researchers. Something about Gray's personality sucks you in, makes you want to become a follower. The word "charisma" doesn't do it justice. It's more that Gray seems completely unguarded, without guile. He will really, *really* tell you what he thinks, and he will tell you ten times over. "I've been in this field fifty years and I'll say what I want"—that pretty much summarizes his attitude. With it comes a mischievous sense of humor that, perhaps now more than before, is tinged by a morbid streak. At one point Gray made me promise that if he turned out to be correct in his prediction that the Earth would begin to cool in five to ten years as part of a natural cycle, I

---

*It has been my policy in this book to preserve scare quotes when referring to global warming "skeptics," or to call them contrarians.

would lay "dandelions on his grave" (a line he repeats often). Later he offered to show me the plot where he would be buried. We never got around to it, but I don't doubt that he would have.

Some of Gray's jokes seemed strained, though. When we first met, I was startled to see that his face was covered with large bluish bruises. Later, Gray explained that the bruises came from falling down during a jog through City Park near his home. But he also joked that his former Ph.D. student Greg Holland, an Australian who is a convert to the notion that global warming is strengthening hurricanes, had been up to Fort Collins and it had come to "fisticuffs."

What made this more painful than funny is that Gray had fallen out with many scientists who had once been peers and friends. Shortly before we met, the *Wall Street Journal* had run a front-page story about how combative the debate had become between Gray and Emanuel, Holland, and other researchers supportive of a hurricane–climate link. What really incensed the other scientists was that Gray would hurl ad hominem attacks and question their qualifications and motives, sometimes implying they had cooked up their results to secure future research funding. During an interview on CNN, for instance, Gray stated of the hurricane–climate issue: "There are all these medicine men out there who want to capitalize on general ignorance on this subject." There are drawbacks, then, to his "I'll say what I want" approach, and at least on some level, Gray seemed aware of them. "I'm becoming persona non grata with more and more people," he told me.

It was hard to tell whether he was hurt by this or simply amused.

To see how Gray became who he is, you need only listen to one of his hilariously entertaining public speeches. In the course of lampooning global warming, he'll practically tell you his whole story.

Gray often discusses his childhood in the presentation. He grew up in Washington, D.C., during the period of warming that caught the attention of scientists and the public alike before coming to an end in the mid-1940s. Gray sometimes relates how he wrote a seventh-grade paper on the "great warming" that occurred roughly between 1910 and 1945 (which scientists have tried to explain by invoking a range of factors including solar intensity changes, greenhouse gas emissions, and internal variability of the climate). "There were all kind of people talking about, although we will likely win the Second World War, we're going to have a Dust Bowl, and all these things," Gray recalls.

As Gray delights in pointing out, however, a cooling period then began around mid-century, even as atmospheric carbon dioxide concentrations continued to rise. Climate scientists today suspect this modest cooling was *also* partly human-caused, as industrial air pollution filled the atmosphere with reflective aerosol molecules like sulfur dioxide, which bounce back incoming solar radiation and thus temporarily offset the warming effects of carbon dioxide (this presumably explains why the cooling was stronger in the more industrially polluted Northern Hemisphere). But some journalists went overboard with the issue, splicing the cooling trend to renewed scientific research on the causes of planetary shifts between glacial and interglacial periods and thus winding up with truly lurid predictions about the possible onset of a new "Ice Age." A few alarmed scientists helped feed these speculations.

"Global cooling" is thus something of a canard, but it's one that climate skeptics like Gray enjoy making endless hay of. After having to deal with global-warming worries in the early part of the century, Gray tells his audiences, suddenly "we had the Ice Age people coming out of the closet." This always draws a laugh.

Growing up, though, Gray wasn't making big crowds titter, unless inadvertently. In adolescence his stutter was debilitating. The way he dealt with it—at least as related by Hugh Willoughby, a longtime hurricane specialist who knows Gray well and formerly directed the Hurricane Research Division at NOAA's Atlantic Oceanographic and Meteorological Laboratory—would come to define his adult personality. "One day, he just said to himself, 'I'm not going to worry about this. I stutter,'" says Willoughby. "And that went over to everything in his life. He is just a sublimely unself-conscious human being."

Around the time the early-century warming trend ended and the mid-century cooling trend began, Gray attended George Washington

University in Washington, D.C. There he majored in geography—a course of study that did not provide a very intensive mathematical or statistical training—and pitched for the baseball team. Gray's early heroes had been Bob Feller and Walter Johnson; "the only thing I wanted in life was to make the major leagues," he's written. But after a college knee injury, a sports career didn't seem possible, so Gray joined the U.S. Air Force in 1953. After basic training, the service sent him to the University of Chicago to study meteorology. At the end of a year, Gray was routed into the field to forecast, but his brief stay in Chicago made a big impression. He took the very first course that used Riehl's *Tropical Meteorology* textbook. The text, Gray would later recall, was a "tour de force" for a young student, especially one who at that time had "none of the advantages of the satellite, computer, etc." Meteorology had not yet been fully transformed by the new technologies.

In the fall of 1957, after several years spent forecasting on the Azores Islands and elsewhere—where he operated as a synoptic meteorologist, working from weather maps with their isobars and isotherms—Gray returned to the University of Chicago. Then, on October 4, 1957, came an event that changed the course of science in America forever: the Soviet launch of Sputnik. In an effort to shore up the nation's competitiveness, Congress responded with a massive wave of funding for the sciences, and meteorology suddenly looked like a very exciting field. Moreover, Chicago had a stunning reputation. Not only did it feature Riehl; the department had been founded by Carl-Gustaf Rossby, who had discoved the large-scale dynamic fluctuations in the atmosphere known as "Rossby Waves." Rossby had attracted many celebrated scientists (including, for a time, Palmén and Charney) to the "Chicago School."

The next year, in 1958, Riehl took Gray down to Florida for his flights into Hurricane Helene, an experience that would prove life-altering. Gray wasn't going to be a ballplayer, but there was another career that featured an on-season and off-season and lots of records and statistics: hurricane research. In 1961, a year after Riehl left Chicago to found the Department of Atmospheric Science at Colorado State University, Gray followed. By 1964 he'd received his Ph.D. for a dissertation entitled "On the Scales of Motion and Internal Stress Characteristics of the Hurricane," based on storm flight data from Helene and two other 1958 hurricanes, Cleo and Daisy. Gray set up as a researcher and defined himself, unmistakably, as a member of the Redfield-Loomis observational school of storm studies. "Some people say only the dullards will stay and have patience to slug it out over the years with data," says Gray, likening his methodology to that of an archeologist. "I guess my mental capacities were such that I would be classified as one of [them]."

Perhaps the epitome of Gray's empirical approach was a technique called compositing: in essence, crunching together hundreds or even thousands of upper-air measurements taken by rawinsondes in the vicinity of hurricanes. Through this method Gray and his students could analyze the large-scale storm structure by computing budgets for energy, water vapor, vorticity, and other quantities. But not content merely to describe how hurricanes worked, Gray also set his sights on a still incompletely resolved issue in hurricane science: genesis. Riehl had successfully described what fully formed hurricanes *are*—heat engines—but what brings them into existence in the first place has proven a much harder question to fully answer.

In 1968, Gray published one of his most famous papers on the genesis problem, one still regularly cited today. Crammed with hand-sketched figures, it presented an overview of the regions where hurricanes regularly form and identified a number of environmental conditions that seem to favor them. Gray opened by announcing his methodology. Unlike other scientists who'd advanced "theories of development" without adequate data, or set up unrealistic models, he would "take the empirical approach and go directly to the observations."

The paper began with a map of global hurricane distribution that had increasingly come into focus as more storm data accumulated. Researchers as far back as Redfield and Piddington had tried to survey the world's cyclone-prone regions, but Gray's 1968 map still remains mostly accurate (with some noteworthy exceptions). It made clear that tropical cyclones largely form in what scientists today often classify as six ocean basins or three "belts" of activity. Within the Western

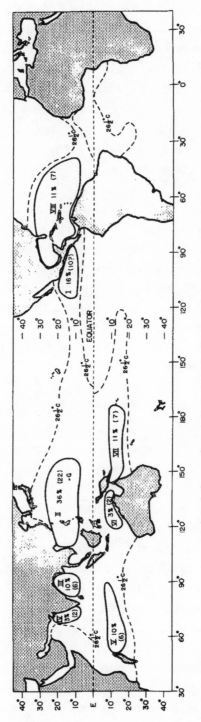

A hand-drawn figure depicting the basins where tropical cyclones form along with the 26.5 degrees C isotherm, from Gray's 1968 paper.

Hemisphere, the Atlantic and the Northeast Pacific basins (the latter off the western and southwestern coast of Mexico) comprise the central sites of hurricane formation. Second, in the Eastern Hemisphere north of the equator, the Northwest Pacific basin (east of China and the Philippines, the home of some 36 percent of all storms in Gray's analysis) and the North Indian basin (the Arabian Sea and the Bay of Bengal; Gray counted this as two basins) provide another zone of tropical cyclone activity. Finally, the Southwest Pacific (to the east and northeast of Australia) and the South Indian (east of Madagascar and west-northwest of Australia; again, Gray counted this as two basins) host the storms that form in the Southern Hemisphere.

Examining why this particular distribution should exist, Gray found several consistent environmental factors across these regions. Surface winds were characterized by strong "relative vorticity" or spin, meaning the rotation of the air in relation to the Earth complemented (rather than negated) the Coriolis effect. The regions also had low levels of so-called vertical wind shear. When winds at different altitudes blow in different directions or at different speeds, they can disrupt the organized structure of a hurricane and force drier air into its humid core. In the South Atlantic and the Central Pacific, where Gray stated that hurricanes "do not occur," high levels of wind shear persisted. This focus on shear would prove one of Gray's most significant contributions to hurricane science, but he'd been wrong to describe these two basins as totally inactive. The world turned out to be stormier than Gray had supposed in 1968.

Gray had powerfully laid out his empiricist methodology and shown what it could do. Then he began extending it. In 1978 he traveled the globe to survey its tropical cyclone forecasting centers on behalf of the World Meteorological Organization, soon concluding that about eighty storms occur each year in the various ocean basins, with the Atlantic representing just a fraction of the total. Gray first published the eighty storms figure in a 1979 paper that's probably best known for describing his six necessary "genesis parameters" for hurricane formation. Palmén had already identified the importance of sea-surface temperature and distance from the equator. Now, Gray introduced four other parameters: low-level relative vorticity, levels of vertical wind shear, the degree of conditional instability, and humidity levels in the middle atmosphere (which affect cumulus growth). He also classified his parameters as either dynamic (the Coriolis force, relative vorticity, and vertical wind shear) or thermal (sea surface temperature down to sixty meters, conditional instability, mid-level humidity). For hurricanes to form, both dynamics and thermodynamics have to line up favorably.

In this early work, Gray had done more than any other scientist to explore where hurricanes form and under what conditions, and he'd done it all by crunching huge piles of data. Even though his theoretical and modeling insights were slight, he'd made tremendous progress. Much of the credit for Gray's success must go to his talents and work ethic; however, he also may have benefited from the lack of competition at the time.

Throughout the prime of Gray's career, hurricanes weren't a very hot topic. Compared with the 1950s and 1960s, Atlantic storm activity had gone into a marked remission. The lull period would run from 1971 to 1994, and during that time hurricane research became something of a backwater. "When I came through school, I would guess the number of professors who had research projects on hurricanes wouldn't have been more than four or five," remembers William Frank, a hurricane specialist at Penn State University who studied under Gray (one of those four or five), receiving his Ph.D. in 1976. But Gray slogged on with his data, largely unnoticed for the time being.

Even in those days, Gray paid attention to the intersection of science and politics. And like a number of scientists (including Emanuel), in the mid-1980s he grew incensed by Carl Sagan's theory of "nuclear winter," which he considered tantamount to the misuse of science to advance the plainly political ends of the antinuclear movement.

In 1983, Sagan and a group of sympathetic scientists theorized that in a situation of nuclear fallout, the atmosphere would fill up with so much dust and smoke that an even greater planetary catastrophe would result. A long period of darkness and freezing temperatures could shut down agriculture and thus starve those remaining humans who'd been lucky enough to survive the nuclear devastation itself. Sagan and allies had used very simplified models to generate their doomsday scenario, however, and other scientists were disturbed by their plainly political foray. Among them was Gray. "He took an extremist view on nuclear winter, which turned out to be correct, and I know I agreed with him at the time," recalls Gray's former student Greg Holland. It was a kind of prequel to Gray's hard line against the theory of human-caused global warming (although Gray limited his grumbling about "nuclear winter" to his peers, rather than making it public).

At around the same time, Gray's methodology led him to another major discovery. Having taught courses covering the subject, Gray knew which years in the past had seen El Niño conditions in the Pacific Ocean. The El Niño phenomenon—the name refers to the Christ Child—was apparently first identified by Peruvian fishermen, who noted a warm ocean current that appeared around Christmas, in some years powerfully enough to dramatically change weather in the region. Eventually scientists linked this local occurrence to a global atmospheric and oceanic fluctuation now referred to as the El Niño–Southern Oscillation, or ENSO. During ENSO, which occurs roughly once every two to seven years, the pool of warm water usually located in the western Pacific spreads eastward all the way to the coast of the Americas, in the process dramatically raising tropical ocean temperatures in the central and eastern Pacific. Examining the data, Gray suddenly saw a pattern: During El Niño years, Atlantic hurricanes tended to be suppressed. The phenomenon occurs for multiple reasons, one of which Gray hypothesized: The warming of the eastern tropical Pacific during El Niño destabilizes the atmosphere above it, generating deep and intense thunderstorm activity. This creates stronger winds aloft, which in turn interfere with the formation of hurricanes in the Atlantic basin.

The strong inhibiting effect of El Niño on Atlantic hurricanes was there waiting to be found, but it took someone like Gray to see it. Along with his data underscoring the significance of vertical wind shear, the El Niño connection may be Gray's most enduring discovery.

It also had large practical implications. Gray found that three-quarters of major hurricane strikes to the U.S. coast occurred during non–El Niño years. No wonder, then, that even as he outlined the El Niño link in 1984, Gray also launched the endeavor that would make him most famous: a seasonal forecasting scheme for the Atlantic basin, which would predict the number of hurricanes and tropical storms months before their actual arrival. The technique was fairly rudimentary: 1) Prior to the June 1 start of the hurricane season, cobble together data on whether El Niño is coming and on other relevant climatological factors (such as oscillations of stratospheric wind and variations in sea-level air pressure); 2) employ statistical formulas, based on correlations between climatology and storm activity during previous hurricane seasons, to determine the likely hurricane activity for the coming year; and 3) issue a prediction. Using this methodology, Gray noted that forecasts could be made "without any expenditure of computer resources." Clearly, this would not be a numerical modeling exercise. Gray also reserved the right to use his meteorological instincts, in addition to the statistics, to shade the forecasts up or down in a way that wasn't precisely quantifiable.

It's hard to overstate the breakthrough that Gray had achieved with his forecasting scheme. Still, it had weaknesses, not the least of which was the difficulty of predicting El Niño far enough in advance. More generally, Gray's forecasts relied on previous correlations between factors like El Niño and hurricane activity, rather than a physically based understanding of why these factors (or other unknown ones) may have influenced the numbers and strengths of storms. "He was doing all of these empirical things, with no understanding, or no physical hypothesis about why this would be," remarks Richard Anthes, president of the University Corporation for Atmospheric Research in Boulder, Colorado. "He's got these empirical predictors, that if the ocean's hot, if there's weak wind shear, if there's lots of disturbances, if there's no El Niño—these indicators are surrogates for physical effects."

If you haven't identified the chain of cause and effect, however, you run the risk of being blindsided when a previously effective predictor of hurricane activity—identified on the basis of statistical correlations detected in past seasons—suddenly stops working. After all, if two factors correlate, that may well be because some third (but un-detected) causal factor influences both of them. This underscores an-other weakness of Gray's forecasting scheme, one he fully admitted: The technique essentially assumed the future would continue to repli-cate the past. But if the world changed significantly—say, because of global warming—the climatology of the past might no longer serve as a reliable guide to future hurricane activity. In that situation, without illumination of the sort provided by theory and computer models, the forecaster could be left with little more than instinct to go on.

Gray's forecasting experiences in the late 1980s and 1990s exposed such weaknesses, even as they also validated his intuitions and made him famous.

For some reason, the Carolinas seem to attract "H" hurricanes. In 1954 came Hazel; in 1958 (almost) came Helene, the storm Gray cut his teeth on. And then thirty-one years later, in 1989, came Hugo, the first in a series of storms that would successively increase the degree of alarm with which Americans view hurricane risks. Throughout that period Gray was there with his forecast, the meteorological equivalent of a bullhorn, warning the Atlantic was about to get very nasty again.

Hugo was a classic Cape Verde–type storm, so named because it formed from a tropical wave relatively near the African coast and the Cape Verde Islands, and so had many days to intensify over the warm waters of the Atlantic's main hurricane development region before threatening the Caribbean and the United States. Sure enough, Hugo lasted for thirteen days and attained Category 5 status, with a minimum sea level pressure of 918 millibars (27.11 inches) over open water. After causing $3 billion in damages in the Caribbean (Puerto Rico was par-ticularly hard hit), Hugo turned north and weakened, but then re-intensified over the warm Gulf Stream just before striking the U.S. East Coast near midnight on September 21. A Category 4 at landfall and the most powerful hurricane to impact the United States since 1969's Camille, Hugo just barely overshot Charleston, South Carolina. The Bulls Bay area north of the city experienced a storm surge of nearly twenty feet, and Hugo was ultimately credited with $7 billion in damage to the U.S. mainland, a record until it was surpassed by Hurricane Andrew in 1992.

Gray's forecast for 1989, the year of Hugo, had been a bust. He predicted only four hurricanes; instead the year saw seven, including one monstrous land-falling storm. The failed forecast had used several key predictors of hurricane activity, including El Niño, but 1989 led Gray to add another that he believed had made the difference: rainfall levels in the Western Sahel region of sub-Saharan Africa. Sahel rainfall, he hypothesized, influences the African easterly waves that Riehl had analyzed back in the 1940s. Gray figured that when there's more rainfall in the Sahel, the waves tend to be stronger and better organized, and therefore more likely to spark the growth of hurricanes.

And Gray went farther: He sounded the alarm. Hugo had been the second extremely intense Atlantic storm of the past two years; 1988 had seen Category 5 Gilbert, which set an Atlantic basin record for its low central pressure (888 millibars; 26.22 inches) and slammed the Yucatán Peninsula, bringing wind speeds of 160 miles per hour. The two years had also seen three additional storms that reached Category 4 strength—and at the same time, a return to more plentiful Sahel rainfall after a period of drought. Gray suspected a change was afoot. "In the next ten to twenty years, we'll see many more intense landfall U.S. storms than we have in the last twenty years in Florida and the East Coast, not so much in the Gulf Coast as in Florida and the East Coast," he told one reporter. "I feel Florida is an absolute sitting duck in the shooting gallery," he added. A great deal was at stake, for during the lull period for Atlantic hurricanes, coastal population and property value had swelled. Now, according to Gray, much destruction might await in the near future.

Meanwhile, Gray dug into studying Sahel rainfall patterns. In a 1990 study, he came up with what sounded like a repeat of the El Niño story: The occurrence of major hurricanes in the Atlantic, he reported, showed a statistically significant linkage to Sahel precipitation, which had been high from 1947 through 1969 (when many intense Atlantic hurricanes formed) but in drought conditions from 1970 to

1987 (when intense Atlantic hurricane activity also declined). Journalists covering the new findings knew just how to play it: "Stock up on candles, dig out the rubber boots and start watching the weather forecasts in Senegal," *Newsday* reported. In the study's conclusion, Gray once again anticipated an end to the Sahel drought and a dramatic new hurricane era. Perhaps less noticed was the swipe at global warming accompanying this prediction: "The historical data imply that such an increase in intense hurricane activity should be viewed as a natural change and not as a result of man's influence on his climate."

With all of this, Gray proved roughly half right. Despite the blip in 1988 and 1989, the hurricane lull wasn't over yet. It wouldn't officially end until 1995 (although 1992's Hurricane Andrew, a Category 5 storm now regarded as an anomaly for its era, caused massive devastation in southern Florida). And while Sahel rainfall levels certainly do change in response to other major climatic factors, they weren't the stellar forecasting tool Gray had hoped for. Later, he would remove the Sahel predictor from the forecast after it "just didn't work in the late nineties," as he put it to me. Today scientists suspect that, while Sahel rainfall and Atlantic hurricane activity do indeed correlate, it's probably due to a third factor—larger-scale patterns in the oceans and atmosphere—influencing both of them.

In short, Gray had successfully predicted the Atlantic would grow more active, although not necessarily with the right timing or for the right reasons. But you had to give him credit for going out on a limb. "Bill in some ways is like a Civil War surgeon," says Hugh Willoughby. "A lot of what he's doing is wrong, but where would we be without the experience those guys got cutting off gangrenous arms and legs?" It's a perspective on Gray echoed by hurricane science pioneers Robert and Joanne Simpson, who knew him from his earliest storm flights with the NHRP. One of Gray's greatest virtues, they noted, is his willingness to throw out ideas, argue over them, and then eat some crow if he's proved wrong.

In the context of the looming debate over hurricanes and global warming, Gray's paper on West African rainfall contained a significant endnote. It referenced the master's thesis of Gray's student Chris

Landsea, who worked on the seasonal forecast and early in his career co-authored numerous studies on Atlantic hurricanes and the Sahel with Gray. The thesis showed that good predictors existed, in advance of the Atlantic hurricane season, for Sahel rainfall levels. A small reference, perhaps, but it underscores that Gray has probably exerted his influence most powerfully through his distinguished students, many of whom have gone on to pursue illustrious careers of their own in hurricane research.

Gray's first Ph.D. student graduated in 1972; since then, he's advised nineteen other successful doctoral students in atmospheric science (not to mention fifty successful master's students). That's quite a lot of hurricane specialists who've heard Gray's endlessly repeated message about the importance of data and the flaws of modeling. Much as Riehl did, Gray encourages them all to experience hurricanes from the inside by taking a storm flight. Not all of them, however, have fully internalized their mentor's scientific philosophy.

Even if he didn't get the precise year right, Gray knew in his bones that the period of relative Atlantic hurricane inactivity would come to an end at some point. He himself had seen a much more active era, the 1950s and 1960s. So he continued to issue warnings.

Then when 1995 finally rolled around, bringing a staggering nineteen storms in the Atlantic, eleven of them hurricanes and five of them major hurricanes, Gray became a true press celebrity. His August forecast that year, worked on by Landsea, had predicted just such an active season: seven more hurricanes (or nine in total), eleven more storms (or sixteen in total), and three major hurricanes. Gray had undershot slightly, especially on the intense storms, but he'd correctly predicted a huge surge in activity. Taking note, ABC News named him Person of the Week in September 1995. Anchor Forrest Sawyer dubbed him "Bill Gray, America's hurricane sentinel, who is sounding a warning siren as shrill as the winds that whipped through the Caribbean this week." Then began a torrent of media profiles, which captured Gray at the high point of a high-achieving career.

He'd demonstrated the importance of vertical wind shear and El Niño to hurricanes. He'd pioneered the empirical study of storm genesis as well as Atlantic seasonal hurricane forecasting. Most of all, he'd trained more than enough students to create a powerful legacy. And all the while he'd remained the data guy, the pattern seeker. "I have never seen anybody who can pick up patterns like he can—including patterns that aren't there, but given his success you're willing to tolerate some false positives," says Willoughby.

Even as Gray had carved out his own scientific space in a (temporarily) quiet field, though, meteorology and climatology were becoming the provinces of sophisticated computer modelers. Today some modelers have even begun to produce their own seasonal hurricane forecasts, a rival to Gray's empirical scheme. But Gray missed the modeling wave, and much of his skepticism today about global warming seems to spring from an utter distrust of the role of climate models in helping to substantiate that theory (as so prominently demonstrated, among other places, by the Charney Report).

That came across when Gray and I went to lunch together at a greasy spoon in Fort Collins called the Farmer's Table, a "proletarian establishment," in Gray's words, where we were served very slowly by wet-behind-the-ears teenagers, and where Gray put down a large helping of eggs and bacon while gently and amusingly trying to indoctrinate me about his new mission in life: "to save the world from worrying over global warming." "Just remain open," Gray lightly hectored me, in a voice that always seemed on the verge of that famous stutter. He couldn't deliver enough praise for Michael Crichton, author of the thinly veiled anti–global warming novel *State of Fear* and Gray's new hero. Like Gray, Crichton distrusts the attempt to use complex computer models to project future climates.

Gray writes that he's been "seething with disgust for 20 years at what was going on with the so called 'science' of global warming." That disgust appears closely linked to his resentment over what he views as the extravagant funding for climate-modeling research. "Modelers drive in stretch limos to their meetings," he told me. By contrast, Gray charges that during the Clinton-Gore years, thirteen of his grant proposals in a row were turned down, requiring him to disappoint promising graduate students and reduce his staff. Gray says he had to make a personal contribution of $45,000 at one point to keep his hurricane research project at Colorado State running.

In critiquing the endeavors of the modelers, Gray goes on at length about how complicated the atmosphere is, far too complicated to be captured within a computer simulation. "Nobody knows how the atmosphere works," he told me over lunch. Yet Gray places great stock in his own intuitive understanding, which he claims can beat the models. His "innate sense of how the atmosphere-ocean functions," he has stated, is what prevents him from accepting global warming.

In fact, even though he describes himself as a "data" guy, Gray has ambitious "theories" of his own. One central reason he rejects the notion of significant human-caused global warming is that he thinks there's a different climate regulator at work: the so-called thermohaline circulation ("thermo" means heat and "haline" means salt). Different scientific commentators mean different things by this phrase, but Gray seems to be referring specifically to the North Atlantic limb of the ocean's great overturning circulation (sometimes also called the "ocean conveyor belt"). As North Atlantic waters flow toward polar regions, they grow colder and thus more dense and heavy; an increase in saltiness caused by evaporation increases density still further. So the waters sink beneath the ocean surface, becoming "deep water" and flowing south again as they join other branches of the global ocean circulation. This in turn pulls more warm surface water northward, helping to heat the North Atlantic region.

Gray and his fellow hurricane scientists have been arguing for some time that Atlantic sea temperatures, hurricane behavior, and much else in the region respond to fluctuations in the strength of the thermohaline circulation, following a natural cycle that has been dubbed the Atlantic Multidecadal Oscillation, or AMO. Given the warm seas and busy hurricane seasons we've seen since 1995, they think the thermohaline circulation is currently in an active phase. During the previous hurricane lull period, they think it was weaker.

Gray himself goes farther still, arguing that such changes in ocean circulation, rather than human interference with the composition of the atmosphere, explain the *global* temperature trends we've seen. For Gray, a strong thermohaline circulation warms the Atlantic (and increases hurricane activity) but cools the rest of the globe. A weak circulation, meanwhile, cools the Atlantic (and decreases hurricane activity) but causes global warming. It's by such logic that Gray concludes global cooling will set in again soon: After all, Atlantic temperatures have been warm and we've seen strong hurricane seasons. To him it's all a big cycle, with everything balancing out everything else and puny humans unable to significantly influence the gigantic forces of nature.

There's much published evidence suggesting that some type of Atlantic oscillation does indeed exist, and climate models link it to the thermohaline circulation. Where the real trouble starts for Gray, though, is when he both asserts that the thermohaline circulation governs global temperatures (ignoring the evidence about human-caused global warming) and then claims to know what that circulation is doing.

In truth, the circulation is exceedingly hard to measure. A surprising 2005 study suggested the Atlantic flow was in decline, even amid record Atlantic warming and hurricane activity; more recently, it has appeared hard to detect any trend in the circulation. Meanwhile, some scenarios have global warming triggering a thermohaline *shutdown* in the future due to increased freshening and thus less dense water at high latitudes (the possibility treated in truly over-the-top fashion in the film *The Day After Tomorrow*). For these and other reasons, the climate-scientist authors of RealClimate.org have charged that Gray's view of the thermohaline circulation is "all seat-of-the-pants stuff of a sort that was common in the early days of climate studies, but which is difficult to evaluate when viewed as a scientific hypothesis. The [thermohaline circulation] is undoubtedly important to climate, because it transports heat from one place to another," they continue. "However it cannot do magical things."

Another of Gray's attacks on current climate science is also under attack. He rejects the concept of a positive feedback between carbon dioxide and atmospheric water vapor, a notion premised on the afore-mentioned Clausius-Clapeyron equation and central to today's concern about climate change. This feedback—one of the central ones pronounced valid by the Charney Report in 1979—is widely accepted today and is contained in all major climate models. Yet Gray rejects it outright, claiming that upper level water vapor will actually decrease as greenhouse gas concentrations rise.

Unlike his work on hurricanes, however, Gray's critiques of climate science in recent years have largely been made in statements to the media and in public speeches and pamphlets, rather than in the published scientific literature. This makes fellow scientists suspicious; one of the most strongly held norms in the scientific community is that one must participate formally in the scientific process, in which new results are reported in journals after they have been critically reviewed by peers. Within the scientific literature, Gray's perspective is tough to find these days; major scientific consensus reports from the National Academy of Sciences, the UN's Intergovernmental Panel on Climate Change, and elsewhere all agree that human beings are contributing to global warming and it's happening now. No major climate simulation agrees with Gray's pronouncement that we will see a cooling trend begin again within the next five to ten years, as part of a natural, ocean-driven cycle.

Sitting in Gray's kitchen just before departing Fort Collins, after spending the better part of a day with him, I noticed that the clock on his stove read 4:24, when in fact it was 3:24. Gray hadn't set it back at the last time change. Then I noticed that the clock on the coffeemaker said 5:25. Then I remembered that the clock in Gray's car had also been an hour fast.

Did any of this provide the final, conclusive proof that Gray was suffering, as the *Wall Street Journal* would later quote one of his critics as saying, from "brain fossilization"? I didn't think so. It's more that Gray's set in his ways and, at seventy-seven years old, not bothered with little things like resetting his clocks. He has greater matters on his mind, like saving the world from global-warming alarmism.

Gray's impressive scientific career notwithstanding, his anti–global warming arguments call to mind that "First Law" of Arthur C. Clarke's: "When a distinguished but elderly scientist states that something is possible he is almost certainly right. When he states that something is impossible, he is very probably wrong." With his late-life climate "skeptic" crusade, Gray has waded into massive controversy with little support. He likes to say that if half (sometimes it's two-thirds) of his Ph.D. students get together to tell him he needs to hang it up, he'll do so. So far, apparently, that critical mass hasn't been achieved.

If Gray is disgusted by the theory of global warming, he's possibly even more incensed by the suggestion that it may change, or has already changed, the storms he's spent half a century studying. That contention began the rise to its current prominence in the late 1980s and 1990s, as an offshoot of the intensifying debate over global warming itself. From the start, it has been closely linked to the work of Kerry Emanuel. Throughout the 1990s, the skirmish over hurricanes and global warming remained at a relatively low level. But even then, the battle lines were quickly drawn, with Gray and Emanuel—and hurricane specialists and climate modelers—on opposing sides.

# 5 • From Hypercanes to Hurricane Andrew

W hen asked late in life about how he came up with the "confluent hypergeometric equation," Jule Charney had a stunning answer. In late 1944 or early 1945, he recalled, he'd gone for a walk in the Brentwood Hills of Los Angeles, performing mathematical transformations in his head as he went along. And then suddenly he "saw"—not derived—the solution. "The equation was so simple," Charney remembered, "that it had to be right."

A similar quest for sublimely simple explanation pervades the research of Kerry Emanuel. In one 2004 essay on the relationship between hurricanes and climate, he wrote of his search for a "satisfying" understanding of the problem, which he described as a "more fulfilling aesthetic under which to perform science." It's clear that Gray's approach—detecting correlations and seeing patterns, never mind the why—could never fully satisfy Emanuel in this sense. According to Gray, we'll never get the atmosphere to reveal all its secrets: It's too damn complicated. "Our philosophy is not to try to understand the physics of hurricane formation," he has stated. Yet achieving such understanding is the driving force behind Emanuel's work.

In an interview in his sixteenth-floor MIT office, next door to that of "butterfly effect" discoverer Edward Lorenz and offering a spectacular view of the Charles River, Emanuel also provided a sharp personal contrast to Gray. He's short and professorial-looking, with wavy graying hair. Rather than loud and unguarded, he's nuanced and sophisticated. Where Gray swears and occasionally stutters, Emanuel talks in complete sentences, his speech as cadenced as carefully honed prose. Once in our conversation he even said "e.g."

In his science, Emanuel clearly works as a theoretician, but he isn't opposed to data-gathering or even above doing it himself. Scientists who want to achieve the fullest understanding, he believes, must be able to wear different hats. In 1985 he flew on several NOAA missions into Hurricane Gloria, a Cape Verde–type storm and a Category 4 at its peak, when it was located off Puerto Rico. Gloria later moved up the East Coast, hit the Outer Banks, and then, as Emanuel remembers, "she followed me home." He experienced the storm's weakened remnants when it passed over Massachusetts, inspiring hurricane parties at Harvard.

Gray seemed to have unlimited time to talk when I met with him; Emanuel was busier. Since publishing a now-famous 2005 paper linking observed hurricane intensification to ongoing global warming, he'd been constantly traveling for lectures and fielding media calls. He'd received some press for previous theoretical work on hurricanes—for example, his suggestion that the asteroid impact that killed the dinosaurs may have generated "hypercanes," runaway super-hurricanes capable of destroying the planet's ozone layer—but nothing compared to the present feeding frenzy. On the day of our meeting, Emanuel gave me over an hour of his time before taking his leave to join a media conference call: It was May 22, 2006, and NOAA was set to release its first forecast for the coming hurricane season (another active year, NOAA predicted, with thirteen to sixteen named storms). Emanuel's conference call was designed to counter the position that NOAA was taking—like Gray, the agency was ascribing the recent spate of active hurricane seasons in the Atlantic to a natural up-and-down cycle.

Emanuel has another hypothesis, one he claims better satisfies the demands of "Occam's razor," the criterion of parsimony or simplicity of explanation that scientists sometimes invoke to argue why one account trumps another. Emanuel thinks the attempt to explain the twentieth century's Atlantic hurricane "cycles" by invoking a so-called Atlantic Multidecadal Oscillation or "mode" (presumably tied to the thermohaline circulation) derives from a misreading of data. He argues instead that the mid-century cooling of the Northern Hemisphere, driven by sulfate aerosols produced through air pollution (here Emanuel accepts the climate scientists' explanation for "global cooling"), also helped to chill the Atlantic enough to suppress many hurricanes. Then, in the mid- to late 1980s, as aerosol cooling diminished, the Atlantic started to warm again under the influence of carbon dioxide, and has been doing so ever since. And the hurricanes have just kept coming.

It's a grim viewpoint because, contrary to the AMO theory or Gray's view of a natural balance that ultimately rights itself, it suggests there may not be any reprieve from strong hurricanes a decade or more down the line. Instead, as we keep heating the planet, the Atlantic storm seasons could steadily worsen.

Mentors matter a great deal in science, but the researchers they train don't always follow in their exact footsteps. Emanuel has been publishing on the relationship between hurricanes and climate for twenty years now, but his initial turn toward the subject came when he decided to criticize the central work on hurricanes published by the man who'd advised him at MIT in the late 1970s—Charney.

As we've seen, Charney proposed an influential but flawed model of hurricane formation generally referred to as "Conditional Instability of the Second Kind," or CISK. More than anyone else, Emanuel is responsible for dismantling it. The debunking occurred after he returned to MIT in the early 1980s, following a three-year stint at UCLA. At MIT, Emanuel occasionally had to teach classes and seminars that involved hurricanes. Just as any other meteorologist at the time would have done, he taught the CISK theory and even published on it. But then something happened: "I realized it couldn't be right after a while," Emanuel remembers, "and that really got my attention."

Although Emanuel's doctoral thesis had focused on winter storms—like a typical dynamically trained meteorologist, he'd begun his career by largely ignoring the tropics—now he started working on hurricanes. "It often happens this way in science," he says. "First I developed my own ideas, and then somewhat later discovered that a lot of those ideas really had already been published many, many years earlier." Emanuel breathed new life into the heat-engine theory that had been propounded by Riehl, Malkus, and Kleinschmidt in the 1950s.

Charney, who had died in 1981, wasn't around to read Emanuel's back-to-back papers in 1986 and 1987 that set out to unseat CISK. In its place, Emanuel introduced his own account of hurricanes, according to which air-sea interaction, rather than the spatial organization of thunderstorm growth, constituted the storms' driving force. In essence, Emanuel presented a dynamically trained meteorologist's reinterpretation of Riehl's heat-engine theory. Then he and his coauthor used a numerical model to test whether the new theory produced a realistic hurricane. It did.

At the outset, Emanuel noted that prior modeling studies of hurricanes had, following CISK, presumed an atmosphere characterized by conditional instability. But Emanuel contended that if that's truly what drives hurricanes, then they ought to form at least weakly over land. On the contrary, Emanuel argued, hurricanes rely upon fluxes of ocean heat for their strength. That doesn't make their deep cumulonimbus thunderclouds unimportant—but they're merely the instrument by which hurricanes transport heat from the ocean up into the atmosphere. The release of latent heat in clouds is "important but it's not causal," as Emanuel puts it.

In distinguishing between these two versions of storms, Emanuel found he could construct realistic hurricanes without initially postulating atmospheric instability (not that it hurt). In this interpretation, hurricanes instead require a "starter," like an easterly wave, to get going. After that trigger, Emanuel found, the storm's intensity depended upon the difference in temperature between the sea-surface boundary layer on the one hand, and the freezing outflow region high in the atmosphere on the other. That's precisely what might be expected in a heat engine, which cycles heat from a warm reservoir to a cooler exhaust area while using it to do work along the way. The greater the temperature differential between these two regions, the more work can be done, and—as "work" in hurricanes means maintaining the storm against friction by driving winds and consequently lowering central pressure—the more powerful the storm can get.

At this point, Emanuel saw his findings had a strong corollary. If you significantly increase the temperature of the initial heat reservoir (the ocean), or if you significantly decrease the temperature of the outflow region (in intense hurricanes, the tropopause or lower stratosphere), you can get much more out of your heat engine. Hurricane intensity will increase. And that quite literally brought global warming into the equation—in this case, an equation Emanuel had derived to describe the "maximum potential intensity" that a hurricane can achieve under various climatic conditions. Within months of the appearance of his second theoretical paper describing hurricanes as heat engines, Emanuel's first paper on hurricanes and climate appeared in *Nature*.

The study used results from the climate model run by James Hansen and colleagues at the NASA-Goddard Institute for Space Studies. For a doubling of $CO_2$, Hansen's model projected sea-surface temperature increases on the order of 2.3 to 4.8 degrees Celsius in the tropics in August. "The prediction of maximum cyclone intensity [is] crucially dependent on estimates of sea water temperature," Emanuel noted, in part because rising air will carry more water vapor, and thus more latent heat, if it is warmer. So Emanuel proceeded to calculate that in the world represented by Hansen's model, the maximum potential wind speeds attainable by hurricanes should increase by about 5 percent for every degree Celsius of ocean warming, with larger corresponding pressure falls and still larger increases in a storm's "destructive potential" (by as much as 40 to 50 percent at the extreme). The study also suggested the theoretical possibility of staggering storms with central pressures of 800 millibars in the Gulf of Mexico and Bay of Bengal—both regions where land-falling hurricanes had wrought tremendous damage in the past.

In 1970, in what is easily the greatest hurricane tragedy of modern times, a tropical cyclone of unknown intensity plowed up the Bay of Bengal and made landfall at high tide in what was then East Pakistan (now Bangladesh), killing between 300,000 and 500,000 people in a twenty-foot or higher storm surge that flooded many miles inland in the low-lying country and swept up everything in its path. In 1991 came an almost-as-awful repeat. An extremely intense cyclone—known only as "02B"—made landfall in Bangladesh packing 155-mile-per-hour winds and again driving a twenty-foot surge. This storm killed well over 100,000 people and left ten million displaced. Clearly, hurricane vulnerability in much of the world greatly exceeds anything found in the wealthy United States. Emanuel's hypothesis had particularly large implications for coastally situated developing countries.

Like any responsible scientist, Emanuel included numerous caveats in his 1987 analysis. Climate projections were uncertain, and a hurricane's maximum *potential* intensity isn't the same thing as intensity in the real world, where any number of dynamic factors can squelch a storm's growth. The study also did not address how global warming

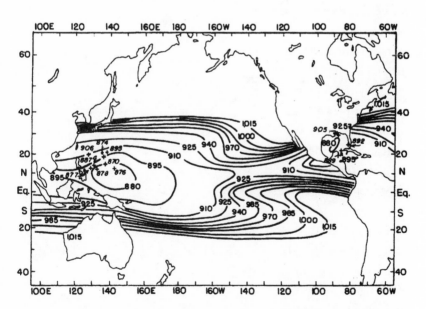

Minimum sustainable pressures, in millibars, that can be attained by September hurricanes in the present climate. *Reprinted by permission from Macmillan Publishers Ltd:* Nature, *Kerry Emanuel, "The Dependence of Hurricane Intensity on Climate," Vol. 326, No. 6112, April 2, 1987.*

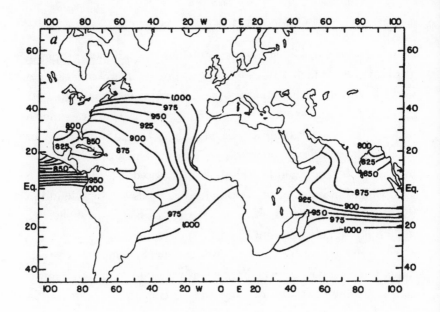

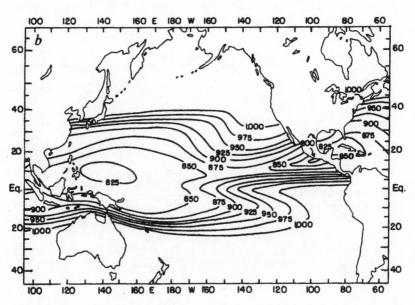

Minimum sustainable pressures, in millibars, that can be attained by
August hurricanes in a future climate, using average sea-surface temperature
increases from a climate model with doubled $CO_2$. The two images
represent the entire globe. *Reprinted by permission from Macmillan
Publishers Ltd: Nature, Kerry Emanuel, "The Dependence of Hurricane
Intensity on Climate," Vol. 326, No. 6112, April 2, 1987.*

might affect the total number of storms—that was a different issue. Emanuel did observe, however, that "there is no obvious reason... to suppose that frequencies would be substantially diminished in a climate with doubled $CO_2$."

This seminal publication on the hurricane–climate connection had a distinctly theoretical rather than empirical character. Emanuel had provided seemingly persuasive reasons to think that hurricanes *would* intensify under enhanced greenhouse conditions, but he had not produced any data suggesting an actual trend. Not yet. Nevertheless, Emanuel's work drew modest media coverage when it came out and much additional attention in the years that followed. The paper's appearance preceded the extremely intense Atlantic hurricanes Gilbert of 1988 and Hugo of 1989, and journalists soon interpreted both storms in the context of Emanuel's analysis. As the subject of global warming itself became increasingly prominent, they would do the same for other strong Atlantic hurricanes, especially those making landfall.

It didn't hurt that Emanuel had given journalists an irresistible catchphrase that telegraphed alarm about strong hurricanes: "hypercanes." Emanuel introduced the concept in a 1988 paper in which he refined the equation he had developed to describe the maximum potential intensity that a hurricane can achieve. For certain very high sea-surface temperatures and/or very low upper-atmospheric temperatures (conditions far exceeding what exists on the planet at the current time), Emanuel found that runaway superhurricanes might occur. They would be characterized by extremely tall storm columns penetrating high into the stratosphere, finely concentrated eyes, mindboggling pressure drops, and surface winds of 500 miles per hour or perhaps more.

To get some sense of how calamitous a hypercane would be, consider tornadoes, which can have stronger winds than hurricanes (albeit much more briefly and on a far smaller scale). The colorfully worded Fujita Scale describes an "incredible tornado"—classification F5—as one whose fastest winds reach 261 to 318 miles per hour. Such storms are capable of tossing cars through the air like tennis balls. Yet still that would pale in comparison to the supposed 500-mile-per-hour winds of hypercanes.

Later, Emanuel and a group of fellow scientists used a numerical model to simulate this theoretical cataclysm, and suggested that hypercanes might emerge if a large object from space struck the ocean and warmed it dramatically. Perhaps they had even played a role in the extinction of the dinosaurs. After all, the site of the Yucatán asteroid strike 65 million years ago, thought to have triggered that extinction, had been underwater at the time. So Emanuel speculated that the asteroid might have set off hypercanes that in turn would have damaged the Earth's protective ozone layer by pumping water high into the stratosphere—thus allowing more deadly ultraviolet radiation to reach the planet's surface and kill off many or most living organisms. It was hard to get more cataclysmic than that. The press loved it.

That journalists made much of Emanuel's theoretical work on hurricane intensity and climate during the late 1980s reflected the political and social tenor of the times. Along with the atmosphere and the oceans, a battle over climate science was heating up.

During the 1980s, Congressman Al Gore—who'd been impressed when one of his professors at Harvard, Roger Revelle, showed him Charles David Keeling's curve of ever-increasing greenhouse gas concentrations in the atmosphere—began to hold hearings on the possibility of climate change. Gore sought to translate this esoteric scientific subject into mainstream politics, and to embarrass the anti-environmental Reagan administration in the process. Yet not until the scorching summer of 1988, amid heat waves and droughts, did global warming have its breakout moment in the United States.

During that summer, NASA's James Hansen came before Congress to testify about climate change. And in a blockbuster statement that Emanuel and many other scientists would later criticize for going too far, Hansen announced his 99 percent certainty that a significant global warming trend had begun, caused by human activities. "It is time to stop waffling so much and say that the evidence is pretty strong that the greenhouse effect is here," he declared in his testimony. To be sure, Hansen cautioned that no specific heat wave could be directly blamed on global warming. But he added that these were the *kinds* of events that we might see more frequently in a globally warmed world.

Accurate or otherwise, the apparent linkage between Hansen's testimony and present-day events affecting real people—including hurricanes Gilbert and Hugo—helped the issue of global warming reach a tipping point. That's the paradox of public communication on this subject. It often seems as if the only way journalists and advocates can draw attention to climate change is in the context of individual disasters and weather events, such as very intense hurricanes. Yet specific weather events can never be "caused" by a statistically averaged change in global climate over time, even if they're precisely the kind of events that should grow more common as global warming sets in.

The attempt to explain and translate such nuances to the public and elected leaders only became more fraught in the years following Hansen's testimony, as politics quickly and predictably infected the science. Those who'd been drumming up concern about global warming also talked about ways of dealing with it, including mandatory restrictions on industrial greenhouse gas emissions. This idea implicated the fortunes of some of the most powerful special interests in the United States: the coal, oil, and automotive industries. Before long, these and other industries organized to combat the global warming forecasters. One of their core weapons involved raising doubts about the validity of the science itself—the same "manufacturing uncertainty" tactic previously employed by many other American industries, ranging from tobacco to lead, when scientific information pointed to adverse consequences from their economic activities.

The first Bush administration, sympathetic to these interests, abetted their attacks on the science. In 1989, Hansen again testified before Congress—but this time, the Bush administration's Office of Management and Budget altered his testimony, against Hansen's consent, to weaken his conclusions. It wouldn't be the last time Hansen, who has been a federal government employee throughout his career, would find a political filter interfering with his ability to state his opinions on climate change.

To prosecute their fight over the emerging science of climate, the fossil fuel interests needed their own scientific arguments, and scientific experts to make them. A group of global warming "skeptics" emerged on the scene, proceeding to dispute either the rising temperature trend itself, the contention that humans had been causing it, or both. Often these "skeptics" aligned themselves, just as Gray had done throughout his career, with a strict adherence to scientific empiricism. After all, much of the concern about global warming derived from projections by global climate models like Hansen's. So the "skeptics" attacked the models and found recourse in the "data," arguing that even if temperatures seemed on the rise, a linear extrapolation of the current trend did not show anything like the model-predicted warming (which included amplifying factors such as the water vapor feedback). The skeptics also focused on what they claimed were anomalous satellite and radiosonde data sets, and used them to argue that warming wasn't happening in the troposphere at the rate predicted by climate models.

These two questions—whether temperatures were actually rising and what might be causing that trend, referred to in the scientific literature as "detection" and "attribution"—became the main battlegrounds in the escalating climate wars of the late 1980s and 1990s. Yet even then, hurricane intensification and other projected consequences of global warming, such as sea-level rise and changing precipitation, comprised a kind of third front (referred to as "impacts"). Emanuel's calculations on greenhouse hurricanes were regularly cited within the climate community and regarded by many as a plausible outcome of climate change. In 1988, the American Meteorological Society and the University Corporation for Atmospheric Research, a nonprofit research organization in Boulder, Colorado, jointly released a major statement discussing potential climate risks, which included "a higher frequency and greater intensity of hurricanes." With mainstream scientific organizations making such pronouncements, the contrarians, or "skeptics," quickly denounced the scientific evidence about any of a number of hypothesized global-warming impacts, including hurricane intensification. Once again, their strategy involved raising doubts about speculative models or theories and prizing hard data.

The fight burst into the open following 1992's Hurricane Andrew, the small but extremely powerful storm that devastated southeastern Florida, destroying 25,000 homes and setting a then record for economic losses from a single hurricane in the United States, on the order of $26.5 billion (in 1992 dollars). Delivering the worst of its punishment to Dade County, Andrew tore through the backyards of many of the nation's hurricane experts, at least one of whom lived through a hellacious night of shrieking winds and later told the tale. The National Hurricane Center, then located in Coral Gables, measured wind gusts of over 160 miles per hour from the roof of the building, and that wasn't even in the eye wall. The storm knocked out the radar antenna on the center's roof and tossed around cars in its parking lot, but that's nothing compared to what it did to neighborhoods to the south. For years Andrew was classified as a Category 4 hurricane at landfall, but a 2004 reanalysis led by Gray's student Chris Landsea determined that maximum sustained winds when the storm hit southeastern Florida near Fender Point had been nearly 170 miles per hour. Andrew had officially been the first Category 5 hurricane to strike the United States since Camille.

Following this incredible storm, a prominent article in *Newsweek* asked, "Was Andrew a Freak—or a Preview of Things to Come?" It quoted Emanuel. Such murmurings drew out Gray with one of his characteristic denunciations: "People who say, whenever there is an intense storm, that this indicates global warming, they don't know what they're talking about." Gray was right: No one, certainly not Emanuel, could argue that one strong storm proves the influence of global warming. Individual storms respond to their immediate environments, and strong storms had been observed in the past. However, Emanuel certainly did contend that over time, the *average* hurricane would grow more intense due to *average* changes in those environments.

Gray was hardly the only critic, and he personally wasn't linked to private industry. Other "skeptics," however, appeared more closely entangled. In an opinion article published in the *Washington Times* following Andrew, the global warming contrarian Patrick Michaels of the University of Virginia—who would later be shown to have received substantial funding from energy interests—also took issue with

Emanuel's work, claiming it "flies in the face of what has been observed in the twentieth century." Like Gray, Michaels often criticized
models and prized "data," so it came as no surprise that he called
Emanuel's calculations "of more theoretical importance than practical
significance." Later, once again in a commentary article for the *Washington Times,* Michaels dubbed Emanuel's work "merely an exercise in
hurricane vortex mathematics."

When the Atlantic kicked back into an active phase in 1995, generating nineteen named storms and eleven hurricanes, the hurricane–
climate battle intensified. Fittingly, for the peak months of August
through October that year, sea surface temperatures in the Atlantic's
main hurricane development region—from 10 to 20 degrees North
latitude and from 20 to 60 degrees West longitude, or stretching from
the coast of Africa to the eastern edge of the Caribbean—had been at
their warmest since records began in 1865.

Once again, the scientific debate wound up being amplified and
sharpened by media coverage—which, in turn, responded to the 1995
hurricane season and then folded global warming into the story line.
Gray quickly sounded a skeptical note. "I don't believe that this hurricane season is a result of anything to do with global warming," he told
the Associated Press. But Gray wasn't the only scientist talking to
the media. In an interview with the *Houston Chronicle,* climatologist
Kevin Trenberth of the National Center for Atmospheric Research delivered a partial rebuttal to Gray's arguments. In particular, Trenberth
cited the effect that global warming could have on hurricane rainfall.
Because warmer air can hold more water vapor, stronger precipitation
theoretically should occur in storms as the planet heats up. And that,
of course, could worsen one key cause of hurricane damage: extensive
flooding and destructive landslides. In Trenberth, Emanuel seemed to
have found an ally.

Meanwhile, Gray and Michaels were joined by conservative think
tanks, which helped battle suggestions of a hurricane–climate linkage.
In 1997 the Competitive Enterprise Institute—a recipient of considerable funding from oil giant ExxonMobil over the years, although
that funding has apparently ceased more recently—published a report

entitled *Calmer Weather: The Spin on Greenhouse Hurricanes,* by climate contrarian Robert C. Balling, Jr., of Arizona State University. "Blaming hurricanes on recent warming is flawed on all fronts—not only is there little to no linkage between global warming and hurricane activity, but there seems to have been no warming in recent decades either," Balling wrote.

Traditional weather forecasters also joined the global warming fight during the 1990s, and denounced the new climate science as it continued to build momentum. In 1995, the UN's Intergovernmental Panel on Climate Change famously declared that the "balance of evidence" suggested that the human impact on the climate system had already become discernible in rising temperatures. Then, in 1997, came the Kyoto Protocol, a treaty designed to put the world on the path to mandatory restrictions on greenhouse gas emissions. To promote Kyoto, the Clinton administration appealed to TV weathercasters to help explain global warming to their audiences. The entreaty backfired: Many forecasters publicly signed a global warming "skeptic" document called the Leipzig Declaration, which stated, "There does not exist today a general scientific consensus about the importance of greenhouse warming from rising levels of carbon dioxide. In fact, many climate specialists now agree that actual observations from weather satellites show no global warming whatsoever—in direct contradiction to computer model results."

Among the Leipzig signatories was Neil Frank, former director of NOAA's National Hurricane Center (a post he held for thirteen years) and now chief meteorologist for Houston's KHOU television station. A leading light of the hurricane community as well as a strong empiricist like Gray, Frank has often denounced fears of human-caused global warming and the flawed computer models upon which those fears are based. Along with Gray, Frank debunked global warming in a speech delivered at the 1998 National Hurricane Conference meeting held in Norfolk, Virginia, contradicting Clinton administration scientists on hand who supported the scientific consensus on climate change. "On numerical models that I can't put faith in for a three-day forecast, we're being asked to simplify and run out [predictions] for two centuries," Frank charged. Gray, meanwhile, went after the Clinton administration's NOAA for not funding his research: "They don't want to give money to people who have a different approach besides climate modeling," he declared.

Why did so many weather forecasters so distrust the theory of global warming? First, TV meteorologists don't necessarily have much theoretical training; their job is to communicate to the public, not to solve equations or conduct cutting-edge research in an academic context. They build their careers around the practical problem of predicting weather day in and day out. They're focused on the immediate, not the long term. And all they've seen from the weather is change, change, and more change, making them understandably suspicious about claims as to trends.

While the influence of fossil-fuel interests may have had much to do with the chorus of global-warming "skepticism" that emerged in the 1990s, then, it hardly constituted the only factor contributing to a gathering political and scientific storm. Inertia among members of the more traditional weather establishment also drove a disciplinary divide among meteorologists. Correspondingly, an anti–global warming constituency emerged in the hurricane-forecasting community. "Tropical meteorologists were probably the last informed people in the atmospheric sciences to take global warming seriously," observes Hugh Willoughby. And some, like Gray, still don't. No wonder Neil Frank's attacks on global warming at the 1998 National Hurricane Conference were well received by the audience and triggered considerable applause.

The media debates over hurricanes and global warming during the 1990s were highly episodic in nature. A big storm appeared somewhere in the Atlantic basin, or struck the United States. Or a very active season occurred. So a journalist called up scientists with different views to get their opinions, and that was about it. Until the next significant hurricane event, anyway.

Within the professional scientific literature, however, a more nuanced dialogue developed, one in which Emanuel had his critics as well as his supporters. In this more rarefied debate, it became clear that while Emanuel had not yet won everyone over to his position, he had inarguably (and pretty much single-handedly) put the hurricane–climate issue on the map, and generated considerable follow-up work as researchers attacked the topic from a variety of angles.

The strongest criticisms came from Gray and his supporters. While acknowledging the importance of sea-surface temperatures to hurricane strength, these scientists repeatedly pointed out that hurricanes depend upon a number of other factors as well, many of which had been highlighted by Gray over the course of his career. Thus much of the criticism of Emanuel amounted to citing Gray's global-genesis parameters, or his findings about regional controls on hurricanes, and arguing that Emanuel's emphasis on ocean heat represented too simplistic an approach in light of all these other factors.

Such arguments were epitomized by a 1994 paper in which Gray and seven other scientists—including his pupils Landsea and Holland (the latter not yet a hurricane–climate convert)—published their own take on hurricanes and global warming. Calling Emanuel's approach a "worst case thermodynamic study," the scientists argued that the postulated effect of increasing sea-surface temperatures upon hurricane intensification (and regions of formation) would be offset in a variety of ways. For example, stronger hurricanes would stir up more cool water from the ocean depths and thereby sap their own strength more than weaker storms. "Even though the possibility of some minor effects of global warming on [tropical cyclone] frequency and intensity cannot be excluded, they must effectively be 'swamped' by large natural variability," the critics concluded.

Gray and coauthors also dismissed entirely the notion that possible changes to hurricanes could be studied in global-climate models. In so doing, they pooh-poohed a trajectory of research dating back to 1970, when Syukuro Manabe of the Geophysical Fluid Dynamics Laboratory had first detected tropical disturbances in such a model. Following Emanuel's first publication on hurricanes and climate, this strand of research had evolved into a series of GCM studies to see how hurricanes might change as atmospheric concentrations of $CO_2$ increased. That included not only whether the storms would intensify but also whether their total numbers would go up.

The results were decidedly mixed. Perhaps the most revealing analysis came in 1990 from Manabe and fellow GFDL modeler Anthony Broccoli, who started out expecting to see hurricanes sprouting up "like mushrooms" in their model once they cranked up the $CO_2$ levels, as Manabe remembers. Yet instead, Manabe and Broccoli found that depending upon how the model treated clouds, it produced either increases *or* decreases in a combined measure of the number and duration of storms. Still, the scientists concluded that climate models were "appropriate tools" for further research on the issue, because modeled storms generally appeared in the right ocean basins and looked more like real hurricanes as model resolution increased. So the GCM research continued, although it produced a scattershot of results, ranging from more and stronger storms for doubled $CO_2$ to substantially fewer (although possibly stronger) storms.

The hurricane empiricists, however, would have none of it, questioning whether these computerized eddies could be safely analogized to storms in nature. Each time a new GCM study that purported to detect hurricane-like storms appeared in a journal, their critical letters seemed to follow. The modelers, in turn, struck back with just as cutting a criticism: Gray's empirically derived genesis parameters certainly weren't any better than models for studying hurricanes in future climates. In fact, they were probably worse. The empirical relationships Gray had uncovered worked for the present climate, but "there is no a priori way of knowing how well they would govern tropical cyclogenesis in a different climate," the modelers noted.

By the mid- to late 1990s, then, a modest debate had begun to brew over hurricanes and global warming within the professional scientific literature. Emanuel had started it, but he certainly hadn't won it. Instead, the scientific process—working just as it so often does—had churned out a small literature of publications that, when surveyed comprehensively, amounted to a collective shoulder shrug from the experts.

The unsettled state of knowledge came across in the 1995 report of the Intergovernmental Panel on Climate Change, which stated: "It is not possible to say whether the frequency, area of occurrence, time of occurrence, mean intensity or maximum intensity of tropical cyclones will change." Following this report, the World Meteorological Organization pulled together a group of experts to outline in more detail what was known about the subject and what wasn't, and to analyze new results. They included Emanuel, Gray, Landsea, Holland, and a number of other scientists, among them Australian tropical meteorologist Peter Webster, a longtime friend of Holland who would have much to contribute to the hurricane–climate debate in later years.

Reviewing the science, this group made the following points: First, there did not appear to be any trends in hurricane numbers, intensity, or regions of formation. Second, neither Gray's empirically derived set of genesis parameters nor the current generation of global-climate models seemed up to the task of studying hurricanes in future climates. Nevertheless, while there was no reason to think the regions of hurricane formation would grow for a doubling of $CO_2$, Emanuel's maximum potential intensity theory (and a similar theory Holland had just published) suggested that storm intensity would increase by 10 to 20 percent when measured by the fall in central pressure (maximum wind speed increases would be smaller, on the order of 5 to 10 percent). Yet various unknowns—such as ocean spray effects, then considered a negative rather than a positive influence on storm strength, or possible atmospheric stabilization from increased warming at upper levels—seemed likely to cut into that potential intensification by an unknown amount. The upshot: Some change in tropical cyclones might occur, but it wouldn't be much, and would be far in the future.

So went the consensus as of 1998. It downplayed any dramatic impact of global warming on hurricanes, without ruling out some possible effect. The extent to which each individual scientist agreed with these conclusions remains unclear, however, especially in the case of Gray. While Gray had his name on the study, it took at least one position he rejected outright. It accepted unquestioningly the 1995

IPCC position that according to the "balance of evidence," humans were causing global warming.

One very important study came out around the time of the consensus analysis, yet apparently not soon enough to be cited by it. Amid all the criticism of low-resolution modeling studies, the Geophysical Fluid Dynamics Laboratory scientists had devised a new angle of approach. Rather than using a global-climate model, this time they used the lab's much more highly resolved regional hurricane tracking and prediction model—the same one the National Hurricane Center had been employing since 1995 to determine where storms will go. Into the hurricane model the scientists imported 51 Northwest Pacific storms from a GCM, and then 51 more Northwest Pacific storms from a GCM simulation run with increased levels of carbon dioxide, in which sea-surface temperatures were about 2.2 degrees Celsius higher. Upon running the higher-resolution hurricane model, they found that the storms from the $CO_2$-heated climate had 5 to 12 percent faster wind speeds on average. Central pressures dropped by an additional 7 to 20 millibars. This result, the study noted, dovetailed nicely with the maximum potential intensity theories of Emanuel and Holland.

The new GFDL study, which broke ground both by its high resolution and by its sole focus on storm intensity rather than storm numbers, had a lead author named Thomas Knutson. It represented the first of a series of modeling studies by Knutson and his colleagues focused on how hurricanes might change under global warming scenarios. No wonder, then, that Knutson would have much more to say about hurricanes and climate in subsequent years—for some, perhaps too much. In 2006, much like James Hansen, he would allege that officials at NOAA had constrained his ability to participate in media interviews on the subject.

Whatever the role of climate change, understanding hurricane intensification itself represented much more than a matter of idle intellectual interest. By the mid- to late 1990s, dynamical models like that of GFDL had shown impressive skill when it came to projecting the paths that hurricanes would take, and thus where they might make landfall. However, modeling attempts to predict either hurricane in-tensification or weakening lagged far behind, and that was deeply troubling. The hurricane forecasters had a nightmare scenario, one with a firm basis in the history of certain notorious storms: a Category 1 hurricane suddenly and unexpectedly strengthens into a Category 4 or 5 killer just before making landfall. Then it hits a populated area that knows a storm is coming but has been led to expect a weak one. So most people haven't evacuated—and now it's too late.

Accordingly, a better understanding of why hurricanes intensify, whether under global-warming conditions or otherwise, became a key focus of research for many scientists. Emanuel led the way, designing a simple atmosphere-ocean model to attack the problem. The gigantic 1999 Hurricane Floyd also increased the impetus to understand storm intensity. Close to 600 miles in diameter, Floyd very nearly reached Category 5 strength as it approached the Bahamas, which meant that unlike many other storms, it had come extremely close to achieving its full potential.

Why did this happen for Floyd but not for every hurricane? In a 2000 statistical analysis of real-world storm intensities, Emanuel showed that every storm that becomes a hurricane has an equal prob-ability of attaining "any given intensity, up to but not beyond its po-tential intensity." So if global warming did indeed increase the maximum potential intensity of hurricanes by 10 to 20 percent, as his theory predicted, Emanuel wrote that "the wind speeds of real events would, on average, rise by the same percentage." Given enough time, that ought to be detectable in storm statistics.

Gray, meanwhile, criticized Emanuel's hurricane intensity predic-tion model, which had a strong thermodynamic emphasis but which Gray called "too simplified." This, in turn, set the stage for a rollick-ing 2000 debate between Gray and Emanuel at the American Meteo-rological Society's biennial conference on Hurricanes and Tropical Meteorology, held that year in Fort Lauderdale. The question posed by the debate did not explicitly involve global warming. Instead, the two scientists squared off over what controls hurricane intensity, with Emanuel focusing more on thermodynamic factors—particularly ocean temperatures—and Gray upon dynamic ones such as vertical wind shear. As neither scientist fully disputed the importance of the factors highlighted by the other, the debate came down to a matter of emphasis—or at least, it should have.

In the recollection of many scientists present, however, it wound up being something of a circus. Gray called Emanuel's attention to thermodynamics a "fixation." He said Emanuel was "playing games." He even likened his fellow scientist to a salesman. "He could sell ice cubes to the Eskimos and steam heat to the Amazonians," Gray declared at one point. The audience chuckled, but this is not how scientific debates are generally expected to go down. "It was sort of like a Kerry Emanuel roast, making fun of me personally," Emanuel remembers. "It was a humorous sort of thing that didn't bring in any science."

Over the course of the coming decade, however, Gray's gags and one-liners would come to seem less entertaining to Emanuel and his supporters, especially in the context of unprecedented hurricane damage in 2004 and 2005, years that dramatically raised the stakes in the hurricane–climate debate and brought to it a new vigor and passion. In the process, the 1998 consensus came unraveled. Numerous scientific and personal realignments quickly followed, even as important new voices dove into the fray.

Gray and Emanuel continued to serve as figureheads for the different sides—but the two would not debate each other publicly again.

# PART II

---

# BOILING OVER

"Because it demands large-scale paradigm destruction and major shifts in the problems and techniques of normal science, the emergence of new theories is generally preceded by a period of pronounced professional insecurity."

—Thomas Kuhn, *The Structure of Scientific Revolutions*

# Among the Forecasters

The scene at the palm tree–lined Rosen Centre Hotel in Orlando, Florida, was bright and active. Suntanned kids chased each other around in swimming trunks, laughing and giggling. It was the Friday before Easter weekend, and a Christian youth conference had just begun taking registration, crowding out the National Hurricane Conference's dwindling display tables. "Lads to Leaders & Leaderettes," the Christian event was called. If it had occurred to the organizers that the slogan might seem to endorse sex-change operations, evidently the thought had not troubled them.

Many of the National Hurricane Center's top forecasters and researchers, including Stacy Stewart, Lixion Avila, and Chris Landsea, had already given their talks here in Orlando. Now, inside the cavernous main conference room, National Hurricane Center director Max Mayfield—a thin man with glasses who was playing the role of emcee for the conference's final session—introduced "our friend professor Bill Gray" to the crowd of hundreds. Mayfield thanked Gray kindly for his "tremendous" contributions to tropical meteorology and to seasonal hurricane forecasting, and for sending talented students like Landsea to work at the National Hurricane Center. Not that Gray needed any introduction before this audience of journalists, insurance experts, emergency managers, and others working on the practical side of hurricane readiness. The crowd loved him.

For years, Mayfield noted, Gray had announced his Atlantic storm predictions in the capstone speech of this annual conference, the chief off-season gathering of the nation's hurricane-preparedness community. But this year, Gray would officially hand off the lead forecasting duties to his latest protégé, a red-haired and freckled Ph.D.

student named Phil Klotzbach. Meanwhile—although Mayfield didn't mention this part—Gray planned to focus much of his energy on debunking global warming.

And so it began: a dramatic two-part anti–global warming polemic from Gray, interrupted briefly for Klotzbach's calmly offered seasonal forecast (predicting seventeen named tropical cyclones in the Atlantic basin) and then continuing until some in the crowd started to leave. "You poor people," Gray commiserated at one point, even as he proceeded to toss up yet another slide. "I can't go another two hours, can I?" he asked later.

The year was 2006. The human fingerprint on the current global-warming trend had been conclusively detected by the world's scientific community. Consensus had been achieved among the vast majority of experts studying the issue. Yet in Gray's audience sat some of the nation's leading hurricane forecasters and emergency planners, who were hearing a very different message—and at least some of whom seemed to be soaking it up like Florida sunshine.

The years 1995 through 2003 had been very kind to the state of Florida. By historic standards, the entire period was extraordinarily active for Atlantic hurricanes (save during the record-breaking El Niño year of 1997, and another El Niño in 2002). Between 1928 and 1965 during the previous active hurricane period, the Florida peninsula had been hit by a major storm roughly once every three years. From 1995 to 2003, however, the worst storm Florida had seen was 1995's Category 4 Hurricane Opal, which rapidly intensified over 28- or 29-degree (Celsius) waters in the Gulf of Mexico in early October, achieving estimated 150-mile-per-hour winds and a central pressure dip down to 916 millibars (27.05 inches). Luckily, Opal shrank back to a weak Category 3 before lifting a storm surge of eight to fifteen feet onto the delicate dunes of Santa Rosa Island, which hosts Pensacola Beach.

And that was it for Florida from 1995 through 2003: one major hurricane strike to the panhandle, none to the peninsula. Meanwhile the rest of the Atlantic was being terrorized by strong hurricanes, none of them worse than 1998's Mitch, which reached Category 5 intensity—with winds of 180 miles per hour and a minimum central pressure of 905 millibars (26.72 inches)—in the western Caribbean in late October. There Mitch sank the *Fantome,* a huge luxury schooner that went down in giant waves off the coast of Honduras with thirty-one people on board after its captain spent days trying to outwit the hurricane. By the time Mitch hit land it had weakened dramatically, but the storm's slow movement allowed it to pour almost three feet of rainfall over mountainous terrain, causing flooding and landslides that swept away some 11,000 people (thousands more were left missing) in Honduras, Nicaragua, and other nearby nations. This death toll surpassed even that of the 1900 Galveston storm. You had to go back to the Great Hurricane of 1780, estimated to have killed 22,000 in the Caribbean, to find a more murderous Atlantic weather event.

And for every full-fledged hurricane disaster during the late 1990s and early 2000s, there were many near misses. As it was, 1998's Hurricane Georges killed hundreds in the Caribbean; had the storm remained a bit stronger and made its final landfall a bit farther west, it could also have delivered a deadly blow to New Orleans. And then there was 2003's Hurricane Isabel, a Category 5 Cape Verde–type storm (915 mb; 27.02 in.) that luckily weakened before reaching the Outer Banks of North Carolina. On September 13, the storm produced the strongest horizontal wind gust ever recorded in a hurricane. A GPS-equipped measuring device known as a dropsonde, released by a reconnaissance plane into the inner edge of Isabel's eye wall, detected a wind of 239 miles per hour—a velocity more like what you'd expect in a strong tornado.

On the other end of the intensity spectrum, meanwhile, 2003 also introduced Tropical Storm Ana. Born as a hybrid between a tropical and an extra-tropical storm but later gaining more clearly defined tropical characteristics, Ana remained at sea and never had sustained winds above about 60 miles per hour. But the storm had a feature distinct from every other Atlantic tropical cyclone on record: A birthday in late April, radically early in the year, more than a month before the start of the official Atlantic season.

Throughout this new period of frequent and intense Atlantic basin activity, Bill Gray had been the rock of the hurricane community—the reliable guy with the forecasts; the source of warnings (and chidings) for those who had built in harm's way. It surely helped that he was a university professor, not an official government forecaster like Max Mayfield. As such, Gray had far more freedom to be the colorful character that he was. He could scare your pants off and make you laugh at the same time. His pivotal speaking role at the National Hurricane Conference, as well as at the annual Florida Governor's Hurricane Conference, reflected this popularity and renown. He was, more than anyone else, "Mr. Hurricane."

Yet in all this time, Gray had never warmed up to global warming. As the years went on, his forecasts also came to contain a boilerplate section debunking any connection between climate change and hurricanes. Gray's rebuttals to the climate worry-worts, however, were neither the source of his fame nor the reason for his steady appearances at these practically oriented mega-conferences. There Gray officially appeared as the nation's top hurricane expert, the guy with the preseason forecast that everyone wanted to hear about. Especially Floridians.

By 2006, however, Gray's two personas—"Mr. Hurricane" and "Mr. Climate Skeptic"—no longer appeared even remotely separable.

That had become clear during Gray's press availabilities at the National Hurricane Conference in Orlando, held daily before his final keynote speech (he was very much in demand). During the second of them Gray was in rare form, decked out in a dark suit, a dandyish purple shirt, and a clashing red tie as he denounced the "baby boomers and yuppies" who'd produced the latest global climate models.

Later, in a witty story on climate skeptics that featured Gray and focused on his Orlando appearance, *The Washington Post*'s Joel Achenbach noted that these press events had been organized by TCSDaily.com (formerly Tech Central Station), a Web site published at the time by a "strategic public affairs" firm in Washington, D.C., called the DCI Group. The site had received funding in the past from fossil-fuel giant ExxonMobil—which also retained DCI's lobbying services—and its "Science Roundtable" offered a kind of clearinghouse for the contrarian arguments of outlier scientists who continued to attack the mainstream understanding of global warming. And now, TCSDaily had appeared at the National Hurricane Conference to help Gray get his message out.

The group must have heartily enjoyed Gray's keynote speech. It opened with his best material: In the 1940s we worried about warming; then came the "Ice Age" scare in the 1970s; and now, lo and behold, we're worried about warming again. And so Gray issued his long-range climate forecast: Global warming, he augured, would go away sometime within the next five to ten years. "I predict—I won't be around to see it, but Phil Klotzbach says he'll put some dandelions on my grave if twenty years from now the Earth is a little cooler than it is now," Gray offered.

After Klotzbach provided the forecast, Gray lumbered back to the podium to ventilate some more. "I think there's been so much foolishness out there over this human-induced global warming," he said— and proceeded to launch yet another assault on the climate modelers. Showing a Rube Goldberg–type image meant to depict the complexity of the climate system, Gray asked the audience: "Do you think people can write equations for all these things?" Later, Gray went on to his water vapor routine and explained his view that ocean circulation is the "fundamental driver for climate change." As more time passed, he started to repeat himself. He performed the water vapor–feedback debunking two times over. At one point he confused "global warming" and "global cooling." He went on too long, and had to be gently cut off after the presentation had passed the 35-minute mark.

Yet despite a somewhat awkward finish, for Gray the speech and especially its reception represented a successfully defiant stand in favorable territory. Given the state of scientific consensus on the subject as 2006, that the National Hurricane Conference would close not just with a debunking of any hurricane–global warming connection, but with a debunking of global warming *itself,* was staggering. Yet Gray ended to thunderous applause.

Gray's speech proved that the rift between the hurricane and climate communities remained alive and well. Their battle had dramatically amplified in 2004, the first major upturn year for damaging *land-falling* hurricanes in the state of Florida; and intensified further still in 2005, a year that increased both the damage levels and the ferocity of debate. And now, the divide seemed set to continue as the 2006 hurricane season approached.

After Gray's speech, it fell to Max Mayfield to pull the curtain on the event. No one knew it yet, but after delivering so many CNN-ready statements about Atlantic hurricanes over the years in his reassuring drawl, the Hurricane Center director would announce his retirement within months. As he sat adjacent to Gray on the stage the entire time, there was no telling what Mayfield thought of the unfolding diatribe, which he had prefaced by glowingly praising its speaker. While Mayfield didn't seem visibly uncomfortable with Gray's talk, he certainly hadn't endorsed any of it.

"I hope to see everyone, including our good friend Bill Gray, back in 2007," Mayfield said in closing. "We'll see you next year."

# 6 • The Luck of Florida

It's probably impossible to have a full-scale battle among meteorologists unless the weather itself cooperates. The 1821 hurricane that hit New York City had fueled the arguments between William Redfield and James Espy, and later the pair also fought over how to interpret other storms, including a devastating tornado that struck New Brunswick, New Jersey. Similarly, the weather of 2004 ushered in a dramatic new phase for the hurricane–climate debate, and gradually identified global warming itself with a new icon: the image of a cyclonic storm.

The year began with a stunning demonstration of how much damage hurricanes can wreak in the developing world. Forming in the South Indian basin about 275 miles south of the island of Diego García on February 29, the storm that would become Cyclone Gafilo meandered southwest toward Africa for several days, slowly strengthening. Then, on March 5, it suddenly bombed into a Category 4 storm, and the next day became a Category 5 with estimated sustained winds of 160 miles per hour and a minimum central pressure of 898 millibars (26.52 inches). At maximum intensity, Gafilo then besieged the northeastern coast of Madagascar—a devastating Category 5 landfall near the city of Antalaha, which was almost completely destroyed. Hundreds of thousands were left homeless by the storm.

Even as international aid agencies began to mobilize, Gafilo swept rapidly across the island, boomeranging in the Mozambique Channel between Madagascar and the African mainland and turning back to strike southern Madagascar from the northwest. On March 7, a weakened Gafilo created a scene straight out of a disaster movie. A ferry named the *Samson* had set out from the tiny island nation of Comoros, situated at the northern opening of the channel, on its way to Mahajanga, a Madagascan port that lay to the southeast. But Gafilo was coming across the island and parts of its circulation stretched out over the channel right around Mahajanga. The ferry sank in the storm and over 100 passengers and crew, who had apparently huddled inside the cabin in their life vests, drowned. Two passengers, who according to one report refused to don life vests and instead jumped overboard, survived to row to shore on a makeshift raft. Later they recalled seeing a huge wave slam into the ferry and sink it.

Gafilo ranks among the strongest known tropical cyclones ever to hit Madagascar. Still, such storms trouble the island (and Mozambique) with some regularity. Not so for Brazil, which, in late March, for the first time in recorded history, saw a hurricane-like storm hit its southern state of Santa Catarina. The storm—which some dubbed "Brazilcane"—stunned the meteorological community in that nation and across the world. Gray's early work on the global genesis of tropical cyclones, which had become more-or-less received wisdom by this point, had stated definitively that this kind of thing just doesn't happen. As he put it in 1979:

> Genesis does not occur in the tropical southeast Pacific and south Atlantic because the background seasonal climatology is so unfavorable. Although short-period positive deviations of genesis potential may be as large at these locations as elsewhere, they can never overcome their strongly unfavorable climatological background.

Yet here was a clockwise spiraling cyclone, characteristic of Southern Hemisphere hurricanes, coming ashore five hundred miles south of Rio de Janeiro with a well-defined eye and outer rain bands. Its peak sustained winds were consistent with those of a weak Category 2 hurricane. The storm damaged more than 35,000 homes, left tens of thousands homeless, and killed several people.

U.S. and Brazilian meteorologists sparred over whether the storm counted as a true hurricane. It had developed, just as some hurricanes do in the Atlantic north of the equator, from an extra-tropical cyclone that had then come to exhibit tropical features. The National Hurricane Center called it a hurricane based upon satellite imagery, but Brazilian forecasters balked at the classification. (Understandably, Brazil does not have a hurricane-forecasting center, much less hurricane-hunter airplanes to measure storm strength from the inside.) Hurricane scientists also found themselves flummoxed over how to name the storm. No rotating alphabetical list of names exists for the South Atlantic; there had never been any need for one. Finally the Brazilians named the storm after the location where it struck: Catarina. The eeriness continued.

Certainly Catarina was not directly *caused* by global warming. But that doesn't mean the two are entirely unconnected. At the United Kingdom's Hadley Centre for Climate Prediction and Research, a branch of that nation's Met Office, scientists pointed out that Catarina formed and struck in a region that, according to their model, might indeed feature more hurricanes in a globally warmed world. In fact, several attempts to study hurricanes in global climate models, whether under increased carbon dioxide scenarios or even under unforced regimes, had shown storms occasionally turning up in the South Atlantic. Before Catarina appeared, "We took this as probably being a problem with the model," remembers Ruth McDonald of the Hadley Centre. After Catarina, one might instead wonder whether the model had exceeded expectations and detected a basin right on the cusp of being hospitable to occasional hurricanes.

Later, two scientists at the University of Melbourne published a study that went further, suggesting Catarina might indeed presage the kind of world that global warming will create. Engaging in a bout of meteorological detective work to identify the conditions that made the storm possible, they found that although sea-surface temperatures had only been 24 to 25 degrees Celsius, the "unprecedented" combination of low wind shear and a "blocking" event—an interruption of normal atmospheric flow—had allowed the storm to transform from an ordinary extra-tropical cyclone into something much more like a hurricane. Did this make the storm a "threshold" phenomenon that pointed to a changing planet? The scientists speculated that global warming could alter Southern Hemisphere circulation patterns to create conditions favorable to more Catarinas, meaning that "other possible future South Atlantic hurricanes could be more likely to occur under global warming conditions."

Catarina thus raised the specter of a very different effect on hurricanes from global warming—not changes in numbers or intensities, but rather, changes to the regions of formation. But it was a specter and nothing more, because Catarina represented a single enigmatic event, not a trend. Scientists, who have caution and skepticism drilled into them over the course of their training, will never draw definitive conclusions based on one data point. At best, they'll give you a range of possibilities. Perhaps Catarina represents an early sign that Gray's empirical research on hurricane formation regions is decreasing in accuracy as global warming sets in. But it's also possible that rare hurricane-type storms have always formed in the South Atlantic but simply went undetected before the dawn of the satellite era. Storms with tropical characteristics had been noticed in the region on several occasions prior to Catarina—in 1991 and in January of 2004—but none had become nearly as intense.

Such ambiguities, however, were lost amid the chatter over a storm that seemed a perfect snapshot of our changing planet. The emergence of Catarina would become a leading argument for those—especially Al Gore—seeking to make the case that global warming has been transforming hurricanes as a way of mobilizing action to deal with the problem. The Brazilcane was the first of many 2004 storms that set the stage for the very public meteorological arguments that followed.

Then there were the Japanese typhoons and tropical storms—all ten of them.

Tropical cyclones churn the seas more violently in the Northwest Pacific than anywhere else in the world, and can do so year round. Traditionally this basin has been the genesis site of fully one-third of these storms globally, and home to the strongest of them all: supertyphoons, which correspond to strong Category 4 or Category 5 hurricanes on the Saffir-Simpson scale but often grow much larger than Atlantic storms and hold the current record for storm intensity. Supertyphoon Tip, of 1979, had a central pressure of 870 millibars (25.69 inches, the lowest pressure ever measured at sea level), and a circulation diameter of well over 1,000 miles, making it about the size of the entire western half of the United States. Fortunately, the storm didn't hit anything at this strength; it weakened considerably before striking the Japanese island of Honshu. "The potential for mass destruction was always there, but from a strictly meteorological standpoint, Tip was also a thing of great beauty," noted the U.S Navy's Joint Typhoon Warning Center at the time.

As Tip's history suggests, Japan—along with China, Vietnam, the Philippines, and many other Pacific nations and islands—faces typhoon threats regularly. Still, the country hardly expected a year like 2004, when fully ten typhoons or weaker tropical storms struck its islands, shattering the previous record of six. That included Supertyphoon Chaba, which had reached an estimated intensity of 879 millibars (25.96 inches) at sea—stronger than anything ever detected in the Western Hemisphere—but weakened considerably before reaching the island of Kyushu. It also included the enormous Typhoon Tokage (Japanese for "lizard"), which peaked at Category 4 status as it approached land and generated eighty-foot waves offshore. By the time Tokage hit the island of Shikoku, it too had weakened, a typical pattern for typhoons that curve northward toward Japan and have to cross colder waters. But the storm's heavy rains still unleashed floods and landslides, killing more than eighty people.

Gafilo, Catarina, and Chaba and Tokage and their many cousins—2004 was a stunning hurricane year globally. Few Americans would have noticed, however, if not for the spate of record-breaking storms that showed up in their own sector of the tropics. These hurricanes ravaged Florida, the most critical swing state in the nation, shortly before a hotly contested presidential election. As a result, it seemed possible that they might literally change the course of U.S. history.

The drama began alphabetically in early August, when Hurricane Alex grazed the Outer Banks but then unexpectedly intensified as it moved north over open ocean, becoming a major Category 3 storm at 38 degrees North Latitude (south of Nova Scotia). In so doing, Alex eclipsed Hurricane Ellen of 1973 as the most intense hurricane so far Pole-ward. "ALEX HAS BECOME ONE FOR THE RECORD BOOKS TONIGHT," National Hurricane Center forecaster Stacy Stewart wrote on August 4. Sea-surface temperatures beneath the storm, he noted, were more than 2 degrees Celsius above average. Despite this record, however, few Americans or Floridians remember Alex—too many other 2004 storms have been seared into their memories.

Even as a ragged tropical storm in the Caribbean, Charley looked ominous. "THERE IS NO OBVIOUS REASON OTHER THAN HITTING LAND THAT CHARLEY SHOULD NOT STRENGTHEN," wrote the hurricane center's Jack Beven on August 10. As the forecasters examined their tracking models, their fears mounted. Not only might Charley grow into a major hurricane; it could strike the low-lying Tampa Bay–St. Petersburg area, notorious for a vulnerability that nearly rivals that of New Orleans. A Category 4 storm approaching the bay at the right angle could drive a tremendous surge that would knock out bridges, flood parts of downtown Tampa under 20 feet of water, and temporarily turn St. Petersburg into an island. And even more than New Orleanians at the time, Tampa's residents suffered from hurricane amnesia. The last significant storm to hit them had come in 1921, long before the metropolitan area mushroomed into a city of over 2 million people.

Tampa Bay–St. Petersburg faced a mandatory evacuation order as Charley moved into the Gulf. Yet instead, the storm veered to the right, sparing the city a thrashing. Just as happened with Hugo, the barometer kept dropping as Charley approached the coast, all the way down to 941 millibars at landfall. That meant the storm jumped from Category 2 to Category 4 strength even as it came ashore over southwestern Florida. Directly in Charley's path lay Punta Gorda and Port Charlotte, where the small but vicious storm lacerated homes with its winds. Then Charley dragged northeast across much of the state, struck Orlando from the southwest, and managed to stay strong enough to exit back into the Atlantic as a hurricane, a rampage that caused an estimated $15 billion in damage (the total would have been much higher but for the fact that the storm tore through many rural areas). Charley had been the second most expensive hurricane in U.S. history after Andrew—temporarily, at least.

Three weeks later came Hurricane Frances, which like Charley had developed from a tropical wave and reached strong Category 4 intensity at its peak north of the Virgin Islands. Reading the forecasters' chatter as the storm moved through the northern Caribbean, one could again sense their anxiety. At least for a while, Frances seemed aimed straight at their Miami headquarters. Stacy Stewart kept warning that the storm might reach Category 5, yet the forecasters couldn't say yet where it would strike. "THE HURRICANE IS NOT A POINT… ESPECIALLY A HURRICANE AS LARGE AS FRANCES," wrote Richard Pasch on August 30. Hurricanes vary so much in size that, as Emanuel has observed, the smallest ones can fit entirely inside the eyes of the largest ones. Frances was about the size of Texas.

Frances presented not one but several worst-case scenarios. First came the possibility of a direct strike on Miami, which grimly called to mind the Category 4 hurricane that hit the beachside city in 1926. Back then, before the storm-flying or satellite era, many people didn't understand the concept of a hurricane eye, and dashed outdoors during a moment of seeming calm in the middle of the storm. Many were killed once the eye passed over and eye wall–strength winds resumed. A storm surge of 8 to 15 feet flooded the city; estimates suggest the same hurricane striking today could cause unprecedented levels of U.S. damage, exceeding $140 billion. But Frances also brought to mind another terrifying analogue from the past: the 1935 Labor Day Hurricane, a Category 5 storm that struck the middle islands of the Florida Keys and is estimated to have had a then-record central pressure for the Atlantic of 892 millibars (26.34 inches, later to be surpassed by 1988's Gilbert and 2005's Wilma). The storm washed over some parts of the Middle Keys entirely, killing a large number of World War I veterans sent there to work on a highway. It also partially destroyed the Florida Overseas Railroad, which once linked all of the Keys but has never been rebuilt.

These parallels may have flitted through the minds of the hurricane experts as they proceeded to set in motion the largest evacuation in Florida's history, of some 2.5 million people. Meanwhile, Frances developed several outer eye walls that then contracted inward, squeezing the inner eye wall and gradually replacing it, causing the storm to weaken. Ultimately Frances came ashore on September 5 at Category 2 strength and spared the most vulnerable areas. It hit southeastern Florida at Hutchinson Island and then took almost exactly the opposite path across the state from that of Charley; their tracks make an imperfect X, centered on Polk County. With its large size, Frances caused an estimated $9 billion in total damage, placing it just behind Charley in terms of its cost record (for the moment, at least). But the most terrifying storm of the 2004 season had not yet arrived: Ivan, which reached Category 5 intensity on three separate occasions and set a record by becoming a major hurricane farther south in the Atlantic than any other storm.

Ivan represented the most feared species of Atlantic hurricanes: a long-lived Cape Verde–type storm. In the end, it wound up lasting in some form or other for an amazing twenty-two days, peaking in intensity with a central pressure of 910 millibars (26.87 inches) and maximum sustained winds of nearly 170 miles per hour. In the process, Ivan maintained Category 4 strength or higher for thirty-two consecutive reports—issued once every six hours—from the National Hurricane Center, or for 192 hours in total. In other words, the storm combined extreme intensity with long duration at that intensity.

As Ivan moved into the Caribbean it kept revving its heat engine, strengthening and weakening and strengthening again. The monstrous storm killed thirty-nine people with a direct strike on Grenada, seventeen more in Jamaica, then washed over Grand Cayman Island, covering most of it with water. Next, Ivan entered the Gulf, where it appeared to fix upon New Orleans. This prompted another evacuation and much fretting about the "Atlantis scenario": a city below sea level actually finding itself below the sea.

Extending the city's luck for one year, Ivan swerved east toward the Florida panhandle, its eye coming ashore near Gulf Shores, Alabama, at Category 3 strength and driving a storm surge of up to fifteen feet in places. East of Pensacola, the huge waves surfing atop the swell knocked out portions of the I-10 span across Escambia Bay, a major conduit for travelers between the Florida panhandle and the Gulf Coast states farther west. Perdido Key, meanwhile, received the brunt of Ivan's powerful right front quadrant and was "essentially leveled," as the National Hurricane Center put it. Ivan also spawned more than one hundred tornadoes over land, and currently rates as the fifth most costly U.S. land-falling hurricane, just behind Charley. (At the time, it was the third.)

If this still isn't enough to convey a full appreciation of Ivan, consider what a storm of its magnitude can do to the ocean. As it crossed the Gulf, Ivan passed directly over six Naval Research Laboratory wave/tide gauges, barnacle-like devices lying 60 to 90 meters below the sea surface some hundred miles south of Mobile Bay. Somehow the gauges survived the storm's pummeling, and the data they registered provide a unique window on its roiling of the ocean. The gauge at one mooring detected a wave that reached an awesome 91 feet in height, the largest ever directly measured. But Naval Research Laboratory scientists confessed that even this probably failed to capture the biggest waves, near the eye wall, which may have reached 130 feet or more.

And 2004 still wasn't over for the Atlantic, or even for Florida. The strongest storm had arrived, but not yet the deadliest. In mid-September, Tropical Storm Jeanne moved into the Caribbean and weakened into a mere tropical depression. On September 18, however, its thick but disorganized clouds passed very slowly over Haiti, dumping rain. The ensuing landslides caused some three thousand deaths, nearly all of them in the city of Gonaives. Then Jeanne moved out into open ocean to the east of Florida and performed a spectacular full loop, tracing the shape of a yellow ribbon almost perfectly while strengthening over warm waters. The hurricane made landfall on September 26 at peak intensity, 950 millibars (28.05 inches) or Category 3 strength, along almost exactly the same path Frances had followed. Polk County, completely landlocked in the middle of Florida, got crisscrossed by its third hurricane of the season. Then Jeanne drove north across the entirety of the state. It was the fourth hurricane for Florida in the space of five weeks.

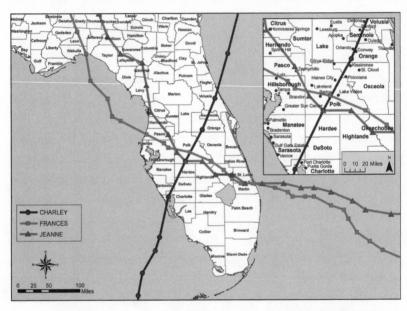

Tracks of hurricanes Charley, Frances, and Jeanne across the Florida peninsula in 2004. From Brian H. Bossak, "X Marks the Spot: Florida is the 2004 Hurricane Bull's Eye," *EOS*, December 14, 2004. *Copyright 2004 American Geophysical Union. Reproduced by permission of the American Geophysical Union.*

And with all eyes still on Jeanne, Ivan suddenly reappeared in the Gulf of Mexico like a deathless creature from a horror film. The storm's remnants had performed a gigantic loop up through the eastern United States, south over the Atlantic, and then west across Florida.

"AFTER CONSIDERABLE AND SOMETIMES ANIMATED IN-HOUSE DISCUSSION," observed forecaster Lixion Avila, the National Hurricane Center had decided the storm was not dead yet. Never stronger than a tropical storm, Ivan the Second ultimately moved over land near Cameron, Louisiana. It caused no damage this time, but it almost seemed to be personally spiting us.

In the end, the number of strikes on Florida in 2004 broke all records, and the combined costs of Charley, Frances, Ivan, and Jeanne reached an estimated $45 billion (in 2004 dollars). As of 2004, all four storms ranked among the top six most damaging hurricanes in U.S. history, a powerful testament to the vulnerability that had built up along the U.S. Gulf and East coasts during the hurricane lull period of the 1970s and 1980s (which Gray and others had been tirelessly warning about). And each storm had its own character, so that collectively they demonstrate the wide range of ways in which hurricanes can cause death and destruction. Charley had been small but intense, most dangerous because of its extreme winds, which occurred over a very narrow area. Ivan had been huge and powerful, driving a large storm surge and then spinning off more than one hundred tornadoes. Jeanne had killed with rainfall.

Following all this, stunned Americans could hardly imagine the possibility of a still more devastating hurricane year. But what they should have recognized is that 2004 could have been far worse. Charley could have hit Tampa. Frances could have reintensified and hit Miami or the Keys. Ivan could have hit New Orleans. Instead of tens of billions of dollars in damage, the total could have exceeded one hundred billion. Many more people could have been killed. Awkward as it is to say, in some sense Florida and the United States had *still* been very lucky.

Meanwhile, given this unparalleled destruction, it seems only appropriate that the 2004 hurricane season touched off the biggest meteorological argument of the decade.

Bill Gray did a pretty good job of forecasting the total number of Atlantic storms that would emerge in 2004. Well in advance, in December

2003, he'd predicted thirteen named tropical cyclones and seven hurricanes, when the actual totals wound up being fourteen or fifteen* and nine, respectively. But Gray had underforecast the number of intense or "major" storms by 50 percent, predicting only three instead of the six that actually occurred (in addition to Alex, Charley, Frances, Ivan, and Jeanne, Hurricane Karl also attained Category 4 strength over the open ocean). "This year did not behave like any other year we have studied," Gray admitted. For one thing, sea-surface temperatures had been anomalously high.

When Gray's October 1, 2004, forecast came out, it included a cartoon at the opening, showing three humanoid figures standing in the middle of a road. One figure shouts, "We must stop GLOBAL WARMING!" and points to the sky. The other two figures scratch their heads quizzically but gaze in the direction he's pointing. Meanwhile, behind their backs, a Mack truck is barreling down on them. "LAND-FALLING HURRICANES," it reads.

Presumably, the stick figures are Floridians.

It's hardly unnatural, in the face of strange or extreme weather, for citizens who have heard of "global warming" to wonder whether it might explain what they're seeing. During and after the staggering 2004 hurricane season, Gray and his colleagues in the hurricane community strove to disabuse the public of this notion. Major media outlets disseminated their message: "2 Storms In Florida Not Seen As Trend; Experts Don't Fault Global Warming," announced a *Washington Post* report following strikes by Charley and Frances. "Storm Activity Part of a Cycle," added the *Los Angeles Times* a week later. The latter story quoted Gray as well as Jim Laver, head of NOAA's Climate Prediction Center in Camp Springs, Maryland. "None of this has anything to do with global warming," Laver told the paper. "These are natural cycles that we see."

If natural cycles presumably explained the warm ocean, the seem-

---

*Depending upon whether you count "Subtropical Storm Nicole," a very weak and short-lived storm that formed in the Central North Atlantic, or not.

ingly unique 2004 devastation owed to many other factors as well—and the hurricane scientists were quick to point them out. The absence of a strong El Niño and weak wind shear had helped generate strong and numerous storms in the Atlantic. Meanwhile, the westward location of the Bermuda High—a large region of relatively higher-pressure sea-level air over the Atlantic—had helped steer them toward Florida. Before they can follow their general tendency to turn northward, Atlantic storms have to move along the south end of the High. So when the High locates farther to the east, hurricanes can turn north sooner, which often takes them up the U.S. East Coast or out into open ocean. But when the High locates farther westward, it can steer hurricanes right into the Florida peninsula and the Gulf of Mexico—which, especially in late summer and early fall, tends to serve as a kind of hurricane trampoline, intensifying storms dramatically.

All of these separate influences played a part in the 2004 destruction. The atmosphere is a complex place; any weather occurrence will necessarily spring from a number of factors acting in tandem, along with chance. Yet for some climate scientists who knew very well that the Earth was already changing in response to global warming, the confident dismissals of *this* factor by the hurricane forecasters and their allies rankled. A new modeling study of hurricanes under greenhouse conditions, published just days after Jeanne made landfall, only added to their concern. The climate scientists saw Catarina, the Japanese typhoons, and the Florida hurricanes as a portent, a harbinger, of global warming's meteorological onset. And they wanted the public to know about it.

The climate scientists staged their attempted rebuttal to the forecasters through a telephone press conference organized by the Harvard Medical School's Center for Health and the Global Environment and held on October 21, just weeks before the 2004 presidential election. The event, in turn, sparked a very public imbroglio between one participant, leading climate scientist Kevin Trenberth of the National Center for Atmospheric Research, and one of Gray's top students, hurricane guru Chris Landsea. At its core, the spat was fueled by differences in scientific methodology and outlook. It also featured plenty of raw animosity.

The Trenberth-Landsea argument, in turn, provided the initial disturbance that would reawaken the hurricane–global warming argument in a much more intense and personal way, engulfing many other experts, scientific societies, and even government agencies in its wake.

# 7. Frictional Divergence

Herbert Riehl had given Bill Gray a spectacular first storm-flying experience with their low-level penetration of Category 4 Hurricane Helene in 1958. But it could hardly rival the experience that Gray passed on, almost like an heirloom, to Chris Landsea thirty years later.

Landsea had grown up in Miami and always had an interest in storms: Category 3 Hurricane Betsy hit in 1965, just two weeks after his family moved there. In 1988, after getting his undergraduate degree in atmospheric science at UCLA and working for a year at NOAA's Aircraft Operations Center (home of the famous Hurricane Hunters), Landsea started graduate school under Gray. He'd only been out in Colorado a month when a hurricane named Gilbert came cruising across the Caribbean, and Gray told Landsea and fellow grad students Jim Kossin and Steve Hodanish, "I can get you guys onto a flight if you want to go." They did. "We just showed up in Miami," Landsea remembers. It probably didn't hurt that he already knew everyone at the Aircraft Operations Center.

And so, on September 13, the three students found themselves hurtling toward an extremely intense Hurricane Gilbert on board one of NOAA's long-range Orion P-3 turboprop research planes, equipped with high-tech instrument consoles for each passenger as well as plenty of barf bags. The timing couldn't have been more perfect. Landsea, Kossin, and Hodanish were just "twenty-three-year-old kids having a good time on board this plane" (their idea of a "good time" being 199-mile-per-hour gusts and 40-mile-per-hour updrafts). But they had managed to get onto the historic flight that, at an altitude of 3 kilometers, recorded (by extrapolation) a central pressure of 888 millibars in

Gilbert's extremely compact eye, which was just ten kilometers across. It was the lowest pressure ever measured in the Atlantic basin and would remain so until the record was broken seventeen years later in Hurricane Wilma. Landsea, Kossin, and Hodanish had hitched their first ride into the strongest hurricane ever observed in the Western Hemisphere.

For Landsea—who would go on to work at NOAA's Hurricane Research Division (the descendant of the National Hurricane Research Project) and later at the National Hurricane Center—this marked the first flight in a long career of airborne storm research. That includes sorties into Opal in 1995, Georges in 1998, Floyd in 1999, and finally Katrina even as it made landfall in Louisiana and Mississippi.

Much like Gray, Landsea is tall, genial, and entertaining—a crowd-pleaser. He sometimes opens his public talks with jokes that turn on his all-too-appropriate last name—for example, observing that if he had a son named "Aaron," the kid's full name would be Aaron Land-sea ("Air and Land Sea"). Bespectacled but tanned and muscular, Landsea is the kind of scientist you'd expect to find living in Miami. At less formal scientific meetings, he wears Hawaiian (or as he calls them, "tropical") shirts, and sometimes a shirt in which hurricane spirals replace floral motifs.

Above all, Landsea is the unrivaled master of Atlantic hurricane data. He heads up the HURDAT project, an ongoing reanalysis of Atlantic storms back to 1851 that aims to get the most precise statistics possible about their tracks and intensities (information that is obviously valuable to insurance companies seeking to assess risks for a particular region). Reanalysis led to the upgrading of Hurricane Andrew from a Category 4 to a Category 5 storm at landfall. But its value is perhaps even better epitomized by Landsea's role in rediscovering the hurricane that affected San Diego, California, in October of 1858, when it was a mere settlement of a few thousand people (today the population of San Diego County exceeds 3 million).

Studying weather records and old newspaper reports in collaboration with an independent scholar named Michael Chenoweth, Landsea helped document a storm in which roofs had been torn off houses and ships had been driven up onto beaches. Los Angeles, too, experienced heavy rains and flooding. Drawing clues from reports of the damage, Landsea and Chenoweth inferred that San Diego had experienced Category 1–force hurricane winds, although the storm that produced them (presumably originating in the Northeast Pacific hurricane basin off the coast of Mexico) had remained just offshore. Such an event had never been recorded before or since, but Landsea and Chenoweth had forever distinguished the unlikely from the impossible. "The risk of a hurricane in southern California is now documented to be real," they wrote. In conclusion, they linked the 1858 San Diego hurricane to seeming record-breaking storms like 2003's Ana and 2004's Catarina. "These are yet additional reminders that if we wait long enough, or dig deep enough in archives, that more surprises are in store to challenge our assumptions about the frequency, seasonality, and location of tropical cyclones," they noted.

This underscored a central theme that would reemerge repeatedly from Landsea as the hurricane–global warming debate intensified in 2004 and beyond: We don't have good enough data to fully grasp the diversity of hurricanes that have existed in the past. As a consequence, we should expect to be continually surprised by apparent "record-breaking" storms or groups of them—like Catarina, or the Japanese typhoons, or the four Florida hurricanes—that would have prior analogues if only we could survey more of meteorological history. So don't blame global warming, the argument goes, blame our skimpy observational records. A "record-breaking" storm, after all, surpasses only what has been *recorded.*

Yet even if Landsea's argument is true—and to some extent it *must* be—climatic changes could also begin to surprise us with unprecedented storms, and it would take many years to determine which factor (poor measurements of the past or ongoing changes in the present) better explained them. The 1858 San Diego hurricane was, assuredly, just a rare event. It may have been made possible by El Niño conditions, which heat sea temperatures off the West Coast, allowing hurricanes to travel farther northward. El Niño represents a natural mode of variability; but if global warming sufficiently increases average sea temperatures off the coasts of San Diego and Los Angeles, it's certainly conceivable that these cities could also face a greater risk of future hurricanes.

As suggested by his reanalysis research, his work on Gray's hurricane forecast, and their collaborative studies of hurricanes and Sahel rainfall, Landsea is a strong meteorological empiricist. Like Gray, he digs down deep into the data—including getting dusty in the historical archives—rather than running models or designing theories reliant upon complex mathematics.

That's not to say that Landsea denies global warming outright or entirely dismisses numerical modeling. He doesn't go nearly so far as Gray on either of these fronts and is willing to criticize his mentor ("I wish he'd publish more," he told me). Still, it's easy to see the overlaps and influences. Landsea, like Gray, has long criticized attempts to link hurricanes and global warming, as well as attempts to study hurricanes in climate models. In one very widely cited 2001 paper, Landsea joined Gray and other hurricane experts in arguing that the uptick in Atlantic hurricane activity since 1995 involved an ocean-driven cycle, the Atlantic Multidecadal Oscillation, rather than climate change.

It came as no surprise, then, that in media interviews during and after the 2004 hurricane season, Landsea joined the other hurricane specialists in refuting any connection between the destruction and global warming. Yet even as they strove to do so, Landsea, Gray, and their colleagues couldn't keep global warming entirely out of the picture. A scientist working within NOAA published a study in late September 2004, with Florida still reeling from Hurricane Jeanne, that made that impossible. It wouldn't be the last time in the hurricane–climate debate that the scientific publication process and the weather seemed curiously synchronized.

In a tour-de-force piece of work, Thomas Knutson of the Geophysical Fluid Dynamics Laboratory and a coauthor, Robert Tuleya of Old Dominion University, went far beyond previous computer studies of hurricane intensity changes for increased concentrations of atmospheric carbon dioxide. They drew upon results from nine different global climate models whose scenarios raised tropical sea-surface temperatures by .8 to 2.4 degrees Celsius. The scientists fed the various climate-model results into the high-resolution GFDL hurricane model, and then ran experiments using four different cloud schemes, three different ocean basins, and so on. In total, the study involved nearly 1,300 simulations of hurricanes under enhanced greenhouse (or control) conditions. Any consistent results uncovered across such a large range of experiments would be very difficult to attribute to the quirks of a single model.

And Knutson and Tuleya found a number of consistent results in response to carbon dioxide–induced global warming. On average, maximum hurricane wind speed increased by 6 percent, central pressure dropped by 14 percent, and, most dramatically, precipitation increased by 18 percent near the storm center (due to the fact that in a warmer climate, the air converging into a hurricane holds more water vapor). This translated into a shift toward stronger storms by "half a category" on the Saffir-Simpson scale, hardly trivial considering that hurricane damage levels spike upward with increasing storm intensity. And the strengthening would surely have been greater but for another partially offsetting effect of climate change: The carbon dioxide increase in the models had the effect of producing an enhanced warming of the upper troposphere relative to the surface in the tropics. This in turn increased atmospheric stability and made it somewhat harder for air to rise in the hurricane eye wall. Finally, the study found that although sea surface and upper tropospheric temperatures rose consistently in the climate models, changes in vertical wind shear were far more erratic. Knutson and Tuleya thus questioned whether this key dynamic factor would shift under global warming in such a way as to systematically affect hurricane intensity. It looked instead like the most important expected changes would be caused by thermodynamics.

All of this seemed to greatly clarify how global warming might change hurricanes. But the upshot for the present moment was simply that there wasn't one. The study made it explicit: Due to their relatively modest magnitude, the carbon dioxide–induced changes to hurricanes "are unlikely to be detectable in historical observations and will probably not be detectable for decades to come." At least according to this work, the effect of global warming on hurricanes seemed a problem for the future. It certainly couldn't be blamed in any meaningful way for the storms in Florida.

Landsea, however, thought even this overplayed the likely effect of climate change. Before long he teamed up with longtime global-warming contrarian Patrick Michaels to critique the Knutson study. They began by posing a question—"Should we trust models or observations?"—and went on to answer in defense of the latter. The Knutson and Tuleya work, they argued, was too idealized, too simplistic. Even its modest results for hurricane intensification were overstated because "observations, rather than models" suggested a more tenuous relationship between sea temperatures and hurricane strength.

In the face of these criticisms, Knutson and his coauthor stood firmly by their study and defended the assumptions they had used to study changing storm intensities in a changing world. "If we had observations of the future, we obviously would trust them more than models," they dryly responded. "But unfortunately observations of the future are not available at this time."

Landsea could counter Knutson's position in the peer-reviewed scientific literature by writing a critique. That's just what he eventually did. But when a group of climate scientists went straight to the media, staging a press conference to make an even stronger linkage between hurricanes and global warming in October 2004, they couldn't be countered in the same way.

When Landsea heard about the upcoming Harvard press conference, he contacted Kevin Trenberth, one of the listed participants, and asked him to rethink. "I said, please don't do this, because there's no science behind such a link," Landsea recalls. But Trenberth—a short, thin, mustached scientist who originally hails from New Zealand and is one of the most widely cited researchers in the climate field—did the event anyway. In fact, during it he stated: "I think one of the reasons we've got this press conference is to perhaps try to add a little bit to other statements that have been made by hurricane forecasters."

Trenberth heads the climate analysis section of the National Center for Atmospheric Research in Boulder, Colorado, and specializes (among other areas) in studying how global warming will change the global water cycle and the character of precipitation in its various forms, ranging from snowfall to the intense downpour generated by hurricanes. It was largely from this vantage point that he approached the hurricane question. In a warmer world, Trenberth reasoned, the atmosphere ought to hold more water vapor, which in turn should bring about stronger precipitation in storms. Warmer seas should also evaporate more water, providing more fuel for the hurricane heat engine. In short, Trenberth was largely relying on basic physical reasoning about how the climate system responds to change on a large scale. On the Harvard conference call, he was accompanied by Harvard biological oceanographer James McCarthy, an expert on the impacts of climate change; Dr. Paul Epstein, associate director of the sponsoring Center for Health and the Global Environment; and Mathias Weber, a senior vice president at the U.S. division of the reinsurance company Swiss Re, a Europe-based firm that has been very open to the notion of a possible connection between climate change and an increase in insured losses due to extreme weather.

In his remarks—which later became the source of fierce controversy—Trenberth did not claim that global warming had *caused* the 2004 hurricane destruction. However, he sought to explain that, as global warming is clearly happening, it's unlikely it would not be having an effect on hurricanes. "We can't say anything really about the tracks which make the hurricanes hit the U.S. or miss the U.S.," Trenberth said. "What we can say is that the high sea-surface temperatures [and] water vapor make for more intense storms and so this is consistent with the evidence that we're seeing." In a press release announcing the call, Trenberth was further quoted as stating that "the North Atlantic hurricane season of 2004 may well be a harbinger of the future." Mathias Weber also included this cautionary remark (which Trenberth echoed): "We believe it is actually impossible to associate a single event such as Hurricane Charley, or even a series of events such as the series we have seen this year, to a climate change trend."

Yet despite such caveats, Trenberth's statements did go beyond where the hurricane–climate debate had wound up by the close of the 1990s by suggesting that a discernible influence on storms already existed. For example, Trenberth called Catarina "the first of its kind and [clear] evidence that things are changing." Citing the Atlantic hurricane increase since 1995, he added that "this kind of evidence is pointing more in the direction that these extremes are occurring and are having a real impact on society." So if Trenberth's remarks were later misinterpreted as suggesting a direct causal connection between global warming and the Florida hurricanes, that's partly understandable in light of how the Harvard press conference—both by its timing and its theme—broadly "linked" the two.

In contrast to Trenberth, Emanuel at this point in time could be found expressing his own position with stronger reservations, and hewing more closely to the 1998 consensus. While still convinced global warming ought to change hurricanes, Emanuel added in a 2004 article that no such change had manifested at the present moment—nor should it have, in light of an average increase in tropical sea-surface temperatures of only .3 degrees Celsius (about half a degree Fahrenheit) since 1950. Using his maximum potential intensity theory, Emanuel calculated that storms should only have strengthened by about 1.3 percent, too small an increase to be detected given large natural variability and the error margins inherent in storm intensity measurements. "I think it's extremely difficult to pin the last season on global warming," Emanuel later said of the 2004 destruction. "That does not preclude that there may be a global-warming signal buried in there somewhere, but nobody in my field thinks that we've seen it."

Knutson's study on hurricane intensification under global warming also argued that the phenomenon would be undetectable for years. But Trenberth suspected that such modeling studies were probably underestimating the sensitivity of hurricanes to climatic changes. Meanwhile, at the Harvard event, Paul Epstein went even further, implying a direct link between global warming and the deaths caused by Jeanne in Haiti. No wonder that in response to such statements, Bill Gray fired back in his typical fashion. "They are all smart guys—I admire them for their talents," Gray told one reporter. "But on this topic, I feel many of them have sort of sold their soul."

Heightening tensions further was the 2004 presidential election that lay on the horizon. No one knew what effect the devastation in Florida might have on the outcome in this most pivotal of states, which had twenty-seven electoral votes compared with twenty for the other key swing state, Ohio. Certainly it was enough of a wild card that both George W. Bush and, later, John Kerry made a point of personally surveying the damage and offering support to those whose lives had just been shattered. In this context, talk of global warming and its impacts on hurricanes could easily be parlayed into an attack on Bush, who had struggled on the climate issue during his first term in office, and whose administration had been repeatedly accused of altering and suppressing scientific information related to climate change and its impacts.

Just a few days after the Harvard press conference, this political subtext ceased to be a subtext at all when two advocacy groups called Environment 2004 and Scientists and Engineers for Change announced they would be displaying billboards along the I-4 corridor linking Tampa and Orlando, as well as in the cities themselves. "Global Warming = Worse Hurricanes," the billboards read. "George Bush just doesn't get it." Alongside this slogan, the billboards depicted a hurricane barreling toward the shell-shocked Florida peninsula.

Judged from the standpoint of political advertising, this certainly constituted a gripping message. It was also a direct, if unsuccessful,

Billboard put up along highways in Florida during the 2004 presidential election by the groups Environment 2004 and Scientists and Engineers for Change. *Credit: Environment 2004.*

attempt to sway an election. Science and politics had merged inextricably in this instance, and that had a serious consequence for the hurricane–climate debate going forward. Scientific divides would harden, while the Bush administration in its second term would dismiss claims that climate change had intensified or might intensify hurricanes, even when some of those claims came from the administration's own scientist employees.

Whatever the impact of the Scientists and Engineers for Change ad campaign in Florida, it did not manage to win the state for John Kerry—we all know how the 2004 election turned out. But the Harvard press conference would have serious repercussions nonetheless.

Shortly prior to the Harvard event, Trenberth had invited Chris Landsea to contribute to a section of the Intergovernmental Panel on Climate Change's Fourth Assessment Report, due out in 2007, which addressed Atlantic hurricanes. The IPCC process marshals the collective contributions of hundreds of global scientists in a loosely hierarchical format, and Trenberth, relatively high on the totem pole, was "coordinating lead author" of his section, a job that entailed getting the world's foremost experts to contribute. Landsea was inarguably an expert on hurricane data, and he had accepted Trenberth's invitation.

But several months after the press conference, Landsea publicly resigned from the IPCC process, e-mailing out a denunciation of Trenberth's Harvard statements in the form of a letter to forty-five colleagues that then made its way onto the Internet. "It is beyond me why my colleagues would utilize the media to push an unsupported agenda that recent hurricane activity has been due to global warming," Landsea wrote. Later he added: "I personally cannot in good faith continue to contribute to a process that I view as both being motivated by pre-conceived agendas and being scientifically unsound." Landsea also questioned whether the scientists involved in the Harvard event had any business speaking about hurricanes: "To my knowledge, none of the participants in that press conference had performed any research on hurricane variability, nor were they reporting on any new work in the field," he observed.

If Landsea's resignation did not immediately follow the Harvard event, it was because first he'd sought internal reassurance that when it came to hurricanes, "what will be included in the IPCC report will reflect the best available information and the consensus within the scientific community most expert on the specific topic." When Landsea complained to the IPCC leadership about Trenberth, however, he did not find a particularly sympathetic response. "Individual scientists can do what they wish in their own right, as long as they are not saying anything on behalf of the IPCC," chairman Rajendra Pachauri had written to him. But Landsea protested that Trenberth had been identified as affiliated with the IPCC at the Harvard press conference. It was only after the IPCC did not deal adequately with his concerns (in Landsea's opinion) that he chose to resign.

After Landsea's open letter appeared in January 2005, the spat between him and Trenberth drew major media coverage. Trenberth called Landsea's charges "ridiculous" in one interview, but said he would welcome him back to contribute to the IPCC report. Landsea said he would work with the IPCC again, but not on a section that had Trenberth as a coordinating lead author. Perhaps the most cutting remark in the conflict came from Landsea in an e-mail later made public:

> The sad thing about this is that it did not have to turn out this way. I did try to caution [Trenberth] before the media event [and] provided a summary of the consensus within the hurricane research community...Dr. Trenberth wrote back to me that he hoped that this press conference would not "go out of control." I would suggest that it was out of control the minute that he and his fellow panel members decided to forego the peer review scientific process and abuse science in pursuit of a political agenda.

In the context of the ongoing global warming debate, the dispute between Trenberth and Landsea had significant political implications. With each of its successive five-year assessment reports, the IPCC had strengthened the conclusion that global warming is happening due to human activities. Meanwhile, each time the climate "skeptics" had sought to undermine the panel's credibility and objectivity. In this sense, Landsea's resignation represented a public relations bonanza to them. He had handed over a big stick with which to beat the IPCC. Among many others, Republican senator James Inhofe of Oklahoma, a leading global warming "skeptic" in Congress, would later cite the Landsea-Trenberth episode as a "stark example of how the [IPCC] process has been corrupted."

Advocates generally took either Landsea's or Trenberth's side in the dispute according to their political predilections. What few recognized, however, was that at the heart of their argument, once again, lay a split between scientific approaches. On the one hand, in his remarks on hurricanes Trenberth had spoken from the perspective of a climate scientist interested in how the overarching system works. Given that global warming is happening, he reasoned, how could that *not* be having at least some effect on storms reliant upon heat and moisture? But Landsea, speaking from the perspective of an Atlantic hurricane analyst and a master of storm data, declared that no evidence could be adduced to demonstrate a "long-term trend up in the frequency or intensity of tropical cyclones." On at least one level, Trenberth and Landsea weren't so much disagreeing as speaking past each other. Had their debate unfolded through the scientific process, rather than through the amplifying, oversimplifying, and often distorting medium of newspaper and other media reports, they might well have been able to find some common ground.

After the dust-up with Landsea, Trenberth talked to the press somewhat, but did not put out a public statement of his position to rebut critics in the media or on the blogs (which were beginning to play a pivotal role in shaping discourse about hurricanes and climate). Instead, he began working on a scientific article detailing the reasoning behind his statements. The paper, which appeared in *Science* in June 2005 with the hurricane season already underway, laid out the basic logic. After citing the 2004 Florida storms and Japanese typhoons, and the global-warming questions that had been raised in relation to them, Trenberth spent most of the paper on caveats. Sure, there's lots of hurricane variability, within and between ocean basins.

And sure, hurricanes are affected by anything from El Niño to vertical wind shear. So far, so good.

But *nevertheless,* Trenberth continued, no one can deny that sea-surface temperatures are rising and that rise has been linked to human-induced global warming. Further, the warming means there is more water vapor in the atmosphere. These two trends should theoretically provide more energy to fuel hurricanes and increase their rainfall. In the face of such changes, Trenberth wrote, it would be surprising if there weren't changes to hurricanes as well, even if no trends had been firmly documented yet. Such a situation often occurs in science, he observed: Researchers lack the data to show that something is truly happening that they suspect ought to be, based on physical reasoning. "Although variability is large," Trenberth wrote, "trends associated with human influences are evident in the environment in which hurricanes form, and our physical understanding suggests that the intensity of and rainfalls from hurricanes are probably increasing, even if this increase cannot yet be proven with a formal statistical test."

It was a fascinating piece of scientific speculation. The title of Trenberth's article—"Uncertainty in Hurricanes and Global Warming"—underscored as much. Trenberth had advanced a scientific hypothesis based on fairly simple physical reasoning, but he had no body of hurricane data to support him. He was also going beyond existing hurricane modeling and theory, as represented by the work of Knutson and Emanuel, which agreed that hurricanes ought to change under global warming but not enough for the change to be detectable yet.

"I was out there by myself," Trenberth remembers. But if he'd gone out on a limb, his statements and his paper also challenged other scientists to dig into global data on hurricanes, in order to determine whether to saw off his support or to clasp his hand.

Meanwhile, even as the Trenberth-Landsea controversy rippled across the media and blogs, another cluster of intense tropical cyclone activity hit a part of the world vastly distant from both Japan and Florida.

In the space of a mere month in February 2005, two Category 4 and two Category 5 storms—Meena, Nancy, Olaf, and Percy—tore through the Cook Islands in the Southwest Pacific basin, to the east of Australia and northeast of New Zealand. Collectively, these cyclones trashed Raratonga, Tokelau, American Samoa, and numerous other small islands. The worst of them, Percy, had a record low central pressure for the region of 900 millibars, and reportedly damaged nearly all standing structures on Pukapuka and Nassau, home to 670 people.

Just two years earlier, Cyclone Zoe had ripped through the Solomon Islands, also in the Southwest Pacific basin, with winds approaching 180 miles per hour and a satellite estimated minimum central pressure of 879 millibars—which, if accurate, would have made it the strongest known Southern Hemisphere hurricane. And now, according to the Cook Islands Meteorological Service, so many intense cyclones appearing in the area, in such a brief period of time, represented yet another "record."

# 8 • Meet the Press

For a number of years, along with two of MIT's other star scientists—oceanographer Carl Wunsch and ocean geochemist Edward Boyle—Kerry Emanuel has co-taught a first-year graduate course, "Climate Physics and Chemistry." One year, it must have been 1999 or 2000, Emanuel found himself listening to Wunsch lecture on the oceans' deep overturning circulation, which transports tremendous amounts of heat from the equator to the poles. Cold, salty water sinks in the North Atlantic because it's more dense—what some call the "thermohaline" circulation—but in order to maintain a global circulation, less dense water must also rise to the surface again elsewhere. As Wunsch pointed out, this in turn requires a process of turbulent upper-ocean mixing that drives warm water downward into the ocean's cooler layers. Most oceanographers thought the necessary mixing occurred through tidal processes, but Emanuel—who knew of hurricanes' powerfully violent churning of the seas, and the cold wakes they leave behind after their passage—started to wonder whether they might play a significant role.

Up to that point, Emanuel hadn't taken very seriously the notion that hurricanes might interact with the climate in two directions, both being shaped by and also shaping it—in short, that they might be a feedback. Wunsch's lecture, though, got him thinking. "I did a very quick back-of-the-envelope calculation," Emanuel remembers, "and then a more thorough publication." And so he became the leading proponent of a fairly revolutionary idea: Far from being isolated and rare—if awe-inspiring—events with no greater planetary significance, hurricanes, by mixing the oceans, might help determine what kind of

Earth we live on. Tropical cyclones, much like extra-tropical ones, could play a fundamental role in regulating the climate.

It's well known that hurricanes draw up cooler waters from below the sea surface, leaving a pronounced cold wake as they pass. But the violent mixing works both ways. Hurricanes also drive warm surface waters down into the colder ocean depths. After a hurricane passes and leaves a cold wake, the sun gradually warms the surface mixed layer (as it's called) up again. The warm water pushed down to the depths, though, persists as an anomalous increase in the net heat content of that particular column of ocean water. So in order to restore equilibrium after a hurricane, Emanuel reasoned, the tropical oceans must redistribute that excess warm water to cooler regions.

This implied that hurricanes might contribute significantly to the overturning circulation, driving heat away from the tropics and toward the poles. The idea had at least two points in its favor. First, hurricanes have a remarkable capacity to churn up ocean waters to considerable depths. And second, like strategically placed turbines, their tropical location puts them in the right place to perform the sort of mixing that would lead to poleward heat transport.

Emanuel first published this big if also speculative idea in 2001, adding that if hurricanes intensified, this could result in a relative cooling of the tropics and a heating of the higher latitudes. He also soon situated this new conceit in the distant past, much as he had done previously by linking hypercanes to the extinction of the dinosaurs. Hurricane-driven ocean heat transport, he speculated, might help explain the oft-noted "cool tropics paradox" of the early Eocene era, roughly 56 to 50 million years ago.

The early Eocene was an exceedingly warm period in the Earth's history that has long puzzled backward-looking climatologists—as well as frightened them, because they suspect that may be where we're heading if global warming continues. Sea levels at the time were dramatically higher, as were atmospheric concentrations of greenhouse gases (carbon dioxide and methane) due to natural causes. The Arctic coastlines were rimmed by temperate forests, and populated by warm-weather plants and animals (including crocodiles in Greenland). Yet based upon the analysis of oxygen isotopes found in the fossilized shells of tiny marine organisms called foramanifera, scientists had found that even as polar temperatures during the early Eocene were dramatically warmer than today, temperatures in the tropics were only slightly higher.

How could this have happened? Emanuel proposed an explanation that, at least to some extent, could be tested: Stronger hurricanes had helped transport large amounts of heat out of equatorial regions. Emanuel's attempt to investigate this idea, however, would lead to a very different kind of turbulent mixing: between scientists.

Emanuel couldn't directly observe many of the central processes stipulated by his hypothesis. He couldn't go out and track ocean heat fluctuations from a boat during or immediately after every strong hurricane. But he could use models and theoretical considerations to calculate how much heat hurricanes might help to transport, and whether it sufficed to bring about a significant climate-scale effect. This, in turn, depended on how extensively these storms mix the ocean; and *that* depended on the collective strength of hurricanes summed over their lifetimes.

Traditional measurements of storm frequency and intensity were ill-suited to such an inquiry, however. Simply focusing on the total number of storms lumped together weak tropical storms with Category 4 and 5 monsters, even though the latter, with gigantic waves like those observed in Hurricane Ivan or Typhoon Tokage, had a much greater capacity to mix the oceans. Simply focusing on a storm's peak intensity, meanwhile, told you nothing about how long it managed to maintain that intensity. The longest-lived tropical cyclone on record, Hurricane/Typhoon John of 1994, lasted for 31 days, during which time it traveled 8,000 miles from its point of origin in the Northeast Pacific basin all the way across the world's largest ocean to the Northwest Pacific basin, and then back east into the Central Pacific again. Along the way, John strengthened and weakened multiple times, spanning the entire gamut of hurricane intensity and at one point becoming a Category 5 storm. Obviously, then, John had mixed the oceans far more than a weak tropical storm that fizzles out within days of its formation.

Frequency and intensity measurements also ignored the important issue of storm size. All else being equal, larger hurricanes mix the oceans more than smaller ones. For all these reasons, traditional frequency and intensity metrics failed to capture how much total hurricane power existed—or, for that matter, the true magnitude of the potential hurricane *threat* to human beings. For a strong overlap exists between hurricanes' capacity to stir the seas and their capacity to destroy outposts of civilization. Both depend on wind speed, with longer periods of high winds making it more likely (all else being equal) that storms hit something when they're at their most dangerous.

To account for all this, Emanuel turned to his equations. He derived a new measurement of hurricane strength that he called the "power dissipation index" (PDI)—some have since labeled it a "potential destruction index"—which measured the total amount of energy released by a hurricane over the course its life. The calculation began with peak sustained wind speeds taken at regular six-hour intervals over the entire history of a storm, and then converted these measurements into a reflection of total storm power by multiplying each wind-speed measurement by itself twice, or cubing it, and adding all the cubed measurements together. Though this might sound like a surprising mathematical move to make, it's actually fairly uncontroversial among hurricane specialists, who know very well that a storm's destructive capacity goes up "as the cube of the wind speed," as it's often put.

When Emanuel examined the new hurricane data, he suddenly saw something very surprising. Increasing storm lifetimes, coupled with increasing intensities, had apparently resulted in a doubling of the amount of power dissipated by Atlantic and Northwest Pacific storms over the past thirty years. "The trend sort of jumped out of the data," Emanuel remembers. Most significantly, he found that increases in PDI correlated closely with rising sea temperatures—themselves generally thought by scientists to reflect the impact of global warming.

And this was no minor trend. Emanuel's data suggested a much bigger increase in storm power than predicted either by Knutson's latest modeling work or Emanuel's own theory of a hurricane's maximum potential intensity. For the first time, actual *data* suggested that hurricanes were intensifying; simultaneously, a huge gulf had opened between that data and preexisting theory, which had postulated a much lower sensitivity of hurricanes to the relatively modest changes in climate that had been seen so far. And now Emanuel, who'd come up with the theory in the first place, listened to the data, and found himself in a position much closer to the one that had been staked out by Kevin Trenberth. As his paper stated: "My results suggest that future warming may lead to an upward trend in tropical cyclone destructive potential, and—taking into account an increasing coastal population—a substantial increase in hurricane-related losses in the twenty-first century." Or as he put it in an interview with *Discover* magazine: "For the first time in my professional career, I got alarmed."

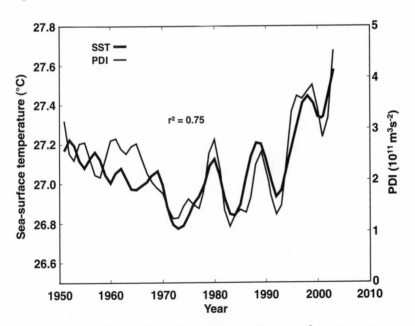

Figure showing the correlation between Atlantic sea-surface temperatures and hurricane power dissipation. *Courtesy of Kerry Emanuel.*

*Nature* published Emanuel's results online on July 31, 2005. The study, which made pretty much everybody's list of top papers for that year, constituted a thunderclap. Here was perhaps the world's leading hurricane theorist—the scientist who had single-handedly generated the concept of hurricane intensification due to global warming as a theoretical possibility, but who had remained unconvinced until now that such intensification had yet made itself manifest—undergoing a very public conversion. "I changed my mind in a big way after 2004," Emanuel would later remark. "I was very open about it, and I think it's a strength of science that when ideas you have are challenged by the data, you be prepared to modify them."

Even before Emanuel's paper came out, the scientific realignment had begun. In July 2005, just as an unprecedented hurricane season began in the Atlantic, Emanuel had his name removed from a group paper downplaying global warming–hurricane concerns and, in essence, seeking to reiterate the 1998 consensus. Emanuel tried to bring his co-authors around to his new view behind the scenes, but they weren't convinced. So he e-mailed one of them, noting that "the problem for me is that I cannot sign on to a paper which makes statements I no longer believe are true." He added, "I see a large global warming signal in hurricanes."

The more skeptical paper read, in part, as a rebuttal to hurricane–climate links made following the 2004 season by Trenberth and others. It ultimately appeared in the *Bulletin of the American Meteorological Society*. Most of its authors worked for NOAA or in the hurricane-forecasting community; they included Landsea, Mayfield, National Hurricane Center forecaster Richard Pasch, Climate Prediction Center director Jim Laver, and lead author Roger Pielke, Jr., a disaster policy expert at the University of Colorado who argues that population growth and economic development in coastal areas are the chief cause of our vulnerability to hurricanes, with or without global warming. (Emanuel doesn't necessarily disagree, but thinks the impacts from global warming will become more pronounced with time.)

The timing of Emanuel's study, his intellectual conversion, and his withdrawal from the paper—together they foreshadowed a coming scientific tempest. The weather also contributed to the organization of this political storm. Emanuel's *Nature* paper appeared online a month before the landfall of Hurricane Katrina, but at a time when the Atlantic had already been behaving oddly when judged by historic standards. Traditionally, July has not been a very active hurricane month in the basin, though it's well within the bounds of the official season. But in 2005, July featured a record *five* tropical cyclones, of which three became hurricanes* and two, Dennis and Emily, were extremely intense hurricanes that impacted populated areas.

Both Dennis and Emily developed from tropical waves, as the most powerful Atlantic storms usually do. One of those scary hurricanes that come up through the Caribbean seeming to ricochet off islands, Dennis kept flirting with early-season intensity records held by 1957's Category 4 Hurricane Audrey, a June storm that devastated the eastern Texas and western Louisiana coasts and killed more than five hundred people. "The bayou folk swam, clung, gasped and prayed for their lives," reads a contemporary *Time* magazine account of Audrey's assault on Cameron, Louisiana. "Those lucky enough to reach specks of dry land found only more terror: with them were alligators and water moccasins, tossed out of the torrent, snapping and striking in their fury." But Dennis surpassed Audrey's record for hurricane strength before the month of August, with a pressure drop down to 930 millibars (27.46 inches) over the Gulf. The storm weakened before coming ashore as a Category 3, but its surge, six to seven feet above normal tides, entirely overwashed parts of Santa Rosa Island.

Dennis overlapped with the season's next extremely intense storm, Emily, whose path through the Caribbean pointed toward the Yucatán Peninsula, which the storm smacked at Category 4 strength on July 18. In retrospect, however, the remarkable development came a day

---

*Hurricane Cindy, the third storm of the year, was classified as such only after the season's end during the National Hurricane Center's reanalysis.

earlier. In a postseason reanalysis, the National Hurricane Center noted that as Emily passed southwest of Jamaica, its maximum sustained winds had briefly topped out at over 160 miles per hour, even as central pressure dropped to 929 millibars (27.43 inches). These measurements meant Emily had snatched away Dennis's record while also setting another one: earliest-forming Category 5 storm in the Atlantic. No previous Category 5 hurricane had ever been recorded in the basin in July.

Dennis and Emily appeared to lend urgency to Emanuel's paper, whose publication followed their landfalls within weeks. Journalists linked the storms and the science, and they also turned to Landsea and Gray for their reactions to the work. Landsea went far easier on Emanuel than he had on Trenberth; he took a critical but measured tone. He praised the study, but said he didn't trust the wind speed measurements at its foundation (a critique he would articulate in much more detail soon enough). Gray, however, let loose, describing Emanuel's work as "a terrible paper, one of the worst I've ever looked at" to the *Boston Globe*.

The substance of Gray's criticism was similar to Landsea's. Emanuel had cubed wind-speed estimates that were themselves prone to considerable error, Gray complained. Emanuel countered that while the data surely did have errors, the strong correlation he had observed between increasing storm strength and increasing sea-surface temperature was very striking (and worrying). These were two different data sets that measured different things. It seemed unlikely to Emanuel that errors in the wind-speed measurements would fortuitously skew the data in such a way that it just happened to closely track an independent rising trend in ocean heat.

Gray's description of Emanuel's work as a "terrible paper" was among the earliest of a volley of barbs, sometimes issued publicly through the media, that would be exchanged as the hurricane–climate debate ramped up in late 2005. Soon Gray told the *Los Angeles Times* that "the people who have a bias in favor of the argument that humans are making the globe warmer will push any data that suggests that humans are making hurricanes worse." "People are jumping out of the woodwork to say that storms are stronger because of global warming, but they're mistaken and most of them don't know what they're talking about," he told yet another paper. And speaking of jumping—Gray told *USA Today*, "If I'm proven wrong, I will jump off the highest peak in Colorado."

Reading these quotations, it sounds as though Gray talked to reporters in the same unguarded way he talks when you're sitting in his kitchen. Saying one's scientific peers are biased and don't know what they're talking about tends to anger them, though—and Gray said more than that. He also both implied and stated that Emanuel, and the authors of another soon-to-be-published hurricane–climate paper, were coming up with these results to advance their careers and get increased research funding. On CNN, Gray said of those linking hurricanes and global warming, "There are all these medicine men out there who want to capitalize on general ignorance on this subject." In an interview with *Discover* magazine he was asked why some scientists support a hurricane–climate link and replied, "So many people have a vested interest in this global-warming thing—all these big labs and research and stuff. The idea is to frighten the public, to get money to study it more."

If Gray called Emanuel's work a "terrible paper," it soon became clear that his long-range forecast for 2005 also had its shortcomings. In December 2004, Gray announced that he did not expect "anything close to the U.S. land-falling hurricane activity of 2004" for the coming season, predicting just eleven named storms, six hurricanes, and three major hurricanes, a slightly above-average year by historic standards. By late May 2005, Gray had upped the forecast to fifteen named storms, eight hurricanes, and four major hurricanes, while NOAA, which had been releasing its own seasonal forecasts since 1998, had similarly predicted twelve to fifteen named storms, seven to nine hurricanes, and three to five major hurricanes. But these final preseason estimates were still too low, almost by half; 2005 ultimately shattered all records, producing twenty-eight storms, fifteen hurricanes, and seven major hurricanes. Four were Category 5 storms, and three were among the six most intense hurricanes ever measured in the Atlantic. Such a large gap between the forecasts and reality clearly called into question whether Gray's or NOAA's statistically based techniques could predict such a record year—in advance of the actual season, at any rate.

Meanwhile, a newer brand of forecasting that Gray would surely view with considerable skepticism—dynamical seasonal hurricane forecasting, which employs global-climate models to project storm numbers—had shown the glint of an ability to perform as well as, or possibly somewhat better than, the statistical techniques. On May 1, 2005, the coupled ocean–atmosphere climate model run by Meteo-France, the nation's weather service, predicted 22 named storms in the Atlantic. By June 1, models run by the United Kingdom's Met Office and the European Centre for Medium-Range Weather Forecasts in Reading, England were also predicting active seasons, and if their results are taken together, these three European models predicted 16.2 storms—still well short of reality, but slightly closer to it than the pre-season statistical forecasts.

The dynamical seasonal hurricane forecasting technique relies upon running ensembles of global climate models to get a sense of the probability, across many model runs, of how many hurricane-like storms will appear. In short, the technique hones in on the same computer-generated storms that empiricists had so criticized for not adequately resembling real-life hurricanes. At present, this method remains in its infancy. Yet just as was the case for standard weather forecasts or forecasts of hurricane tracks, it's possible or perhaps even probable that numerical models will get better and better over time and eventually eclipse statistically based techniques for the purposes of predicting seasonal hurricane activity. After all, the numerical models have an advantage: They're not tied to past history. They simply solve the equations. If global warming is dramatically changing hurricanes, as Emanuel's work suggested, such models may stand a far better chance of producing accurate forecasts.

And so with a high-profile new paper linking global warming to strengthened hurricanes, and with statistical and dynamical forecasts alike predicting a busy season, August arrived for the Atlantic basin. Hurricane Irene, a long-lived Cape Verde–type storm, spent nearly half the month dissipating its store of power over open ocean. And then came Katrina, the most damaging hurricane in U.S. history, with an estimated cost of over $80 billion and more than 1,500 killed. When it hit land—while Chris Landsea rode through the storm in a NOAA plane—Katrina also drove a record storm surge, twenty-four to twenty-eight feet in some places in Mississippi, higher even than the surge driven by Hurricane Camille (a fact attributable to Katrina's enormous size). And there were other shocking measurements: sustained winds of nearly 175 miles per hour over the Gulf produced during a rapid bout of intensification once Katrina hit the infamous Loop Current; and a minimum central pressure measurement of 902 millibars (26.64 inches), temporarily placing the storm fourth among the most intense hurricanes ever measured in the Atlantic basin, ahead of Camille and Mitch (both 905 mb; 26.72 in.) and just behind 1980's Hurricane Allen (899 mb; 26.55 in.). But Katrina's intensity ranking would drop to sixth after hurricanes Rita and Wilma. If the 2005 hurricane season had been an Olympic race, it would have been one in which multiple runners set world records.

A brace of books about Katrina and its aftermath have since been written. As a result, the appalling incompetence of the Federal Emergency Management Agency following the storm has been well established. So has the negligence of the U.S. Army Corps of Engineers (and, let us not forget, the members of Congress who ultimately oversee it). Not only had the Corps constructed faulty levees; it had redirected the Mississippi to starve protective wetlands and built worse-than-worthless projects like the Mississippi River Gulf Outlet ("MR. GO," it's not-so-amusingly called), which helped channel Katrina's storm surge straight into New Orleans. By contrast, one government agency that did a stellar job during Katrina was the National Hurricane Center. Its stressed and overworked forecasters had nevertheless produced track and landfall predictions that were stunningly accurate many days in advance—giving other agencies, like FEMA, ample time to prepare. But the hurricane center's performance was the exception, not the rule.

The broad failings by our government helped ensure that Katrina had a far more devastating impact than it would have had otherwise.

For contrary to the words of George W. Bush, what occurred could not simply be chalked up to the "whims of nature." Had Katrina hit New Orleans directly as a Category 5 hurricane, surely nothing could have prevented the utter destruction of the city. But that's not what happened. Instead, the storm weakened before landfall and swerved away. It can't be emphasized enough: Katrina *missed*. "Overall, it appears likely that most of the city of New Orleans experienced sustained surface winds of Category 1 or Category 2 strength," the National Hurricane Center concluded.

This was hardly a worst-case-scenario hurricane, meaning that only human failure can explain how Katrina still managed to take such a toll. No one knew at the time about the poorly constructed levees, but New Orleans's general vulnerability had been discussed ad nauseum, especially during Ivan only a year earlier. There was no excuse for Bush or for FEMA to be so fundamentally unprepared, so clueless.

Without a doubt, humans can make themselves starkly vulnerable to extreme weather events based upon where they live (often at dangerous sites where land meets sea) and how they alter their environments (such as by destroying wetlands). But nature must also cooperate to engender true catastrophe. Usually it will do so eventually, provided favorable conditions prevail—and an extremely hospitable atmospheric and oceanic environment had made Dennis, Emily, Katrina, and later Category 5 storms Rita and Wilma possible in the first place. That environment had been supercharged for hurricanes due, among other factors, to its anomalously warm sea temperatures. Might humans have had something to do with that as well?

In a later retrospective, a team of NOAA scientists that included Landsea pointed out the many hurricane-ripe conditions that prevailed in 2005: record sea-surface temperatures in the main hurricane development region, La Niña–like conditions in the tropical Pacific (the opposite of El Niño), and low levels of wind shear. NOAA didn't say anything about a role for global warming, however; rather, the analysis favored an explanation that invoked natural cycles. (Emanuel might have called it a reiteration of the agency's party line.) The 2005 hurricane season also featured relatively weak easterly trade winds across the Atlantic. Stronger trade winds cause more evaporation from the sea surface and thus more cooling; weaker winds leave the oceans warmer. So it seems that in 2005, hurricanes took up some of the slack for the trade winds in ventilating the oceans.

But why had the oceans gotten so hot in the first place? In the region of the tropical Atlantic central to hurricane formation, the June-to-October temperature anomaly broke all records: .92 degrees Celsius above normal. If we step out of the chronological sequence of events for a moment, we can consider the scientific paper that has linked this most closely to climate change: a 2006 study by Trenberth and his colleague Dennis Shea, who tried to break down how much of the 2005 anomaly could be connected with a global trend of ocean warming attributable to human influences. Through statistical analysis, they credited .45 degrees Celsius, or roughly half of it, to the global trend. The rest they attributed to the aftereffects of the 2004–05 El Niño and the Atlantic Multidecadal Oscillation, which in their analysis had only a small impact.

Trenberth had statistically tied a central environmental factor underlying the record hurricane year—sea-surface temperature—to global warming. Assuming that's correct, it's significant. But it's still a far cry from asserting that any single storm, such as Katrina, could be attributed in any meaningful way to climate change. For members of the public, however, who often conceptualize global warming in a visceral rather than a statistical sense, and who invariably connect it to whatever weather extremes they might be experiencing at a given time, this point hardly came across so clearly in Katrina's aftermath. It didn't help that many journalists and commentators stoked the confusion.

First came the various pundits and politicians who went overboard. In an opinion article published in the *Boston Globe* on the day after Katrina's final landfall, veteran global warming reporter Ross Gelbspan wrote, "The hurricane that struck Louisiana yesterday was nicknamed Katrina by the National Weather Service. Its real name is global warming." The German environment minister Juergen Tritten went even farther with an attack on President Bush, writing (according to the *Washington Post*'s translation), "The American president closes his eyes to the economic and human damages that are inflicted on his country and the world economy by natural disasters, like Katrina, through neglected climate protection."

On a scientific level, such assertions are indefensible. As Greg Holland says of those who claim global warming strengthened or otherwise affected Katrina: "It's just unadulterated garbage. That cyclone was reacting to the immediate environment that it was in." When it comes to global warming, Holland adds, "All you can say is that as time goes on, if you were hit by a tropical cyclone, the chances are now higher it's going to be a Category 4 or 5 than they were before." Emanuel has similarly stated that attributing the Katrina disaster to global warming would be "absurd." But given that Gelbspan was writing only a day after Katrina and amid the national alarm and horror over the event, we should probably forgive him for overstepping a bit. No one was thinking in a very nuanced way at the time.

Talking heads weren't the only ones connecting Katrina to global warming. In a considerably more subtle but perhaps also more powerful way, the major media did so as well. During prior active Atlantic storm seasons, journalists had written occasional "he said, she said" stories about global warming and hurricanes, quoting the scientists on either side of the debate. This coverage had often been highly episodic in nature, frequently following in the aftermath of destructive landfalling storms like Hurricane Andrew. Such a pattern of reporting, by its very nature and timing, helped to foster the misleading impression of a direct causal link between individual weather events and long-term climate trends.

Katrina took this pattern to a new extreme, triggering unprecedented media discussion of the hurricane–climate relationship. The storm produced saturation news coverage of people stranded on rooftops and suffering in the Superdome and at the New Orleans Convention Center. Amidst this round-the-clock stream of information, the hurricane–climate relationship represented just one theme among many—including race, poverty, leadership failings, and government incompetence. Nevertheless, the attention to it far exceeded anything that had come before.

If you plot the number of articles over the years discussing the hurricane–global warming relationship in two major agenda-setting newspapers, the *New York Times* and the *Washington Post,* the resultant figure bears a striking resemblance to the wind-speed measurements of a hurricane that remains relatively weak for many days, then suddenly runs over deep warm water and explodes into a Category 5 storm. From 1985 through 2003, discussion of this subject, whether brief or in-depth, remained at a relatively low level. Those slight blips that did occur were perhaps partly tied to the occurrence of noteworthy hurricanes, or to higher levels of attention to the broader global warming issue (for example in 2001, when President Bush withdrew from the Kyoto Protocol). But there were no major media feeding frenzies, not even following destructive land-falling storms like Hugo and Andrew.

In 2004, however, coverage started to rise precipitously, linked to the Florida storms. The next year that rise became meteoric, almost certainly thanks to the combination of alarming new research (like Emanuel's) and Katrina. Some forty articles discussing the connection between hurricanes and global warming appeared in the month of September 2005 in these two publications alone. Other highly influential media outlets reflected the trend as well. In October 2005, a *Time* magazine cover asked, "Are We Making Hurricanes Worse?"

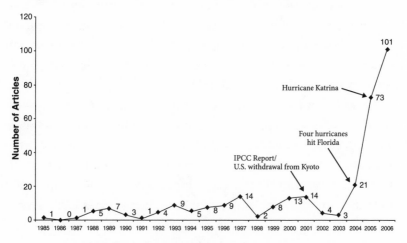

Combined articles in the *Washington Post* and the *New York Times* discussing the relationship between global warming and hurricanes, plotted over time.

Emanuel himself missed much of this frenzy. Just after publishing his *Nature* paper, he headed off for a long-planned sabbatical to the Mediterranean island of Majorca. The experience, he would later note, helped provide a nice "filter." But in Emanuel's absence, a major new environmental factor invaded the hurricane–climate argument: the media. Journalists made the debate public as never before, and the scientists involved became newsmakers whose every word seemed fraught with significance. They in turn started worrying about how they came off in news articles, and what other scientists were saying about them—particularly Gray, who frequently slammed others' work.

Media coverage that folded global warming into the Katrina story line also seemed to parallel changes in public opinion. In a survey by the Pew Research Center released on September 8, shortly after Katrina, 25 percent of respondents said the storm's severity had been "caused by global climate change." Democrats and Independents were far more likely than Republicans to make such an attribution in the poll, underscoring the partisan nature of the global warming issue.

In turn, widespread links between global warming and Katrina—sometimes articulated directly by misguided commentators, sometimes merely implied by the timing and tenor of media coverage—triggered a fierce backlash. To cite just one example, on September 9, 2005, the conservative *Washington Post* columnist Charles Krauthammer baldly asserted, "There is no relationship between global warming and the frequency and intensity of Atlantic hurricanes. Period." In light of the emerging science, such an absolute decree was at least as incautious as Gelbspan's claim that Katrina's "real name is global warming."

Those opposing mandatory cuts on greenhouse gas emissions had good reason to fear that Katrina could prove a pivotal event, forever altering the views of Americans on climate change. And in the wake of the storm, it certainly looked as though they were trying to do something about it. The think tanks of the political right, ever battling over the science of climate, became hurricane experts. The George C. Marshall Institute, partly funded by ExxonMobil and long a hub for global warming skepticism and contrarianism, fired out a news release on September 6 declaring, "Linkage Between Hurricanes and Global

Warming Tenuous." Tech Central Station (as it was then called) and the Competitive Enterprise Institute put out similar messages.

The next month, the Marshall Institute followed up with an event at the glitzy National Press Club in Washington, D.C., entitled "Atlantic Hurricanes: The True Story." The event featured Florida State University oceanographer James O'Brien, an El Niño specialist, as the expert on hand. O'Brien proceeded to propose the most narrow metric conceivable for assessing storm changes: He would examine whether a trend could be seen in the intensity of U.S. land-falling hurricanes, which comprise only 3 percent of the global total of storms. It's true virtually by definition that we have more reliable data on land-falling storms than on any others. But global warming should affect storms regardless of whether they happen to make landfall, which meant that focusing arbitrarily on such a tiny subset of hurricanes could greatly obscure the real issue.

Sure enough, O'Brien could find no trend in land-falling storm data. But this absence could hardly be said to invalidate Emanuel's vastly different approach. And then O'Brien went farther, acknowledging a global trend of ocean warming but questioning what might have caused it. "It is warming up in many places in the ocean. Whether it is man-induced or whether it is natural variability—who knows?" he remarked.

In fact, the scientific literature strongly demonstrates that, just as for warming surface-air temperatures, the current trend of warming sea temperatures cannot be explained without invoking a significant role for human-induced changes to the climate. Only a few months before O'Brien's pronouncement, around the start of the Atlantic hurricane season, a major study attributing the warming of the world's oceans to human influences had been published by leading oceanographers and climate scientists in the journal *Science*. Noting a substantial ocean-by-ocean warming trend, the scientists had run various climate-model studies seeking to replicate the signal. They found that only models that factored in greenhouse gas and sulfate aerosol emissions could do so successfully. Models that merely took into account natural variability, whether springing from causes internal to the system or external phenomena (such as volcanic eruptions and changes in solar intensity), failed to explain the data. "The immediate conclusion is that human influences are largely responsible for the warming signal," the study found.

At the time, this was the definitive study attributing the heating of the oceans to human influences. O'Brien didn't mention it. But the hurricane–climate skeptics would find themselves increasingly on the defensive as the 2005 hurricane season progressed.

What had begun, then, as Emanuel's attempt to test a somewhat esoteric hypothesis about a hurricane–climate feedback had suddenly translated into the biggest scientific story of the year—and it was about to get bigger. Scientific papers get published in the thousands, but with this particular one all the stars had been aligned. Emanuel already knew the hurricane–climate issue carried with it a unique political sensitivity; the 2004 hurricane season and its aftermath had amply demonstrated as much. But he couldn't have known that his intellectual conversion would go hand in hand with an even more staggering hurricane year, leading the media to take up the subject as a new obsession. Moreover, another scientific bombshell would soon explode, this one with direct origins in the Trenberth-Landsea argument from the previous year.

As a result of all of these independent developments, the issue of hurricanes and global warming, once a side subject among the vast array of concerns that fall under the rubric of global change, was about to become virtually coterminous with global warming itself. The sublime image of a hurricane as glimpsed from space would become the new icon of climate change wielded by environmental groups and their supporters. Meanwhile, industry and conservative think tanks would harden their skepticism, and a group of not-entirely-suspecting scientists would soon be swept into the fight of their lives.

# 9 • "The #$%^& Hit the Fan"

Peter Webster remembers well the 2004 Miami conference on Hurricanes and Tropical Meteorology, sponsored by the American Meteorological Society, where he had a run-in with Bill Gray. Regarded as one of the most talented tropical meteorologists of his generation for his studies of the dynamics and forecasting of monsoons, Webster had just returned from a research trip to Bangladesh, and he was still recovering from the malaria that he had contracted there. The lanky Gray put his arm around the much shorter Australian scientist—Webster resembles a slightly weather-beaten version of Sting—and told him he really ought to get working on hurricanes.

"He said, 'You know, you can really solve these problems,'" Webster remembers. Gray was referring in particular to the still incompletely resolved question, grappled with in his own work and by Riehl even earlier, of why some disturbances grow into hurricanes while others do not.

Before long, Webster did what Gray suggested. He got into hurricane research. Gray, however, would abhor the result.

Webster had followed the Trenberth-Landsea spat, and his initial instinct had been to side with Landsea. Webster felt especially skeptical about what he viewed as Trenberth's attempt to "look regionally and infer globally" about trends in tropical cyclones. "Only 11 percent of hurricanes form in the Atlantic Ocean," Webster explains. And so, suspecting a global overview of hurricanes would show that the 2004 Atlantic anomalies weren't matched elsewhere, he set out to test what he called the "Trenberth hypothesis." For help, Webster turned to a student of Gray's who also happened to be an Australian friend going back decades—Greg Holland.

As Webster related this story to me in his office in Georgia Tech's airy Ford Environmental Science and Technology Building, it suddenly seemed as though it was happening all over again. Webster's cell phone went off with an oddly festive ring tone. It was Holland on the line, calling from Boulder, Colorado.

Not only are Webster and Holland golfing buddies who talk on the phone regularly. Before ever setting out to work together on hurricanes, they had been involved in working on the Aerosonde, a small remote-operated aircraft designed to obtain hard-to-get meteorological data—for instance, from the perilous air–sea boundary region of a hurricane, where better observations could help resolve some of the remaining mysteries about hurricane intensification (particularly concerning the role of sea spray). The Aerosonde can also stay in storms far longer than manned aircraft, and thus can take more continuous observations. Along with a colleague, Holland had conceptualized these mini-planes back in 1992 while still in Australia working for that nation's Bureau of Meteorology Research Centre. Then he started a company to produce them, which he ran for half a decade. (The first Aerosonde flight into a tropical cyclone came in 2005—into Tropical Storm Ophelia, which performed a flirtatious dance with the Carolina coast before dying out at sea.)

In Holland, Webster had brought on board a longtime hurricane expert (particularly on storms affecting Australia) who had studied under Gray but originally trained as a mathematician, and who in 1997 had published a thermodynamic theory of the maximum potential intensity achievable by hurricanes under different environmental conditions that is the leading rival to Emanuel's account (although the two versions have far more similarities than differences). A white-bearded scientist with bushy eyebrows and a very quotable Australian wit, Holland also happens to be a rare witness to one of the world's most infamous tropical storms, having lived through Cyclone Tracy as it tore apart the city of Darwin, Australia, early on Christmas Day in 1974. Holland was on duty at the time, working as a forecaster at the ten-story Darwin Tropical Analysis and Regional Forecasting Centre. He was on the eighth floor when Tracy hit. The building "was jumping around, and I literally mean jumping around," he remembers. "It was moving around so much—and it wasn't just swaying, it was actually literally sharp moves—that there were times when it was actually hard to walk. You'd take a step and the building would walk out from underneath you." Although an exceedingly tiny hurricane of a type sometimes called a "midget storm," Tracy—whose true intensity remains unknown—uprooted every tree and entirely destroyed most of the buildings in Darwin with its winds. Holland's building took a "fair hiding" but was one of the few that remained standing.

In 2004, Holland moved to the National Center for Atmospheric Research in Boulder, Colorado, to take over the directorship of the Mesoscale and Microscale Meteorology Division. There, he helped Hai-ru Chang, a senior research scientist at Georgia Tech who works with Webster, to assemble a data set on global hurricane intensities. Later, after the data had been compiled, Webster's partner Judith Curry, a climate scientist who is also chair of the Georgia Tech School of Earth and Atmospheric Sciences, joined the project. Their cross-disciplinary team thus brought together a hurricane specialist (Holland), a theoretically inclined tropical meteorologist who had previously paid little attention to hurricanes (Webster), and a climate researcher (Curry) whose best-known work to that point involved studies of Arctic climate and weather (in which she had employed Holland's Aerosondes).

The team had gone into the project expecting to disprove Trenberth. But the data weren't cooperating. Instead, they increasingly suggested that Trenberth had been on to something. No one on the Webster team had had much public involvement in the politico-scientific quagmire that is the American global warming fight. But they were about to venture into an arena where most researchers never go—the scientific equivalent of appearing on *Hardball with Chris Matthews* or *The O'Reilly Factor*.

Later, reflecting on the experience, Holland remarked that he planned on becoming a "bloody hermit on a mountaintop" the next time one of his papers on hurricanes and climate came out.

Although officially submitted on June 22, well before the peak of the hurricane season, the Webster group's study appeared in *Science* two months after Emanuel's work came out, only weeks after Katrina, and just days before Hurricane Rita moved into the Gulf of Mexico. The timing, which the scientists could never have planned, had an incalculably massive impact on the amount of attention the results received. As Curry later put it in a blog comment: "When our paper was published right between Katrina and Rita, the #$%^& hit the fan."

Emanuel's study had limited itself to two major ocean basins. But the *Science* study surveyed every regularly active basin using so-called best track records from the world's hurricane forecasting centers spanning the official satellite era, which began in 1970—a fact that lent at least some consistency to the data. This more conventional methodology had little overlap with Emanuel's PDI approach. It certainly didn't require cubing wind-speed measurements taken over the lifetime of each storm. Instead, the satellite-era records could be expressed in the familiar Saffir-Simpson categories of hurricane strength.

In some basins, particularly the Atlantic, the "best track" records reflected measurements from airplane reconnaissance missions, the most reliable means of sampling storm intensities. But that wasn't possible for every basin. Seeking to cut budgets, the U.S. Department of Defense had terminated military aircraft reconnaissance of Northwest Pacific typhoons in 1987. In other basins there had never been reconnaissance in the first place. Forecasters had instead learned to determine storm strength by examining satellite images and employing a cloud pattern recognition scheme known as the Dvorak technique. As Webster and his colleagues acknowledged, this methodology had been created specifically for an operational setting in the mid-1970s, and had undergone changes over time in its manner of application. In short, the "best track" records were the best available, but only in a far-from-perfect world.

Examining these records from the satellite era, Webster's team did not find any trend in the total number of tropical cyclones. Instead there had been a large upturn in Atlantic storm frequency since 1995, counterbalanced by a downturn in other basins. When it came to hurricane intensity, though, a different story emerged. The study detected a "thirty-year trend" toward more frequent and intense hurricanes. Category 4 and 5 storms had apparently almost doubled in number and in proportion to weaker storms—a trend, again, closely following rising sea-surface temperatures. In conclusion, Webster and his co-authors noted that their findings were "not inconsistent with recent climate model simulations that a doubling of $CO_2$ may increase the frequency of the most intense cyclones," citing the work of NOAA's Thomas Knutson. And that was pretty much all they said about it.

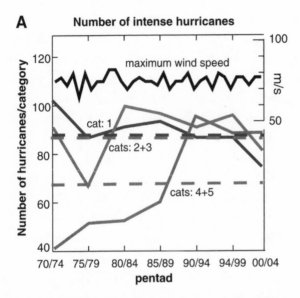

Figure depicting a large global increase in the number of the strongest hurricanes. From Webster et al., "Changes in Tropical Cyclone Number, Duration, and Intensity in a Warming Environment," *Science,* Vol. 309 (2005), pp. 1844–46. *Reprinted with permission from the AAAS.*

Compared to Trenberth or Emanuel, the Webster group hadn't pointed the finger very directly at global warming. That's partly because the authors didn't agree among themselves about how to address the contentious subject. Holland in particular had previously linked his name with those of Landsea and Gray on papers debunking a strong hurricane–climate link. As Curry remembers: "Peter when he was first writing it essentially said, 'Well, it looks like global warming to me.' And then Greg Holland in his revision crossed it out and said, 'Of course this has nothing to do with global warming.' And my reaction was, 'Oh my gosh, this is a tar baby.'" So the group wound up with a fairly weak statement, hardly one that directly attributed the changes they had detected to human influences. You had to read between the lines. But that wasn't hard to do—and Holland, following Emanuel, was even then in the process of becoming the second major climate convert in the longtime hurricane-research community.

As for their take-home message to the public, Webster, Holland, and Curry had hoped to issue a warning for coastal cities while remaining relatively agnostic about the climate issue. Storms like Katrina, they stressed, might not be "once-in-a-lifetime events," but rather might become more frequent. Knowing how the risk of intense hurricanes making landfall was changing could have enormous implications for how we decide to protect low-lying areas (or whether we decide to abandon them). As their original press release put it, a risk-assessment study should be undertaken for "all coastal cities in the southern and southeastern U.S.... the southeastern U.S. needs to begin planning to manage the increased risk of category-5 hurricanes."

But that message got lost in the subsequent furor. As Webster, Curry, and Holland would later write, "Even senior scientists are ill-prepared for their first major experience with mixing politics, science, and the media." With the press already in high gear over Katrina, and with Rita soon to make landfall, their paper immediately got sucked into the sharp and ever-intensifying global-warming debate that followed upon those storms' destruction. That included radio and television showdowns (Curry versus Landsea on *The News Hour with Jim Lehrer* on PBS; Curry versus Gray on *The Diane Rehm Show;* Webster versus Patrick Michaels on CNN's *Lou Dobbs Tonight,* and so on). It included congressional hearings. And it included environmentalist advertising campaigns that used arguments about hurricanes to raise concern about global warming, coupled with strong backlash from the community of climate "skeptics."

So instead of getting to talk about coastal policy, Webster and his coauthors found themselves drawn into the global-warming crossfire and baited into conflicts with colleagues like Gray. As Curry recalls of her experience with television interviews by satellite: "You're strapped in like you're in an electric chair with all these wires. You're staring at this camera. People start asking you things you are totally unprepared for. We didn't know how to be effective in that environment." On one occasion she got a press call from *Hustler* magazine. "The guy was intelligent and asked good questions," she remembers.

And their immersion in a high-stakes, very public battle over the content of the science was just beginning.

The disturbance that would become Hurricane Rita formed east of the Turks and Caicos Islands on September 17, arising from the interaction of a tropical wave and an old cold front. The thick cloud cluster moved through the Florida straits on September 20, passing just south of Key West as it became a hurricane and then intensified to Category 2 status. The warm waters of the Gulf lay in wait. Just like Katrina, Rita soon hit the infamous Loop Current and rapidly began to intensify. By September 21, the storm had transmogrified into a Category 5 monster, having spun up from a tropical storm in just thirty-six hours—a rapid deepening that the forecasters did not anticipate.

The next day Rita reached peak intensity, with maximum sustained winds approaching 180 miles per hour. Pressure is estimated to have dropped all the way down to 895 millibars (26.42 inches), making Rita the strongest known hurricane in the Gulf and the third-most intense storm ever detected in the Atlantic basin. But soon that rank would drop to fourth.

Rita was also a very large hurricane, occupying much of the breadth of the western Gulf at its height. Luckily, the storm ultimately targeted a relatively less populated area just east of the Louisiana–Texas border for landfall. Like Katrina, Rita also weakened considerably as it approached shore, so that maximum sustained winds at landfall were only about 115 miles per hour, or Category 3 strength. Despite the storm's weakened state, however, Rita drove a large surge, possibly as high as fifteen feet in places. The storm's final destination fell very close to the site struck in 1957 by Hurricane Audrey, and the surge destroyed entire coastal communities in Louisiana's Cameron Parish, with the circle of destruction spreading into the city of Lake Charles, with its mix of refineries and casinos, and Vermilion Parish. The ultimate damage total was on the order of $10 billion.

Rita's impact cannot be judged solely from this tale of destruction, however. Psychologically, a hurricane even stronger than Katrina, appearing only weeks later, shocked Americans. It seemed as though every time they saw a satellite picture of the Gulf on television they found themselves staring into a huge vortex. Furthermore, Rita's earlier track had pointed straight at Houston, Texas, prompting the largest evacuation in that state's history. "Unless the storm turns south or north in the next 24 to 48 hours we are set up for a truly horrific event," *Houston Chronicle* science reporter and hurricane-beat specialist Eric Berger wrote on his weblog on the evening of September 21. "I am not going to sugar-coat this, my friends."

Some two million people crowded the interstates as Rita approached, some of them Katrina evacuees who had fled *to* Houston less than a month earlier. The evacuation was a disaster: People sat in traffic for as long as sixteen or eighteen hours to get to nearby cities like Austin. Cars broke down or ran out of gas, leaving their drivers stranded along roadsides in 100-degree heat. CNN filmed the chaos—including images of standing traffic on one side of highways and no cars at all on the other—and its reporters demanded to know why more lanes weren't open. Finally, Texas officials implemented a "contra-flow" regime they had never rehearsed. In the end many of the more than one hundred deaths attributed to Rita arose indirectly, in the context of the evacuation. Twenty-four nursing-home evacuees died when their bus burst into flames along the highway outside Dallas.

As this disorganized mobilization suggested, Houston, like so many U.S. coastal cities—including nearby Galveston, situated on a barrier island and protected after the 1900 storm by a fifteen-foot sea wall—faces a catastrophe if directly hit by a powerful hurricane. Located across Galveston Bay from the Gulf, Houston could find itself staring down a giant wall of water if a strong hurricane approaches leading with its right front quadrant. "Within an hour or two, a storm surge, topping out at 20 feet or more, would flood the homes of 600,000 people in Harris County," wrote Berger in a February 2005 warning article for the *Chronicle* that, had Rita taken a more southerly course, would have been unendingly praised for its clairvoyance (just as all the articles predicting the destruction of New Orleans later were). The sea wall protecting Galveston Island would valiantly fight off the surge, Berger noted, but fail as water crept behind it and engulfed the island from the bay side. Near the Port of Houston, meanwhile, chemical and water treatment facilities would also find themselves underwater—leaking God knows what. Damages could reach $40 or $50 billion, and hundreds or even thousands of people could perish.

So while Houston may not be quite as vulnerable as New Orleans to a hurricane's devastation—at least it would drain more quickly—it will someday experience a storm that changes its history forever. It's only a matter of time.

Rita drove the public and media dialogue about global warming and hurricanes—keyed, once again, to land-falling storms—to an even more frantic pitch. Everyone had an opinion on the issue. On the one hand, a who's who of Democratic leaders, including Al Gore and Jimmy Carter, cited the recent findings by Emanuel and the Webster group to warn that global warming had contributed to the hurricane problem and to argue that action on greenhouse gas emissions must follow promptly. Skeptics responded by continuing their campaign to dispute the scientific evidence and insisting that no serious cuts in emissions were needed. At one point in Congress, New Mexico Republican Pete Domenici called California Democrat Dianne Feinstein's suggestion of a hurricane–global warming link "nuts."

Public opinion, too, seemed on the move. In an ABC survey taken just after Rita, 39 percent of respondents said they thought the hurricanes were the result of climate change, a considerable increase since polls taken just after Katrina. Posing the question differently—"Thinking about the increase in the number and strength of hurricanes in recent years, do you think global warming has been a major cause, a minor cause, or not a cause of the increase in hurricanes?"—a *USA Today/*CNN Gallup poll found that 36 percent of the public viewed global warming as a major cause, 29 percent viewed it as a minor cause, and 30 percent felt it was not a cause. Yet the poll's question wording conflated the different scientific issues of hurricane frequency and hurricane intensity, and did not specify whether the question referred to the undisputed upturn in Atlantic hurricanes or to a global increase. Assuming the latter, that means the question assumed at face value the validity of the Emanuel and Webster results. Yet many hurricane specialists, particularly Landsea and Gray, strongly disputed those results. Or as Gray barked at Curry when the two appeared together on *The Diane Rehm Show* on September 21, 2005, the day of Rita's rapid intensification in the Gulf: "I question whether the authors are that expert in the analysis of this data that they can make these conclusions."

Unmistakably, the Emanuel and Webster papers suggested a very different view of the hurricane–climate relationship than had existed before. Previously the consensus had been: Sure, global warming might strengthen hurricanes—but not by that much, and not in a measurable way in the near future. Now, however, a new vision was coming to life, and it was much more disturbing.

One thing hadn't changed. The relationship between hurricane *frequency* and global warming remained murky. Some modeling studies generated more storms, and some fewer, for a doubling of $CO_2$ concentrations. And except in the Atlantic, which had seen a dramatic upswing in storm numbers since 1995, there didn't appear to be an appreciable trend in storm frequency. Neither was there a very reliable theory to explain why there should or shouldn't be one. Given that large and intense hurricanes do much more to cool down the oceans than weak tropical storms, it's perfectly conceivable that global warming might lead to stronger storms but fewer of them in total—precisely the result produced in one GCM study using Japan's Earth Simulator, which ranks among the world's most powerful supercomputers.

Any individual hurricane, however, can cause harm to life and property in four basic ways. And now it seemed possible that *each* of these destructive storm characteristics might be worsened in the future—or, perhaps, had already worsened—due to global warming.

The deadliest aspect of a hurricane is its storm surge, which can easily exceed twenty feet in a land-falling Category 5 storm—and that's not counting the huge waves that ride atop such surges. Hurricanes Camille of 1969 and Katrina of 2005 presented dramatic examples of deadly surges, the worst the U.S. Gulf Coast has seen. But for sheer carnage, neither can begin to rival the 1970 storm that struck present-day Bangladesh, whose surge killed over 300,000 people, even more than the 2004 tsunami.

Considering that winds play the most central role in driving the wall of water that hurricanes propel toward shorelines, this destructive aspect of storms should worsen if the average hurricane grows more intense. Furthermore, one of the most certain outcomes of global warming is a rise in sea level, caused both by the melting of ice and by thermal expansion of seawater. If all hurricanes ride atop higher seas, then barring some dramatic retreat from coastal areas, all hurricanes pose a greater threat to human lives and property in those areas—whether or not the storms have independently intensified.

After storm surges comes the next chief source of hurricane damage: winds, which can be powerful enough to tear down trees and all but the sturdiest of human-built structures. Some famous examples of purely wind-driven hurricane destruction occurred in 1974's Cyclone Tracy, 1992's Hurricane Andrew, and 2004's Charley. The Emanuel and Webster work most obviously suggested that the average hurricane's maximum sustained wind speed is increasing due to global warming—a particularly troublesome outcome in that wind damage increases steeply as velocity rises.

Third, in addition to storm surges and wind destruction, hurricanes cause heavy rains and, in some cases, catastrophic flooding. The canonical example here is Hurricane Mitch, which came ashore as a very weak storm and yet killed more than 11,000 people through rainfall alone. Another major rainfall killer was Tropical Depression Jeanne of 2004, and there have been many, many others. In a globally warmed world, hurricane precipitation, too, is expected to increase, because the air converging into the storm center should carry more water vapor—thus potentially upping the chance that a given hurricane will create a rainfall-related disaster. Thomas Knutson's modeling study of hurricane intensification under global warming scenarios predicted an eventual 18 percent increase in rainfall near the storm center for increased concentrations of atmospheric $CO_2$.

Changes to the final major source of hurricane damage—hurricane-spawned tornadoes—are probably the most speculative. Such tornadoes were discussed in early empirical work by Gray, which noted that among many other factors, hurricanes making U.S. landfall from the Gulf of Mexico tend to generate many more tornadoes than those striking from the Atlantic—presumably because hurricanes approaching from the Gulf lead with their powerful right front quadrant.

Most U.S. land-falling hurricanes generate at least some tornadoes, and although these tend to be fairly weak whirlwinds on the Fujita scale (in the F0 or F1 range) and no rival to Great Plains tornadoes, they can sometimes be stronger. Tropical Storm Beryl of 1994 spawned three F3 tornadoes, with winds up to 206 miles per hour. But the fundamental fact is this: Stronger hurricanes tend, on average, to spin off more numerous tornadoes at landfall. As Gray and a co-author put it in 1974: "There appears to be a direct relationship between tropical cyclone intensity and tornado incidents." If so, it stands to reason that these incidents should increase in number if hurricanes grow more intense (and continue to make landfall at similar frequencies). There's some evidence that, in conjunction with more active Atlantic hurricane seasons since 1995, the number of hurricane-spawned tornadoes has also gone up, reaching a high number of 302 in 2004 followed by 194 in 2005. So if global warming is contributing to the Atlantic hurricane uptick since 1995, it may also be linked to increased tornadic activity.

Temporarily assuming, for the sake of argument, the validity of the Emanuel and Webster studies, what does all of this add up to? Fifty years from now, even if all four sources of hurricane damage have indeed worsened as suggested above, we still won't be able to point to a particular storm and say, "Aha, global warming!" Rather, we'll be in the same position we're in now, forced to argue over statistics to detect trends.

So far, data on damage from U.S. hurricanes that has been "normalized"—i.e., adjusted for changes in population and wealth, as well as for inflation—does not show any trend over time. The 1926 Miami hurricane, if it happened today, would be expected to cause considerably more damage than 2005's Hurricane Katrina. However, U.S. damage levels may not be a very good indicator of whether hurricanes themselves are changing in response to global warming. Any damage study must inevitably limit itself to the relatively small number of U.S. land-falling storms; moreover, damage levels depend on countless factors besides storm strength itself, ranging from storm track to tide at the time of landfall. Perhaps most important of all is societal change. If more people are living in the paths of hurricanes, and putting valuable homes and possessions along those paths, then storms will inevitably cause much more damage—and that's precisely what we've seen happen in the United States.

It stands to reason, however, that if storms also change in a major way, then barring some other major countervailing change, that will eventually show up in damage statistics. In turn, those analyzing such statistics, including insurance and reinsurance companies, could find themselves shocked by the new world in which they're trying to write coverage. Whether or not global warming can be blamed, that already seems to be happening. In the wake of the 2005 Atlantic hurricane season, Risk Management Solutions, a "catastrophe modeling" firm that works for insurance companies, revised its estimate of hurricane risks to Florida and the Gulf Coast upward after calling together a panel of scientists including Emanuel and Knutson.

Finally, it's not enough merely to consider that all four vectors of hurricane destruction could worsen as a result of global warming. We must also weigh still more ambiguous evidence about how the world and its storms may change—evidence about the possible linkage between the occurrence of South Atlantic hurricane-type storms and global warming, for instance. If, as some scientists suspect, the South Atlantic is a "marginal" basin that generally can't support hurricanes, but with slight climatic changes could begin to host them more regularly, this could have serious consequences for Brazil and perhaps other nations in the region. Similarly, we must weigh the possibility that by raising sea-surface temperatures, global warming would increase the chance that already-formed hurricanes will be able to strike regions where they have never or only rarely made landfall in the past, such as Southern California.

Such possibilities are hard to express in terms of a statistical likelihood—many have not been studied in detail—but not, for that reason, acceptable to ignore. Now, the Emanuel and Webster studies, combined with hurricanes Katrina and Rita, had brought them all into sharp focus.

# 10 • Resistance

L ongtime hurricane specialist Hugh Willoughby has described the Emanuel and Webster studies as precipitating a "paradigm shift"—albeit possibly a false one—within the world of hurricane research. This now ubiquitous and over-applied phrase, which traces back to the theoretical physicist turned historian of science Thomas Kuhn's famous 1962 book *The Structure of Scientific Revolutions,* once had a very specific meaning. According to Kuhn, most of the time researchers in various fields go about conducting "normal science." They study a generally agreed-upon set of questions within an agreed-upon intellectual or methodological framework built upon past achievements. Normal science is predicated, wrote Kuhn, "on the assumption that the scientific community knows what the world is like." So the researchers engaged in normal science go about filling in details, solving puzzles, confirming their theories. They're working within an accepted paradigm.

Sometimes, though, scientific revolutions occur. Kuhn's examples include the Copernican, Newtonian, and Einsteinian ones. In scientific revolutions, an existing paradigm proves unable to account for the anomalies that scientists begin to detect. Eventually, as anomalies accumulate, some scientists start forging a new paradigm. The transition between paradigms is never easy or smooth, however, because other scientists cling to the old paradigm more tightly. In science, wrote Kuhn, "novelty emerges only with difficulty, manifested by resistance, against a background provided by expectation." In fact, in Kuhn's account the resistance to new theories—what some scientists might call institutionalized skepticism—could be said to have a healthy and productive role to play. "By ensuring that the paradigm will not be too easily surrendered," wrote Kuhn, "resistance guarantees that scientists will not be lightly distracted and that the anomalies that lead to paradigm change will penetrate existing knowledge to the core."

In hurricane science, one paradigm has been built upon the work of Gray and the storm-flying researchers who preceded him. Some of its governing assumptions include empiricism and a practical, life-saving orientation. Hurricanes, in this worldview, are to be studied so as to better understand their formation, structure, and the seasonal variation in their strength and numbers—all of which should, in turn, help save lives and manage risk through the steady improvement of forecasting abilities (whether of storm tracks, intensities, or seasonal frequencies). But the "Gray paradigm" does not include the assumption of systematic changes in hurricanes over time as a result of human-caused climate change. Neither, for that matter, does it pay much attention to the possibility of a dynamic interactive relationship between hurricanes and the large-scale climate system.

In 2005, however, a different set of scientists—Emanuel, Webster and his colleagues—identified what they viewed as dramatic anomalies. And so began the intellectual realignment that defines the early stages of a possible paradigm shift or scientific revolution. To hear Webster's coauthor Judith Curry describe their work is to see this perfectly. "If left to their own devices, the card-carrying tropical cyclone people never would have done the Webster et al. study," Curry commented in an early 2006 interview. "They never would have done it. They knew the answer. There is no change. I didn't realize they hadn't done the work, but they knew the answer. We didn't know the answer so we did the work."

They did the work, and then, as Kuhn would have predicted, resistance set in—a necessary application of professional scrutiny that helps prevent false paradigm shifts from taking hold. There's just one problem: Necessary as it is, resistance isn't always friendly. As Kuhn put it: "Because it demands large-scale paradigm destruction and major shifts in the problems and techniques of normal science, the emergence of new theories is generally preceded by a period of pronounced professional insecurity." In the case of the hurricane–climate debate, that took the form of attacks on motives and credentials, sometimes very nasty ones.

From today's perspective, however, there's a notable absence in Kuhn's account of scientific revolutions—one of which Kuhn himself seemed well aware. A predominantly historical treatment written well before the evolution of the twenty-four-hour news cycle or the blog-driven chatterological media, Kuhn's study understandably does not explore what happens when possible scientific revolutions get covered live in play-by-play format. Neither does it outline how their dynamics might parallel partisan political commitments during a time of national crisis—so that "resistance," in Kuhn's terminology, takes place on the floor of the U.S. Senate.

Bill Gray quickly fired out detailed rebuttals to the papers by Emanuel and the Webster team. "I just can't have people using data incorrectly," he explained, "particularly if they don't have the experience with it."

Dismissing Emanuel's study, Gray called it "not valid" and "not realistic." He took particular aim at Emanuel's use of data from the Northwest Pacific "over a 3–5 decade period of changing maximum wind measurement techniques." By cubing wind-speed measurements that were of "questionable accuracy," Gray wrote, Emanuel's procedure "greatly exaggerates" any preexisting measurement errors. Gray went on to detail how inconsistent the various methods for determining typhoon intensity—ranging from airborne guesstimates to satellite-based techniques—had been during past decades.

As for the Webster study, Gray once again targeted the data, not only for the Northwest Pacific this time but for every basin but the Atlantic (where he agreed storms had grown more intense but attributed the finding to the Atlantic Multidecadal Oscillation). Here, Gray related his 1978 experience of visiting global tropical cyclone forecasting centers, and remarked that particularly for the North Indian basin and basins in the Southern Hemisphere, "satellite tools and forecaster training" had been inadequate for the task of distinguishing accurately between different storm intensities. Gray even argued that for the period from 1975 through 1989, forecasters in these regions could not always tell Category 4 and 5 storms from far weaker Category 1 and 2 hurricanes.

Gray also got invited to broadcast his skepticism before Congress. Just days after Rita's landfall, on September 28, he appeared before the Environment and Public Works committee, then chaired by James Inhofe, an Oklahoma Republican who has suggested that the whole climate fuss might be a "hoax." Inhofe continually professes his regard for "sound science," however, and the hearing itself would investigate the "Role of Science in Environmental Policymaking." The headlining witness that day was Gray's hero Michael Crichton, whose novel *State of Fear* involves eco-terrorists conspiring to bring about phony natural disasters and thereby (falsely) convince the world that global warming is underway.

At six foot five and six foot nine respectively, Gray and Crichton towered over the other witnesses, even as they all sat together behind a polished table. Inhofe opened by announcing his delight at having the novelist and film and television producer on hand: "I think I've read most of his books. In fact, I've read them all." "While *State of Fear* is a novel, it is fiction, the footnotes are incontrovertibly scientific," Inhofe added. The Democrats and environmental supporters who followed with their opening statements weren't impressed. Independent James Jeffords of Vermont, the ranking minority member of the committee, demanded to know why, in the face of the disasters that had just befallen the Gulf Coast, Inhofe had called a hearing "that features a fiction writer as a key witness." "It's a work of fiction even if it has footnotes, Mr. Chairman," added Senator Hillary Clinton.

Crichton drew most of the ire from the assembled Democrats, and yet in his presentation he merely read a staid statement criticizing the lack of "independent verification" of many results in climate science (including those of climate models) while never taking on the theory of human-induced global warming directly. By contrast, Gray's testimony was improvised, boomingly loud, confrontational, and occasionally profane. He shouted "damn" and "damn it"; like Henry Piddington, he spoke in language any sailor could understand. He seemed staggeringly out of place in the somber and ornate Senate Dirksen Building hearing room.

Gray began by observing that he'd been "simmering for twenty years" over hyped-up subjects like nuclear winter and global warming. He'd been a lifelong Democrat "until Al Gore ran for president," he explained. Then he outlined his expertise: "I come at this from having spent fifty-two years of my life working very hard down in the trenches, looking at data, working. I've been around the world. I've done forecasting. I've done all these things. And I am appalled at what has come forth." Yet even as Gray denounced expert assessment bodies like the Intergovernmental Panel on Climate Change—"These people that sit on these boards don't know much about how the atmosphere ocean ticks"—he also cracked up the room:

> Just because two curves go up—because we've seen some modest warming in the globe the last three decades and the human-induced greenhouse gases have gone up—does not mean these are necessarily related, that one causes the other. There's a very nice curve I could show that if you look at sunspots and the number of Republicans in the Senate, they go up on about a 10- or 12-year cycle.

From here the testimony only grew more theatrical. A few minutes into his presentation, Gray suddenly sprang up from the witness table and tripped over a microphone cord as he darted across the room to his posterboard and slide presentation. Unselfconscious as ever, he didn't miss a beat. His voice growing louder and louder, Gray launched into his routine about the complexity of the earth-atmosphere system and the shortcomings of modelers who don't issue yearly climate forecasts because "they know they have no damn skill at it." "Should we believe them fifty, a hundred years down the line when they can't forecast six months or a year in the future?" asked Gray. "It's ridiculous," he said, plopping back into his seat but never ceasing to talk for a moment. Before long Gray had likened global warming to the eugenics movement, an inflammatory analogy that he might have picked up, among other places, from Crichton's novel.

Senator Barbara Boxer, a liberal Democrat from California who would later take over the committee chairmanship after the Democrats regained control of Congress in 2006, did not seem amused. She cross-examined Gray about whether his articles on global warming—not his distinguished hurricane work—had gone through the normal scientific process and been published in peer-reviewed journals. Not seeming to get a straight answer, Boxer pressed further: "Would you not agree, Dr. Gray, that there [are] some very talented people who believe that global warming is a phenomenon, it is occurring?"

"I would agree to that," Gray replied, "and the trouble with that is they don't know how the atmosphere ticks. They're modelers. They're people that make assumptions that are not valid, and they believe them."

"Your attitude is not really very humble," Boxer soon replied. Before long she asked Gray's opinion of NASA's famed climatologist James Hansen.

"I don't know what he knows about the atmosphere," Gray said. "He's not trained as a meteorologist." By the end of the interrogation, Gray was still struggling to keep talking as Boxer cut him off. The transcript speaks for itself:

> BOXER: You just brush away everybody who doesn't agree with you, which I think going in isn't a very scientific thing to do, to prejudge...
> GRAY: There's a lot of us out there that don't agree with...
> BOXER: Dr. Gray, I understand. I understand. But I'm just trying to say something in a friendly way to you. It doesn't help your case to demonize everyone who doesn't agree with you because you wind up [without] very much credibility.
> GRAY: No, it's not everyone doesn't agree with me.
> BOXER: I would like to ask Dr. Crichton a question.
> GRAY: I represent a lot of meteorologists who think very much like I do.
> BOXER: Dr. Gray, my time is running out.

The 2005 Atlantic hurricane season wasn't about to slow down for the month of October. There were many more records to be shattered. The question was, did each represent a Kuhnian anomaly, or could it be integrated into the existing paradigm?

In mid-month came Hurricane Vince, which originated as a storm with a mix of tropical and extra-tropical attributes but took on clearer tropical features as it moved northeast across the Atlantic. Vince lasted just three days as an official tropical cyclone, and only briefly developed into a weak hurricane northwest of the Madeira Islands. However, this location meant it had achieved hurricane status farther eastward than any other known Atlantic storm. Even though Vince quickly weakened, it held together long enough to come ashore near Huelva, Spain, as a tropical depression, thereby becoming the first recorded tropical cyclone to strike the Iberian peninsula. Vince had weakened so much by then that it didn't cause any real damage, but it did dump significant precipitation. In his final report on the storm, one wag at the National Hurricane Center couldn't resist having a little fun with this. "The rain in Spain was mainly less than 2 inches, although 3.30 inches fell in the plain at Cordoba," wrote forecaster James Franklin.

What Franklin didn't say was that Vince, like all the other seemingly unprecedented storms of 2004 and 2005, posed an unanswered question: Were so many records toppling all at once simply because technology now allowed for better observations of hurricanes? Or might there be some other reason—perhaps a changing climate?

At the very least, the clustering of new records seemed suggestive. If global warming is changing the global distribution or collective characteristics of hurricanes, you would expect to see a slew of storm records broken, just as you would expect to see many temperature records broken. None of these records in and of itself could be *blamed* on global warming, but each would have been made more likely to occur because of it. "In the context of a warming planet," observes Judith Curry, "you see a lot of year-to-year variability, but you'll probably see progressively more records being broken"—specifically, she expects, records for hurricane intensity, season length, and the regional distribution of storms. And those were precisely the kinds of records set in the Atlantic in 2005.

If Vince was an oddity, Hurricane Wilma, the next record-breaking storm, wasn't the kind of meteorological event that one jokes about. Few were invoking the Flintstones when Wilma, having formed to the east-southeast of Grand Cayman and meandered weakly through the Caribbean for several days, suddenly put on an extraordinary burst of intensification from late on October 18 through early the next day. In only twenty-four hours, Wilma strengthened from a tropical storm with maximum winds close to 70 miles per hour to a Category 5 storm with winds upwards of 170 miles per hour, deepening even more quickly than Rita had a month earlier. This behavior blew out intensity forecasts from the National Hurricane Center, although the experts there knew something dramatic was about to happen. "WILMA HAS DEVELOPED THE DREADED PINHOLE EYE," wrote Jack Beven at 11:00 P.M. on the night of October 18, before the explosion had nearly run its course.

By the next morning, a U.S. Air Force reconnaissance flight that managed to find and penetrate that tiny eye—little more than two miles in diameter at one point, the "smallest eye known" to staff at the National Hurricane Center—had recorded central pressure measurements of 881 and 884 millibars, both unprecedented for the Atlantic basin. The first measurement came from the on-flight meteorologist's extrapolation, the second from a dropsonde released into the tight vortex from the plane. (Later the corrected estimate was given as 882 millibars, or 26.05 inches, although the real value may have been lower.) "THIS IS PROBABLY THE LOWEST MINIMUM PRESSURE EVER OBSERVED IN THE ATLANTIC BASIN AND IS FOLLOWED BY THE 888 MB MINIMUM PRESSURE ASSOCIATED WITH HURRICANE GILBERT IN 1988," wrote forecaster Lixion Avila, the first Miami specialist to comment on the stunning new observations. Avila proceeded to add that "WILMA IS NEAR ITS MAXIMUM POTENTIAL INTENSITY AND FURTHER STRENGTHENING IS NOT ANTICIPATED"—this at a time when maximum sustained winds were estimated at just over 170 miles per hour.

But in fact, the National Hurricane Center's post-season report on Wilma bumped the storm's sustained winds on October 19 up to about 185 miles per hour. It also noted that intensity forecasts during the hurricane's entire lifetime had a persistent low bias, and added that Wilma's pressure drop, 97 millibars in only twenty-four hours, obliterated the previous Atlantic record of 72 millibars in twenty-four hours set by Gilbert. "Wilma's deepening rate over the northwestern Caribbean Sea...was incredible," the report noted. It went without saying that Wilma had been the strongest October Atlantic storm, easily besting Mitch.

As for the destruction: Wilma directly struck the island of Cozumel as a strong Category 4 hurricane and then slowly crossed the northeastern Yucatán peninsula, where the storm expended much of its strength upon the landscape. Then it turned sharply northeast across the Gulf, regained strength in the face of vertical wind shear, and shook southern Florida as a midrange Category 3 storm. Tearing rapidly across the state, Wilma most strongly affected the highly populous Dade, Broward, and Palm Beach counties and caused the largest power outage in Florida history.

In September of 2006, the National Hurricane Center revised Wilma's U.S. damage estimate upward to $20.6 billion, a stunning total that made it the third most destructive storm on record after Katrina and Andrew, and more costly than any of the 2004 storms. To explain this surprisingly large figure, we must look to Wilma's particular path across Florida, as well as its large size. Wilma "had this enormous eye and eye wall that covered the entire southern third of the peninsula," observes National Hurricane Center forecaster Richard Pasch, whose own roof was torn off by the storm.

Although Wilma didn't cause nearly as much death and destruction as Katrina, it was certainly the year's most disturbing hurricane in a purely meteorological sense. The records that it broke—minimum sea level pressure, rate of intensification—were the ones that truly mattered, for they captured the storm's ability to dissipate power and to potentially cause catastrophic damage. If the future would feature storms like Wilma more frequently, then that future sounded like a terrifying place.

Tracks of hurricanes
during the 2005 Atlantic
season, showing few large
stretches of water that did
*not* see a storm.
*Image credit: National
Hurricane Center.*

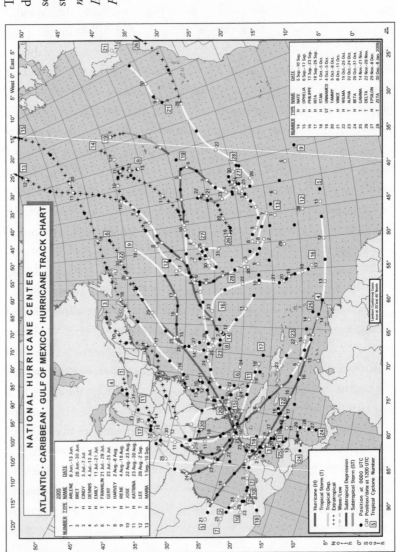

Furthermore, according to the research of Webster, Curry, and colleagues, global warming also appeared to be lengthening the average tropical cyclone season. This made a kind of intuitive sense, as in a warmer world, the tropical oceans would be warmer both earlier and later in the year. For an analysis of season length, the record-breaking 2005 Atlantic hurricane year provided only one data point and could not in itself justify broader conclusions. Still, the fact that the season ran on for more than an extra month, to the very end of the calendar year and even a bit beyond it, is consistent with their argument.

Even before Wilma—which bore the last storm name available—had fully dissipated, the National Hurricane Center turned for the first time to naming storms "after fraternities," as Max Mayfield would later joke. And so came Tropical Storm Alpha (which killed twenty-six people in Haiti and the Dominican Republic), Hurricane Beta (which briefly reached major hurricane strength), Tropical Storm Gamma (which killed thirty-seven in Honduras and Belize), Tropical Storm Delta (whose remnants affected the Canary Islands), and finally Hurricane Epsilon and Tropical Storm Zeta, which stretched into January. All in all, the year featured a total of twenty-eight hurricanes or tropical storms—so many that it almost seemed reasonable to mistake the Atlantic for the Northwest Pacific. In fact, the Atlantic had spawned more total storms than that most active of basins for this particular year.

The previous Atlantic record for storm numbers, set in 1933 before the satellite and storm-flying era, had been twenty-one. Maybe, as Landsea and Gray like to argue, we failed to observe a lot of storms that remained out at sea that year. Or maybe the number of storms and general behavior of the Atlantic in 2005 hinted at the onset of a new climate regime. If true, such a result would not merely have upended an existing paradigm in the world of hurricane science. Within the Bush administration—which had already fumbled in response to Katrina while the entire nation watched, and which wanted nothing less than to see global warming written into that already damaging narrative—the conclusion was so politically explosive that its mere discussion had to be carefully controlled and, in some cases, suppressed outright.

# 11 • "Consensus"

The Geophysical Fluid Dynamics Laboratory of the National Oceanic and Atmospheric Administration occupies a squat, dark building set against an open field on Princeton University's Forrestal Campus, several miles from the main campus. Founded by Joseph Smagorinsky, who had worked with Jule Charney to develop numerical weather prediction at the nearby Institute for Advanced Study, the office now known as GFDL originally served as the most forward-looking scientific branch of the U.S. Weather Bureau in Washington, D.C. In 1967, in one of its most famous efforts, scientists Syukuro Manabe and Richard Wetherald published the first modern calculations of the climate system's sensitivity to a doubling of atmospheric carbon dioxide concentrations. The next year Smagorinsky moved the lab back to Princeton, where numerical modeling had originated.

Today GFDL is one of the premiere climate and weather-modeling centers in the world. Its high-powered supercomputers consume half the lab's budget and are constantly being replaced with the latest hardware. Twenty-four hours a day, they're solving equations. At the same time, though, GFDL shares with Princeton the ethos of a university. On a sunny day in late August 2006, there were plenty of open spots in the lab's parking lot, and some of the scientists wore shorts and sandals. One of them, Thomas Knutson, came downstairs to greet me for an interview that, just half a year earlier, he might not have been able to give—or at least not without prior clearance, or perhaps a "minder" from the NOAA public affairs office listening in. For while GFDL may have the feel of a college campus, it's a government laboratory, and under the Bush administration, its climate scientists were kept on such a tight leash that eventually, you might say they decided to rebel.

Knutson became the hero of this rebellion, though you wouldn't know it from his meek and soft-spoken demeanor. He wears a short hair-cut that looks almost (but not quite) military, and talks with a marked accent that signals his rural southwestern Virginia origins. Of all the scientists at GFDL, he works in what's arguably the most politically fraught area: right at the intersection of hurricane and climate research.

In addition to its climate models, GFDL boasts one of the top hurricane forecasting models in the world. During the 1990s, encouraged by Jerry Mahlman, the lab's director at the time, Knutson led an effort to bridge the two research groups. The collaboration, which in all likelihood could only have taken place at GFDL, resulted in a series of high-resolution experiments exploring how hurricanes would change in a warmer climate, culminating in Knutson's previously discussed 2004 study, which used some 1,300 simulations. The most famous figure

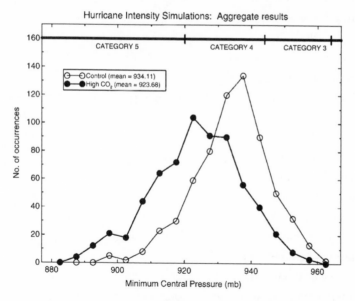

Figure showing storms strengthening by half a category on the Saffir-Simpson scale for increased $CO_2$ conditions. From Knutson et al., "Impact of $CO_2$-Induced Warming on Simulated Hurricane Intensity and Precipitation: Sensitivity to the Choice of Climate Model and Convective Parameterization," *Journal of Climate*, Vol. 18, No. 18 (Sept. 15, 2004).

from the paper, showing storms growing stronger by about half a Saffir-Simpson category, hangs on his office door.

That paper came out during the 2004 hurricane season, even as Gray and storm experts from some of GFDL's sister offices within NOAA debunked links between the recent destruction and global warming. Knutson didn't see any scientifically defensible connection to the Florida storms either, and said so to the press at the time. Still, under a media policy for all NOAA scientists, he had to inform agency public-affairs officers about requests to interview him before responding to those requests. And not just that. Internal e-mails revealed following a Freedom of Information Act request by the environmental group Greenpeace give a sense of how the protocols worked in practice.

On one occasion, a NOAA public-affairs official based in Washington, D.C., apparently traveled up to Princeton to sit in on an interview that Knutson did with ABC News. In another instance, an official e-mailed Knutson a series of talking points "in anticipation of possible media inquires regarding climate change and the recent hurricane season"—sound bites that, according to the e-mail, had been prepared at NOAA's National Hurricane Center and the Hurricane Research Division of the Atlantic Oceanographic and Meteorological Laboratory (where Landsea worked at the time). The message they articulated was the one the hurricane community broadcast during and after the 2004 season: No studies conclusively link observed hurricane behavior and global warming; hurricane trends in the Atlantic instead spring from a "natural multi-decadal cycle"; and increased hurricane damage to the United States can be attributed to "massive development and population increases" in coastal areas. The talking points even described Knutson's own study for him.

But Knutson wasn't rocking the boat back then. During the 2005 season as the Emanuel and Webster studies emerged, however, he shifted his view slightly. Knutson wasn't necessarily convinced that the new results, which contradicted his own more modest findings about the sensitivity of hurricanes to climate change, were correct. But he certainly considered it within the range of possibilities. As he told a reporter with the *Los Angeles Times* just days after the landfall of Hurricane Rita: "If that's what the climate system is really doing, I find the implications to be rather alarming." In short, Knutson was now willing to give at least a lukewarm endorsement to the notion that a trend might be emerging in intense hurricanes, linked to global warming.

"That seemed to trip some wires somewhere," he remembers.

The administration of former oilman George W. Bush had problems with climate science, and with its climate-scientist employees, almost from the outset. While campaigning for the presidency, Bush had endorsed mandatory restrictions on industrial emissions of carbon dioxide. But just months after taking office he reversed his position, calling scientific knowledge about global warming "incomplete" and shortly afterward rejecting U.S. participation in the Kyoto Protocol. Meanwhile, Bush's administration called upon the National Academy of Sciences (NAS), whose experience with global warming studies dated back to the Charney Report, to provide a rapid independent evaluation of early 2001 findings released by the United Nations' Intergovernmental Panel on Climate Change. In its Third Assessment Report, the IPCC had attributed greater certainty than ever before to the conclusion that humans were driving global warming.

In practice, Bush's request to the NAS meant that a small group of American experts (including, among others, NASA's James Hansen) spent a month reviewing the collective work of more than a thousand global experts, carried out over several years. They returned, unsurprisingly, with an endorsement of the IPCC's central findings. When the press then asked for the president's reaction, Bush and his administration were put in an awkward position. The president had already called the science of global warming into question and dismissed Kyoto. And yet here was the nation's leading scientific advisory body warning that global warming was, indeed, just as real and severe a problem as everyone had been saying—and doing so in a report requested by the White House itself.

The administration responded with what amounted to a multi-year holding pattern. When the topic came up, the president always described global warming as a serious issue that needed to be addressed.

But the administration never endorsed anything beyond voluntary measures, combined with research initiatives, to deal with it. Occasionally, Bush would mouth an apparent endorsement of the scientific consensus as represented by the IPCC and the NAS reports. At other times, however, he would brazenly mislead the public by suggesting that a serious debate still existed over whether global warming might be "natural."

Meanwhile, at the various government agencies involved in some form of climate research—ranging from the Environmental Protection Agency (EPA) to NOAA to NASA—the media began to expose science scandals at regular intervals. White House officials were caught editing scientific documents to downplay the urgency of the information. Public-affairs officers were caught interfering with government scientists' ability to speak to the media. Evidently having taken a page from Senator James Inhofe, Bush himself was revealed to have met with novelist Michael Crichton to discuss climate science.

One of the most stunning flaps occurred in 2003, when the *New York Times* reported that officials at two White House branches, the Council on Environmental Quality and the Office of Management and Budget, had bowdlerized a forthcoming EPA report on the state of the environment, reducing its global-warming section to "a few noncommittal paragraphs." In a leaked memo, EPA staff complained that the edited report "no longer accurately represents scientific consensus" on climate change. They added that the White House had "discarded" conclusions from the NAS report that the administration had itself requested. Ultimately the EPA decided to drop the global warming section from the report rather than put out misleading information.

A similar story emerged two years later. Rick Piltz, a former employee of the Climate Change Science Program, an interagency group directed out of NOAA, revealed that the White House had repeatedly sought to edit program reports, once again in such a way as to raise doubts about human-caused global warming. The man with the red pen was a lawyer who had previously worked for the American Petroleum Institute, now stationed at the Council on Environmental Quality. After the lawyer resigned amid the scandal, he went to work for ExxonMobil.

Piltz went further in his accusations. Toward the end of the Clinton administration, an ambitious scientific report known as the U.S. National Assessment had sought, for the first time, to comprehensively study the effects that global warming could have upon the United States. Projected impacts included a reduction in mountain snow pack (and therefore water supplies) in the West and a rise in sea level that would slowly swallow coastal areas. The report also considered whether hurricanes might intensify or increase in number, though it merely cited the many uncertainties surrounding this issue.

The National Assessment had also been endorsed by the National Academy of Sciences in its report for Bush. Yet the administration worked to prevent its disturbing scenarios from coming before the public in a prominent way. Piltz charged that references to the Assessment had been "systematically" deleted from documents and reports put out by the Climate Change Science Program. The Assessment, he wrote, had been sent into a "black hole" by the Bush administration. It hardly seems a coincidence that conservative think tanks at work on the climate issue had spent much of their fury attacking the National Assessment and, in particular, the climate models that formed the basis of its conclusions.

Tales like these contributed to a widespread sense of suspicion among the nation's scientists. It seemed clear that the Bush administration wanted to control the flow of information about climate science, presumably to keep the issue out of the news and off the agenda. But it wasn't only the stories that made their way into the press that troubled members of the science community. It was also the stories they heard by word of mouth. Many came from their friends and colleagues who worked within branches of the Bush administration, including the GFDL. These government scientists were growing increasingly uncomfortable with administration policies and practices that seemed to constrain them from freely sharing their knowledge about climate change with the media and the public. As government employees, federal climate scientists ultimately receive their salaries from American taxpayers. Yet those taxpayers were being prevented from hearing about the scientific knowledge their money had funded.

The issue appears to have first reared its head right at the beginning of the Bush administration. On January 24, 2001, only days after Bush's inauguration, Jana Goldman, a NOAA public-affairs officer assigned to GFDL, had requested to be forwarded all media requests concerning the key climate-related news story of the day (and a particularly sensitive one at that): the newly released IPCC report. "If you get *any* press requests for IPCC please bump them to public affairs before you agree to an interview," Goldman e-mailed to GFDL climate modeler Ronald Stouffer, one of Knutson's colleagues. In retrospect, Stouffer's reply reads like the opening salvo in what would become a years-long struggle over how journalists' requests to interview GFDL scientists would be handled:

> Can I ask why this is the policy? It seems cumbersome at
> best. If this policy is implemented, it will greatly cut down
> on NOAA scientist interviews. We scientists are hard to track
> down. I think a reporter will just go somewhere else if we make
> it hard for them. The IPCC story is widely available...
>
> What would happen if I sent a reporter to you or Scott?
> Assuming they still wanted to talk with me, they would then
> have to re-contact me. Seems a lot more work for me. It is at
> least one if not 2 more interruptions in my day.
>
> —Ron

The issue did not appear to escalate right away, however. Despite her initial request concerning the IPCC report, by mid-2001 Goldman was asking merely to be kept "in the loop" about interview requests. GFDL researchers like Stouffer took less issue with that type of a policy, which did not bring the public-affairs staff into the process in a way that might delay or otherwise impede press interviews. And so the scientists wrote regular e-mails describing their interactions with the media.

In late 2003, though, a flare-up occurred that seemed to presage a tighter press policy. Kevin Trenberth had collaborated with NOAA scientist Thomas Karl on an article for *Science* magazine that strongly attributed recent warming to human activities. "Anthropogenic climate change is now likely to continue for many centuries," it read. "We are venturing into the unknown with climate, and its associated impacts could be quite disruptive." But when the study came out, media calls to Karl were apparently routed instead to a senior NOAA official who debunked and criticized the article. Usually that's a take journalists hear on their second or third phone call (if they get that far), not their first. Trenberth called what had happened "unconscionable."

By mid-2004, rules for interacting with the press had been officially codified and published. A written NOAA policy required agency scientists to refer all national media requests, as well as all requests on "controversial" issues, to public-affairs officers *prior* to responding. It was no longer okay for the scientists simply to fire off notification e-mails after they'd already talked to reporters.

And in terms of its actual implementation, the new policy seems to have been even more constraining. Scientists like Stouffer were now having to get prior approval or clearance before doing press interviews. This represented a considerable step beyond mere notification, and potentially placed public-affairs officials, sensitive to various political pressures (including those coming from the Department of Commerce, under which NOAA is subsumed), in the position of deciding which scientists could speak and which could not. In fact, in many cases the scientists first had to write out long explanations of what they would say *if* given permission to be interviewed. Meanwhile, public-affairs officers sometimes sat in on or listened to these interviews, reinforcing the sense that the scientists had better be careful what they say.

Also in relation to the new policy, Goldman asked to know about any papers coming out in scientific journals on which GFDL scientists were lead or second authors. When GFDL deputy director Brian Gross asked whether the request "pretty much covers every possible scientific and technical publication," Goldman responded, "You betcha, especially in the current political 'climate' (pun intended)."

It's not unreasonable for a government agency to require some type of notification from its scientists when they have a paper coming out, or when they do a media interview. If these scientists are generating news through their comments or their work, administration officials may have to respond to that news, and could be blindsided if not kept in the loop about it. And of course the Clinton administration had had media policies of its own. But in practice these do not appear to have been nearly as constraining, notes climate modeler Anthony Broccoli, who worked at GFDL during both administrations, leaving for Rutgers in 2003. From Broccoli's perspective, something changed during Bush's first term in office but after his own departure from GFDL. "My experience prior to that time was not as restricted," he comments. Adds Stouffer: "It evolved from notification to clearance over time." Stouffer can understand the need for the former, but he bristled under the latter—especially because he believes that pre-clearance often effectively prevented him from speaking to the press.

In some cases, the information-control processes forced upon NOAA climate researchers can only be called ridiculous. For example, GFDL atmospheric scientist Venkatachalam Ramaswamy—"Ram," as his fellow scientists call him—co-authored a study published in February 2006 in *Science* on the cooling of the lower stratosphere, which the study explained by invoking both greenhouse gas emissions and natural factors. Ramaswamy is a leading climate scientist highly involved with the IPCC process, and his results can hardly be called controversial—certainly not by the standards of much else in climate research (such as the Emanuel and Webster papers). Yet curiously, the NOAA press release that was supposed to announce the paper didn't appear until several days after the study had come out. Ramaswamy had to liberate his non-NOAA coauthors to write their own press releases because he could not get clearance for his own in time.

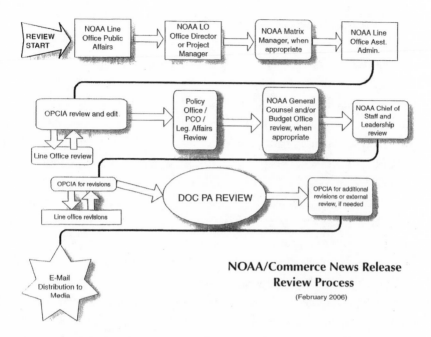

**NOAA/Commerce News Release**
**Review Process**
(February 2006)

February 2006 diagram depicting protocols for review of
a press release at NOAA and the Department of Commerce,
as revealed by a Freedom of Information Act request.

Later, the cause of the delay became apparent: NOAA and the
Department of Commerce had set up a Byzantine thirteen-step review
process for the clearance of press releases. A document had to wend its
way through public-affairs, policy, and political branches of NOAA,
and finally past the Department of Commerce's public-affairs office as
well, before being disseminated. Not only did this process give ample
opportunities for political figures to edit the text; it took about three
weeks from start to finish. As Ramaswamy wrote to Goldman:

> Any updates on the "clearance"? I suppose there are 2 sorts of
> clearances—one for the press release itself and the other for me
> to talk to the "press" should they call.

Unlike some of his colleagues, Ramaswamy has not had many problems with the public-affairs process while working at GFDL (though

an official did listen in on one of his interviews). But of the press-release incident he says: "I don't know why it was delayed beyond the publication date, but whatever the reason was, those kinds of things should not really happen."

Compared with Ramaswamy, GFDL climate modeler Ron Stouffer, a frank and even at times blunt researcher who is an expert on the thermohaline circulation, had more colorful (and troubling) encounters with the NOAA public-affairs process. At least as of mid-2004, Stouffer was having his interview requests pre-cleared by Goldman. (She happened to be GFDL's main public-affairs contact during the Bush administration, but she had also worked in the Clinton administration and the scientists don't blame her for the NOAA policies she had to implement.) As Stouffer wrote to a reporter with *National Geographic News* in response to a request in April of that year, "If there is no problems from above, I would be willing to do the interview." When the interview did happen, a NOAA public affairs official named Kent Laborde listened in. A month later, another official sent Stouffer "internal noaa talking points" on how to address the subject of abrupt climate change, as might result from a hypothesized shutdown of the thermohaline circulation.

"How close to the talking points do I need to stay?" Stouffer asked in reply.

All of this happened *before* NOAA's 2004 media policy kicked in. When it did, the transition wasn't exactly comfortable. As Stouffer confessed to Andrew Revkin of the *New York Times* that September, he had knowingly broken the "new rules" by failing to clear an interview they had done about computer modeling of the climate—and indeed, was "breaking the rules yet again by replying directly to you." While Stouffer said he was "not in any trouble that I know of," the chilling nature of the situation—as well as its absurdity—was well captured in a parody of the *Times* article that fellow researcher John Lanzante sent to Stouffer:

> Ronald J. Stouffer, a modeler at the Geophysical Fluid Dynamics Laboratory in Princeton, N.J., noted that many competing simulations had been created by independent teams using differ-

ent methods—and they all showed warming, as he picked up his hat, pink slip in hand, and headed out the door of his spacious office for the last time....

And somewhere, John Lanzante, the sun about to set, was sticking his head out of his hole in the ground, counting his blessings that they didn't quote him saying pretty much the same thing while in his semi-comatose state, having jumped out of bed to answer the phone to talk to the NY Times reporter...

"The bad news for you all, is that you are still stuck with me," Stouffer wrote back.

Parody aside, it seems unlikely that Stouffer would have been fired for doing the *New York Times* interview without permission. But in light of the sensitivity of the climate issue in the Bush administration, he had good reason to be worried about other consequences. As he explained in an interview, "If you break one of the NOAA rules, I guess there's a whole wide range of disciplinary things that NOAA can do to you, from a letter in your personnel folder, to nothing, to being fired at the extreme."

As of mid-2005 Stouffer was playing by the rules, having his interview requests preapproved. By late that year, however, reporters weren't merely asking about the science; they were also following up on rumors that NOAA's researchers had been effectively muzzled. Stouffer refused to talk to one of these muckrakers. As he later summarized for Goldman (without naming the journalist):

The reporter got quite upset with me. I asked what did he expect? He knew I could not talk, yet he called anyway. It was not the most positive NOAA scientist–reporter interaction.

The time wasn't quite ripe for the problems at NOAA to burst into the media. Discomfort, however, was mounting. Stouffer's own experience included having NOAA officials sometimes listen in on his media interviews and having to provide detailed advance write-ups of what he *would* say if interviewed. Furthermore, he had seen the number of interviews in which he actually ended up participating drop off steeply. The preapproval process—which took, on average, two to three days—was evidently too great a deterrent, given reporters' short deadlines. Stouffer characterized cases in which a journalist's interest in interviewing him disappeared before he'd received approval as a "pocket veto." This may have been the most pervasive effect of the NOAA policy: Journalists, knowing how it worked, stopped requesting interviews in the first place.

"You quickly train the reporters not to call NOAA scientists, right?" explains Stouffer. "And that's exactly what happened."

Following the landfall of Hurricane Katrina and the subsequent media storm—which included, as one of its subsidiary narratives, questions about the role of global warming in hurricane intensification—the tensions at NOAA rose dramatically. When Goldman notified GFDL that the Commerce Department wanted to "coordinate" on all "Katrina-related, national inquiries," hurricane modeler Morris Bender commented: "Most of the national media seem to understand the restrictions being placed on government scientists." Bender added that journalists were already going to an outside scientist who collaborated with GFDL when they needed quotes for their stories, and "maybe that is all for the better." Within weeks another e-mail had gone out to ensure that NOAA employees complied with the official media policy. By late November there was no mistaking it—interview requests were going to be closely scrutinized. As GFDL director Ants Leetmaa informed one of the lab's climate scientists, Isaac Held, "in theory jana needs to approve of the interviews ahead of time."

Yet at the same time, scientists from other parts of NOAA—especially the National Hurricane Center—not only seemed to be talking more freely, but were putting out what sounded like an official line on hurricanes and global warming, just as they had during the 2004 season. They were attributing increased hurricane activity since 1995 to a "natural cycle" in the Atlantic basin, and nothing more. And their statements were, in turn, being used by anti–global warming activists as well as some in the media—including in a major editorial in *USA Today*—to debunk the notion of a strong hurricane–climate link.

On September 20, 2005, the day that Hurricane Rita passed Key West and headed into the Gulf, National Hurricane Center director Max Mayfield testified before the U.S. Senate. The period of intense Atlantic hurricane activity that had begun in 1995, Mayfield said, had not been "enhanced substantially" by global warming. Mayfield did not even cite or mention the recently published papers in *Science* and *Nature,* which suggested otherwise, in his written testimony. In response to a question from Alaska senator Ted Stevens, Mayfield stated: "Without invoking global warming, I think that just the natural variability alone is what [recent hurricane activity] can be attributed to."

In October 7 testimony before the House of Representatives Committee on Science, Mayfield truly bent over backwards to keep global warming out of the picture. He was asked by Republican congressman Vernon Ehlers of Michigan for "a little futurism.... What is the future outlook with respect to both hurricane frequency and intensity during the next fifty to one hundred years?" Knutson's modeling studies, as well as the maximum-potential-intensity theories of Emanuel and Holland, suggest that global warming can be expected to influence hurricanes *in the future* even if it is not yet clearly influencing them. Indeed, the uncontroversial 1998 consensus had stated as much. But Mayfield dodged any mention of global warming in his reply, in the process ignoring that prior consensus as well as the newly published work. His words on this occasion were truly extraordinary, because even as he noted the importance of sea-surface temperatures to hurricane activity, Mayfield then ascribed Atlantic sea-temperature changes exclusively to "cycles" that would "very likely continue," entirely omitting the role of global warming in heating the oceans.

Mayfield's adherence to what Emanuel has called the NOAA "party line" was reflected by other scientists at the agency. As the record 2005 hurricane season drew to an apparent close on November 29—at the time, no one expected to see a Hurricane Epsilon or a Tropical Storm Zeta—NOAA held a press conference that featured its administrator, Vice-Admiral Conrad Lautenbacher, Jr., and Gerry Bell, a meteorologist with NOAA's Climate Prediction Center who produces the agency's seasonal hurricane forecasts. Unsurprisingly, Bell found himself peppered with questions about global warming and hurricanes from assembled reporters. In response, he entirely dismissed the notion that global warming might have played any role in the pattern of increased storm activity since 1995 or in the record 2005 season, stating that although Atlantic waters were "two to three degrees Fahrenheit warmer than normal" that year, this change could be attributed solely to a "multi-decadal cycle" and was "not related to greenhouse warming." Bell, again, didn't acknowledge that ongoing global warming was causing warmer ocean temperatures.

In a simultaneous article published on its Web site, NOAA went still farther, asserting that the views expressed by Bell and Mayfield were a matter of broad agreement at the agency: "There is consensus among NOAA hurricane researchers and forecasters that recent increases in hurricane activity are primarily the result of natural fluctuations in the tropical climate system known as the tropical multi-decadal signal." Nowhere did the release mention the work of NOAA's own Tom Knutson suggesting that global warming might increase the risk of Category 5 storms in coming decades. In fact, even then Knutson and the other GFDL modelers were working on a study attributing the warming of the Atlantic's main hurricane development region to human influences.

If Knutson seemed a probable dissenter from his agency's "party line," it's worth noting that during the Clinton administration, NOAA had taken a far less dismissive view on the basis of what, at the time, constituted considerably less evidence. In a February 12, 1998, press release, NOAA announced, "Hurricanes May Be Intensified by Global Warming," citing earlier work by Knutson and his colleagues. And on April 18, 2000—Earth Day—the former administrator of NOAA, Dr. D. James Baker, gave a speech alongside Lake Pontchartrain in New Orleans to highlight the risks posed to the city by global warming. Noting that storm-surge models suggested that New Orleans's levees could be overtopped during a bad storm, Baker said, "With sea level rise, the danger to New Orleans becomes even greater." He also discussed changes to hurricanes that might be brought about by global warming: "The scientists cannot say if we will have more hurricanes, but mostly agree that the hurricanes that we do have will be more severe."

International experts also seemed more open-minded than the present leaders of NOAA. At a December 2005 news conference Michel Jarraud, secretary-general of the World Meteorological Organization, was asked whether global warming was linked in some way to the dramatic 2005 Atlantic hurricane season. "The honest answer is: we don't know if it is," Jarraud stated.

Eventually, the internal and external grumblings over NOAA's hard line made their way into the press, and the agency became case study number two of the Bush administration's repression of government climate scientists. The first was the public revelation by NASA's James Hansen, in early 2006, about attempts by his agency's own public-affairs staff to clamp down on his statements about "dangerous" global warming.

As reported by Andrew Revkin in a *New York Times* page-one story on Sunday, January 29, Hansen claimed NASA public-affairs officials had tried to block his ability to speak out about the urgency of addressing climate change. In particular, Hansen said he'd been targeted following his speech at the American Geophysical Union (AGU) conference in December 2005—the talk delivered just before Emanuel's own not entirely apolitical presentation, which had drawn attention to an apparent crackdown on GFDL scientists in relation to the hurricane–climate question. Hansen's story had an easy-to-grasp narrative that prompted immediate and sustained outrage. It turned out that his would-be oppressor was an officer in the NASA press office, George Deutsch, who was in his early twenties and (it was later revealed) had not officially graduated from college at the time. The notion that the Bush administration would empower someone like Deutsch to block a legend like James Hansen from speaking out about climate risks was staggering.

The *Times* story set in motion a series of events that gave new legs to the narrative of scientist suppression in the Bush administration. When *Times* global warming ace Revkin broke the Hansen story, he knew of similar allegations about NOAA. They had already been made public by Emanuel at the AGU meeting, and Revkin also knew firsthand the constraints under which Ron Stouffer had been laboring at GFDL. Still, Revkin and other reporters had been unable to get a NOAA scientist to go on record with complaints until Hansen blazed the trail. "The Hansen piece uncorked a bottle," remembers Revkin. "It clearly made it easier for a lot of scientists to talk more freely."

Hansen continued to stir the pot in statements made at a conference in New York, where he claimed, just as Emanuel had previously, that he knew NOAA scientists who were afraid to speak out about efforts at information control. Rather hyperbolically, Hansen liked the situation to "Nazi Germany." As for having "minders" on press calls, Hansen noted that while NOAA claimed this was to protect the scientists doing the interviews, "if you buy that one please see me at the break, because there's a bridge down the street I'd like to sell you." The words were quoted in the *Washington Post*.

And so the pressure on NOAA began to build. Around the same time, another article, this one in the *New Republic*, exposed the agency's one-sided public claims on the hurricane–climate issue and contained further allegations from Emanuel, Curry, and others that there had been a clampdown on government scientists' ability to speak to the media. Climate scientist Jerry Mahlman, who had worked at the Geophysical Fluid Dynamics Laboratory for thirty years and had been its second director (after Smagorinsky) from 1984 to 2000, was quoted as saying to the *New Republic*'s John Judis: "I know a lot of people who would love to talk to you, but they don't dare. They are worried about getting fired."

Internally at GFDL, meanwhile, Mahlman's successor, Ants Leetmaa—an oceanographer perhaps best known for his successful long-range prediction of the extremely strong El Niño event of 1997—watched the gathering media storm. In an e-mail about the *New Republic* article to a number of agency officials, Leetmaa voiced his frustration:

> This is an embarrassment that NOAA could have easily avoided
> by inserting something like "impacts of global warming cannot
> be precluded" in the various press releases and Hill testimonies.
> A "one-NOAA" approach to press releases would have
> prevented this from happening. A more humble-not knowing

everything approach would also have enabled us to highlight
our research program, e.g. we are actively trying to understand
the phenomena.

"One NOAA" was Vice-Admiral Lautenbacher's slogan to signify how
the agency ought to be unified across its many disparate branches. In
the e-mail, Leetma also bluntly called into question the assertions of
the hurricane specialists about natural cycles:

> It is also disconcerting scientifically that synoptic meteorologists
> were making decadal hurricane projections based on a
> phenomenon (Atlantic Decadal 'Oscillation') of which they
> know nothing and which might or might not in recent years be
> forced by anthropogenic effects. The arguments on both sides
> of this "debate" rely on correlating hurricane activity with
> tropical Atlantic SST anomalies. We were taught early in our
> careers that correlation does not prove causality.

This e-mail powerfully demonstrates that a very distinguished scientist at NOAA dissented from the "party line" that had been articulated by the agency. But the GFDL perspective was not getting into the
media nearly as easily as the other point of view. Judis's reporting, and
the work of other journalists following the story, had been right on the
money in this respect. Following the *New Republic* story, GFDL modeler Tom Delworth even drafted an internal critique of the NOAA
Web site article that claimed a "consensus" on hurricanes and global
warming. The cautiously written note warned that "to state in absolute
terms that greenhouse warming has no role is premature at best," especially given the strong evidence of warming seas due to climate change.
"To the extent that ocean warming plays a role in modulating hurricane
activity, the role of greenhouse warming cannot be excluded," Delworth
continued. He recommended that the NOAA Web site posting be updated to reflect a more complete view of the science, or to state that the
positions it expressed weren't a matter of consensus at the agency.

Reporters couldn't see all of this activity going on behind the scenes,
but they heard the rumors and smelled blood. The media couldn't necessarily be counted upon to avoid misleading the public—and jerking it

around—by episodically bringing up the subject of global warming in the context of land-falling hurricanes. As Andrew Revkin has put it, journalists succumb all too easily to the "tyranny of the news peg," and Katrina was about as big a news peg as they come. Yet at the same time, reporters excel at exposing wrongdoing and malfeasance in government. And now they had NOAA in their sights.

All the reporters needed to break the story wide open was a source, a way of substantiating the claims that scientists were being suppressed. In short, they needed a courageous whistleblower. It was only a matter of time before more revelations appeared, and NOAA higher-ups seemed to get the hint. Lautenbacher ("the Admiral," as internal e-mails dubbed him) soon sent out a message to NOAA employees saying the reports of muzzling were false and encouraging the agency's scientists to speak "freely and openly." Meanwhile, the offending NOAA Web site article was changed through the addition of an online editor's note, which backed away from the previous claim of "consensus" on the hurricane–climate relationship.

All of this, however, seemed something of a forced concession. The update to the NOAA site, for example, ungenerously added a hard-to-see clarification at the very bottom of the Web page containing the article. As the GFDL scientists e-mailed the revised link around, they noted the placement. "You will find near the bottom of the article a newly inserted Editor's note," wrote Tom Delworth. "Look carefully because it is easy to miss."

Lautenbacher's assertion that no agency scientists had been discouraged from speaking was also about to be undermined. In a February 16 article in the *Wall Street Journal*, Antonio Regalado and Jim Carlton reported the first on-the-record allegations from NOAA scientists regarding agency efforts to control their statements to the media. Their story prominently featured Tom Knutson, who had several troubling tales to relate. In October 2005, Knutson said, public-affairs officials turned down a request from CNBC television to interview him after calling and asking how he would respond to questions about hurricanes and climate. One question concerned whether a trend was emerging in Atlantic hurricanes. "To that, I said I would respond that I think there's a possibility of a trend emerging, even in the Atlantic," remembers Knutson. "And this person said they would get back to me, and then I just got a voicemail a few minutes later, saying, 'Tom, about that interview, it's been turned down.'" On another occasion, Knutson had been invited to appear on Ron Reagan's show on MSNBC. But after notifying public affairs, he says he got another voice mail saying, "The White House said no."

Later, e-mails exposed by Salon.com showed what had happened to Knutson's CNBC interview. The media request had passed on from NOAA public-affairs officials to the Department of Commerce, where another official, Chuck Fuqua, had asked to know "what is Knutson's position on global warming vs. decadal cycles? Is he consistant [sic] with Bell and Landsea?" An e-mail from NOAA's Kent Laborde replied:

> He is consistant [sic], but a bit of a different animal. He's purely a numerical modeler. He takes existing data from observation and projects forward. His take is that even with worst case projections of green house gas concentrations, there will be a very small increase in hurricane intensity that won't be realized until almost 100 years from now.

To this Fuqua responded, "Why can't we have one of the other guys on then?" In addition to being an empiricist on matters of science, Fuqua had previously been in charge of running media for the Republican National Convention.

When he learned of this smoking-gun e-mail, Landsea—to his credit—was outraged. In an interview, he said, "I would hope that this [Department of Commerce] guy would leave or be fired or something, 'cause that's just not appropriate for scientists to be censored like that." Landsea added, "I feel like I've been kind of used like a little pawn in this...I didn't know what was going on." What was going on was this: Through the public-affairs process, NOAA and the Department of Commerce had made it much easier for Landsea to express his scientific opinion than for Knutson to do so. While Knutson had interviews turned down when he sought clearance, Landsea had been given free rein to answer any and all press calls. "I was instructed, basically, if a reporter asked you, you just do the interview, and you let us know about [it]," he told me. In fact, Landsea had been all over the media, including high-profile appearances on *The News Hour with Jim Lehrer* and CNN.

If only by their starkly unequal treatment of interview requests concerning these two scientists—who were *both* leading experts on the subject of hurricanes and global warming—NOAA and the Department of Commerce were gaming the release of information and trying to shift debate in their favored direction. At the time he told his story to the *Wall Street Journal*, however, Knutson had nothing but his word to back up what had happened to him. Still, his decision to talk to the media had been partly inspired by Hansen's example. "I felt a certain sort of kinship to that, that here he was being muzzled, and it had happened to me as well," Knutson explained. Knutson was younger than Hansen, however, and not as famous—differences that were not lost on Hansen himself, who e-mailed Stouffer when the news came out: "Very courageous of Tom, as a mid-career person, to come out so strongly!"

And in effect, by talking to the media, by drawing attention to abuses and forcing the Bush administration to deal with the subsequent storm of negative press, Hansen and Knutson won out in the long term. They had gone public, and they had not been fired (after all, firing them would have generated even more negative publicity). Instead, they had generated outrage as well as solidarity.

And so, citing Lautenbacher's statement about NOAA scientists speaking "freely and openly," GFDL and its researchers stopped cooperating with any preapproval process for their interview requests. (They did not participate in one for this book.) The apparent contradiction between the official NOAA public-affairs policy and the loftier statements of "the Admiral" about speaking "freely and openly" still left them in a "crappy situation," as Stouffer puts it—at least as long as that much criticized policy remained in place. (As this book went to press the Department of Commerce had just released a new policy that triggered further controversy.)

Still, the scientists had learned to fight back. Furthermore, at least if Lautenbacher's words were to be taken at face value, NOAA would be cleaning up its act. Scientists would be allowed to speak, and the agency would no longer try to control the flow of information on controversial subjects. After all, the bad publicity should have made it obvious that trying to artificially shape the way knowledge gets released, though it might be essential at a government intelligence agency, is quite simply bad policy at a scientific one. Soon enough the press finds out, and the ensuing scandal causes far more trouble than it's worth from a public-relations standpoint—not to mention damaging the credibility of the agency as a whole.

Revelations during the 2006 hurricane season, however, would subsequently prove that NOAA had not, in fact, learned this most obvious of lessons. Or perhaps the agency's leaders had learned it, but simply lacked the power to rein in politicos at the Department of Commerce. Either way, the hurricane–climate fight, in addition to setting scientists against one another, would further contribute to the undermining of one of the leading scientific agencies of the U.S. government.

# PART III

# STORM WORLD

"The scepticism that I advocate amounts only to this: (1) that when the experts are agreed, the opposite opinion cannot be held to be certain; (2) that when they are not agreed, no opinion can be regarded as certain by a non-expert; and (3) that when they all hold that no sufficient grounds for a positive opinion exist, the ordinary man would do well to suspend his judgment."

—Bertrand Russell, "On the Value of Scepticism"

# 12 • Preseason Warm-Ups

Chris Landsea had a packed room to handle. It was late January 2006, and Landsea and fellow Gray alum Greg Holland were preparing to present back-to-back on a panel about hurricanes and climate at the annual meeting of the American Meteorological Society in Atlanta. It was standing room only; people lined the walls. Most of the audience members were scientists, along with a few reporters. Many of them expected, perhaps even hoped, to see fireworks.

Landsea and Holland wouldn't be officially debating on this panel; they were merely slated to speak consecutively. In fact, a planned debate at this Atlanta meeting that was to feature Gray and Holland had been canceled by the conference organizers, who feared the showdown would get too nasty.

After the Webster paper came out, Holland had been up to Fort Collins, and he and his old teacher wound up in a shouting match. Not surprisingly, their memories of it differ. Gray's joking aside, there don't seem to have been actual "fisticuffs," but it's apparent nonetheless that they had a falling out.

"I said, 'Greg, you need a tongue-lashing,'" Gray remembered. And then, according to Gray, Holland "gave me hell." Why, Holland wanted to know, hadn't Gray stood by his own student as the hurricane–climate debate unfolded? "He came in the office and we really argued," said Gray. "He said he is going to come back the next day and show me data. He never showed." In Holland's recollection (shortly after it happened), the exchange sounds a bit different. "Bill and I have argued about scientific issues from day one," he said.

"That's what scientists do. The unfortunate thing is that, in the last twelve months, it's become personal, and I have to say, it's become personal entirely on one side."

The public debate scheduled for the Atlanta meeting wasn't the only one undermined by a scientific conflict that, under the combined influences of politics, the media, and the weather, had grown too frictional. Two other proposed events had to be reorganized as Emanuel, Holland, Webster, and Curry vowed to no longer appear alongside Gray.

The meltdown happened in the context of planning another conference panel, for the American Meteorological Society's more specialized Hurricanes and Tropical Meteorology meeting, slated to take place in April 2006 in Monterey, California. In November 2005, Elizabeth Ritchie, a University of New Mexico hurricane expert charged with chairing the meeting, had invited Gray, Webster, Emanuel, Landsea, and Max Mayfield to participate in a panel discussion that sounded like the conference's main draw. Ritchie merely said the panel would address the "causes" of the dramatic 2005 Atlantic hurricane season. But given who'd been invited, global warming would clearly take center stage.

Webster and Emanuel quickly expressed concerns. Emanuel recalled his debate with Gray at a Hurricanes and Tropical Meteorology meeting in 2000. "While this sort of thing plays well with certain tropical groupies and with the press, I think it does lasting damage to the image of our profession," he wrote. "If Bill Gray is prepared to act professionally then we will see," added Webster, complaining that Gray had accused his team of "all types of malfeasance including cooking the data to get money."

Quoting all this, Gray then fired back a lengthy e-mail to the group, stating that he would be happy to sit on the panel so long as he was given an assurance that Emanuel and Webster "will behave themselves and try not to make derogatory and paranoid statements about me as contained in their recent e-mails." Gray went on to suggest that the two scientists had indeed come up with their data to advance their careers. (As he put the point in a later e-mail: "Had their data showed no TC increase or a TC decrease, they would not have had papers of media interest or justification for further grant support for research on this topic.") Gray signed off by invoking a disciplinary divide and his own special expertise as a card-carrying hurricane scientist: "How were Emanuel and Webster et al. able to see trends in the global data that the rest of us long-time TC researchers presently working on these same data sets do not find?"

Ritchie quickly swooped in and tried to save the panel. She promised there would be special "rules" to govern the discussion and keep everything above the belt—rules to be enforced by moderator and longtime hurricane scientist Russell Elsberry, who like Gray was a former student of Riehl. And she emphasized that she wanted everyone she had originally invited to participate: "The media know and respect all of you, and the panel will be seen to be incomplete without any of you." But it was too late. Emanuel and Webster refused to sit on the panel with Gray. "To disagree with science is one thing but to question motivation and accuse one of ethical malfeasance is another," wrote Webster.

Ritchie wasn't giving up. She suggested disinviting Gray and instead asking someone like Gray's student Johnny Chan—a professor at the City University of Hong Kong, an expert on Northwest Pacific typhoons, and a skeptic of the Webster research—to participate. Apparently she then did so, because in a later e-mail to the group Gray suggested he had been "blackballed" and added to Ritchie: "There is still time to backtrack."

At this point Landsea—who had started off the thread with a joking message promising not to "throw anything or hit anyone ;-)" at the debate—stepped in. "Bill, please, stop," he wrote. "Liz had no choice but to drop you from the program because of your public accusations," he continued. Now, Landsea said, he would have to "carry the banner" in Gray's absence.

And so in a sense Landsea became the group's diplomat. Not only would he have to keep explaining why the new studies' findings about hurricanes and global warming weren't reliable. He'd have to do so without triggering another meltdown.

When the Atlanta meeting finally rolled around, Landsea seemed up to the challenge. He started the panel off smoothly, joking that as first speaker he would be allotted twenty-five of the panel's thirty minutes, and Holland, who would follow, would get five.

A surge of laughter diffused the tension in the room, and Landsea launched into his presentation (which he limited to a reasonable fifteen minutes). First he underscored the discrepancy between Knutson's modeling work—which suggested that although hurricanes should intensify due to global warming, that intensification shouldn't be detectable yet—and the data-based studies of Emanuel and the Webster group. "Theory and models," Landsea claimed, gave grounds for doubting the latest data (not that Landsea trusted the models, either).

Landsea's chief argument, however, lay with the data itself. Especially when it came to the Webster study, Landsea said, satellite records of hurricane intensities weren't dependable enough to support its striking conclusions. In particular, he noted that the application of the Dvorak cloud pattern-recognition technique, which is regularly used to evaluate hurricane intensity from satellite pictures and has been especially relied upon in basins lacking aircraft reconnaissance, had changed over time. Landsea contended that the strong trend of storm intensification observed in the Webster study probably reflected a change in techniques for measuring hurricanes, rather than a change in hurricanes themselves.

Satellites, Landsea explained, had grown more numerous over time, and their images had increased in resolution. The Dvorak method itself had matured into an infrared technique in 1984, meaning it could be used at night as well as during the day. Landsea even flashed satellite images of a few North Indian basin cyclones from previous decades that, he said, would have been classified as stronger storms in a later era. Therefore, Landsea concluded, the "problem is with the data sets."

Unlike Gray, Landsea never once in the discussion questioned the existence of global warming. Nor did he dispute that evidence of it was apparent in the oceans (a subject Knutson would discuss at the meeting the next day) or even in the specific ocean regions that serve as hurricane breeding grounds. Rather, he sought to set observations of hurricane intensities in historical context and explain how they'd grown much more reliable over time.

Another way Landsea makes this point is to contrast hurricane intensity measurements at fifty-year intervals. The 1900 Galveston hurricane, he explains, had its central pressure sampled only once— by a ship. In 1954, Hurricane Carol had its intensity measured seven times, still not nearly enough for us to know how strong it was during significant parts of its lifetime. (Carol, which knocked a tree onto Jule Charney's car at Woods Hole, isn't even officially classified as a hurricane in Massachusetts, although Landsea thinks it ought to be.) Hurricane Wilma in 2005, by comparison, had its pressure and winds measured 280 times over the storm's lifetime. So it's far more likely that Wilma was observed at or around peak intensity.

Without a doubt, Landsea had articulated a serious criticism. Yet he had not directly disproved the work of Emanuel and Webster; he had merely given reasons to doubt their conclusions. And Emanuel and Webster's team had counterarguments. While acknowledging weaknesses in the historic "best track" hurricane databases, Emanuel also ventured that they ought to be little more than random errors, in which storm intensities were overestimated or underestimated in roughly equal proportion. Webster and colleagues, meanwhile, responded in Jerry Maguire fashion: Show me the money. Given the size of the trend they claimed to have uncovered (a near doubling of Category 4 and 5 hurricanes), only the reclassification of a very large number of storms would significantly undermine their results. In the meantime, they wrote, "There is no evidence that we cannot, for the vast majority of hurricanes since 1970, distinguish between category-4 and -5 hurricanes and category-1 and -2 hurricanes."

Interpretations of the flawed hurricane data, then, took on a half-full/half-empty aspect. Landsea looked at the data and saw reasons to doubt. Webster and colleagues looked at the data and saw reasons to worry.

Holland followed Landsea on the panel. On paper, the two scientists sound like twins, and they share the distinction of being Gray's only students to have won the same two American Meteorological Society awards while studying under him. Yet in person the contrast couldn't be sharper. Landsea is tall and clean-shaven, bluntly American in speech and style; in suit and tie, he looked ready to meet the president (as, in fact, he later would). Holland is shorter and thick-bearded, and talks much more rapidly, with a strong accent. He dressed in a rumpled academic style—blazer but no tie.

Holland began on a personal note: Since he'd moved to the United States, he had grown acutely interested in the Atlantic and its hurricanes. And so he sought to defend his team's controversial results and, simultaneously, to reconcile them with preexisting hurricane-intensity theory (which he and Emanuel had done much to create). One reason we've seen more intense storms in the Atlantic, Holland argued, is that the seedbeds of Atlantic hurricanes had changed. The storms had been forming farther to the south over warmer waters, a phenomenon that had created a higher proportion of Cape Verde–type storms. "The whole damn lot have moved towards the equator and become more intense," Holland said. But theoretical and modeling studies of hurricane intensity, he pointed out, hadn't been designed to analyze such a shifting storm population.

Holland also challenged the notion that a natural oceanic cycle could explain the warming Atlantic, which had fostered these stronger hurricanes. Given all the research showing that human activities had been driving a global ocean-warming trend, he stated, there was "no way any rational being can say that high SSTs in the North Atlantic are entirely natural."

Emanuel didn't attend the 2006 Atlanta meeting, but like Holland, he was busy trying to reconcile his prior theory with his new observations. In particular, Emanuel was investigating why the apparent response to global warming seemed different in the Atlantic than in the Northwest Pacific, the other basin he'd studied. For the Atlantic, he found that four key factors controlling how much power hurricanes dissipate—sea-surface temperatures, wind shear, trade-wind speed, and temperatures in hurricanes' outflow region (the tropopause)—all seemed to be changing in a synchronized fashion. But for the Northwest Pacific, the four were "doing their own thing." If warming oceans were having a more pronounced effect in one basin than in another, the response of hurricanes to global warming might be far more complicated than originally supposed.

If the scientists were finding that the link between hurricane intensity and a warming world was a tough riddle to crack, they were also learning that dealing with a swarming media—especially after the disastrous 2005 hurricane season—could be fraught with peril.

Prior to 2004, journalists had generally been content to discuss hurricane–climate linkages episodically, usually in the context of landfalling storms during hurricane season. Then they would largely drop the subject until the next storm showed up. After the 2004 and 2005 hurricane seasons, however, the public wanted to know what the hell was going on with the atmosphere and the oceans, and this appetite continued to drive news even in the absence of storms. Without dramatic weather or fresh scientific publications on hurricanes and global warming to report on in early and mid-2006, reporters turned to novel story angles. Not only did they fixate on the budding scandals at NOAA, but they began haunting scientific conferences and reporting on the increasingly nasty and personal nature of the debate between Gray and his adversaries. It was a form of journalism that the scientists themselves despised, because it suggested that there might be more driving their stances than an objective assessment of the data—and because it moved the coverage toward an emphasis on drama and conflict.

The trend was epitomized by a *Wall Street Journal* page-one story by Valerie Bauerlein, published in early February 2006. "Cold Front: Hurricane Debate Shatters Civility of Weather Science," screamed the headline. Reporting on the American Meteorological Society meetings in Atlanta, Bauerlein opened her story with the canceled Holland–Gray panel and put a heavy accent on character and conflict. At the Atlanta conference, she wrote, the reasons for the deadly 2005 hurricane season were "almost too hot to handle." She soon quoted Gray saying that Webster's coauthor Judith Curry "just doesn't know what she's talking about," and then quoted Curry saying that Gray suffered from "brain fossilization."

Clearly, if the weather and ongoing scientific research did not provided anything juicy, journalists would be looking elsewhere for the fodder they needed.

The 2006 global hurricane season began where it always does, in the Southern Hemisphere, which experiences summer first. In late February, the South Atlantic hosted what looked like another tropical disturbance, though certainly no Catarina this time. The storm remained organized for only a few hours before getting blown apart by shear. Still, its 35-mile-per-hour winds were enough to prompt leading meteorology blogger Jeff Masters to suggest that the time had come to consider a naming system for South Atlantic cyclones and to speculate about whether climate change might be systematically weakening wind shear in the region. Two weeks later, another weak but tropical-looking disturbance showed up briefly in the South Atlantic.

Meanwhile, the Australian region was already in the midst of a terrible year for severe tropical cyclones, as the strongest hurricanes there are called. Australia can be hit by storms forming in either the South Indian or Southwest Pacific basins (which merge together more or less seamlessly as one progresses farther east). The intensity scale used to classify these cyclones differs from the one used in the United States, but translated into Saffir-Simpson categories, the 2005–2006 Australian season saw either two or three Category 4s (Bertie-Alvin, Floyd, and possibly Larry) and two Category 5s (Glenda and Monica). The most destructive of them, Larry, formed in the eastern Coral Sea and slammed the populous northern coast of Queensland near Innisfail on March 20, leaving half of the homes damaged. At Silkwood, which received the worst of the storm, the figure was much worse: 99 percent of homes lost their roofs or suffered some form of assault to their structural integrity.

Larry—and the difference between the Australian and Saffir-Simpson hurricane scales—did provide for some comic relief, however. In April 2006, *Time* magazine ran a cover story on global warming. "Be Worried. Be Very Worried," it intoned. Announcing that "the crisis is upon us," the lead article then continued:

> It certainly looked that way last week as the atmospheric bomb that was Cyclone Larry—a Category 5 storm with wind bursts that reached 180 m.p.h.—exploded through northeastern Australia.... Disasters have always been with us and surely always will be. But when they hit this hard and come this fast—when the emergency becomes commonplace—something has gone grievously wrong. That something is global warming.

Although there's some dispute about its strength, it seems clear that Larry was either a Category 3 or possibly a Category 4 storm by the hurricane scale Americans are used to. According to the National Climatic Data Center, the storm's maximum wind gusts only reached about 145 miles per hour (and maximum sustained winds were closer to 115 miles per hour). Not only did *Time* make the perennial mistake of linking global warming to a single land-falling storm; it didn't even choose one of the strongest ones.

Meteorologically, Severe Tropical Cyclone Glenda told a more frightening tale. It was a rapid intensifier like Wilma. The storm formed off Australia's northwestern coast on March 27, and within a day had swelled into a Category 4 storm, en route to Category 5. Moving to the southwest along the coast, Glenda weakened to a Category 3 storm before making landfall in the Pilbara region of western Australia near the town of Onslow. This de-intensification prevented more severe damage at landfall, but at Glenda's peak, one estimate based upon satellite imagery put the storm's central pressure at 898 millibars (though the Australian Bureau of Meteorology put it at 910 mb).

Still more powerful was Severe Tropical Cyclone Monica, which churned from April 17 to April 24, 2006, very late in the season by Southern Hemisphere standards. Originating in the Coral Sea, Monica was a small storm, not unlike Cyclone Tracy of 1974; at one point it even seemed similarly aimed at the city of Darwin. And Monica could have been even more devastating. Despite its late-season formation, it was one of the two strongest tropical cyclones ever recorded in the Southern Hemisphere, with maximum sustained winds approaching 180 miles per hour—what might be considered Category 6 strength if we assume that Category 5 runs only from 155 to 175 miles per hour or so (a similar span to the categories below it).

Monica's minimum central pressure reading is disputed. Just before its landfall in the Northern Territory, as the storm left the Gulf of Carpentaria and moved into the Arafura Sea, satellite-based estimates put its intensity at a stunning 879 millibars. For the Southern Hemisphere, such a measurement would tie the satellite estimate for 2002's Cyclone Zoe (which also had maximum sustained winds of 180 miles per hour at its peak). In fact, using an automated method called the Advanced Dvorak Technique, scientists at the University of Wisconsin at one point estimated Monica's minimum pressure to be as low as 868.5 millibars—which, if accurate, would be the lowest pressure ever measured anywhere on Earth at sea level.

The 868.5-millibar estimate doesn't count as an official record, however, and isn't necessarily reliable. Australia doesn't send reconnaissance flights into tropical cyclones as the United States does, and intensity estimates from satellite images have many problems. The Australian Bureau of Meteorology apparently judged Monica's lowest pressure to have been considerably higher—905 millibars, a huge discrepancy. The storm's true intensity will always remain a mystery, a fact that lends strength to Landsea's arguments about the immense difficulty in tracking down reliable and consistent intensity figures for storms across the globe. If we can't get dependable measurements for Monica in 2006, how could we have done it for storms in the 1970s?

Severe Tropical Cyclone Monica just north of Australia on April 23, 2006, possibly the most intense storm ever observed in the Southern Hemisphere. *Image credit: Naval Research Lab*

April 24 was the day Monica made landfall in Australia's Northern Territory, west of the Aboriginal township of Maningrida (sparing Darwin another blow). It also happened to be the day William Gray was slated to appear before a crowd of scientists at the Hurricanes and Tropical Meteorology conference in Monterey, California. As per the e-mail dialogue several months earlier, Gray had been removed from the panel debate scheduled to occur the next evening, but he had submitted a paper to present instead. The online write-up suggested it would be a full-on attack on the theory of human-induced global warming.

Earlier in the day, meteorologist David Nolan of the Rosentiel School of Marine and Atmospheric Science at the University of Miami, who sometimes collaborated with Emanuel, had presented perhaps the scariest idea yet about the relationship between hurricanes and the climate system. Using a computer model, Nolan and Emanuel explored the possibility of "spontaneous" genesis of tropical cyclones in a warmer world (perhaps one that had been sufficiently heated thanks to an enhanced greenhouse effect). The scientists accepted the view, dating at least back to the work of Riehl, that hurricane development must be sparked by an independent disturbance. But they suggested that this constraint, while important in our present climate, might not always exist in the future, and might not have existed in previous warmer eras of Earth's history. In a hot enough world, seas conducive to hurricanes might stretch much farther pole-ward, into regions where the Coriolis force deflects winds more strongly than it does nearer to the equator (the effect of the Earth's rotation increases towards the poles). This might allow hurricanes to come together from "random convection" and thus—it went without saying—occur far more frequently and in locations where we are unaccustomed to seeing them in the current climate.

Nolan didn't have the misfortune of having to compete head-on with Gray's speech later that afternoon. Former NOAA Hurricane Research Division director Hugh Willoughby, however, wasn't so lucky. As Willoughby ruefully recalls, "I sure knew who the people who were interested in my work were. All six or seven of them." It certainly seemed as if a large proportion of the more than 550 scientists on hand for the conference—many more than would have attended the same event in the decades before hurricane research became sexy— had piled in to hear the grand old man of tropical meteorology.

For the assembled scientists—who, just like crowds of hurricane preparedness experts, liked a little entertainment now and again— Gray didn't disappoint. He started with a slide in black and red type, set against a light green background:

SOCIETY'S PROGRESS CAN CONTINUE ONLY AS LONG AS ITS OLD MEN PERSIST IN DECRYING THAT "EVERYTHING IS GOING TO HELL"

This quotation Gray attributed to an "unknown philosopher." Then he launched into a favorite routine—recalling yesteryear.

"As I look out over the crowd, I think I'm the oldest guy here," he began. "Where were you all in 1961, June, in Miami?" That was the month, Gray recounted, that he had attended the second-ever incarnation of this now-biennial Hurricanes and Tropical Meteorology conference. He had missed the first conference in the fall of 1958, he added, because "I couldn't get Herbert Riehl to agree to pay my travel down."

"All you young people are reinventing the wheel, you know, in '61 we had it all worked out," Gray continued, to much laughter. "And then the damn computer and satellites came along and ruined everything. And that's where we are today." He turned back to his slide. "When I give you hell…it is *real* hell," he warned. "And that's what I intend on doing."

And so it went, on into Gray's dismissal of concerns about human-caused global warming and the global climate models upon which they are based. He had toned down his presentation to this highly trained—and critical—audience not a whit; if anything, he had amped up the humor. He had even added a new schtick to his standard "Ice Age" joke recapping alarmist quotations about "global cooling" from the 1970s: a PowerPoint presentation of a succession of *Time* magazine covers. First, a faux cover purporting to be from 1945 clarioned the possibility of global warming. The second, an actual cover from 1977, announced "The Big Freeze" with a photo of a man wearing a ski mask with snow encrusted on it. The third was the aforementioned "Be Worried. Be Very Worried" cover from that very month, showing a polar bear on a dwindling ice floe.

But Gray wasn't finished roasting *Time*. In a final slide, he presented a cartoon of a person standing in what looks like an ice cube, thinking "It's Cold! Burrr!," with the familiar *Time* magazine logo above. "I've projected this," Gray said. The date: 2036.

As the talk continued, so did the patter. Gray—the "Howard Stern of meteorology," as one scientist described him to me—slammed entire communities of researchers with lines like "Anybody, any experienced meteorologist that believes in a climate model of any type should have their head examined, they really should." He accused climate scientists of being "Prisoners of the Clausius-Clayperon equation," the well-known law of physics. Finally, he gave his audience a quotation from Michael Crichton:

> Historically, the claim of **consensus** has been the **first** (*not last*) refuge of scoundrels; it is a way to avoid debate by claiming that the matter is already settled. Whenever you hear the **consensus** of scientists agrees on something or other, reach for your wallet, because you're being had.

And there Gray nearly ended, to laughter and great applause from the audience. Basking in the response—feeding off it, just as a hurricane feeds off the ocean—Gray couldn't resist one more comment. "I'm sorry I'm so reluctant to express my views on things," he said.

As this was a professional scientific meeting and not the National Hurricane Conference, there was a second act: questions from the audience. The first came from Peter Webster, whom Gray had embraced and urged to get to work on hurricanes at the same event two years before.

In a very civil tone, Webster—the type of scientist who always seems to ask the first question after a lecture—challenged Gray's account of the role of the thermohaline circulation in driving the recent Atlantic warming. In particular, Webster referenced a recent study in the journal *Nature* that had detected an apparent slowdown of this circulation. He didn't get to phrase a fully formed question before Gray cut in.

Oceanographers cannot directly measure whether the thermohaline circulation is speeding up or slowing, Gray countered, and then his voice began to rise. "We've been working fifteen or twenty years on this," said Gray, "and you come in, right the last year, and throw all this out the window! Do you really know what you're talking about, Peter?"

"Bill, I think I do," continued Webster calmly. In Gray's presentation, he said, "the thermohaline circulation looks nothing like anybody's ever seen. So, I think I know what I'm talking about."

"You know what you're talking about most of the time, Peter, I have great admiration for this," said Gray. "But on this you don't know what you're talking about."

"I think that will have to be settled outside," said the moderator.

The next questioner was Holland, Gray's former student and Webster's friend. The tag-team approach sparked uncomfortable laughter from the audience.

"I always love Greg Holland's questions," Gray said gamely. "They're wonderful."

"This was highly entertaining," Holland began. "But unfortunately you obfuscate the real issues at hand." Holland then launched into an impassioned defense of climate models and the integrity of the researchers working with them—who included many of his own colleagues at the National Center for Atmospheric Research (NCAR) in Boulder. For Gray to denounce so many hard-working researchers in such an absolute fashion, Holland argued, "does the science a disservice." The statement drew Holland his own round of applause.

But Gray had the microphone and the stage, and he had the last word.

"Oh Greg," Gray responded, "I didn't know you as a highly religious person. That's a belief. That's a belief, not a reality." It was one of the worst slights one scientist can bestow upon another—the accusation that one's conclusions have been determined by a preconceived opinion, a theology. It echoed Redfield's attacks on Espy more than a century earlier.

"They're trying hard, they're good scientists—some of my best friends are modelers. But it can't be done," Gray went on. "No, Greg," he finished. "Since you've joined NCAR, you've come to religion."

The next speaker was Emanuel.

"Those of you who are here because you think you're going to hear a rebuttal will be disappointed," he said, quelling another ripple from the audience. Then he launched into an equation-intensive talk that sought to reconcile his theoretical understanding of hurricane intensification with the latest observations. A decline of trade-wind speeds over the main development region, Emanuel suggested, seemed to have amplified the sensitivity of Atlantic hurricanes to global warming. So had a poorly understood but apparent cooling of the tropical tropopause, which had decreased the temperature in hurricanes' outflow regions even as temperatures at the sea-surface heat reservoir had increased (thus upping the potential intensity achievable by storms in two separate, complementary ways).

Emanuel's presentation limited itself almost entirely to purely scientific content. It was highly theoretical, geared toward the scientifically advanced audience. Emanuel did, however, make one side remark about the "previous speaker"—who he never mentioned by name, but who he described as being "in denial" about global warming.

The next evening's debate, featuring Emanuel, Webster, Landsea, and Johnny Chan, went off without a hitch. The moderator, Russell Elsberry of the Naval Postgraduate School, cautioned at the outset that there were to be "no personal comments as to character or any other thing." "Everyone involved in this panel discussion is searching for the truth, and I want to compliment everyone for doing that," offered Landsea, once again playing the role of conciliator, and once more using humor to that end. "I get along personally with everyone involved and I want to continue that—even if they're wrong," he continued.

Emanuel, too, had a gloss on the state of affairs. "I think the people you see up here in front of you have conducted this debate in a very civilized way, I hope we can say we're the models," he said at one point during the discussion. "It's not us who have been the problem. It's certain members of the press and certain people you don't see up here." In slamming the press, the scientists mostly seemed to have in mind the *Wall Street Journal* story that had depicted such a nasty conflict between Gray and Curry. "They like to try and make it look like everybody's fighting everybody," said Webster, who seemed particularly incensed at journalists. (Earlier at the conference, spotting me walking and talking with Richard Kerr, a reporter for *Science,* Webster had joked, "Oh my God, now there's two of them.")

Gray was in the audience for the debate. Even if he'd wanted to speak, though, he wouldn't have been allowed to. The organizers, not taking any chances, had stipulated that questions from the audience would be submitted in writing and read aloud by the moderator.

And so there followed a lengthy, substantive discussion. One memorable moment came when Landsea publicly apologized for the behavior of NOAA, his employer. Insofar as the agency had claimed a "consensus" on hurricanes and global warming on its Web site, Landsea said, "that was a mistake to do." He continued: "I think that was a misguided attempt by the public affairs folks to try to provide a broad-brush answer to a pretty complex problem."

Johnny Chan, meanwhile, limited his case to the storms of the Northwest Pacific, where, inspired by Gray, he had introduced a statistical forecasting system for seasonal typhoon activity. In the context of the debate over hurricanes and global warming, this basin had huge significance because it hosts such a large number of storms (and so many very intense ones). Sea-surface temperatures in the Northwest Pacific, Chan argued, are "so high that a little bit of change is not going to do anything." In much of the basin, he noted, these temperatures exceed 28 degrees Celsius for most of the year, well above the general 26- to 27-degree threshold for storm formation in the current climate. Chan argued that, at least for the Northwest Pacific, storm intensity seemed more strongly controlled by factors like wind shear: "Thermodynamics cannot really explain the variations."

What emerged most strongly from these exchanges was that until someone carefully reanalyzed the global storm intensity data and provided a record that both sides could accept, they would remain at an impasse. Fortunately, it now came up that an outside scientist, Jim Kossin of the Cooperative Institute for Meteorological Satellite Studies at the University of Wisconsin–Madison—who'd flown with Landsea on the record-setting Gilbert flight back in 1988 and was in the audience listening to the debate—had volunteered to undertake a comprehensive satellite-data reanalysis. "Jim, get back to work," Landsea joked at one point.

The next morning at the conference, I sought out Gray to hear his impressions of the debate. True to form, he said he thought Chan and Landsea had done a "great job." He also said once again that Emanuel could sell ice cubes to the Eskimos and steam heat to the Amazonians. Then I got my turn as target practice when Gray jokingly asked if he could call me a "hired gun of the left." I replied that I wouldn't sue him. Then he said, "Well, maybe I can call you a hired gun of the middle." It felt strangely pleasant to be the subject, however briefly, of one of Gray's jibes.

I asked Gray if he felt bad that he hadn't been included in the debate. My notes say: "he said, no, he was just proud of his students, but also that they kicked him off the panel—but he was proud of his students."

A few weeks later, at the twentieth annual Florida Governor's Hurricane Conference, held in Fort Lauderdale, Gray was again in his element. He'd been the final speaker of this massive event (with 3,800 attendees this year) since 1994. Now, his long arms planted on either side of the podium, he was passing the torch to Klotzbach.

Having listened to a string of the previous speakers—including Florida's Secretary of Community Affairs, Thaddeus Cohen, who could not seem to complete a sentence without including the phrase "in terms of"—I had a better understanding of why any sane audience would respond enthusiastically to an irascible old guy with a humorous slide show. And I could better appreciate that such crowd-pleasing was one of the skills Landsea had taken care to pick up from his teacher. I'd missed Landsea's workshop the previous day on "hurricane myths," though at the National Hurricane Conference I'd seen him give a similar talk. Alongside the concept that global warming might strongly influence hurricanes, he had tossed in hilariously dumb ideas, such as the notion that we might defeat hurricanes by arming our coasts with giant fans to blow them back out to sea, or towing Arctic icebergs into their paths, or even hitting the storms with nuclear bombs. (This last conceit, Landsea noted, would simply create a "radioactive hurricane.")

Having heard Gray's routine multiple times by now, I listened for elements that might be different. But I quickly saw that every Gray talk is new. It all tumbles out a bit differently each time, sometimes more strident, sometimes less. Today seemed a relatively mild day. Although Gray gave his standard anti–global warming talk with its three pillars—the weaknesses of numerical modeling, the erroneous water-vapor feedback loop, natural cycles driven by the thermohaline circulation—he also tailored his words specifically to Florida, the most hurricane-exposed state in the nation. Gray's central message was simple: Floridians had been lucky for a long, long time. From 1966 until 2003, the peninsula had seen only one major hurricane landfall, that of Andrew in 1992. "What was happening those thirty-eight years?" Gray asked. "You were all moving down here, having children; they were growing up, expanding their houses."

Gray's contention that Florida's vulnerabilities sprang from societal factors like population growth and increased development of valuable coastal property repeated a mantra of the hurricane community whose validity is tough to dispute. But then he told Floridians to drop global warming from their litany of concerns as they contemplated their future: "Worry about nature. Nature's tough enough. It's going to do a lot of harm to Florida, and that's your main threat I think."

What Gray modulated in tone, however, he made up for in length. After forty minutes, he was just beginning a dive into paleoclimatology. He kept right on going; as he had jokingly told the crowd earlier, "I have a little more views I want to get off my chest." And then once again, Gray finished to a standing ovation (albeit from a somewhat thinned-out audience).

The reception reminded me of an encounter before the talk, when I'd been sitting and chatting with Gray about the history of hurricane science. Two men came up to us, with a boy who looked about ten years old. One of the men obviously knew Gray, and he asked if Gray would pose for a picture with the boy, presumably his son.

The boy, the man explained, wanted to be a weatherman when he grew up.

# 13 • Where Are the Storms?

N o more Katrinas, NOAA tell the truth!"
"No more Katrinas, Mayfield must go!"
"No more Katrinas, Lautenbacher must go!"
The protesters were in a chanting mood on the morning of May
31, 2006—although the four-syllable word "Lautenbacher" threw off
their cadences. Trying to recover, they sounded like a group of people
struggling to get the timing right at the start of "Happy Birthday."
They didn't seem to have practiced ahead of time.

Still, some fifty to one hundred of these demonstrators, clad in life
preservers, had staked out a cordoned-off area in front of NOAA's offices in Silver Spring, Maryland, where they were surrounded by police officers and eyed warily by a team of red-shirted security guards
on bicycles. The protesters had framed their podium between two large
NOAA buildings and just below the organization's logo: the white
bird with wings outstretched, soaring over the ocean. At the base of
the podium rested a poster showing a man dragging a boat across a
flooded area—presumably in New Orleans.

As a work of political theater, this was fairly ingenious: On the day
before the June 1 start of the 2006 Atlantic hurricane season, the protesters aimed to hold NOAA accountable for suppressing scientific
information about the relationship between hurricanes and global
warming. As with the science-related political scandals that had be-
deviled government agencies ranging from the Environmental Protection Agency to the Food and Drug Administration, the media exposés
of recent months had badly damaged NOAA's credibility. The protest
perfectly exploited this weak spot. Demonstrators vowed to camp out
in front of the agency's offices until the hurricane season began and to

ply employees with information. Cameras were well placed, and ABC News ran a story about the event.

The protest had been the work of Mike Tidwell, a suntanned journalist-cum-climate activist who wore a salt-and-pepper goatee and sunglasses propped atop his head as he emceed the event. If Tidwell's spectacle showed political savvy, though, it also demonstrated a certain excess in its depiction of scientific knowledge. Not only did the protesters talk as if the science linking global warming to stronger storms was a done deal (despite vigorous debate at the Monterey meeting only a month earlier), but the event's speakers and literature drew an untenably direct connection between climate change and the damage inflicted upon New Orleans by Hurricane Katrina. In one statement Curtis Muhammad, of the People's Organizing Committee in New Orleans, dubbed the storm a "natural disaster made worse by global warming." Another speaker, Casey DeMoss Roberts, former chair of the New Orleans Group of the Sierra Club, declared herself a "climate refugee." Then Tidwell swept back up to the podium and declared, "Arguably we have about two million climate refugees in this country."

If Tidwell's rhetoric flew beyond the science, his call for the resignation of National Hurricane Center director Max Mayfield seemed truly over-the-top. True, Mayfield had neglected to seriously discuss possible global-warming influences on hurricanes in testimony before Congress the previous year. He hadn't given elected representatives the full picture, and in failing to do so, had helped set the stage for the subsequent, very valid criticisms of NOAA's "party line" treatment of the issue.

Still, in the run-up to the 2006 hurricane season I'd seen Mayfield at the Monterey conference listening closely to the panelists' debate. He was well aware of the arguments transpiring in the world of science and better informed about them than most. But he claimed not to have been convinced yet by Emanuel, Webster, Curry, and Holland. That hardly seems a firing offense, especially since, when it came to protecting coastlines and vulnerable areas, Mayfield had performed more than admirably during the 2005 hurricane season. Not only had he provided a reassuring and dependable voice on television while deadly storms sat perched in the Gulf; he had also briefed the president in an accurate and timely way about the huge threat posed by Katrina. (In any event, Mayfield would presently announce his resignation anyway, understandably burned out by the previous two grueling hurricane seasons.)

But Tidwell had another target. A search of the National Hurricane Center Web site, his literature complained, had yielded "at least 104 hits" for Bill Gray's name. So Tidwell demanded that "no U.S. taxpayer funded website...should have any links to the flawed and dishonest climate information carried on the website of discredited meteorologist William Gray." The protesters didn't seem to see a contradiction between this demand and their vociferous opposition to the censorship of NOAA scientists.

Still, given the fear they inspire and the attention they attract, you could see why those worried about global warming, like Tidwell, might be in a particularly agitated state on the topic of hurricanes. At the time, Al Gore's *An Inconvenient Truth* had already successfully debuted in New York and Los Angeles and was expanding to other major cities. Posters for the film showed the emissions from a smokestack organizing, in the dark sky above, into a cyclonically shaped storm—but one with a clockwise, rather than counterclockwise, rotation. Did that signify an attempt to make a subtle point about Southern Hemisphere hurricanes like Catarina?

Perhaps. More likely, though, it was just a mistake.

But as I furiously scribbled notes, beginning to sour on Tidwell and the demonstrators, I realized that I was in the presence of the "other side." The man next to me turned out to be none other than Bill Riggs, with the Web site TCSDaily.com. Riggs gave me an information sheet that asked, "Is Global Warming to Blame for Another Powerful Hurricane Season? Leading Climate Scientists Remain Unconvinced." There followed a list of five scientists that Riggs would presumably love to set journalists up with for interviews. I noted Florida State's James O'Brien and Patrick Michaels on the list, although notably, not Gray or Klotzbach. TCSDaily.com, apparently, thought winning on the merits wasn't enough. Scientists skeptical of a strong hurricane–climate link had to be foisted on the media in an organized fashion.

With the arrival of hurricane season, the prospects for serious discourse on hurricanes and global warming—from either side of the aisle—seemed dim.

The season itself soon opened with a scare, as Tropical Storm Alberto moved into the Gulf and revved up to near-hurricane strength. The storm's sudden burst of intensification on Monday, June 12, took forecasters by surprise; apparently Alberto had run over the Loop Current. "GIVEN THE UNCERTAINTIES IN PREDICTING INTENSITY CHANGE WE MUST NOW ALLOW FOR THE DISTINCT POSSIBILITY THAT ALBERTO COULD BECOME A HURRICANE," wrote forecaster Richard Pasch, even as the National Hurricane Center put out a hurricane warning for the Florida Gulf Coast. In the end, only a few relatively arbitrary miles per hour prevented Alberto from reaching the hurricane threshold, but psychologically it made all the difference: Had Alberto come ashore as a "hurricane" it would have been the earliest to strike Florida in forty years, and the chatter would have been dramatic. Instead, the storm weakened and made landfall with winds of less than 50 miles per hour (still enough to drive a four-foot storm surge at Cedar Key). Hurricane or no hurricane, the season seemed off to a vigorous—and early—start.

So did the rhetoric. While Alberto brewed in the Gulf, in a Democratic Party fundraiser speech in Florida former president Bill Clinton stated, "It is now generally recognized that while Al Gore and I were ridiculed, we were right about global warming. It's a serious problem. It's going to lead to more hurricanes." Unless he was trying to make the fairly nuanced point that a general strengthening of the average storm will lead more tropical storms to reach the hurricane class—which seems doubtful—Clinton had confused the question of storm intensification with that of storm numbers.

As it happened, Alberto and another land-falling tropical storm, Ernesto, turned out to be the worst the 2006 Atlantic hurricane season had to throw at the United States. Those expecting yet another banner year of destruction were proven incorrect, as this time around both Gray's and NOAA's forecasts turned out to have dramatically overpredicted the season's activity levels. In part due to a very slow August, the Atlantic saw only ten total storms, five hurricanes, and two major hurricanes, Gordon and Helene, both of which reached Category 3 intensity but remained at sea. Hurricane Florence did give some modest trouble to the tiny Atlantic island of Bermuda, and Gordon to the Azores. But 2006 was the first year since 1997 that did not feature a single Category 4 or 5 storm in the Atlantic.

In anticipation of another nasty season, however, the National Hurricane Center had hired four new forecasters in early 2006. In a year whose biggest dramas featured arguments over storm names rather than nail biting and mass evacuations, they put in almost no overtime. In July, Stacy Stewart touched off a big debate when he declared: "THE CORRECT PRONUNCIATION OF TROPICAL STORM BERYL IS BERLE...LIKE THE LAST NAME OF MILTON BERLE." Twelve hours later, this necessitated a partial retraction from James Franklin:

REGARDING THE PRONUNCIATION OF BERYL...A REVIEW OF SEVERAL DICTIONARIES SHOWS THAT BOTH BER'-IL AND BURL ARE ACCEPTED PRONUNCIATIONS...AND IN FACT THE NATIONAL WEATHER SERVICE DIRECTIVE SPECIFIES THE FORMER...TWO SYLLABLE...PRONUNCIATION. THE ONLY BERYL I PERSONALLY KNOW ALSO PRONOUNCES IT BER'-IL. WE APOLOGIZE FOR ANY CONFUSION.

Then in early August came Tropical Storm Chris, which led to invocations of the "curse" of Chris: Storms that receive this name have traditionally been pretty wimpy. (As Chris Landsea observed, it's a good curse to have.) Sure enough, although initially Chris seemed on a dangerous path aimed at the Gulf, it dissipated without reaching hurricane status.

The considerably less active 2006 season did not vindicate anyone in the hurricane–climate debate. "We're going to have quiet years for sure," Kerry Emanuel explained, "but we probably won't see a quiet decade." Simply put, natural and random variability remain powerful enough that any single hurricane season can buck any trend, whether up or down. In 2006, a number of factors helped create an inhospitable environment for Atlantic storms. In downgrading their forecast for September—they admitted their August forecast had been a "bust" and now expected a slightly below-average year—Gray and Klotzbach remarked upon some of them, including mid-level dryness over the tropical Atlantic and large amounts of atmospheric dust blown off Africa. The surprise onset of El Niño then further shut down hurricane activity for October and November. (The European three-model forecasting ensemble, which successfully picked up El Niño, predicted a 12.1 storm season in the Atlantic by June 2006, thus beating the statistical forecasts by a significant margin for that year.)

But although the Atlantic was calmer in 2006, one cannot extrapolate a global picture from a single season in a single basin. The Northeast Pacific, on the other side of Central America from the Caribbean, had a very active year in 2006, so much so that at moments it seemed the U.S. West Coast and Southwest had more to fear from hurricanes than the Gulf and East coasts. In particular, Hurricane John, a Category 4 at its peak, closely hugged the Mexican coast as it tracked northwest toward an ultimate landfall at the southern tip of the Baja California peninsula. It's possible to imagine a storm with similar origins cutting west of the peninsula and then following the coast north as far as Southern California, as the unnamed 1858 San Diego storm may have done.

Instead, as John moved inland it caused flooding in El Paso. Not long afterward, another intense coast-hugging hurricane, Category 3 Lane, slammed Mexico and once again delivered anomalous rainfall to Texas. Finally in mid-November came Hurricane Sergio, very nearly a Category 3, which sounded a lot like one of the November–December Atlantic storms of 2005. Sergio wound up being the strongest known Northeast Pacific hurricane for so late in the year, as well as the longest-lived November storm in the basin—two more "records." All in all, the Northeast Pacific, where hurricane activity had previously been trending downward, saw eighteen named storms and five major hurricanes.

Just a bit farther west, meanwhile, August 2006 brought one of the most spectacular tropical cyclones in known history. The hurricane and supertyphoon called Ioke shattered numerous records, most notably by virtue of its long lifetime at strong intensity. Emanuel might have considered the storm a kind of free advertisement for his power dissipation index.

Ioke, whose name is the Hawaiian version of "Joyce," formed in a "basin" that doesn't rank among the traditional six where hurricanes regularly develop—the Central Pacific, which is officially the region north of the equator between 140 W Longitude and the International Date Line (180 Longitude). Although in his 1968 paper Gray had asserted that hurricanes "do not occur" in the Central Pacific, we now know that's far too absolute a statement. Storms often travel there after forming in the Northeast Pacific off the coast of Mexico and then drifting across the ocean. But they do not originate in the Central Pacific with a very high frequency, which is a good thing, because storms in this region can pose a severe threat to Hawaii (especially during El Niño years). In 1992, Hurricane Iniki delivered one of the most intense U.S. landfalls ever after it directly struck the island of Kaua'i at Category 4 strength, causing nearly $3 billion in damage. Because of storms like this, an official Central Pacific hurricane naming system exists, and Honolulu hosts a Central Pacific Hurricane Center. Before Ioke, though, the basin had not given birth to a storm since 2002.

Ioke developed 745 miles south of Honolulu on August 19; a day later, it was a rapidly intensifying hurricane. By August 21, it was launching so much of the lower atmosphere into the air above that it ranked as a Category 4 storm with a central pressure of 945 millibars (27.91 inches). Ioke then weakened as it struck Johnston Atoll, a U.S. possession comprised of four islands moored atop a coral reef that hosts a wildlife refuge, on August 22. But these were still the storm's early days.

On August 24 and 25, as Ioke moved west over warm and open waters, it deepened again, ultimately growing into a Category 5 storm with sustained winds estimated at 160 miles per hour. A discussion from forecaster Robert Burke of the Central Pacific Hurricane Center conveyed the significance of this development:

THIS IS THE FIFTH CATEGORY 5 HURRICANE ON RECORD IN THE CENTRAL PACIFIC...AND THE FIRST ONE SINCE 1994. IOKE IS THE FIRST STORM TO DEVELOP WITHIN THE CENTRAL PACIFIC AND ACHIEVE CATEGORY 5 STATUS. JOHN...EMILIA AND GILMA MOVED IN FROM THE EASTERN PACIFIC BEFORE STRENGTHENING...WHILE PATSY CAME IN FROM THE WEST PACIFIC. AT THE SAME TIME...THE ESTIMATED SURFACE PRESSURE FROM SATELLITE ANALYSIS WAS 921MB OR 27.20 INCHES. THIS UNOFFICIALLY IS THE LOWEST SURFACE PRESSURE FOR A SYSTEM IN THE CENTRAL PACIFIC.

The next day, as Ioke approached the International Date Line and therefore the Northwest Pacific, the storm improved upon the final record by tipping the mercury down to 920 millibars (27.17 inches). Meanwhile, in the Central Pacific Hurricane Center's final bulletin as Ioke moved beyond its area of responsibility, lead forecaster Jeffrey Powell noted that another first might be in the offing: "IOKE COULD ENTER THE RECORD BOOKS FOR LONGEVITY AS A CATEGORY 4 OR GREATER STORM."

Ioke didn't disappoint. It crossed the date line as a Category 5 storm, becoming Supertyphoon Ioke on August 27. Then it weakened down to Category 4 again, but restrengthened to Category 5 for a third time on August 29. The final weakening began the next day, even as Ioke prepared to pass directly over (and apparently submerge) tiny Wake Island, whose 188 personnel, mostly military, were evacuated. Later, when the Central Pacific Hurricane Center tabulated the data, it became official:

THE 198 CONSECUTIVE HOURS IOKE EXISTED AT OR ABOVE CATEGORY 4 INTENSITY WAS THE LONGEST

CONTINUOUS TIME PERIOD AT THAT INTENSITY
EVER OBSERVED FOR ANY TROPICAL CYCLONE ANY-
WHERE ON EARTH.

Two years earlier, Hurricane Ivan had lasted at this intensity for 192 hours. But now the champion was Ioke. While other hurricanes had certainly been stronger for periods of time, none on record had remained so intense for so long. Later, Ioke approached Japan but recurved northward well before reaching the islands, ultimately slamming Alaska as a powerful extra-tropical cyclone.

In 2006 it was not Japan but the Philippines that experienced the most relentless onslaught of typhoons. From late September through mid-December 2006, the island nation suffered a stunning five major typhoon strikes, four of them from storms that had undergone bouts of rapid intensification prior to landfall (Xangsane, Cimaron, Chebi, and Durian). "It's unusual to see one storm do this in a season, let alone three—and all in the same place!" wrote an amazed Jeff Masters during Chebi. And that was well before the arrival of Supertyphoon Durian, the deadliest tropical cyclone of 2006. Once again rapidly intensifying and hitting the Philippines, Durian poured down rain over the Mayon Volcano on the island of Luzon, dislodging volcanic ash from its slopes that coursed downhill and buried villages. The precise number of resulting deaths will probably never be known, but it may well have exceeded 1,000. And then little more than a week later the fifth typhoon, Utor, hit the island, piling on still more suffering.

In sum, despite what happened in the Atlantic, 2006—like 2004 and 2005—featured many incredible hurricanes. That includes what may have been the strongest Southern Hemisphere storm ever observed (Monica), and what is officially the longest-lived intense storm, Ioke. The records set were yet again consistent with—though still not proof of—a global warming–induced intensification of hurricanes. They didn't make you certain, but they certainly made you wonder.

In the United States in 2006, the highest-profile political leaders acknowledged the potency of the hurricane–climate issue. On July 31,

George W. Bush himself stopped by the National Hurricane Center (for a "P.R. tour," the Florida Democratic Party charged). There, Bush met with Max Mayfield and Chris Landsea, who explained his reasons for being skeptical that global warming is dramatically intensifying hurricanes and told Bush there was "not a consensus" on the issue. Landsea also got to place in the president's hands a copy of a paper he'd published in *Science*, criticizing the Emanuel-Webster work.

Landsea dressed sharply for the occasion; the official White House photo shows him in crisp white shirt and tie. But he wasn't above having a little fun with the encounter. On his office door, a doctored image shows Landsea and Bush, the latter patting the former on the head as he sits in front of a computer. Instead of suits, they're wearing Hawaiian shirts. Bush looks like a *South Park* character with his clumsily doctored torso. Landsea remembers the president being "short"— he certainly is compared to Landsea—and does an impression of his folksy voice. He's not sure Bush fully grasped the point that if we want to study how hurricanes are changing, we must also take into account how our means of perceiving them have changed.

Peter Webster and Judith Curry, too, got their high-profile meeting with a politician in 2006. Two months earlier, they'd had an audience in Tallahassee with then-governor Jeb Bush as well as current governor Charlie Crist, who was the state attorney general at the time. Webster and Curry took the opportunity to tell both leaders that global warming might be increasing Florida's hurricane risks. According to Curry's notes from the encounter, Crist was very attentive and in a later interview "made it clear that he bought our arguments." As for Bush, the first thing he apparently said was: "Georgia Tech? Are you two the ones that got in the pissing match with Bill Gray that [I] read about in the newspaper?" The governor was amused because "you didn't typically see this kind of behavior from scientists."

Bush paid close attention to the scientists' presentation, asked intelligent questions about the data, and apparently agreed that even if the Webster-Curry results weren't conclusive, the possibility of an increased risk to Florida had to be taken seriously. He told the scientists that the 2004 and 2005 hurricane seasons had "changed his life."

And he called for climate researchers and Florida's hurricane specialists to jointly get to the bottom of the issue, to "take the politics out
of this." The climate scientists seemed to leave the encounter considerably more impressed by the governor than Landsea had been by the
president.

Most revealing, though, is the contrast between how the two
politicians treated the science (at least according to the recollections of
the scientists who met with them). George took the opportunity to
selectively hear about scientific uncertainty and doubt from Landsea.
There's no indication he heard another side at all. But Jeb, who'd governed Florida through two disastrous hurricane seasons, seemed more
open to the subtler but significant point that scientific uncertainty
notwithstanding, the possibility of an increased risk remained deeply
worrisome.

Broadly speaking, the two brothers' contrasting attitudes toward
a potential hurricane–climate risk tracked two opposed positions about
the proper role of science in political decision-making, which we might
dub "sound science" and the "precautionary principle." And those two
positions, in turn, map (albeit imperfectly) onto our current political
divide in the United States.

"Sound science," generally although not exclusively associated
with the political right (the slogan has in fact been linked in part to
the efforts of the tobacco industry), emphasizes satisfying a very high
burden of proof before scientific information can serve as the basis for
significant political action—especially *expensive* action. By contrast,
the "precautionary principle" asserts that we cannot always wait for
all the evidence to come in before we respond or take action. If we
wait, the problem suggested by the latest data—however tentatively—
could worsen while we study it. The idea here is that scientific knowledge is always incomplete, but what else is new? Policymakers must
constantly make decisions in the face of scant evidence, and the best
they can do is commit to revising those decisions, if necessary, once
more evidence comes in.

Both principles can be taken to extremes or abused. The decision
to go to war in Iraq, despite at best tentative evidence of dangers posed

by that country to the United States, could be considered an extreme application of the precautionary principle. ("Preemptive war" is inherently a precautionary policy.) At the other end of the spectrum, the calls for "sound science" by global-warming deniers like Senator James Inhofe—even in the face of broad scientific consensus across the expert assessment bodies that have ascribed ongoing warming to human activities—clearly impose an unreasonable burden of proof before action can be taken to address the problem.

For some scientists involved in the hurricane–climate debate, the magnitude of the battle, and the degree of not-always-desirable visibility that it brought them, prompted much soul searching. They responded in different ways, but one of the most intriguing reactions came from Judith Curry of Georgia Tech, whose personal experience with science in the public arena she alternatively likened to "Alice falling down the rabbit hole" and to "falling out of the Ivory Tower." Curry's encounters drove her to reflect not only on the science but on the politics, the sociology, and (as one scientist has put it) the "mediarology" of the situation.

Curry had been shocked by the media blitz that followed the publication of the Webster-team paper. As the circus unfolded, she began to think about how poorly prepared her scientific training had left her for such high-profile conflicts. At the same time, Curry wondered why the formal scientific publication process seemed incapable of providing information about hot-button issues, such as hurricanes and global warming, in either the form or at the pace that the public and media desired.

In general, scientific training and scientific publication alike seemed, to Curry, to deemphasize the practical or useful. Most scientists are taught little if anything, during their formative years, about how to communicate their findings to the public. Instead, they're inculcated into an ivory-tower culture of *publish, publish, publish.* They learn how to communicate with one another in highly technocratic language, but not how to talk to middle America (indeed, having a scientific training probably makes it *harder* to talk to middle America). The scientific journals, meanwhile, are often more inclined to publish papers that perform some sort of nifty analytical trick or introduce a complex new methodology than papers that present simple but useful analyses, or outline the big picture in a way that's comprehensible to policymakers and the general public. The hurricane–climate debate had exposed a large disconnect between the way scientists approach their work and the way politicians, advocates, and journalists approach it.

Especially journalists: Curry had been most stung by the *Wall Street Journal* article that quoted her accusing Gray of "brain fossilization." She doesn't recall using those words in the interview (although the *Journal*'s Atlanta bureau chief, Doug Blackmon, says the paper stands by the quotation). But more important, Curry regretted both the widespread perception created by the article that the debate had descended into mud-slinging and the implication that she'd helped to bring that about. So she began to explore different means of communicating about science, and before long committed a heresy that's growing increasingly common among researchers. She began to contribute heavily to discussions about the hurricane–climate issue taking place upon a number of blogs that, in the temporary absence of many fresh results from the official journals, had become the dominant sources of high-level commentary on the subject (despite the lack of a formal peer-review system for blog content).

Perhaps the top blogs for debate on hurricanes and global warming were RealClimate (www.realclimate.org), started by a group of leading climate researchers, and Prometheus (http://sciencepolicy.colorado.edu/prometheus/), run by Roger Pielke, Jr., a political scientist and hurricane policy expert. The two had different tones. RealClimate warned against attributing any individual storm to global warming but took the general results of the Emanuel and Webster studies very seriously, and scathingly criticized Gray; while Pielke generally took a more sympathetic approach to the hurricane specialists (with whom he'd coauthored papers). Pielke also repeatedly made the argument that has become his trademark: Even if hurricanes are intensifying due to global warming, so what? For as Pielke noted, the largest source of hurricane vulnerability in the United States sprang from societal and demographic trends—namely, a mass movement of persons and property to vulnerable coastal areas, such as the state of Florida. We had made ourselves into sitting ducks, Pielke argued, and whether or not climate change was amplifying the problem, the proper fix resided not in the Kyoto Protocol (although greenhouse gas reductions could be justified on other grounds), but rather in improvements to building codes, emergency-preparedness plans, and other lower-profile but more practical solutions.

When I dropped in to speak with Curry at her office at Georgia Tech in March 2006, she described herself as a "lurker" on the blogs: She read but didn't comment. But before long lurking led to commenting, and then commenting became very frequent indeed, until by late 2006 Curry had given one of her classes an assignment to evaluate another heavily read global-warming blog, ClimateAudit.org, which has a generally contrarian take on the science and where she had been posting comments in a kind of field experiment in science communication. (The students didn't seem to appreciate the medium nearly as much as she did.)

Curry's partner and coauthor Peter Webster also experimented with blogging. Following Gray's speech in Monterey—where he had publicly questioned the hurricane expert's depiction of the thermohaline circulation—Webster went farther by posting an essay-length critique of the presentation to RealClimate. There he scathingly summarized Gray's approach to the science as analogous to "putting together a jigsaw puzzle, ignoring the picture on the box and using a hammer to force the pieces together irrespective of what the final picture finally produced."

But Webster wasn't the blog denizen that Curry had become. In one revealing episode, Curry used a thread of blog comments on Real-Climate to post material that she had been "asked to remove" from a peer-reviewed article that she, Webster, and Holland had published about their experiences following the appearance of their attention-grabbing 2005 paper on hurricane intensification. The excised material included this notable passage:

> The prevailing views on the topic of hurricanes and global change differ considerably between hurricane forecasters and climate researchers. The consensus view of hurricane forecasters is

to attribute the warming in the North Atlantic and the associated [increase] in hurricane frequency and intensity to natural variability. The consensus view of climate researchers is to attribute the warming, particularly since 1970, to have a substantial component associated with greenhouse warming. These discrepancies can be understood at least in part by clarifying the source of these differing perspectives. The hurricane forecaster focuses on predicting the path and intensity of land falling hurricanes, and also makes seasonal forecasts. They work on verifying their forecasts, and they are also experts on hurricane data. On the other hand, the climate researcher does not focus on forecasting but rather applies the scientific method to understanding the underlying physical processes and causes of climate variability. The climate researcher has expertise on climate data records and statistical methods.

Curry went on to describe how the fragmentation of NOAA—which contains branches heavily populated by researchers of both specialties (such as the Geophysical Fluid Dynamics Laboratory and the National Hurricane Center), but with far too little communication or collaboration between them, in her view—exacerbated this divide. "A dichotomy has developed in the U.S. between the operational forecasting community and the meteorological research community, a dichotomy that does not exist in Europe," she noted in another passage removed from her paper. For instance, while GFDL and the National Hurricane Center are located hundreds of miles from one another, at the United Kingdom's Met Office in Exeter, climate researchers and weather forecasters work within the same large building, quite literally sharing office space.

Yet such sociological observations, although pivotal to understanding the climate–hurricane debate, apparently weren't "scientific" enough to be included in Curry's paper (for the *Bulletin of the American Meteorological Society*). So she threw them up on RealClimate instead. "We certainly live in interesting times, and the blogosphere adds a unique element to this," Curry wrote in conclusion to her post. "I appreciate the opportunity for a venue to post what I couldn't publish on the topic."

Eventually new scientific papers did begin trickling out, many inspired by the findings of Emanuel and Webster. Some—further work by the Webster group, for instance—seemed to bolster the original results. Others—papers by Patrick Michaels, Chris Landsea, and Gray's student Phil Klotzbach—cast doubt upon them. NOAA's Gerry Bell, who had dismissed hurricane–climate linkages during the 2005 season, also co-authored a paper suggesting that natural "modes" of variability were controlling Atlantic hurricane activity. In short, the scientific process was once again working—and not going anywhere quickly.

The most striking thing about the new papers was where many were originating. There apparently had been a mass movement of climate researchers into the hurricane field—a development that Curry, for one, welcomed. "To me the fundamental significance of our paper, whether it's right or wrong, is that we've now brought climate scientists and oceanographers into hurricane research, rather than just leaving it to the card-carrying tropical cyclone people plus Kerry Emanuel," she told me.

Trenberth had been one of the earliest dyed-in-the-wool climate researchers to take up hurricanes. He'd done a 2005 study reporting an increase in atmospheric water vapor over the global oceans, and now had a new paper downplaying the magnitude and significance of the Atlantic Multidecadal Oscillation. Michael Mann, another climate researcher best known for his attempts to reconstruct historic temperature trends stretching back before the period of thermometer readings, collaborated with Emanuel on a paper that did likewise. They attributed the relatively cool conditions in the tropical Atlantic during the 1960s through the 1980s (linked to a downturn in hurricane activity) to a competition between a long-term global warming trend and a human-induced regional cooling associated with the emission of sulfate aerosols. In this account, the abrupt warming in the 1990s, and the associated increase in hurricane activity, came about when aerosol cooling diminished and the global-warming signal was finally unmasked. Thus for Mann and Emanuel, a "natural cycle" had little or nothing to do with patterns of Atlantic hurricane activity.

Perhaps the tour de force from the climate community, however, came in September 2006, after a quiet August for hurricanes in the Atlantic. Ben Santer of the Lawrence Livermore National Laboratory and Tom Wigley of the National Center for Atmospheric Research led a massive team of researchers that used twenty-two different climate models to explore the reasons for warming sea temperatures (ranging from .32 to .67 degrees Celsius during the twentieth century) in the key Atlantic and Pacific regions of hurricane formation. They found that while natural variations may have played a role, human factors had to be invoked as the "dominant influence" to explain the warming trend, especially in recent decades. The study helped further cement the conclusion that humans have been heating the oceans, and especially the tropical waters that serve as hurricane breeding grounds; its great advance was to hone in on these particular zones, rather than studying temperature changes across the entire world ocean.

Yet the work was very misleadingly sold to the press by Resource Media, an environmentalist public relations firm that organized a conference call to announce the results. The group's news release stated that the new research "provides the final link in the warming/hurricane causal chain by showing that global warming, not a natural cycle, is heating the oceans in the key hurricane formation regions, and driving intensified hurricane activity." In a subsequent media conference call, Wigley stated that his work "kind of closes the loop here"—again suggesting that the central remaining issue in the hurricane–climate debate was whether humans are causing tropical oceans to warm.

In truth, that's one of the *least* unresolved questions. Far more disputed are the reliability of the past hurricane-intensity data and the issue of precisely how warmer seas will affect hurricanes in the varying basins, and the study didn't address either subject. Not surprisingly, Gray fired out his own release, calling the new work's significance "grossly exaggerated." "It is expected that increased federal funding for tropical cyclone research is in the works," Gray added. But while Gray still disputed whether human beings were actually responsible for ocean warming—or any other kind of significant warming—Landsea was more than willing to concede the point. "To me, that's not a big issue," he explained.

The Santer-Wigley paper caused another blip in hurricane–climate media coverage, even without any land-falling storms to accompany it. Journalists covered any news in this area now. And following the cue of Resource Media, some misleadingly framed the findings as cementing the link between human activities and hurricane intensification. The scientists themselves had partly enabled this. They had become caught up in a losing political strategy employed by too many environmentalists and activists generally: tout each new study in a scientific journal that seems consistent with your goals. That may be a safe practice when a strong consensus exists on a subject, such as the basic question of whether global warming is happening and caused by humans. But when the scientific peer-review process is producing what *New York Times* reporter Andrew Revkin has described as a "windshield wiper" effect—one study pushes the debate one way, another pushes it back—this tack can't be defended. If serious environmentalists want to capitalize on the hurricane–climate issue without overplaying the still-developing science, they need to learn a new playbook.

And indeed, environmental advocates had a better way of advancing their cause. They were about to be given a huge gift by the Bush administration: yet another NOAA scandal over the suppression of science. Thinking as a strategic communication specialist might, environmentalists didn't need a "scientific" angle to frame their story and advance their interests. They had a "public accountability" angle that was far more powerful.

In light of the controversies of early 2006, the protesters on its doorstep calling for resignations in late May, and the obvious fact that scientists and journalists alike were scrutinizing NOAA and expecting improvement, one might think the agency would strive to clean up its act. Instead, while some well-meaning scientists launched an internal attempt to achieve precisely that objective, they were once again thwarted.

In the fall of 2006, as the Atlantic hurricane season failed to rage, yet another NOAA scandal emerged, and it uncannily echoed the previous one. It was suddenly revealed (by a reporter writing for *Nature*) that several months earlier, timed for the start of the hurricane season,

NOAA had prepared a fact sheet to release to the public about hurricanes and global warming. The document had been drafted by an internal group of government experts, headed up by GFDL director Ants Leetmaa and including GFDL's Tom Knutson, Tom Delworth, and Ron Stouffer, the National Hurricane Center's Chris Landsea, Gerry Bell of the Climate Prediction Center, and Tom Karl of the National Climatic Data Center. The list may sound like a roundup of the usual suspects, but the grouping was significant: Two offices with disparate scientific outlooks, GFDL and the National Hurricane Center, had teamed up.

The group hammered out a compromise-oriented and not particularly controversial statement. It certainly did not endorse the findings of Emanuel and the Webster group. The statement merely noted the results of Knutson's modeling studies, and cited other research suggesting the Atlantic had been warming under the influence of global warming (which in turn provided "more fuel" for hurricanes). And that's it. Hardly controversial stuff, at least when judged by the standards of what was then under open debate within the world of science.

And yet amazingly, NOAA had failed to release the fact sheet at the start of the hurricane season as originally planned. Somewhere at the Department of Commerce it hit a snag, and Leetmaa got an e-mail on May 18 suggesting the document was "too technical" and not to be released. There followed nothing but silence—until the *Nature* exposé four months later, whereupon NOAA quickly released the document, as it should have done in the first place. But by then it was too late. Another media frenzy began, and the blogs swelled with indignation. Fourteen senators called for an investigation. As Democratic senator Frank Lautenberg of New Jersey charged, "The administration has effectively declared war on science and truth to advance its anti-environment agenda...The Bush administration continues to censor scientists who have documented the current impacts of global warming."

Meanwhile, NOAA administrator Lautenbacher acted as though he took the public for utter fools. First he asserted that the fact sheet had never been intended for distribution, and was promptly contradicted by Leetmaa and internal e-mails. Then he put out a statement in which he claimed, in contradiction to his previous statement, that the fact sheet "was being prepared for this year's hurricane season rollout" and was intended as an "easy-to-understand public document." This was an obvious attempt to skirt the issue, and while the admiral denounced the "mischaracterizations and falsehoods" in the latest media reports, he never bothered to explain why the fact sheet—which he described as scientifically accurate—had not been released as planned.

Leetmaa was outraged that a document that had been intended to increase NOAA's credibility—and surely would have—was having exactly the opposite effect, thanks to its suppression. The initial push to draft the fact sheet had grown out of the scandals earlier in the year, and the GFDL scientists' internal critiques of NOAA's skewed information on hurricanes and global warming. "It was basically trying to recoup from the bad PR NOAA got from that, coupled with the whole general issue that NOAA is muzzling its scientists," Leetmaa explains. "From that perspective, it was a goddamn disaster that somebody sat on it. I don't understand what the hell they were thinking. I don't know how they thought this would not come to light."

The Bush administration's repeated interferences with scientific information pertaining to global warming are so well documented at this point that it's impossible to claim there has been nothing unusual going on in the government in this regard. Yet whether these abuses are fully intentional remains debatable. The administration's misbehavior hardly seems the result of an intelligible—or intelligent—strategy. Once the act of scientific suppression comes to light, as it inevitably does, the ensuing negative publicity far exceeds any conceivable consequences of simply releasing accurate information in a timely fashion. Most likely, then, the repeated abuses spring not from some conscious conspiracy, but rather from the collective behavior of a large number of politicized bureaucrats who think they're doing the White House's bidding and who've been given far too much power over scientific information.

The result, alas, has been the shredding of an otherwise stellar agency's credibility. Interviewing Leetmaa about the fact-sheet episode in October of 2006, I asked what he thought should be done to restore NOAA's reputation. "I honestly don't know," Leetmaa said. "I think the hole is pretty deep right now."

On the morning of October 23, 2006, a few days after I spoke to Leetmaa, two protesters used an extension ladder to climb atop the NOAA building in Silver Spring, Maryland. Above the entrance they hung a banner: "Bush: Let NOAA Tell the Truth." They then spent several hours "perched on a ledge," according to the *Washington Post*. Apparently they brought food and drink along—and suction cups to keep themselves in place. They were planning to stay awhile.

Protesters on the ground, meanwhile, plied NOAA employees with information and once again called for the admiral's resignation. Unable to convince the rooftop protesters to come down, the police reportedly borrowed a cherry picker from a nearby construction site to fetch and arrest them (peacefully, of course). The men were members of Mike Tidwell's U.S. Climate Emergency Council, which had a press release at the ready. It cited the fact-sheet saga and new revelations about how Tom Knutson had been blocked from talking to the media about his research—"something the White House clearly wants to keep from wide public scrutiny," the release said.

One can question Tidwell's tactics, but NOAA had directly enabled them. At the start of the 2006 hurricane season, the agency could have released a careful and defensible fact sheet that would have undercut both the overwrought claims of Tidwell's group and claims that the agency was suppressing science. Instead, NOAA not only remained silent but—we now know—guiltily so.

No wonder environmentalists were scaling its roof.

# 14 • Hurricane Climatology

There was no hurricane swirling in the Atlantic on December 15, 2006, when Kerry Emanuel once again spoke at the American Geophysical Union meeting in San Francisco. It was just over a year since he'd issued his dramatic challenge to NOAA, telling the agency to stop censoring its scientists. A lot had changed since then. A lot hadn't.

NOAA had, once again, been caught gaming the dissemination of scientific information. The agency's lesson apparently had not been learned; perhaps the architecture of the Bush administration made such growth impossible. But Democrats had recently retaken Congress and stood poised to bring about a more significant shaming than either Emanuel or the news media could muster. Already, talk was circulating about congressional hearings to determine why political appointees seemed to be guiding the dissemination of sensitive scientific information across so many branches of the government. Democrats would be looking into the "war on science" that had been waged over the past six years, and NOAA and the Department of Commerce would not escape their attention. Democratic senator Frank Lautenberg of New Jersey, home to the GFDL, had said explicitly that he would press for hearings on the agency's behavior.

On the scientific front, there were also signs of movement. For starters, Emanuel had to some extent modified his thinking over the course of the year. He'd become less confident about some of his previously published conclusions, while he stood strongly by others. And he'd shifted his outlook for what any scientist would recognize as the right reason: New research made him change his mind.

Both sides had been eagerly awaiting the aforementioned study by meteorologist Jim Kossin of the Cooperative Institute for Meteorological Satellite Studies at the University of Wisconsin-Madison. Kossin, too, had been a student of Gray's at one time. As the hurricane–climate debate began to whirl wildly in 2005, he had volunteered to reanalyze the disputed storm-intensity data and help sort matters out. Both groups of scientists saw Kossin as a fair, unbiased arbiter.

The resulting study hadn't been officially published when Emanuel spoke in December. But it had gotten around, and Kossin had presented the results publicly. He and his team had created a homogenous global database of hurricane satellite images from July 1983 through December 2005—169,000 pictures of some two thousand storms, all of them at the same coarse resolution. Then Kossin's team applied an unvarying automated algorithm to each image to determine the storm's intensity. The whole approach was designed to get around the problem of changing human measurement practices over time—"primate change," as one of the study's coauthors had jokingly put it. The method might not be as accurate as storm flights, but it had the advantage of being entirely consistent.

When Kossin's results came out, they seemed to have something for everyone. Hurricane intensity had indeed been trending strongly upward in the Atlantic. And it had apparently been trending downward in the Northeast Pacific (the year 2006 had bucked both trends). This suggested that the data maintained by the National Hurricane Center, which tracks both basins and is the only global forecasting center to perform regular aircraft reconnaissance into storms, was highly reliable.

For the other basins, though, aircraft reconnaissance had either been canceled (as occurred in 1987 for the Northwest Pacific) or never carried out in the first place. And here Kossin's analysis suggested— in marked contradiction to the Emanuel and Webster studies—no significant upward trend in storm intensity. At least based upon this slicing of the data, then, the hurricane response to global warming *globally* didn't look nearly as predictable as anyone had thought. Kossin's was just one attempt to reanalyze the contested records, but if nothing else it certainly showed that they remained contested. As this book went to press, debate over the global hurricane intensity record showed no signs of any quick resolution.

Kossin's work had prompted Emanuel to modify his outlook. "I'd have to step back from part of those conclusions," he told me frankly when we talked in late October 2006 and I asked how his 2005 study stood up in light of Kossin's research. But Emanuel certainly wasn't stepping down on the Atlantic, the basin where the data were the most reliable and the trend best documented. Alongside Webster, Holland, and Curry, Emanuel increasingly suspected that when it came to hurricanes, the United States, Central America, and the Caribbean might be getting the worst of global warming—or at least might be seeing the effects of climate change in the most easily demonstrated fashion.

Storm numbers in the Atlantic basin had risen sharply since 1995, tracking rising tropical ocean temperatures; and more numerous storms had also meant more numerous intense ones (not because the proportion of intense to weak storms had changed, but simply because there were more storms in total). As Holland now put it in his presentations, looking toward the future, he could think of "no rational reason" to expect a decrease in Atlantic hurricane activity. Indeed, Holland's and Webster's growing confidence that the increase in Atlantic storm numbers could not be explained without invoking global warming had drawn them into a new data-centric argument with Landsea, this time over storm count records rather than storm intensity records.

That debate, too, remained unresolved, but its very existence signaled an evolution in scientific thinking since the 2005 hurricane season, and since the first appearance of the Emanuel and Webster team studies. While those famous papers had sought to demonstrate trends *across* global hurricane basins, it now seemed possible that global warming was affecting different parts of the world differently. In short, there might be winners and losers; the Atlantic might respond much more sensitively to warming oceans than, say, the Northwest Pacific. Given the complexity of the ocean-atmosphere system and the varied environmental factors that affect hurricanes, such an unpredictable response did not seem at all implausible. In fact, a climate-modeling study performed using Japan's powerful and high-resolution Earth Simulator had found a similar result: The Atlantic might have both more frequent and stronger storms, even as global storm numbers decreased on average (but global intensity increased).

If so, that probably meant only more trouble for the United States in the coming years.

It was in this context—of developing and changing knowledge—that Emanuel spoke in San Francisco. It was the day after Al Gore himself had held forth at the AGU conference, decrying political interference with climate science and telling thousands of geoscientists that they must learn to become better communicators, to explain and defend the knowledge they had brought into the world. So many scientists had shown up to hear Gore that they couldn't all fit into the San Francisco Mariott's giant lecture salon, and hundreds wound up watching the speech on video screens. For this crowd, global warming was a foregone conclusion.

Attendance at the meeting itself was higher than ever this year—more than 14,000—and the number of scientists giving papers on hurricanes and climate had also spiked. There were so many presenters that they'd been split up into separate panels. New results were coming in about everything from model-projected changes in future vertical wind shear to the quality of the hurricane database. This profusion of interest, more than anything else, showed that the process of science was ultimately working in the way it's designed to—despite the many interferences over the past year by the media, government agencies, and special-interest groups, and despite scientists themselves sometimes making matters worse.

By the time Emanuel's talk began, the presentation room at the Moscone Center was full. But anyone expecting fireworks this time around had come to the wrong place. Emanuel spoke in his trademark well-punctuated complete sentences and refrained entirely from political remarks. Matters were considerably calmer after the 2006 hurricane season than they'd been after the 2005 one, and the talk reflected that mood.

Instead, Emanuel presented a sublimely simple review of what we know about hurricanes and climate, especially as it concerns the Atlantic. Storm numbers there had been rising; so had hurricane power dissipation; and it all closely followed a trend of rising sea temperatures. Emanuel particularly emphasized that we must stop focusing narrowly on traditional measurements, such as storm numbers and intensities, to gauge overall hurricane activity: "I happen to think that's not what nature really cares about." Weak tropical storms shouldn't be viewed as "in the same league" as Category 5 hurricanes, Emanuel explained. Look at how much total power storms were dissipating in the Atlantic—that was the measure that followed sea surface temperatures most closely of all.

At this juncture Emanuel introduced an equation, a long and complicated hieroglyphic that governed the maximum theoretical wind speed that a given hurricane has the potential to achieve. For those who could not decipher it, he explained some of its terms: the sea-surface temperature, the outflow temperature, the speed of the trade winds, the greenhouse effect itself. The equation plainly showed that sea-surface temperatures aren't the only factor controlling a hurricane's theoretically achievable intensity. But for the Atlantic's main hurricane-formation region, sea temperatures were unmistakably trending upward.

Some scientists, Emanuel had noted, had postulated a natural cycle to explain all this. In fact, the presenter who had preceded Emanuel, modeler Tom Delworth of GFDL, had argued that a global warming trend had been laid atop a natural oceanic cycle in the Atlantic. But Emanuel didn't think Delworth's more middling approach could cut it, at least when it came to the regions of the Atlantic critical to hurricanes. For as he explained in his talk, "You can't see much difference between the tropical summertime North Atlantic, where the hurricanes develop, and the Northern Hemisphere temperature." This suggested a simpler explanation, Emanuel said: Whatever was causing the

Northern Hemisphere temperature change was also causing temperature changes in the hurricane development region.

That thing, of course, was global warming.

There Emanuel ended, without even driving home the point, because he didn't really need to. The implication was clear, and what remained unsaid was just as powerful as what had been stated. The global picture of how hurricanes were responding to climate change still posed many mysteries; but for the Atlantic, much seemed to be coming into focus. And it didn't look hopeful at all.

Something else remained unsaid, at least for the moment. It hadn't yet been announced, but Emanuel had been named the 2007 recipient of the American Meteorological Society's Carl-Gustaf Rossby Research Medal, the society's highest honor and the meteorological equivalent of being inducted into baseball's Hall of Fame. In Emanuel's case, it was hard to imagine that the timing of the award could be purely coincidental. Not after the 2005 hurricane season, and the high-level science fight that had followed it.

Two decades earlier, Emanuel had fundamentally linked hurricanes to the climate, and to the greenhouse effect, through his thermodynamic account of how hurricanes work, why they intensify, and the maximum potential intensity they can achieve under different environmental conditions. And now, thanks to innumerable factors that included not only the significance of his work but also politics and the weather itself, these ideas had become some of the most influential in all of meteorology.

When two simultaneously churning hurricanes move close to one another, they can sometimes get drawn into an elaborate cyclonic dance known as a Fujiwhara interaction, in which the storms seem to lock arms (or at any rate, rain bands) and twirl around a central point even as they also move together in the same direction.

One theme that emerged from much of the research presented at the December 2006 AGU meeting was that hurricanes and the climate system might, in a very broad sense, be locked in their own interactive dance. Even as the climate changed hurricanes, hurricanes might also change the climate. It was just the sort of idea you'd expect to see emerge as a bunch of climate scientists stampeded into a field like hurricane research. And once again, it represented a potential change in paradigm from what had gone before.

In the 1979 paper that introduced his famous six genesis parameters, and the even more famous 80-storms-per-year figure, Gray had discounted the idea that hurricanes play an essential role in the climate system on a mega-scale. "The tropical cyclones' contribution to the globe's mass, moisture and energy budget could probably be accomplished (were their formation not to occur) by a greater number of weaker tropical disturbances existing in their place," he wrote. But scientists like Emanuel, Trenberth, Holland, and Webster had now begun to think about the matter very differently.

As usual, Emanuel had been the first. For half a decade, he'd been arguing that hurricanes shape the climate by stirring the seas and driving ocean heat transport, with stronger storms helping to drive more heat to the poles than weaker ones and with stronger storms occurring in warmer climates. New research on this subject now appeared at the AGU meeting, where it became apparent that Emanuel had inspired a number of younger scientists—his own band of protégés—to take up the matter. As one of them, Matthew Huber of Purdue University, put it to me, "The good news is that the world may have a tropical thermostat that helps keep the planet cool. And the bad news is that that may be tropical cyclones running around all the time."

At the same time, Trenberth, Webster, and Holland had been advancing a complementary account of the role of hurricanes in the climate system. They started out from the fundamental observation that hurricanes are a powerful mechanism for extracting the ocean's warmth and transporting it many miles into the air, using some of that energy to drive winds in the process. In short, hurricanes do a great deal to transport heat out of the tropics, where especially during the summertime, energy from the beating sun accumulates in the oceans. That heat cannot simply radiate back up to space due to the strong greenhouse effect of water vapor over the oceans. This makes convection—in the form of both tropical thunderstorms and hurricanes—a critical mechanism for keeping the system in balance.

Compared to individual thunderstorms, however, hurricanes do a far more efficient job of pumping heat above the lower parts of the atmosphere and cooling down the oceans. So the climate scientists reasoned that hurricanes might in some sense be a "release valve," a way of ventilating the tropical oceans and redistributing heat. "Would the climate system notice if they didn't occur? I think it would," says Trenberth. If so, that could have a very large bearing on how hurricanes might change as the climate changes. Indeed, it suggested that they would *have* to change, perhaps quite dramatically, to keep pace with a warming world.

Collectively, then, Webster, Trenberth, Holland, and Emanuel were postulating that hurricanes might play a role in the climate system similar to—if perhaps less obvious than—the role played by extra-tropical cyclones, which mix together warm tropical and cold polar air and thus also redistribute heat. Emanuel focused on how hurricanes might perform this climate-scale task through the oceans; Webster, Holland, and Trenberth focused on the atmosphere. But they converged on this point: Hurricanes might be having a nontrivial impact on the global climate system, and this effect had not previously been taken into account, especially in climate models.

This kind of thinking, in turn, seemed to finally promise a way of solving a great mystery: Why are there about 80 or 90 tropical cyclones per year, as opposed to 8 or 9, as opposed to 800 or 900? The climate scientists suspected this general regularity existed because, in some sense, that was the right number of storms to perform a particular "job" within the present climate. In the context of a changing climate, however, there was no guarantee these numbers would remain the same—especially since when it comes to stirring the oceans, or pumping heat out of them and into the atmosphere, all storms aren't equal. "If you think of hurricanes as the cart horses of taking energy away from the tropics, then you need less of them if they're stronger," Webster explained. Along similar lines, Emanuel's approach emphasized that the strongest hurricanes perform much more ocean mixing and thus theoretically ought to bring about much more heat transport.

To be sure, much of this reasoning remains at a fairly early and speculative stage. But we'll get firmer answers about the role of hurricanes in the climate system soon enough, and some may come from the field of "paleotempestology"—also a prominent focus at the AGU meeting. The term, originally coined by Emanuel, refers to the study of how hurricanes have varied in past eras of the Earth's history, including periods characterized by very different climates. It's a new field and faces significant hurdles. Tracing hurricane activity back into the past, whether through historical archives or through other types of naturally preserved records (so-called proxies), is tough work. Yet here, too, intriguing results seem to be rolling in.

In particular, scientists have learned that some coastal lakes, marshes, and ponds preserve evidence of "overwash" events, in which powerful hurricane storm surges deposited sand layers that can be detected in sediments and dated, thus providing a sense of how frequently the strongest storm events recurred. Given enough paleotempestological records, a picture might emerge of how hurricane activity had varied in climatic regimes dating back thousands or even hundreds of thousands of years.

In fact, that's starting to happen. Taking sediment cores in western Long Island, Jeff Donnelly of the Woods Hole Oceanographic Institution has been able to identify the sand record left behind by the 1821 hurricane that gave William Redfield the idea of rotary storms. Other cores from the northeastern United States reflect the impact of the great 1938 New England Hurricane, 1954's Hurricane Carol, and others. Collectively, meanwhile, Donnelly's sediment cores taken from New England as well as from Vieques, Puerto Rico, suggest an apparent period of strong hurricane activity up until a thousand years ago, followed by a period of inactivity, followed by another period of strong activity starting around the year 1700 and running to the present.

Just as with research on hurricane–climate feedbacks, the study of hurricane variations on long time scales remains in its infancy. Still, it's hard to overstate the potential significance of this growing body of work. Call it the field of "hurricane climatology." Thermodynamic theories like Emanuel's and Holland's can calculate, for a given set of conditions, how powerful a single hurricane has the potential to become. But that's just one hurricane. The ability to understand global hurricanes in a global climatic context, however, could lead to a far more satisfying and complete theory of how storm numbers and intensities alike would change—would *have* to change—under varying climatic regimes. As Webster and Holland have put it, without understanding how hurricanes fit into the climate system or whether there's some type of trade-off between storm frequencies and storm intensities, "predicting the future characteristics of hurricanes in a warming world is merely statistical extrapolation."

At last, then, hurricane climatology may offer a way of integrating two fields of research that have remained at odds for too long. Hurricanes—unwisely ignored for many years by most climate scientists and meteorological dynamicists and taken up instead by a group of tropical meteorologists, many of whom didn't trust global warming—were finally being set into their grand climatic context.

In the fullest sense, the storms were being made part of the world.

In late 2006, Bill Gray, man of the Rockies, could be found hanging out in the swamps of Washington, D.C., a lot.

First, in October, the lifelong Democrat gave a talk at the Capitol Hill Club—also known as the "National Republican Club of Capitol Hill"—a predictably glitzy place with oil paintings of George H. W. Bush and Ronald Reagan on the walls, and a huge blown-up photograph of a grinning W. in the lobby. Behind a podium adorned with an elephant, in a room whose walls boasted still more paintings of great Republicans (Eisenhower and environmentalist Teddy Roosevelt this time), Gray discussed the 2006 hurricane year, his busted forecast ("we didn't do so well this season"), and of course, global warming. The talk was sponsored by the George C. Marshall Institute, a conservative think tank that had been undermining global warming concerns for over a decade, and that has been partly funded in recent years by ExxonMobil.

Despite his professed financial independence from fossil fuel interests, Gray has no problem doing events with industry-supported think tanks. As he sees it, the global warmers—especially the high-tech modelers with their expensive computers—get so much government research funding that this is just a way of evening out the ledger (though he says he doesn't accept direct industry payments). And to be fair, despite the many special interests circling the climate debate like sharks, it's impossible to believe Gray has in any sense been bought off. Clearly, his scientific conclusions about global warming spring from his particular empiricist philosophy and the course his career has taken, not from any sort of quid pro quo. Still, the help he gets in disseminating his arguments isn't necessarily disinterested.

At least by Gray's usual standards, the Marshall Institute talk didn't seem to go over very well. No one kept him to time, so he just kept on going for at least an hour as the lunchtime audience steadily dwindled. Many people had difficulty hearing him, because Gray kept lowering the hand-held microphone away from his mouth, sometimes all the way down to his waist, or even holding it behind his back. Later, he started trying to stuff the mike into his blazer breast pocket to free his hands. But it kept drooping, and once tumbled all the way to a floor with a loud crash. Gray also messed up the slide show. "I get worked up and press the wrong button," he said.

He had added some new content to his talk this time—theological content. One slide discussed "The Ascendancy of the Religion of Numerical Modeling and the loss of Meteorological Judgment and Reality." "I'm an older guy," Gray explained. "But when the computer came along…the younger people started to build models." Then came a cartoon depicting the "Climate Model Department" of the Oracle at Delphi, with stick-figure modelers bowing before a computer framed amid Greek columns.

"We prostrate ourselves before our all knowing GOD," said the scientific supplicants. "We humbly accept your GLOBAL WARMING judgment."

Back in Colorado a few weeks after the Marshall Institute speech, Gray unsurprisingly got into a spat with Kevin Trenberth at a workshop on the subject of climate diagnostics and prediction. The *Rocky Mountain News* was there watching, eating it up:

> Colorado State University's William Gray, one of the nation's preeminent hurricane forecasters, called noted Boulder climate researcher Kevin Trenberth an opportunist and a Svengali who "sold his soul to the devil to get (global warming) research funding."
>
> Trenberth countered that Gray is not a credible scientist.
>
> "Not any more. He was at one time, but he's not any more," Trenberth said of Gray....

Then, on November 7, 2006, the Democrats swept back into control of Congress. A week later, there was Gray—the secular scientist who didn't go to church, who'd accused climate modelers and even his own student Holland of having "come to religion," of believing on faith rather than evidence—standing beside Republican James Inhofe at a press conference on Capitol Hill. In addition to being a global warming denier, Inhofe is a right-wing evangelical Christian who has stated on the Senate floor:

> I believe very strongly that we ought to support Israel; that it has a right to the land. This is the most important reason: Because God said so. As I said a minute ago, look it up in the book of Genesis... This is not a political battle at all. It is a contest over whether or not the word of God is true.

At the event with Gray, Inhofe declared that even though the Senate and House of Representatives had changed hands, "our government is not going to embrace economy-killing carbon caps next Congress." He pledged to fight to kill them. As for Gray and the two other scientists who joined him, Inhofe offered them as proof that "climate skepticism—or evidence-based science—is alive and well."

And then Gray did his routine again—the water-vapor feedback was wrong, the thermohaline circulation controlled everything, the models were worthless. Cooling would come again soon. He was joined on the occasion by meteorologist Joe D'Aleo, who had co-founded the Weather Channel and also questioned the scientific consensus on global warming. As part of his presentation, D'Aleo flashed a slide declaring, "Only Constant in Nature is Change." The presentation added that "a great many climate scientists who work with the actual data see natural cycles at work."

It was all getting a little old by now.

Inhofe had made a stand with a few scientists backing him, but it was increasingly clear that he—and they—were the losers now. Soon Senator Barbara Boxer, who had given Gray some "real hell" of his own on the Senate floor a year earlier, would take control of what had been Inhofe's committee. Meanwhile, the UN's Intergovernmental Panel on Climate Change would, in its soon-to-be-released Fourth Assessment Report, attribute a greater than 90 percent certainty to the conclusion that human activities were driving the recent global warming trend—and even the Bush administration would start pretending that it had always accepted this scientific conclusion.

In short, although the world was changing, Gray hadn't. Whereas Emanuel had modified his view on global hurricane intensity trends in the face of new evidence, Gray—never reluctant to admit when he'd busted a forecast—couldn't seem to give any ground on global warming. Here was a man who never wanted to stop talking and arguing—and so he didn't. But he didn't seem to realize that his own words could hurt him.

Still, I'd come to admire Gray. After seeing him speak in locations across the country, having long talks with him about the history of hurricane research, and experiencing the occasional ribbing from him myself, I'd developed a liking for a man who, in his late seventies, had much more life to him than some people ever do, and could still overwhelm those around him by his sheer presence. Even as I knew I could never agree with Gray, I recognized that on some level I wanted him for my own mentor. I envied the scientists who'd had the fortune of studying under him.

That's what made it so hard to draw the line that had to be drawn.

No matter how much I might like Gray—or want to hang out with him and hear his jokes and stories—I couldn't recommend his view of the science of global warming to the public, or to the people in power who make decisions on behalf of us all. There's just too much at stake, and too little support for Gray's views among the broader scientific community.

For despite Gray's and Michael Crichton's sneering at scientific "consensus," it's really all we have—we laypersons, we journalists, we politicians—to go on. We watch scientists battle, and no matter how much of their debates we think we understand, if we're honest we know they're always a little bit ahead of us, knowing a little bit (or a lot) more. We can't presume to reliably guess which scientist is right and which is wrong as it all unfolds in real time. That would be the height of arrogance and foolishness. We can't pick winners—not unless the broader scientific process, in which they all participate, pulls them (or the bulk of them) together in a conclusion they strongly and collectively accept. On global warming itself, that has happened already. On global warming and hurricanes, it hasn't yet.

When it comes to this critical question of determining what science to trust if you're not a scientist yourself, Peter Webster likes to cite the philosopher Bertrand Russell:

> The scepticism that I advocate amounts only to this: (1) that when the experts are agreed, the opposite opinion cannot be held to be certain; (2) that when they are not agreed, no opinion can be regarded as certain by a non-expert; and (3) that when they all hold that no sufficient grounds for a positive opinion exist, the ordinary man would do well to suspend his judgment.

Russell added, "These propositions may seem mild, yet, if accepted, they would absolutely revolutionize human life."

Implicit in Russell's pithy statement is the principle that even when the "experts are agreed," it remains wholly possible that their consensus conclusion will turn out to be entirely wrong. It might, at any time, be overturned by other scientists who successfully initiate a true paradigm shift. Unless and until that happens, though, the "consensus" represents, better than anything else, the most fully developed scientific understanding that humanity possesses at a given point in time. It's synonymous with knowledge itself, as best we can discern it.

And we ignore that at our peril.

# CONCLUSION

# Home Again

There's no doubt about it: Global warming—which is already happening—*will* change hurricanes. If we know anything about these storms, it's that they respond sensitively to conditions in the atmosphere and oceans. Human beings are already changing the environments in which hurricanes form and attain their terrifying strength, which means hurricanes will inevitably change, too. Precisely how and to what extent remains very much unsettled, however, and that makes all the difference.

Despite everything they've learned about hurricanes during the decades since World War II, scientists still do not completely understand all the environmental factors that cause them to develop and deepen. And global warming, which ought to intensify the average hurricane, could also change the regions of storm formation or the numbers of storms that form in the first place. Despite troubling signs, the evidence simply isn't in on all of these changes—not yet. And whatever does ultimately happen, it is unlikely to be simple or straightforward. "Welcome to the wonderful world of projections," says Greg Holland.

To further complicate matters, the extent of global warming itself depends on our own choices about energy use, population size, and much else in the coming century, including the policies we adopt (or fail to adopt) to restrain greenhouse gas emissions. With all of these variables, the precise global average temperatures that we'll see by 2100, or 2200, can't possibly be predicted. That makes their ultimate impact on hurricanes all the more uncertain.

To grasp just how complex it all really is, consider the well-established effect of El Niño upon hurricanes, which is brought about, among other factors, by the modulation of wind shear over the Atlantic. Thanks to the pivotal discoveries of scientists beginning with Gray, we now know that El Niño tends to suppress hurricanes in the Atlantic but increase their activity in the Pacific. But how will global warming alter the frequency and strength of what scientists refer to as the El Niño–Southern Oscillation, or ENSO? At this point the question isn't remotely settled, though it makes sense that some type of change ought to occur. If it does, that throws another huge curve ball into the hurricane–global warming discussion, particularly as it affects the United States.

Clearly, then, we can't give an exact answer about how global warming will modify hurricanes. Yet just because we can't perfectly quantify changing levels of risk doesn't mean we have no right to feel concerned.

It's an increasingly well-established result of climate science that the heating up of the world's oceans, including the warm pools of the tropics where hurricanes spin up after being triggered by various types of disturbances, has a large human component to it. Meanwhile, scientists going back to Riehl have taught us that hurricanes are natural heat engines reliant upon ocean warmth for their power, even as modern theoretical and modeling accounts—including the work of Emanuel, Holland, Knutson, and others—agree that global warming ought to intensify the average hurricane (though these theoreticians and modelers are still trying to work out precisely how much). Finally, although skeptics remain, at least for the Atlantic there are grounds for suspecting that global warming is contributing to a sharp rise in the total number of storms that form each year, as well as—inevitably— the number of very powerful hurricanes. Not only has a trend emerged; some leading scientists think we're its cause.

In late 2006, many of the experts involved in this debate came together under the auspices of the World Meteorological Organization to reach a new consensus, albeit a temporary one, on hurricanes and global warming. They included Emanuel, Knutson, Landsea, Holland, Willoughby, Chan, and numerous others who traveled to Costa Rica to pore over the science and figure out what they could reliably say about it. The scientists assembled agreed that there was still plenty of uncertainty all around—the debate had not been resolved—and the summary statement subsequently issued by the World Meteorological Organization in response to their endeavors was quite cautious (see Appendix IV). "No firm conclusion" could be made yet about whether hurricanes had changed in a detectable way due to human-induced global warming, it read. But the summary added that "it is likely that some increase in tropical cyclone peak wind-speed and rainfall will occur if the climate continues to warm." It also noted: "If the projected rise in sea level due to global warming occurs, then the vulnerability to tropical cyclone storm surge flooding would increase."

When the Fourth Assessment Report of the United Nations' Intergovernmental Panel on Climate Change emerged in early 2007, meanwhile, it took a somewhat stronger stand on the hurricane–climate relationship. The report's "Summary for Policymakers" judged it "more likely than not"—in other words, the confidence in the conclusion was just above 50 percent—that there had already been an increase in intense hurricane activity, partly caused by global warming. A footnote, however, cautioned that this conclusion was based on "expert judgment rather than formal attribution studies." Other parts of the IPCC document mentioned the ongoing data difficulties, the detection of a trend in the Atlantic (correlated with rising sea surface temperatures), and the expectation of future storm intensification based upon modeling studies like Knutson's.

While these statements clearly depict a field of science that's in flux, they also more than justify worry on the part of a journalist, a citizen, or a decision-maker. We don't know yet the precise "hurricane sensitivity" to climate change, but it could be very significant. By the time we successfully quantify it, we may already be well within its range. Perhaps we're seeing hints of that sensitivity kick in already in the form of spates of record-breaking storms. Perhaps we're seeing it in the Atlantic. And even if we haven't yet, we're likely to in the coming years.

But how should such knowledge, such worry, translate into action? The answer is tricky for one key reason: We're so disturbingly vulnerable to hurricanes in the United States (and for that matter, globally) that with or without global warming, we're virtually certain to see more disasters in the future. It's a staggering statistic: Half of the U.S. population lives within fifty miles of the coast. And they're not anywhere close to being ready to withstand a major hurricane's impact. "They don't even have building codes in some of the unincorporated areas of Texas and Louisiana," Chris Landsea points out. "So, much less getting ready for any potential scary changes [due to] global warming, we're not prepared for hurricanes as they are today."

Over the course of this book, we've repeatedly followed hurricanes as they coursed towards vulnerable coastal cities. Mercifully, most of them missed, but they won't always in the future. Many parts of the United States face a dramatic hurricane risk, with New York/Long Island, Miami/Fort Lauderdale, and Galveston/Houston probably topping the list if we judge by the potential for large-scale destruction and economic impacts to major population centers (and if we conveniently but arbitrarily ignore the possibility of another major storm hitting New Orleans). As for large loss of life: We're better off than some poorer parts of the world, but still extremely vulnerable in this regard as well, as Hurricane Katrina amply demonstrated.

And New Orleans is just one high-risk area. Among the U.S. regions vulnerable to the type of hurricane devastation that could trigger not only expensive damage but mass fatalities, the Florida Keys hold a special place. They can be overrun by storm surges and can't be evacuated without a lot of lead time, since a narrow two-lane highway must be relied upon to transport evacuees back to mainland Florida. That means the carnage from a powerful hurricane that makes a sudden turn—or one that rapidly intensifies—could be very great. The waters of Florida's Lake Okeechobee, meanwhile, have killed once before in a hurricane, in 1928, and scientists at Florida International University's International Hurricane Research Center suggest that the 140-mile earthen dike that protects 40,000 people from the lake could be breached again during a storm. Tampa/St. Petersburg and Cape Hatteras and Wilmington, North Carolina, also appear on the center's top-ten list of places most susceptible to a hurricane strike.

In light of this stark vulnerability—combined with a steady movement of persons and property into harm's way—Landsea, Roger Pielke,

Jr., and many others have strongly argued that we must focus our primary attention on addressing the demographic and societal aspect of our hurricane quandary. It represented a landmark in the hurricane–climate debate when, in July 2006, most of the scientists involved put aside their differences and agreed that even as the scientific argument continues, "it should in no event detract from the main hurricane problem facing the United States: the ever-growing concentration of population and wealth in vulnerable coastal regions." As they explained:

> These demographic trends are setting us up for rapidly increasing human and economic losses from hurricane disasters, especially in this era of heightened activity. Scores of scientists and engineers had warned of the threat to New Orleans long before climate change was seriously considered, and a Katrina-like storm or worse was (and is) inevitable even in a stable climate.

The scientists refreshingly continued by extending their knowledge to make some general political observations and recommendations, something too many scientists are afraid of doing even when those recommendations are fairly basic and obvious:

> Rapidly escalating hurricane damage in recent decades owes much to government policies that serve to subsidize risk. State regulation of insurance is captive to political pressures that hold down premiums in risky coastal areas at the expense of higher premiums in less risky places. Federal flood insurance programs likewise undercharge property owners in vulnerable areas. Federal disaster policies, while providing obvious humanitarian benefits, also serve to promote risky behavior in the long run.
>
> We are optimistic that continued research will eventually resolve much of the current controversy over the effect of climate change on hurricanes. But the more urgent problem of our lemming-like march to the sea requires immediate and sustained attention. We call upon leaders of government and industry to undertake a comprehensive evaluation of building practices, and insurance, land use, and disaster relief policies that currently serve to promote an ever-increasing vulnerability to hurricanes.

The statement signers included Emanuel, Curry, Holland, Landsea, Webster, and Knutson, as well as Phil Klotzbach, Max Mayfield, Richard Anthes of the University Corporation for Atmospheric Research, and James Elsner of Florida State University. They deserve our applause for trying to translate their knowledge into meaningful action, and for managing to converge on this critical matter despite the ongoing uncertainty in the hurricane–climate debate. For especially when it comes to the Atlantic, the fact is that whether you think the recent uptick in hurricane activity is the result of global warming or a natural cycle—or some combination of both—we have every reason to expect more bad years ahead. To a large extent, we can let the scientists haggle it out while we just start protecting ourselves.

Yet even as we focus on the demographic and societal aspects of hurricane vulnerability, we can't ignore the possibility that long-term changes in hurricanes (or short-term changes if they're big enough) might also amplify our collective exposure. For someone with a coastal home in Florida, notes Roger Pielke, Jr., global warming really doesn't make a lot of difference in terms of how you deal with hurricanes: "You just have to adapt." But for those who are concerned not about one house but about overall trends in damage, and who are capable of studying and responding to future risks in an aggregate sense—large reinsurance companies, for example, or states and nations—the possible impacts of global warming can and should factor into the calculus. That's the world we now live in. Indeed, the very fact that our society has put so many lives and so much property in harm's way means that our leaders should worry *even more*, not less, that global warming could be making it all even more vulnerable.

Suppose, merely for the sake of argument, that we decide it's worth the money and resolve to undertake a massive engineering project to make New Orleans entirely safe from another hurricane storm surge for the next hundred, five hundred, or one thousand years. Any defense plans would then have to take into account not only projected sea-level rise due to global warming (perhaps well over a foot by the year 2100) but also the possibility of hurricane intensity and frequency changes. Because of scientific as well as societal and political uncertainties, no fixed number could be ascribed to either risk. Rather, the risk assessment would have to consider a range of possibilities (nothing new to risk assessors).

Hurricane Katrina, it seems safe to say, would not be the worst-case scenario in such an exercise.

None of this should be taken to mean that hurricanes *alone* justify imposing mandatory caps on emissions of industrial greenhouse gases, whether through the Kyoto Protocol or some other climate-change mitigation policy. Such policies are inherently slow-acting and long-term in nature. For the short term, though, we're committed to significant global warming that's already "in the pipeline." If that warming is going to change hurricanes further, it's a done deal and there's nothing the Kyoto Protocol or any other emissions policy can do to change that. So whatever we do about global warming, we should be preparing ourselves for hurricanes (including possibly stronger ones) no matter what.

It's a bit simplistic to offer up hurricanes as a reason for dealing with global warming anyway. By definition, if you change the climate you're changing almost *everything*—agriculture, sea level, the extent of ice and glaciers, the character of precipitation, the distribution of species and the likelihood of their extinction—the list goes on and on. If we're going to act to prevent such changes, then, we should do so because on balance we oppose *most or all* of them, not because of any one of them in isolation; and because we think it's worth preventing such wholesale alterations to the planet.

Still, there's no denying that amid all these hypothesized (and increasingly actualized) changes, the possibility of human-induced alterations to hurricanes has a unique way of grabbing the public's attention. The potency of this symbol has been, and will surely continue to be, misused by some environmental advocates who pay too little heed to the complexity of the science in their rush to make the powerful image of a cyclonic storm do political work on their behalf. We must oppose this exploitation and demand that advocates remain honest on both sides of the aisle. Still, it's easy to understand why hurricanes have become emblematic of many citizens' discomfort over our changing planet. Altering the Earth is scary; so are hurricanes; and provided we state the science properly, it's entirely defensible, on the basis of current knowledge, to conjoin these two types of concern. Hurricanes *will* change as a result of global warming. We don't know precisely how, but (as with so much else about global warming) it seems doubtful that it will be in a way that we like.

So we must address both hurricane vulnerability *and* global warming; we must do so simultaneously and yet in significantly different ways; and we must act not so much because of the linkage between the two, but rather because each poses intolerable risks to us individually. If we act promptly on both fronts, perhaps such action will have the added benefit of helping to preserve a world in which, even as we're better protected against hurricanes, the worst-case hypothetical scenario—souped-up storms surfing atop dramatically higher seas to many locations they couldn't reach when the world was cooler—never has a chance of becoming a reality.

The hurricane–climate debate contains lessons stretching beyond hurricane or climate policy, however. It's emblematic of a situation that occurs repeatedly at the intersection of science and policy: Scientists appear to *disagree* about something very important—the science of global warming, the biomedical potential of different types of stem cells, the risk posed by bird flu, and dozens of other things. How should citizens, journalists, policymakers, and politicians respond when faced with these increasingly frequent scenarios?

The answer is that while the scientific disagreement may or may not be entirely honest—and the hurricane–climate debate is more honest than some—it need not be paralyzing. We should stop thinking we'll ever achieve scientific certainty (we won't), and instead realize that when making decisions at a societal or personal level, our duty is to take current knowledge into account. If a decision then results whose scientific basis later gets called into question, we should be open to revisiting that decision at that time. But we needn't apologize for the fundamental fact of science and reality that everything is, to a greater or lesser degree, uncertain and debatable.

The hurricane–climate debate demonstrates this perfectly: While we don't know *precisely* how global warming will change hurricanes, that's not really the point. What matters is that today, we know enough to be worried. Granted, it so happens that the most immediate policy implication for the United States—*get ready; take evasive action*—is probably the same whether or not global warming is significantly changing storms. But as we've seen, if we look to the longer term, or take a broader international view—recognizing that for poorer countries with exposed populations, expensive adaptation or coastal retreat isn't necessarily possible—then precautionary measures are certainly needed.

One key reason for this lies in the history of meteorology itself. Again and again, knowledge advances most reliably when theory, observations, and modeling all get taken into account and all converge upon a consistent answer. And in this case, all give grounds for worry.

The great virtue of theoreticians lies in their ability to distill a complex reality down to its fundamental components—to *explain* what's happening. Yet this very talent inevitably means that theoreticians (and modelers) will sometimes oversimplify. Witness Jule Charney and Conditional Instability of the Second Kind, or James Espy with his "centripetal" theory of storm winds. That's why theoreticians need "data" guys to keep them honest, to point out observations that complicate or contradict their theories—precisely what has happened in the hurricane–global warming debate.

Yet data alone, without a physical *understanding* of what's happening, can also blind and mislead. Correlations don't prove causation. Sahel rainfall can change in lockstep with Atlantic hurricane activity without causing changes in that activity. Temperatures can go up and down and up again without these wiggles reflecting a natural cycle.

That's why any healthy science will inevitably balance both theoretical and empirical approaches. And when you take both approaches into account in the hurricane–climate debate, you once again wind up with reasons to worry. For example, in the opinion of one scientific observer—Hugh Willoughby—modeling studies (like those of Thomas

Knutson) present a "conservative estimate" of how hurricanes will change due to global warming, while the famous data-based Emanuel and Webster studies may, in some aspects, show too dramatic an increase. "And of course," Willoughby continues, "the truth lies somewhere in the middle."

So while it would be uncharitable not to respect and admire Gray for all he's achieved over the course of his scientific career, it remains hard to swallow his rejection of climate modeling. These models provide plausible projections, rooted in our most up-to-date physical understanding, of how the future may develop. No such model result should be considered an unerring prediction; instead, climate models are perhaps most useful when employed to test hypotheses that scientists come up with about how the real world works, and what is likely to happen if various natural or human influences occur in the future. Whatever the inevitable shortcomings of a given model, if it contains the relevant physical processes and gives the expected result, the hypothesis has at least been confirmed within the constraints of that particular model. And if multiple teams of scientists, running slightly or even considerably different models, all hit upon similar fundamental results—that, say, temperatures will rise several degrees Celsius for a doubling of atmospheric carbon dioxide concentrations—then confidence in their estimates increases accordingly.

In short, climate models, just like empirical analyses, are tools that help advance our understanding. We need as many such tools as we can get. We should admit their flaws and imperfections, and that's precisely what modelers do. But we shouldn't throw them out, any more than we should throw out empirical studies. As Emanuel told me in May 2006:

> I try to tell this to my students, that it's dangerous to start considering yourself a theoretician, or a modeler, or a field observationalist, because you're pigeonholing yourself, and you're restricting yourself unnecessarily. A good scientist ought to try to use any means at his disposal, and not be territorial about, "Well, I'm not going to do this because it involves modeling and I don't consider myself a modeler." You're drawing a cultural distinction that's unnecessary.

Emanuel has flown into storms, derived and transformed complicated equations, and run numerical models. That doesn't mean he has perfectly described—yet—the sensitivity of hurricanes to global warming (though he's working on it). But it does mean that he combines, in one scientist, a set of abilities we should generally expect from the scientific community as a whole.

Luckily the world hosts a broad enough diversity of scientists, with varying backgrounds and different creative ways of approaching problems, that we can usually trust them, collectively, to help us solve important issues (given adequate time, research support, and so forth). Scientists are great at doing *science,* without a doubt. But they too often fall into a trap very similar to the false theory/observations dichotomy when yanked outside of a purely scientific context and thrust into media and political debates, such as the global warming battle. In this respect, it's hard not to groan a bit to over a statement by Curry, Webster, and Holland about how they initially approached presenting their controversial findings to the public. They write that they consciously sought to emphasize information from the "peer-reviewed literature" in their media interviews, "although this often placed us at a considerable debating disadvantage." Of course it did. If you play by boxing rules in a kick-boxing match, you're bound to lose.

After their media trial-by-fire, Curry and her colleagues changed their view of the scientist–media–public interface. Curry in particular realized that scientific training does not contain an adequate media component, and that the scientific publication process (that hallowed "peer-reviewed literature") often deemphasizes the delivery of the most policy-relevant information. As a result, especially on hot-button issues, the public tends to want such information faster than science seems able to provide it. In such situations, scientists would be well advised to stop pretending that they're purely objective fact machines and nothing more. And they can't simply limit their statements to the peer-reviewed literature, because there's not enough there for public consumption. Rather, scientists must carefully, strategically step up to the plate and offer more general interpretations that, without betraying existing knowledge, help to contextualize it for the public and the media.

The scientists of the hurricane–climate debate ultimately did this when they jointly explained that their ongoing arguments should not distract from the pressing issue of our society's "lemming-like march to the sea." By then, however, journalists—with little else to cover in the face of little newly published science—had amplified personal battles and honed in on scientific disagreements, rather than writing more policy-oriented stories that would have helped to set the developing knowledge in context. Some scientists helped fan these flames by publicly attacking each other. But the scientists' bigger mistake—one for which they cannot simply blame the media—lay in allowing the hurricane–climate issue to be framed around scientific uncertainty and contentious debate, rather than around common ground and solutions. And that framing failure, in turn, traces back to scientists' too frequent unwillingness to step outside a narrow, technocratic mode of discourse and explain more broadly why it is that their results matter.

That's why all scientists working in controversial areas—and who knows what tomorrow's controversy will be!—should pay attention to the hurricane–climate battle and learn from it about how to proceed in such fraught contexts. Scientists mustn't allow their fields of research to become polarized along disciplinary or methodological lines. And they mustn't let fights over how to interpret the latest findings—fights that will eventually get resolved—distract the media and public from the big picture.

In order to achieve these goals, however, scientists are going to have to stop being *only scientists,* and realize that they must be communicators—and leaders, and examples—as well. Scientific institutions, especially universities but also overarching scientific societies, must take steps now to train future researchers so that they can survive a fall from the ivory tower. As the controversy over the Emanuel and Webster team studies amply demonstrates, scientists have tremendous power, simply by publishing certain findings at certain times, to drive public discourse and shape societal decision-making. And yet too many of them cling to the antiquated myth that their job is merely to put the "facts" out there, and nothing more—and then the facts will speak for themselves, and we'll all be better off because of it.

They won't, and we won't, either. Rather, as we've seen, those "facts" will get spun by advocates with opposed interests, attacked by politicians, and even suppressed by agenda-driven government agencies. Scientists can complain about this all they want, but they'd be better off taking actual measures to prevent and counter it. If the hurricane–global warming conflagration teaches nothing else, it surely teaches us this.

For Thanksgiving 2006, I went home to New Orleans. And there was no choice: I had to visit the scene of Mom's house again. I knew what I would see, but that didn't lessen the shock upon arriving. There was no swampy, spongified home to look on any more. I stood on the curbside regarding the absence of one.

The little house—"the size of a postage stamp," Mom used to say—had been bulldozed, just like about a third of the other properties in the neighborhood. The razing made sense in Mom's case; her home hadn't been even remotely salvageable. Some of the neighbors had busily started to rebuild on their lots and snatch up additional property. "We're Coming Home To Lakeview," read the signs on some lawns. But my mother had a different plan: She wanted to sell. That was proving difficult, though.

When we arrived at the lot, which was littered with Coke cans and junk left behind by work crews, we quickly realized someone had swiped Mom's "For Sale By Owner" sign. It was a scorching day for late November, and as we trudged across the dry, uneven ground picking up the trash, Mom angrily denounced the sign theft. "That's pretty low," she said. This probably explained why she hadn't received any calls recently about the lot.

It's a daily struggle, but in many ways, New Orleans seemed to be bouncing back, emboldened by a tame hurricane season and the little triumphs that accumulate with the passage of time. The city looked much cleaner than before, though crime remained a terrible problem and National Guard Humvees still patrolled the streets. But amidst all these changes, I wanted to know how New Orleanians were—or weren't—taking global warming into account as they made decisions about their futures.

What I learned was heartening in some ways, but troubling in others.

I already mistrusted the city's leader on this subject. "Katrina is the standard" when it comes to rebuilding the city's levees, New Orleans mayor Ray Nagin had declared at a White House press conference in late 2005. Not only did this make no mention of the possibility of long-term hurricane intensification or ongoing sea-level rise; it ignored the fact that Katrina was not a worst case–scenario hurricane for New Orleans.

Nagin's statement, if translated into policy, would amount to repeating the same error that was made following Hurricane Betsy of 1965, sometimes called "Billion-Dollar Betsy" because it was the first storm to rack up that much damage. Betsy hit New Orleans at Category 3 strength and flooded much of the city, killing some eighty people and stranding many more on rooftops. So the Army Corps of Engineers went to work building levees to protect New Orleans, but only tall enough to fend off a "Standard Project Hurricane" that today we would call a fast-moving Category 3 storm (Betsy hit before the creation of the Saffir-Simpson Scale). The protections ignored worst-case scenarios, including a storm like Category 5 Camille, which struck Mississippi only four years after Betsy. Treating the large, Category 3 Katrina as a worst-case storm strike would amount to the same error.

If Nagin didn't inspire much confidence, the New Orleans public simply didn't seem very engaged with the issue of global warming. It hardly represented a major topic of daily debate or discussion in the city. What New Orleanians worry about, local *Times Picayune* environmental reporter Mark Schleifstein explained to me while I was in town, is "Are the levees protecting them from the next storm?" He added, "And what causes that, they don't care." But if they don't care, they can't bring adequate pressure to bear upon their local leaders, or their congressional representatives, to ensure that nothing gets excluded from long-term planning.

Finally, there were the technocrats charged with figuring out how to rebuild and redefend New Orleans: the much maligned U.S. Army Corps of Engineers. Here, the signs were actually somewhat brighter. The Corps had completed restoring the city's levees to pre-Katrina strength and was in the process of determining what constitutes a "100-year hurricane" for the New Orleans area. Congress had demanded that such additional protections be complete by 2010, and the agency had promised to comply. And in the context of conducting that risk assessment, the Corps had been factoring global warming into the equation, rather than merely assuming that future storm activity would resemble what had been seen in the past. To be sure, scientists like Webster and Curry are skeptical that the agency is doing an adequate job of taking climate change into account. But at least the *Times-Picayune*'s Schleifstein, a visionary reporter who was writing stories about the city's hurricane vulnerability long before Katrina, got a Corps scientist named Don Resio to admit that because of global warming's possible impact on hurricane frequency and intensity, "down the road, maybe the 100-year storm is the 86-year storm."

Thinking in this way is the only responsible thing to do, given our current knowledge. As Greg Holland puts it, when it comes to Atlantic hurricanes and the current increase in activity, "there's no evidence we're going to go back to the 50s and the 60s." We can't simply assume any more that the past will serve as a reliable guide to the future.

The Corps of Engineers' "100 year hurricane" risk assessment had not been completed when this book went to press. After finishing it, the agency was set to consider what it would take to secure the ultimate protections for New Orleans and the Louisiana Coast—defenses against killer storms estimated to occur more rarely than once in a hundred years (but still possible in any given year). Here again, global warming must figure into long-term planning; after all, we're talking about worst-case scenarios. Meanwhile, any successful defenses would probably entail costly projects like major coastal restoration, still higher levees, and even the construction of huge gated structures to block storm surges from entering Lake Pontchartrain.

The major constraint on all of this—besides the Corps' own bureaucratic slowness—seems certain to be a lack of money (and vision). Shortly after Katrina, the Bush administration announced a $3.1 billion plan to restore the city's hurricane protections; Category 5 storm protections had been estimated to cost $32 billion or more at the time. Later, the tab for even these modest initial protections went up to nearly $10 billion, the administration balked at the cost, and Category 5 defenses didn't seem even worth occasionally dreaming about. You can fret about global warming all you want in the context of some long-term scenario or other, but if better hurricane protections aren't affordable or a priority, it will make little difference.

And that's just the outlook for New Orleans. Every American and global city vulnerable to hurricanes has to set its own priorities, and make its own hard choices. Those priorities and choices will differ from place to place, but they share this commonality: You can't even begin to make such decisions without the best available information. All of it. And we live in a world now where global warming is a *part* of that information. You can't deny it any more, and you can't censor it out of government reports. It's time to deal.

In a sense, it goes back to the original Webster-Curry-Holland press release issued at the time of their now famous 2005 study. The press release interpreted the scientists' results by suggesting that a series of risk-assessment studies should be conducted to determine the vulnerability of various coastal cities to hurricanes under changing meteorological and climatic scenarios. Unfortunately, however, to a significant extent that message was obscured or even lost. The proposal that we move forward constructively, by translating existing knowledge into action, got buried as personal and political battles shrouded the latest results under an impenetrable cloud of scientific uncertainty, and the entire issue got swept up into the global warming fight.

Yet whether or not the Webster study's conclusions ultimately hold up, the press release itself couldn't have been more insightful.

Even as we act immediately to curtail short-term vulnerability, every exposed coastal city needs a risk assessment that takes global warming scenarios into account. What states and cities should have been doing, as the scientists carried on their battle, is assess their risks, get a range of scenarios, and then respond to them as best they could, checking back with the scientists now and again for any new updates or developments.

The activities of the Corps of Engineers suggest that's already happening in New Orleans, and so much the better. Similarly, scientists at the NASA Goddard Institute for Space Studies in New York have been studying that city's vulnerability to hurricane impacts in a changing world, and calculated that with 1.5 feet of sea-level rise, a worst case–scenario Category 3 hurricane could submerge "the Rockaways, Coney Island, much of southern Brooklyn and Queens, portions of Long Island City, Astoria, Flushing Meadows–Corona Park, Queens, lower Manhattan, and eastern Staten Island from Great Kills Harbor north to the Verrazano Bridge." (Pause and think about that for a second.) Finally, large insurance and reinsurance companies are also reanalyzing their exposure. In a 2006 report on hurricanes, Munich Re called for "a process of fundamental rethinking... in the evaluation of hurricane risks" and focused on the possible influences of climate change.

These are all heartening developments and should be embraced more broadly, even in the face of considerable scientific uncertainty. For the truth is that in the end, we never know everything, and we never will. There is only evidence and the various lenses through which it's interpreted. And then there's action and inaction—both of which have consequences.

# ACKNOWLEDGMENTS

This book would not have been possible without the help and feed-back of many friends, colleagues, and dedicated and thoughtful indi-viduals. First, I'd like to thank the law firm Taggart, Morton, in New Orleans, for allowing me to use office space and get online during a crucial period when the idea for this book was being hatched—which is essentially tantamount to thanking Cory and Jim Morton, who made it possible, and even took me to lunch afterward. Later, I used the Taggart, Morton office spaces again as I burrowed into the writing and revision process. It was an inspiration to look out upon New Orleans from high above as I worked, all the way to distant Lake Pontchartrain and then across to the nearby Hyatt Regency hotel, whose north side windows had been blown out by Katrina's winds and were still covered with white plastic ten months later.

In a life cluttered with obligations and distractions it can be diffi-cult to find writing time, so I also want to thank those who helped me escape. They include the stylish Hempel Hotel in London, where I wrote a significant chunk of this book as the staff (particularly Mr. Finnegan) made the stay beyond comfortable (despite the heat wave!); and my late grandparents Jean and Gerald Cole, who built the wonder-ful rustic house north of Flagstaff, Arizona, where I secluded myself and also got a great deal of writing done—not once but twice in 2006. There's nothing like waking up in the morning, scattering elk when you open the front door, taking a look at a mountain in your backyard, and then realizing that there's nothing to do all day *but* write.

Some people helped me escape; others kept me awake. In my pre-vious book I thanked the servers at Tryst, in Adams Morgan in Wash-ington, D.C., for all the late-night chais. This time around, I needed chaipuccinos to get by—and then, when things got really rough, just a straight large coffee. They once again obliged, as did the servers at sister restaurant Open City.

My agent, Sydelle Kramer, once again guided me through this process masterfully and also provided critically helpful comments on the manuscript—with a quick turnaround time when it really mattered. So did Tim Bent and Becky Saletan of Harcourt, who became my deadline-crashing buddy. Meanwhile, many people, including friends, colleagues, and scientific experts, offered feedback on parts of the text in its various stages of development. For this I'd like to thank Katharine Anderson, Richard Anthes, James Bradbury, James Rodger Fleming, Eli Kintisch, Doug Lilly, Michael MacCracken, Jerry Mahlman, Michael Mann, Michael Mooney, Sally Mooney, Pedro Mulero, Antonio Regalado, Gavin Schmidt, Paul Thacker, David Thompson, and Spencer Weart.

For fact-checking and research help, meanwhile, I'd indebted to Cathy Davies, Rick Desper, Norman Doering, Jim Easter, Matthew Ficke, Laurel Kristick, Kate Moran, Susanna Wegner, and various John Does who know who they are. I have also profited from conversations with, and feedback from Harold Brooks, D. Graham Burnett, Jerry Mahlman, Rick Piltz, and Tony Socci. I must also thank Nicole Smith for help on preparing my PowerPoint presentation, Kert Davies at Greenpeace for allowing me access to Freedom of Information Act documents, Matthew Nisbet and Heather Benson for research on media coverage, and Matthew Nisbet for lots of helpful conversations while jogging.

I'd also like to thank the blogs whose discussions of hurricanes and global warming I have found particularly enlightening: Real Climate (http://www.realclimate.org/), Prometheus (http://sciencepolicy.colorado.edu/prometheus/), Dr. Jeff Masters' WunderBlog (http://www.wunderground.com/blog/JeffMasters/show.html), and Eric Berger's SciGuy (http://blogs.chron.com/sciguy/). Additionally, I have voraciously consumed the products of many of the tropical cyclone forecasting centers of the world, including the U.S. National Hurricane

Center, the Joint Typhoon Warning Center, and the Central Pacific Hurricane Center. I can't thank them enough for their critically important work.

The historical parts of my research would not have been possible without Martin Kidds of the National Meteorological Library and Archive at the UK Met Office; Judy Dayhoff and Terry Murray of the National Center for Atmospheric Research (NCAR) library; NCAR archivist Diane Rabson; librarians at the U.S. Library of Congress as well as David Meyer, who did research for me there on more than one occasion; and Dr. Suzanne Gray of the University of Reading.

Most of all, I'd like to thank the scientists at the center of this story who took the time to give me repeated interviews over the course of 2006. I know they're a little nervous about my claim that they've done "extraordinary things at high wind speeds." But after reading this book, I trust they'll see that I mean the word "extraordinary" in the best possible sense.

# The Saffir-Simpson Hurricane Scale; Note on Units of Measurement

The Saffir-Simpson Hurricane Scale is a 1–5 rating based on the hurricane's present intensity. This is used to give an estimate of the potential property damage and flooding expected along the coast from a hurricane landfall. Wind speed is the determining factor in the scale, as storm surge values are highly dependent on the slope of the continental shelf and the shape of the coastline, in the landfall region. Note that all winds are using the U.S. 1-minute average.

**Category One Hurricane:** Winds 74–95 mph (64–82 kt or 119–153 km/hr). Storm surge generally 4–5 ft above normal. No real damage to building structures. Damage primarily to unanchored mobile homes, shrubbery, and trees. Some damage to poorly constructed signs. Also, some coastal road flooding and minor pier damage.

**Category Two Hurricane:** Winds 96–110 mph (83–95 kt or 154–177 km/hr). Storm surge generally 6–8 feet above normal. Some roofing material, door, and window damage of buildings. Considerable damage to shrubbery and trees with some trees blown down. Considerable damage to mobile homes, poorly constructed signs, and piers. Coastal and low-lying escape routes flood 2–4 hours before arrival of the hurricane center. Small craft in unprotected anchorages break moorings.

**Category Three Hurricane:** Winds 111–130 mph (96–113 kt or 178–209 km/hr). Storm surge generally 9–12 ft above normal. Some structural damage to small residences and utility buildings with a minor amount of curtainwall failures. Damage to shrubbery and trees with foliage blown off trees and large trees blown down. Mobile homes and poorly constructed signs are destroyed. Low-lying escape routes are cut by rising water 3–5 hours before arrival of the center of the hurricane. Flooding near the coast destroys smaller structures with larger structures damaged by battering from floating debris. Terrain continuously lower than 5 ft above mean sea level may be flooded inland 8 miles (13 km) or more. Evacuation of low-lying residences with several blocks of the shoreline may be required.

**Category Four Hurricane:** Winds 131–155 mph (114–135 kt or 210–249 km/hr). Storm surge generally 13–18 ft above normal. More extensive curtainwall failures with some complete roof structure failures on small residences. Shrubs, trees, and all signs are blown down. Complete destruction of mobile homes. Extensive damage to doors and windows. Low-lying escape routes may be cut by rising water 3–5 hours before arrival of the center of the hurricane. Major damage to lower floors of structures near the shore. Terrain lower than 10 ft above sea level may be flooded requiring massive evacuation of residential areas as far inland as 6 miles (10 km).

**Category Five Hurricane:** Winds greater than 155 mph (135 kt or 249 km/hr). Storm surge generally greater than 18 ft above normal. Complete roof failure on many residences and industrial buildings. Some complete building failures with small utility buildings blown over or away. All shrubs, trees, and signs blown down. Complete destruction of mobile homes. Severe and extensive window and door damage. Low-lying escape routes are cut by rising water 3–5 hours before arrival of the center of the hurricane. Major damage to lower floors of all structures located less than 15 ft above sea level and within 500 yards of the shoreline. Massive evacuation of residential areas on low ground within 5–10 miles (8–16 km) of the shoreline may be required.

*Source: National Hurricane Center; Shortened Version.*

**Note on Units of Measurement:** In addition to the wind-speed measurements that are so critical to determining a hurricane's Saffir-Simpson rating—and which in this book are expressed in the familiar "miles per hour"—several other units of measurement are also employed throughout this text and merit some further explication here.

I have often found the need to discuss atmospheric pressure, or, more specifically, minimum central pressure (or minimum sea-level pressure) estimates in hurricanes. Atmospheric pressure is simply the force exerted by the weight of air molecules over a particular area. To express pressure, I have followed the practice of U.S. National Hurricane Center public advisories and used "millibars" (mb) as well as "inches" (in), the latter being short for "inches of mercury." A conversion from millibars to inches of mercury can be achieved by multiplying millibars by .02953. Thus, a hurricane whose minimum central pressure in millibars is 902 would have a minimum central pressure in inches of mercury of 26.64, rounded to two decimal places (902 × .02953 = 26.64).

I have also often found the need to discuss temperatures, most frequently at the sea surface. Here, following the United Nations' Intergovernmental Panel on Climate Change (and for general convenience and simplicity), I have used degrees Celsius rather than degrees Fahrenheit or some other unit of measurement (although I have occasionally provided a Fahrenheit conversion in the text as well). A conversion from Celsius to Fahrenheit can be achieved by multiplying a Celsius measurement by 1.8 and then adding 32. Thus, if sea-surface temperatures are 30 degrees C, they are 86 degrees Fahrenheit; [(30 × 1.8) + 32] = 86.

# APPENDIX II

# Cyclone Typology

"Nature is not the slightest bit interested in our classifications of cyclones," National Hurricane Center forecaster James Franklin has observed. Although they obviously must employ some type of terminology to describe storms, modern meteorologists generally recognize that "tropical" and "extra-tropical" do not denote absolute categories. Instead, such terms are better thought of as representing opposite ends of a spectrum, with hybrid "subtropical storms"—which have both tropical and extra-tropical characteristics, drawing energy from the oceans as well as from the temperature contrast between air masses—lying in between.

Further complicating matters is the fact that storms can move along the spectrum over the course of their lifetimes. Hurricanes traveling far enough northward often undergo "extra-tropical transition" and become cold-core cyclones, while storms originally forming outside the tropics can develop into hurricanes. A certain form of extra-tropical cyclone, the infamous Nor'easter, can even come to exhibit "blizzicane" features, including dramatic drops in central pressure and an eyelike structure. The "Halloween Storm" of 1991, memorialized in Sebastian Junger's book *The Perfect Storm*, started out as a Nor'easter, absorbed Hurricane Grace, drifted south over the warm Gulf Stream and became subtropical, and then transitioned into a full-fledged hurricane that remained officially unnamed—so as to prevent confusion.

Nineteenth-century meteorologists could hardly have detected such metamorphoses, and thus we cannot fault them for failing to distinguish adequately between different types of large-scale storm systems (as discussed in the first chapter). Scientists at the time simply didn't have access to investigative tools, such as radar and satellite observations, that would have allowed them to fully appreciate that complexity. As National Hurricane Center forecaster Richard Pasch explains, one chief way that he and his colleagues distinguish tropical from subtropical storms lies in their satellite signature. In a satellite image, Pasch observes, "the subtropical cyclone could have a broad band of clouds and thunderstorms and heavy showers, that is comma shaped, and is not so much concentrated over the center. Whereas a classical tropical cyclone, the strongest thunderstorm activity and convection is concentrated right nearer the center." Not only do subtropical storms tend to have a broader field of strong winds; they also often form over cooler ocean waters.

Meteorologists have learned a great deal about cyclone typology in the modern era, yet even today, strange storms occasionally boggle their minds. In early November of 2006, an oddball cyclone formed over the cold waters off the coast of Oregon. Leading hurricane and meteorology blogger Jeff Masters described the storm as "a hybrid between a warm-cored tropical cyclone, cold-cored extra-tropical cyclone, and an uncommon type of winter storm called a Polar Low." He dubbed it "Thingamabobbercane."

# Early Hurricane–Climate Speculations

Kerry Emanuel wasn't the first scientist ever to postulate that hurricanes might intensify in a warmer world. He was merely the first to perform the detailed theoretical work necessary to flesh out that speculation. The concept itself, however, had emerged on several prior occasions, including one very unexpected one just after the turn of the nineteenth century. These episodes—which are based upon the author's research but should not be taken to represent a complete historical survey—suggest that there may have always been something fairly intuitive about the relationship between hurricanes and heat.

No one today remembers Alfred Russel Wallace as a scientist who offered any particular insight into hurricanes. If he is remembered at all, it's usually as one of history's classic second fiddles—the man who mailed Charles Darwin an essay describing the very concept of evolution by natural selection that Darwin had been holding close to his chest for well over a decade, fearful of publishing because of the reaction he knew it would provoke.

But if Wallace nearly beat Darwin, he was many decades ahead of his time in speculating, albeit only briefly, that changes to the Earth's climate might strengthen the planet's most powerful and destructive breed of cyclonic storms. The thought appeared in 1903's *Man's Place in the Universe,* a book in which Wallace expounded a theory of how the Earth had been perfectly designed to accommodate human life, and which included a remarkable paragraph about hurricanes:

> It is outside the zone of the equable trade-winds, and in a region a few degrees on each side of the tropics, that destructive hurricanes and typhoons prevail. These are really enormous whirlwinds

due to the intensely heated atmosphere over the arid regions already mentioned, causing an inrush of cool air from various directions, thus setting up a rotatory motion which increases in rapidity till equilibrium is restored. The hurricanes of the West Indies and Mauritius, and the typhoons of the Eastern seas, are thus caused. Some of these storms are so violent that no human structures can resist them, while the largest and most vigorous trees are torn to pieces or overturned by them. But if our atmosphere were much denser than it is, its increased weight would give it still greater destructive force; and if to this were added a somewhat greater amount of sun-heat—which might be due either to our greater proximity to the sun or to the sun's greater size or greater heat-intensity, these tempests might be so increased in violence and frequency as to render considerable portions of the earth uninhabitable.

From a modern scientific perspective, much of Wallace's logic here seems foreign. Today scientists view hurricanes as natural heat engines that draw their energy from warm ocean water and moist air. So contrary to Wallace's assumptions, an "inrush of cool air" would weaken a hurricane, as would greater atmospheric "density" or mass (which would reduce wind speed by increasing the pressure, which is simply the weight of air molecules from above). Still, it's striking that Wallace thought an increase in heat from the sun, bearing down on the Earth, might strengthen these deadly storms. Perhaps he knew of the theories, not uncommon at the time, that invoked variations in solar intensity to explain changes in weather as well as longer-term climate cycles. It's tantalizing to imagine Wallace going one step farther and surmising that the planet might warm, and hurricanes strengthen, not because of direct changes in solar intensity but due to an increased atmospheric capacity to "trap" heat that originated from the sun as it radiated back upward from the Earth.

In a 1954 essay on hurricanes, the Swedish meteorologist Tor Bergeron, who had been a key member of the Bergen School and is perhaps best known today for his discovery of so-called occluded fronts, echoed

Wallace by speculating about possible changes in hurricane intensity. Then he took an added cognitive step. As Bergeron wrote:

> Another problem, of much more far-reaching consequences, presents itself. What kind of secular changes may have existed in the frequency and intensity of the hurricane vortices on our Earth? And what changes may be expected in the future? We know nothing about these things, but I hope [to] have shown that even quite a small change in the different factors controlling the life history of a hurricane may produce, or may have produced, great changes in the paths of hurricanes and in their frequency and intensity. A minor alteration in the surface temperature of the sun, in the general composition of the earth's atmosphere, or in the rotation of the earth, might be able to change considerably the energy balance and the balance of forces within such a delicate mechanism as the tropical hurricane. During certain geological epochs, hurricanes may have been just as frequent as the cyclones of our latitudes, or they may have occurred all over the oceans and within all coastal regions, and they may have been even more violent than nowadays. During other periods they may have been lacking altogether.

Not only does this passage predict avenues of hurricane research being pursued today, such as paleotempestology (see Chapter 14, "Hurricane Climatology"). Bergeron echoes Wallace's speculation about the relationship between solar temperatures and hurricane strength but then goes farther, explicitly mentioning the effect of possible changes in the "general composition of the earth's atmosphere," as might occur due to increasing concentrations of greenhouse gases like carbon dioxide. Bergeron's discussion of the "energy balance" within hurricanes implies a thermodynamic understanding of these monster storms, a perspective that inevitably lends itself to the notion that hurricane intensity might increase with more heat added to the system.

Apparently Bergeron also lectured on the hurricane–climate linkage in the 1960s. Florida State University meteorologist T. N. Krishnamurti

290 • Appendix III

recalls a Bergeron seminar given at the University of California–Los Angeles in the 1960s that discussed global warming and its potential intensifying effect upon hurricanes. Krishnamurti, who was teaching at UCLA at the time, distinctly remembers Bergeron describing the storms as heat engines and discussing how they might grow stronger. "Back then it was surprising to hear," Krishnamurti says. Perhaps Bergeron's thoughts in this area sprang from familiarity with the work of a mentor, Svante Arrhenius, a fellow Swede and one of the first scientists involved in early discoveries about the greenhouse effect. (Arrhenius recommended Bergeron to his friend Vilhelm Bjerknes, who in turn brought the young scientist to Norway to join the Bergen School.)

Finally, in addition to Wallace and Bergeron, the scientists who originally came up with the heat-engine theory of hurricanes also mooted the implications of their work for hurricane intensification. In an interview, Joanne Simpson (formerly Malkus) recalled that back in the days when they published their influential work on hurricane structure and energetics, she and Herbert Riehl had "played around" with the idea that the strength of the hurricane heat engine they had described might be altered by a change in the climate. "We thought, well, if the ocean gets a lot warmer, would we have more hurricanes, or more intense hurricanes?" says Simpson. But, she continues, "This was just talk, we didn't write anything up about it, although we showed clearly that the local heat source is necessary for the storm to deepen."

Given their timing, such speculations about a hurricane–climate linkage by Bergeron, Malkus, and Riehl shouldn't seem entirely surprising. By the 1950s and 1960s, two central pieces of scientific theory could sustain such thinking. First, hurricanes had been described as heat engines; and second, there were reasons to suspect that humans might be involved in a heating of the world's oceans. In tandem with an active Atlantic hurricane era and Herbert Riehl's introduction of the heat-engine theory, global warming itself was reemerging as a subject of inquiry and, for the first time, of at least limited public concern.

Nevertheless, the idea of hurricane intensification caused by climate change was not destined to be built upon at the time, for a multitude of reasons. Soon CISK would emerge on the scene in the world of hurricane science, deemphasizing the role of the oceans. As the mid-century cooling period began, meanwhile, global warming slipped from the political and scientific radar. So did hurricanes themselves, as the frequency of major storms declined significantly in the Atlantic basin. Neither subject would become a matter of much significant public attention again until the late 1980s, when Emanuel's hurricane theory linked them permanently, even as global warming became a topic of political discussion—and very intense Atlantic hurricanes began to reappear.

# APPENDIX IV

# Consensus Statements by Participants in the World Meteorological Organization's 6th International Workshop on Tropical Cyclones, San Jose, Costa Rica, November 2006

1. Though there is evidence both for and against the existence of a detectable anthropogenic signal in the tropical cyclone climate record to date, no firm conclusion can be made on this point.
2. No individual tropical cyclone can be directly attributed to climate change.
3. The recent increase in societal impact from tropical cyclones has largely been caused by rising concentrations of population and infrastructure in coastal regions.
4. Tropical cyclone wind-speed monitoring has changed dramatically over the last few decades, leading to difficulties in determining accurate trends.
5. There is an observed multi-decadal variability of tropical cyclones in some regions whose causes, whether natural, anthropogenic or a combination, are currently being debated. This variability makes detecting any long-term trends in tropical cyclone activity difficult.
6. It is likely that some increase in tropical cyclone peak wind-speed and rainfall will occur if the climate continues to warm. Model studies and theory project a 3–5% increase in wind-speed per degree Celsius increase of tropical sea surface temperatures.
7. There is an inconsistency between the small changes in wind-speed projected by theory and modeling versus large changes reported by some observational studies.

8. Although recent climate model simulations project a decrease or no change in global tropical cyclone numbers in a warmer climate, there is low confidence in this projection. In addition, it is unknown how tropical cyclone tracks or areas of impact will change in the future.

9. Large regional variations exist in methods used to monitor tropical cyclones. Also, most regions have no measurements by instrumented aircraft. These significant limitations will continue to make detection of trends difficult.

10. If the projected rise in sea level due to global warming occurs, then the vulnerability to tropical cyclone storm surge flooding would increase.

# NOTES

## PROLOGUE: 6229 Memphis Street

**PAGE**

1 **many residents**...Based upon a survey reported on by the *New Orleans Times-Picayune* in April 2006, nearly three-quarters of Lakeview residents planned to return to the shattered neighborhood. See Lynne Jensen, "Lakeview Survey Finds Hundreds Are Returning," *New Orleans Times-Picayune,* April 6, 2006.

1 **couldn't imagine living anywhere else**...For an example of the determination on the part of some Lakeview residents to return and rebuild, see Brian Thevenot, "Family Ties," *New Orleans Times-Picayune,* November 25, 2005.

2 **a front-page feature article**...Martha Karr and Jeffrey Meitrodt, "What Will New Orleans Look Like Five Years from Now?" *New Orleans Times-Picayune,* December 25, 2005.

2 **Katrina was a mid-range Category 3 storm**...For the definitive meteorological history of Katrina, see the National Hurricane Center, "Tropical Cyclone Report: Hurricane Katrina," updated August 10, 2006. Available online at http://www.nhc .noaa.gov/pdf/TCR-AL122005_Katrina.pdf.

3 **an article I published**...Chris Mooney, "Thinking Big About Hurricanes," *American Prospect Online,* May 23, 2005. Available online at http://www.prospect .org/web/page.ww?section=root&name=ViewWeb&articleId=9754.

3 **"We only have one Earth"**..."Hurricanes and Global Warming: Is There a Connection?" *RealClimate.org,* September 2, 2005. Available online at http://www .realclimate.org/index.php?p=181.

## INTRODUCTION: "The Party Line"

**PAGE**

5 **Twelve thousand scientists**...Figures on the AGU event were provided by public information officer Harvey Leifert, e-mail communication, March 3, 2006.

5 **security guards had to police**...This description of escalator overcrowding at the American Geophysical Union's San Francisco meeting relies upon an account of the event by attendee Mika McKinnon, available online at http://www.sigmapisigma .org/societynews/agu_05.htm.

5 **a *Time* magazine cover story**...Jeffrey Kluger, "Global Warming: The Culprit?"

*Time,* October 3, 2005. Available online at http://www.time.com/time/magazine/article/0,9171,1109337,00.html.

**5 the top science story of the year**..."Year in Science: Hurricanes Intensify Global Warming Debate," *Discover,* Vol. 27, No. 1, January 2006. Available online at http://www.discover.com/issues/jan-06/cover/.

**5 five to ten media calls**...Interview with Kerry Emanuel, April 26, 2006.

**5 one of the hundred "Most Influential"**..."Kerry Emanuel: The Man Who Saw Katrina Coming," Jeffrey Kluger, *Time,* May 8, 2006. Available online at http://www.time.com/time/magazine/article/0,9171,1187251,00.html.

**6 all the world's electricity generators**...See Kerry Emanuel, "The Power of a Hurricane: An example of reckless driving on the information superhighway," available online at ftp://texmex.mit.edu/pub/emanuel/PAPERS/hurrpower.pdf. Emanuel estimates that an average Atlantic hurricane dissipates 3 terawatts of power ($3 \times 10^{12}$ watts) and an extreme Pacific supertyphoon dissipates 30 terawatts ($3 \times 10^{13}$ watts). According to the U.S. Energy Information Administration, "worldwide installed electricity generating capacity" was 3.71 terawatts in 2003 (or 3,710 gigawatts). (See http://www.eia.doe.gov/oiaf/ieo/electricity.html.) So in fact some hurricanes dissipate much more power than the worldwide electricity-generating capacity as of 2003.

**6 Hurricane Epsilon**...See National Hurricane Center, Tropical Cyclone Report, Hurricane Epsilon, January 7, 2006. Available online at http://www.nhc.noaa.gov/pdf/TCR-AL302005_Epsilon.pdf.

**6 the twenty-seventh storm**...For many months Epsilon was thought to have been the season's twenty-sixth storm. However, a postseason reanalysis by the National Hurricane Center detected a short-lived and previously unnoticed storm with tropical characteristics, never named, that formed in early October.

**6 built to withstand**...Interview with Richard Pasch, November 8, 2006.

**7 "I HAVE RUN OUT"**...National Hurricane Center, Hurricane Epsilon Discussion Number 28, December 6, 2005. Available at http://www.nhc.noaa.gov/archive/2005/dis/al292005.discus.028.shtml.

**7 weather communiqués**...Interview with Richard Pasch, November 8, 2006 (in person).

**7 "EPSILON APPEARS"**...National Hurricane Center, Hurricane Epsilon Discussion Number 29, December 6, 2005. Available online at http://www.nhc.noaa.gov/archive/2005/dis/al292005.discus.029.shtml.

**7 "THE END IS IN SIGHT"**...National Hurricane Center, Hurricane Epsilon Discussion Number 31, December 6, 2005. Available online at http://www.nhc.noaa.gov/archive/2005/dis/al292005.discus.031.shtml.

**7 the audience had heard**...James Hansen, "Is There Still Time to Avoid 'Dangerous Anthropogenic Interference' with Global Climate?: A Tribute to Charles David Keeling," lecture delivered at the American Geophysical Union meeting, December 6, 2005. Available online at http://www.columbia.edu/~jeh1/keeling_talk_and_slides.pdf.

**7  a seemingly typical scientific talk**...Kerry Emanuel, "Trends and Variability in Tropical Cyclone Activity," PowerPoint presentation at the American Geophysical Union meeting, December 6, 2005. On file with the author.

**8  the flux of energy**...For more on the role of greenhouse gases in regulating the planetary energy balance, see J. Hansen et al., "Earth's Energy Imbalance: Confirmation and Implications," *Science,* Vol. 308 (June 3, 2005), pp. 1431–35.

**8  This hypothesis**...Kerry Emanuel, "The Dependence of Hurricane Intensity on Climate," *Nature,* Vol. 326, No. 6112 (April 2, 1987), pp. 483–85.

**8  Hurricane damage**...Interview with Greg Holland, February 13, 2006.

**8  It has been estimated**...William Gray, "Twentieth Century Challenges and Milestones," in *Hurricane!: Coping with Disaster,* ed. Robert Simpson (Washington, D.C.: American Geophysical Union, 2003).

**10  an agency publication**...*NOAA Magazine,* "NOAA Attributes Recent Increase in Hurricane Activity to Naturally Occurring Multi-Decadal Climate Variability," November 29, 2005, noting, "There is consensus among NOAA hurricane researchers and forecasters that recent increases in hurricane activity are primarily the result of natural fluctuations in the tropical climate system known as the tropical multi-decadal signal." Available online at http://www.magazine.noaa.gov/stories/mag184.htm.

**10  what came next**...The substance of Emanuel's remarks on this occasion and the audience reaction were reconstructed through telephone interviews with Richard Somerville, who chaired the panel (February 21, 2006); Judith Curry, who was present (February 21, 2006); and Emanuel himself (January 4, 2006).

**10  "I HOPE THIS IS"**...National Hurricane Center, Tropical Depression Epsilon Discussion Number 37, December 8, 2005. Available online at http://www.nhc.noaa.gov/archive/2005/dis/al292005.discus.037.shtml.

**10  Tropical Storm Zeta**...National Hurricane Center, Tropical Cyclone Report, Tropical Storm Zeta, March 17, 2006. Available online at http://www.nhc.noaa.gov/pdf/TCR-AL312005_Zeta.pdf.

**10  "THE CALENDAR WILL SHORTLY"**...National Hurricane Center, Tropical Storm Zeta Discussion Number 2, December 30, 2005. Available online at http://www.nhc.noaa.gov/archive/2005/dis/al302005.discus.002.shtml.

**11  hundreds of overtime hours**...Interview with Chris Landsea, November 8, 2006; e-mail from Dennis Feltgen, National Weather Service, January 4, 2007.

**11  "I SUPPOSE IT IS ONLY FITTING"**...National Hurricane Center, Tropical Depression Zeta Discussion Number 30, January 6, 2005. Available online at http://www.nhc.noaa.gov/archive/2005/dis/al302005.discus.030.shtml.

## PART I: Warming and Storming

PAGE

**13  [This] seems to be a rule**...Tor Bergeron, "Methods in Scientific Weather Analysis and Forecasting: An Outline in the History of Ideas and Hints at a Program," in *The*

*Atmosphere and the Sea in Motion: Scientific Contributions to the Rossby Memorial Volume,* ed. Bert Bolin (New York: The Rockefeller Institute Press, 1959), pp. 440–74.

## CHAPTER 1: Chimneys and Whirlpools

PAGE

15 **The ancient Mayans**...As related in Dr. Bob Sheets and Jack Williams' *Hurricane Watch: Forecasting the Deadliest Storms on Earth* (New York: Vintage, 2001), pp. 5–6.

15 **The thirteenth-century Japanese**...See Kerry Emanuel, *Divine Wind: The History and Science of Hurricanes* (New York: Oxford University Press, 2005), Chapter 1, "Kamikaze."

15 **the fleet of Christopher Columbus**...Emanuel, *Divine Wind,* Chapter 5, "Columbus's Hurricane."

15 **scattered accounts from mariners**...For a list of such descriptions, see Henry Piddington, *The Sailor's Horn-Book for the Law of Storms* (London: Smith, Elder, & Co., 1848), pp. 1–2, noting, "Hence we see that, up to the first ten years of the present century, all that appears known and published of tropical storms and hurricanes was, that they were often great whirlwinds."

15 **images from Caribbean civilizations**...Emanuel, *Divine Wind,* Chapter 3, "Huracán."

15 **Benjamin Franklin first conceived**...For an account of Franklin's insight, see John D. Cox, *Storm Watchers: The Turbulent History of Weather Prediction from Franklin's Kite to El Niño* (Hoboken, N.J.: John Wiley & Sons, 2002), Chapter 1.

15 **An accurate meteorological taxonomy**...As Gisela Kutzbach notes in *The Thermal Theory of Cyclones: A History of Meteorological Thought in the Nineteenth Century* (Boston, Mass.: American Meteorological Society Historical Monograph Series, 1979): "No clear distinction had yet been made between storms of various scale size and origin; in fact, throughout the first half of the nineteenth century authors often used the same general, non-specific term storm, while referring to quite different phenomena, such as hurricanes, tornadoes or large-scale cyclones" (p. 16).

16 **American Storm Controversy**...My discussion of the controversy draws upon original sources as well as a number of different secondary accounts. The authoritative version is James Rodger Fleming, *Meteorology in America, 1800–1870* (Baltimore, Md.: The Johns Hopkins University Press, 1990). Other accounts appear in Kutzbach, *The Thermal Theory of Cyclones;* Cox, *Storm Watchers;* and Jeffrey Rosenfeld, *Eye of the Storm: Inside the World's Deadliest Hurricanes, Tornadoes, and Blizzards* (New York: Basic Books, 1999).

16 **Rutherford famously put it**...In J. B. Birks, ed., *Rutherford at Manchester* (New York: W. A. Benjamin Inc., 1963). Rutherford is quoted in a reminiscence by P. M. S. Blackett, who writes, "Rutherford's single-minded and passionate interest in the nucleus led him sometimes to decry the importance and interest of other

branches of physics and still more so of other sciences. Though this depreciation was more jocular than serious, his prestige was such that even a joke from Rutherford's mouth was apt to become a dogma in lesser men's minds. No very young physicist could be totally unaffected by his famous crack: 'All science is either physics or stamp collecting,' or by the often implied assumption that it only needed some further progress in physics to allow us to deduce from first principles the facts and laws of the lesser sciences like chemistry" (p. 108).

16 **has long dogged meteorology**...For a historical account of the growth of meteorology that highlights battles between empiricists and theoreticians, see Frederik Nebeker, *Calculating the Weather: Meteorology in the 20th Century* (San Diego, Calif.: Academic Press, 1995).

17 **William Redfield**...For a detailed account of Redfield's life, see Cox, *Storm Watchers,* Chapter 4.

17 **a very important study**...William C. Redfield, "Remarks on the Prevailing Storms of the Atlantic Coast, of the North American States," *American Journal of Science and Arts,* Vol. XX (July 1831), pp. 17–51.

17 **a range of evidence**...In his paper, Redfield generalized his observations, arguing that "most storms, if not all, exhibit in a greater or less degree a circumrotative character" (p. 29).

18 **rather than beginning with a commitment**...As Redfield wrote in one rebuttal to Espy: "The attempt to explain nearly all the physical phenomena of the atmosphere by the theory of aqueous condensation, is not unlike that of him, who, in essaying to climb, should commence at the last and highest step in the ladder. In so diffuse and complex a science as meteorology, it is not by this inverted Baconian process that we can expect to 'ascend from effects to their causes.'" (W. C. Redfield, "Remarks on Mr. Espy's Theory of Centripetal Storms," *The Journal of the Franklin Institute,* 1839.)

18 **a pot being stirred**...As Redfield put it in his 1831 article: "Let a cylindrical vessel of any considerable magnitude, be partially filled with water, and let the rotative motion be communicated to the fluid, by passing a rod repeatedly through its mass, in a circular course. In conducting this experiment we shall find that the surface of the fluid immediately becomes depressed by the centrifugal action, except on its exterior portions, where, owing merely to the resistance which is opposed by the sides of the vessel, it will rise above its natural level, the fluid exhibiting the character of a miniature vortex, or whirlpool. Let this experiment be carefully repeated by passing the propelling rod around the exterior of the fluid mass, in continued contact with the side of the vessel, thus producing the whole rotative impulse by external force, analogous to that which we suppose to influence the gyration of storms and hurricanes, and we shall still find a corresponding result...."

18 **"analogy between the tides and currents"**...William C. Redfield, "Remarks on the Prevailing Storms of the Atlantic Coast," p. 18.

**18 "mechanical gravitation"**...W. C. Redfield, "On the Gales and Hurricanes of the Western Atlantic," *U.S. Naval Magazine,* 1836.

**18 a book for sailors**...Henry Piddington, *The Sailor's Horn-Book.*

**19 Redfield-Reid-Piddington school of storm studies**...Many insights about the behavior of hurricanes offered by Redfield and his devotees over a century and a half ago remain valid today. Not only did these researchers identify the rotary nature of hurricanes; they were also aware of the reversal of cyclonic rotation in the Southern Hemisphere. Moreover, they attempted to survey global storm behavior, observing the close similarity between Atlantic hurricanes and Pacific typhoons and noting that storms in the Atlantic often follow parabolic or "recurving" paths, moving west, then north, then back to the east.

Granted, these empiricists could not know what we know now, and many of their statements seem alien or even disorienting when read today. Not drawing a modern distinction between hurricanes and extra-tropical cyclones, Redfield lumped the two together. Some of the storms that he dubbed "hurricanes" originated over land, and some of them dumped snow. For instance, in "On the Gales and Hurricanes of the Western Atlantic," published in the *U.S. Naval Magazine* in 1836, Redfield included a chart of the "route of twelve storms, or hurricanes, which have visited the American coasts and seas, at various periods, and at different seasons of the year." Most of the storms originated over the ocean and followed tracks that seem very representative of the behavior of Atlantic hurricanes. However, Redfield's storm No. X is described as a "violent hurricane and snow-storm" occurring in December, and storm No. XI was a "violent inland storm" that crossed lakes Erie and Ontario. Neither was a hurricane by modern definitions.

Redfield also thought hurricanes were simply a larger version of tornadoes. As he wrote in one essay, "A full and just consideration of the facts which have been stated, will show conclusively...that the storm operates in the same manner and exhibits the same general characteristics, as a tornado or whirlwind of smaller dimensions; the chief difference being in the magnitude of the scale of operation." (William C. Redfield, "Observations on the Hurricanes and Storms of the United States and the West Indies," *American Journal of Science and Arts,* Vol. XXV, No. 1 [1834], p. 6.)

**19 "common sailor-language"**...Piddington, *The Sailor's Horn-Book,* p. ii.

**19 James Pollard Espy**...For detailed accounts of Espy's life, see James Rodger Fleming's entry on James Espy in *American National Biography,* eds. John A. Garraty and Mark C. Carnes, 24 vols. (New York: Oxford University Press, 1999); an entry on Espy in the *Dictionary of Scientific Biography,* Charles Coulston Gillispie, editor-in-chief, Vol. 4 (New York: Scribner, 1971); and Alexander Bache, remarks made to the Regents of the Smithsonian Institution, in *Annual Report of the Board of Regents of the Smithsonian Institution* (Washington, D.C.: The Institution, 1860), pp. 108–111. See also L. M. Morehead, *A Few Incidents in the Life of Professor James P. Espy* (Cincinnati, Oh.: R. Clarke & Co., Printers, 1888).

21 **a major step**...For this description of Espy's significance in the context of the growth and history of meteorology, see Rosenfeld, *Eye of the Storm*, p. 61. Espy's theoretical innovation seems particularly noteworthy in light of the fact that it preceded the discovery of the First Law of Thermodynamics, which states that energy cannot be created or destroyed, but only converted into a different form. By contrast, Espy worked from a "caloric" theory, which envisioned heat as a substance rather than as being interchangeable with work as stipulated by the first law. (See Kutzbach, *The Thermal Theory of Cyclones*, pp. 43–44.)

21 **all storms were the same**...As Espy put it, "it is believed that all the phenomena of rains, hails, snows and water spouts, change of winds and depressions of the barometer follow as easy and natural corollaries from the theory here advanced, that there is an expansion of the air containing transparent water vapour when that vapour is condensed into water." Quoted in Cox, *Storm Watchers*, p. 37.

21 **writing in 1835**...Quoted in Rosenfeld, *Eye of the Storm*, p. 56.

21 **a bile-filled 1839 rebuttal**...Redfield, "Remarks on Mr. Espy's Theory."

21 **the growth of American meteorology**...On the institutional changes brought about by the American Storm Controversy and its long-lasting nature, see Fleming, *Meteorology in America*.

22 **the most memorable commentary**...Quoted in Fleming, *Meteorology in America*, p. 23.

22 **the conflict turned**...For the differing scientific methodologies of Redfield and Espy, see Rosenfeld, *Eye of the Storm*, pp. 69–70.

22 **Matters came to a head**...For an account of this episode, see Fleming, *Meteorology in America*, pp. 97–98.

23 **Elias Loomis**...For an account of Loomis's life, see Cox, *Storm Watchers*, Chapter 6.

23 **intensively studying**...Loomis decided to undertake a detailed retrospective study of a particularly well-documented winter snowstorm that had occurred in December 1836. (See Kutzbach, *The Thermal Theory of Cyclones*, pp. 29–35.) Examining data on barometric pressure, temperature, and other measurements from dozens of outposts and locations across the country, he pieced together an image of a storm very different from the hurricanes that had drawn most of Redfield's attention. It was a mid-latitude or extra-tropical cyclone, and as Loomis realized, its winds blew at one another in such a way that cold air lifted warm air above it—which, in turn, led to condensation of water vapor and thus precipitation.

Like hurricanes, extra-tropical cyclones have spiraling winds. But Loomis's observations of this particular storm were too limited in extent to actually detect them (a defect he would remedy in later studies). Already, however, he had done a good job of describing what meteorologists now call a cold front. In subsequent examinations of other mid-latitude cyclones, meanwhile, Loomis detected the storms' spiraling winds. But like Espy, he also highlighted the importance of latent heat release, postulating a storm that, thanks to rising heated air, pulls in additional moist air from below and thus "gains violence by its own action." (Quoted in Kutzbach, *The Thermal Theory of Cyclones*, p. 34.)

**23 statistical studies**...See Kutzbach, *The Thermal Theory of Cyclones*, pp. 123–24.

**23 a synoptic chart or weather map**...For an account that complicates the standard narrative of how the practice of mapping the weather developed, see Katharine Anderson, "Mapping Meteorology," in *Intimate Universality: Local and Global Themes in the History of Weather and Climate*, Fleming, Jankovic, and Coen, eds. (Sagamore Beach, Mass.: Science History Publications, 2006).

**24 George Bliss**...Quoted in Mark Monmonier, *Air Apparent: How Meteorologists Learned to Map, Predict, and Dramatize Weather* (Chicago, Ill.: University of Chicago Press, 1999), p. 10.

**24 William Ferrel**...For more on Ferrel's life, see Cleveland Abbe, "Memoir of William Ferrel, 1817–1891," with Ferrel's "Autobiographical Sketch," *National Academy of Sciences. Biographical Memoirs* (Washington, D.C.: National Academy of Sciences, 1895), pp. 265–309.

**24 "dynamical meteorologist"**...See Nebeker, *Calculating the Weather*, p. 28. For more on Ferrel, see Fleming, *Meteorology in America*, pp. 136–40.

**24 the Coriolis force**...See Anders Persson, "How Do We Understand the Coriolis Force?" *Bulletin of the American Meteorological Society*, Vol. 79, No. 7 (July 1998). Available online at http://www.ap.cityu.edu.hk/Ap8813/References/Coriolis/Coriolis.pdf. See also Persson, "The Coriolis Effect: Four centuries of conflict between common sense and mathematics, Part I: A history to 1885." *History of Meteorology* 2 (2005), pp. 1–24. Available online at http://www.meteohistory.org/2005historyofmeteorology2/01persson.pdf.

**25 "to the right"**...Quoted in Fleming, *Meteorology in America*, p. 138.

**25 did not draw firm distinctions**...For Ferrel's failure to distinguish between tropical and extra-tropical cyclones, see Kutzbach, *The Thermal Theory of Cyclones*, pp. 141–42.

**25 popular misconceptions**...For a debunking of myths associated with the Coriolis force, see Pennsylvania State University meteorologist Alistair Fraser's "Bad Coriolis" Web page at http://www.ems.psu.edu/~fraser/Bad/BadCoriolis.html.

**26 in a modified form**...According to James Rodger Fleming, Ferrel was "'a supporter,' with modifications, of Espy's convective theory of storms. He held that gyratory storms were maintained by 'Espian thermal processes,' but he did not support Espy's centripetal wind patterns...." *Meteorology in America*, p. 138.

**26 "First Law"**...Arthur C. Clarke, *Profiles of the Future: An Inquiry into the Limits of the Possible* (New York: Holt, Rinehart and Winston, 1962), p. 29.

**26 the aging James Espy**...See Fleming, *Meteorology in America*, p. 139.

**26 one of Espy's contemporaries**...Alexander Bache, remarks made to the Regents of the Smithsonian Institution, in *Annual Report of the Board of Regents*, pp. 108–11.

**27 meteorological midgets**...See Emanuel, "A Century of Scientific Progress," in *Hurricane!: Coping with Disaster*, ed. Simpson.

**27 the lower part of the Earth's stratosphere**...Interview with Kerry Emanuel, October 19, 2006.

**27 and especially Europe**...Europe does not experience tropical cyclones at all—or at least, had not recorded any until Hurricane Vince, by then weakened to a tropical depression, made landfall in Spain in October 2005. (See National Hurricane Center, "Tropical Cyclone Report: Hurricane Vince," February 22, 2006. Available online at http://www.nhc.noaa.gov/pdf/TCR-AL242005_Vince.pdf.)

**27 types of cyclones**...See Appendix II, "Cyclone Typology."

**28 a famous 1921 paper**...Quoted in Kutzbach, *The Thermal Theory of Cyclones*, p. 212.

**28 found inadequate**...Few scientists at the time appear to have made what now seems the obvious move: Use the thermal theory to explain hurricanes and the frontal theory to explain extra-tropical cyclones. However, the Austrian physicist Max Margules did precisely that. See Kutzbach, *The Thermal Theory of Cyclones*, p. 193.

In general, though, the ideas that had begun with Espy, centering upon phase changes of water molecules, went out of fashion even as most meteorologists devoted relatively little energy to understanding the cyclones of the tropics (where those ideas would have proven much more useful). See Emanuel, "A Century of Scientific Progress": "The great success of the Norwegian School, led by Vilhelm Bjerknes, and the subsequent linear theories of extratropical cyclogenesis by Charney and Erik Eady in the late 1940s showed that most of the observed properties of middle latitude storms could be explained without reference to condensation of water vapor" (p. 183).

**28 scientific observations were scarce**...See, e.g., Christopher Landsea et al. "The Atlantic Hurricane Database Reanalysis Project: Documentation for 1851–1910 Alterations and Additions to the HURDAT Database," in Richard J. Murnane and Kam-Biu Liu, eds., *Hurricanes and Typhoons: Past, Present, and Future* (New York: Columbia University Press, 2004). As the paper notes: "The tropical storms and hurricanes that stayed out at sea for their duration and did not encounter ships (or tropical cyclones that sunk all ships that they over-ran) are, of course, undocumented for the period of 1851 to 1910. It was estimated that the numbers of 'missed' tropical storms and hurricanes for the 1851 to 1885 period are between zero and six per year. The estimate is a bit lower for the 1886 to 1910 period, when it is thought that between zero and four storms were missed. The higher detection for the latter period is due to increased ship traffic, larger populations along the coastlines, and more meteorological measurements being taken" (p. 195).

**28 a powerful hurricane**...My account of the Galveston hurricane and Isaac Cline's story relies upon Cox, *Storm Watchers*, Chapter 15; Emanuel, *Divine Wind*, Chapter 13; and Neil Frank, "The Great Galveston Hurricane of 1900," in *Hurricane!: Coping with Disaster*. See also Erik Larson, *Isaac's Storm: A Man, a Time, and the Deadliest Hurricane in History* (New York: Vintage, 1999).

**28 the Galveston strike**...Behind the catastrophic destruction and loss of life lay multiple failures. The U.S. Weather Bureau, which had been formed only ten years earlier and took responsibility for issuing hurricane warnings, ignored seasoned Cuban forecasters as well as considerable data about the storm's trajectory, incorrectly predicting it would curve past Key West and threaten the East Coast. Instead, the storm cut across the Gulf of Mexico toward Texas. Thus poor forecasting abilities were compounded by jealousy and xenophobia, a particular deadly combination. Meanwhile, Isaac Cline, Galveston's chief forecaster, did little better. Cline firmly believed that the city, despite its location on a barrier island separating the Gulf of Mexico from Galveston Bay, would be immune to a hurricane's storm surge. "It would be impossible," he had written in 1891, "for any cyclone to create a storm wave which could materially injure the city." (Quoted in Cox, *Storm Watchers*, p. 120.) Cline went even farther and argued that the Texas coast was generally "exempt" from hurricanes. On September 8, 1900, he was proven utterly wrong. And for this, Cline's punishment was considerable: His pregnant wife died in the surge that destroyed the city. Again, for Cline's story, see Larson, *Isaac's Storm*.

**28 a Category 4 storm**...According to NOAA's analysis of the "Deadliest, Costliest, and Most Intense United States Hurricanes from 1900 to 2000," that's the estimated strength of the Galveston storm. See http://www.aoml.noaa.gov/hrd/Landsea/deadly/Table4.htm.

## CHAPTER 2: Of Heat Engines ...

PAGE

**31 a tropical depression**...As reported in Herbert Riehl, "On the Formation of Typhoons," *Journal of Meteorology*, Vol. 5, No. 6 (December 1948).

**32 "a bit of life"**...American Meteorological Society/University Corporation for Atmospheric Research Tape Recorded Interview Project, Interview with Herbert Riehl, September 9, 1989; Joanne Simpson, interviewer.

**32 Born in Munich**...For obituaries of Herbert Riehl, see William Gray, *Meteorology and Atmospheric Physics*, 67, 1998, pp. 3–4, and Joseph B. Verrengia, *Rocky Mountain News*, June 10, 1997.

**32 a powerful December typhoon**...See Emanuel, *Divine Wind*, Chapter 23, "Bull Halsey's Typhoons."

**33 an entire generation of weather experts**...See William A. Koelsch, "From Geo- to Physical Science: Meteorology and the American University, 1919–1945," in James Rodger Fleming, ed., *Historical Essays on Meteorology* (Boston, Mass.: American Meteorological Society, 1996). See also Roger Turner, "Teaching the Weather Cadet Generation," in *Intimate Universality: Local and Global Themes in the History of Weather and Climate*, Fleming, Jankovic, and Coen, eds. (Sagamore Beach, Mass.: Science History Publications, 2006).

**33 a very different problem**...In 1945, Robert Simpson worked with the U.S. Air Force to establish a school of tropical meteorology in Panama, very similar to the institute in Puerto Rico. As Simpson later described it, "This was a program to provide an educational retread for A-course graduates who had been taught temperate latitude meteorology but found themselves ill-equipped to deal with the tropical weather they had to forecast in the western Pacific." (American Meteorological Society/University Corporation for Atmospheric Research Tape Recorded Interview Project, Interview with Robert H. Simpson, September 6 and 9, 1989; Edward Zipster, interviewer.)

33 **catching up to do**...For more historical context on the wartime training of U.S. meteorologists and their encounters in the Pacific, see Edward N. Rappaport and Robert H. Simpson, "Impact of Technologies from Two World Wars," in *Hurricane!: Coping with Disaster.*

33 **Riehl led the way**...In a later interview, Riehl made it sound like almost an accident: "Somehow, once you get going in some subjects, everybody keeps shoving projects to you in that area, and the line of least resistance is to do it. So that was what it was with tropical meteorology." (American Meteorological Society/University Corporation for Atmospheric Research Tape Recorded Interview Project, Interview with Herbert Riehl, September 9, 1989; Joanne Simpson, interviewer.)

33 **He served as mentor**...As Joanne Malkus (later Simpson) has put it, "I didn't really get the real devotion to meteorology until Herbert Riehl's course in tropical meteorology in 1947." (American Meteorological Society/University Corporation for Atmospheric Research Tape Recorded Interview Project, Interview with Joanne Simpson, September 6, 1989; Margaret LeMone, interviewer.)

33 **his foundational 1954 textbook**...Herbert Riehl, *Tropical Meteorology* (New York: McGraw-Hill Book Company, 1954).

33 **an "observational assault"**...Richard Anthes, "Hot Towers and Hurricanes: Early Observations, Theories and Models," in "Cloud Systems, Hurricanes, and the Tropical Rainfall Measuring Mission (TRMM)—A Tribute to Dr. Joanne Simpson," Chapter 10 in AMS Meteorological Monograph, Vol. 29, Tao and Adler, eds., January 2003, pp. 139–48.

33 **glowingly reviewed**...Robert D. Fletcher, Review of *Tropical Meteorology, Science,* Vol. 120 (1954), p. 600.

34 **such devices**...Interview with William Frank, May 30, 2006.

34 **radiosonde measurements**...In Riehl's "Waves in the Easterlies" report he discusses only radiosonde and pilot balloon measurements. In later work, research using rawinsondes gets reported. See, for example, Herbert Riehl and Ralph Higgs, "Unrest in the Upper Stratosphere Over the Caribbean Sea During January 1960," *Journal of Meteorology,* Vol. 17 (October 1960), pp. 555–61.

34 **a pioneering report**...Riehl was not the first scientist to detect the existence of African easterly waves, despite this definitive early report on them. They were first detected by meteorologist Gordon Dunn in 1940, whose findings inspired Riehl's paper. See Dunn, "Cyclogenesis in the Tropical Atlantic," *Bulletin of the American Meteorological Society,* Vol. 21 (June 1940), pp. 215–29.

**34 African easterly waves**...Herbert Riehl, "Waves in the Easterlies and the Polar Front in the Tropics," Misc. Rep., No. 17, Department of Meteorology, University of Chicago, 1945, 79 pp.

**34 "preexisting disturbances"**...Quoted in *Tropical Meteorology*, p. 332.

**35 a national weather radar network**...Edward N. Rappaport and Robert H. Simpson, "Impact of Technologies from Two World Wars," in Simpson, ed., *Hurricane!: Coping with Disaster.*

**35 satellite imagery**...See Christopher Velden et al., "The Burgeoning Role of Weather Satellites," in Simpson, ed., *Hurricane!: Coping with Disaster.*

**35 The first deliberate hurricane flight**...For discussions of airplane reconnaissance of hurricanes, see Emanuel, *Divine Wind,* Chapter 25, and Rappaport and Simpson, "Impact of Technologies from Two World Wars," in Simpson, ed., *Hurricane!: Coping with Disaster.*

**36 "Around us was an awesome display"**...R. H. Simpson, "Hurricanes," *Scientific American,* Vol. 190, No. 6 (1954), pp. 32–37.

**36 "In the eye of a hurricane"**..."Eye of a Hurricane" is included as part of The Edward R. Murrow Collection, Disc 2, *The Best of See It Now.*

**37 the National Hurricane Research Project**...Again, see Rappaport and Simpson, "Impact of Technologies from Two World Wars," in Simpson, ed., *Hurricane!: Coping with Disaster.* See also, in the same volume, Robert C. Sheets, "Hurricane Surveillance by Specially Instrumented Aircraft," pp. 63–101.

**37 "every pier"**...Walter R. Davis, "Hurricanes of 1954," *Monthly Weather Review,* December 1954, pp. 370–73. Available online at http://www.aoml.noaa.gov/hrd/hurdat/mwr_pdf/1954.pdf.

**38 abrasive personality**...Interview with Robert and Joanne Simpson, October 12, 2006.

**38 he rejected all of them**...As Robert Simpson related in a 1989 interview: "One of the people quite anxious to head this project was Herbert Riehl, without question the most notable tropical meteorologist of the time. While Dr. Reichelderfer recognized that Dr. Riehl had scientific credentials for the job, he was concerned whether Riehl, as a line manager, would be able to interface effectively with such diverse groups as he would have to deal with persuasively, not only on the scientific front, but with political figures, engineering groups, the military, contract support groups, and others across the nation upon whom the success of the project would depend. While I didn't know at the time what was happening in the recruitment effort, I learned later that Riehl had been offered a number of options for playing a leading role in the project, but not that of director. He rejected them all. His failure to be appointed director was unquestionably a bitter disappointment—understandably so. Unfortunately, his bitterness led to his refusal to have anything to do with the project during its formative months, both in Washington and later at West Palm Beach, despite my entreaties for him to join us. It was not until Erik Palmén and Joanne

Malkus visited the project at Palm Beach and became enthusiastic about it that Riehl was persuaded (by Palmén) to associate himself with the project." (American Meteorological Society/University Corporation for Atmospheric Research Tape Recorded Interview Project, Interview with Robert H. Simpson, September 6 and 9, 1989; Edward Zipster, interviewer.)

**38 NHRP hurricane flights**...The planes flew at three different levels: 6,000 feet, 14,000 feet, and 35,000 feet, the latter being "comfortable cruising altitude," remembers Robert Simpson (who was offered the NHRP directorship in place of Riehl). Interview with Robert and Joanne Simpson, October 12, 2006.

**38 "You were supposed"**...Interview with William Gray, October 12, 2006.

**38 a hurricane's strongest winds**...Interview with Charlie Neumann, November 8, 2006.

**38 a wide range of observations**...Working in this way in 1958, Riehl and Joanne Malkus came up with a famous (and somewhat poetic) notion in hurricane science: the concept of "hot towers." The key convective activity in hurricanes, the scientists argued, takes place in a relatively few regions of deep cumulonimbus cloud growth that become more prevalent toward the storm's eye wall, where large amounts of heat are transported high up into the atmosphere. In later studies, including examinations of data accumulated from several days of NHRP flights into 1958's Hurricane Daisy, Riehl and Malkus confirmed their "hot tower" hypothesis, as well as analyzing other aspects of hurricane structure and the flow of energy through these storms. See, for example, J. S. Malkus and H. Riehl, "On the Dynamics and Energy Transformations in Steady-State Hurricanes," *Tellus,* Vol. 12, No. 1 (February 1960), pp. 1–20, noting: "These temperature deficiencies suggest, however, that the moist adiabatic ascent does not take place by means of uniform and gradual ascent of the whole mass in the hurricane but, as postulated by Riehl and Malkus (1958) for the equatorial trough zone, it is largely concentrated in regions of rapidly ascending buoyant hot towers."

For a history of the development of the "hot towers" concept, see Anthes, "Hot Towers and Hurricanes: Early Observations," pp. 139–48.

**38 "He wasn't entirely"**...Interview with Robert and Joanne Simpson, October 12, 2006.

**39 women weren't allowed**...As Joanne Simpson put it in 1989: "I was just involved as a consultant to the hurricane project. To learn about hurricanes and how they worked, I went down a number of times to Palm Beach when they had the project. The hurricane flights there were made by military planes, and, of course, no women could go. A couple of years after that they took along a woman reporter, but they didn't take women scientists, which made me very mad." (American Meteorological Society/University Corporation for Atmospheric Research Tape Recorded Interview Project, Interview with Joanne Simpson, September 6, 1989; Margaret LeMone, interviewer.)

**39 attempts to create storm models**...See, for example, Herbert Riehl, "Some Relations Between Wind and Thermal Structure of Steady State Hurricanes," *Journal of the Atmospheric Sciences,* Vol. 20 (July 1963), pp. 276–87. The paper outlines a model of a "steady state, symmetrical hurricane" and then examines whether the observations from a number of storm flights match the model.

**39 considerable progress**...Some of the insights that arose from the early days of storm-flying are now better remembered than others. In 1960, Riehl helped generate one of the more notorious ideas associated with hurricane science: the notion that seeding clouds at the outer part of the hurricane eye wall with silver iodide crystals might weaken the storm by causing more growth farther away from its center—in other words, hurricane modification. Riehl himself was never a great fan of the idea. But his observations during a 1960 navy flight into the outflow regions of the intense and long-lived Hurricane Donna—which devastated the Middle Keys of Florida as a Category 4 storm and later also struck North Carolina and finally New England—helped to set it in motion. Riehl had noticed that the storm's outflow appeared to arise from a relatively small area, which suggested to Robert Simpson that cloud seeding might actually be feasible. (American Meteorological Society/University Corporation for Atmospheric Research Tape Recorded Interview Project, Interview with Robert H. Simpson, September 6 and 9, 1989; Edward Zipster, interviewer.)

Before long, such speculations led to the establishment of Project STORM-FURY, which attempted hurricane-seeding missions. There have been many questionable ideas about how to weaken hurricanes over the years (a tradition that continues to this day), but the U.S. government actually invested in this one. While STORM-FURY appeared to show some positive results, in retrospect the observed weakening in seeded hurricanes probably arose from the storms' natural behavior rather than anything we humans had done to them. Meanwhile, the project grew controversial, with Fidel Castro claiming in the 1960s that the United States was modifying hurricanes so that they would hit Cuba. It eventually ended in 1983. See Willoughby et al., "Project STORMFURY: A Scientific Chronicle, 1962–1983," *Bulletin of the American Meteorological Society,* Vol. 66, No. 5 (May 1985), pp. 505–14. See also Sheets and Williams, *Hurricane Watch,* Chapter 7, "Controlling Storms."

**40 a seminal 1948 paper**...Erik Palmén, "On the Formation and Structure of Tropical Hurricanes," *Geophysica,* Vol. 3, 1948, pp. 26–38. In addition to his remarks on sea-surface temperature, Palmén also drew a firm distinction between tropical and extra-tropical cyclones and postulated that an "upper limit" must exist for the strength that a hurricane can achieve.

**40 Ernst Kleinschmidt**...For information on his German-language publications, I am indebted to two internal reports from the Joint Centre for Mesoscale Meteorology of the United Kingdom's Meteorological Office. The first, Internal Report 11, is entitled "An Appreciation of the Meteorological Research of Ernst Kleinschmidt," by A. J. Thorpe, May 1992. The second, Internal Report 40, is entitled

"Theory of Mature Tropical Cyclones: A Comparison Between Kleinschmidt (1951) and Emanuel (1986)," by Suzanne L. Gray, and contains a full translation of Kleinschmidt's 1951 paper.

The first report provides an overview of Kleinschmidt's work on atmospheric dynamics and his career in general. Interestingly, it notes that he visited the University of Chicago in 1959/1960 at the invitation of Herbert Riehl. However, Kleinschmidt's work on hurricanes as heat engines had been published much earlier, in 1951. In that paper, just as Kerry Emanuel would decades later, Kleinschmidt noted (in translation), "The heat removed from the sea by the storm is the basic energy source of the typhoon. In comparison to it, the latent heat of water vapour, which the air carries with it from the outside, plays no more than a secondary role." The paper is "Principles of the Theory of Tropical Cyclones," *Archiv für Meteorologie, Geophysik und Bioklimatologie*, Vienna, Vol. 4a (1951), pp. 53–72. It shows a strong familiarity with the works of Riehl.

**40  a 1950 paper**...Herbert Riehl, "A Model of Hurricane Formation," *Journal of Applied Physics*, Vol. 21 (September 1950), pp. 917–25.

**40  "heat engine"**...In later work, Riehl combined the heat-engine model with other observational data to further elucidate the energetic and wind structure of hurricanes. In 1960, he and Malkus published a paper on the inflow of air into a hurricane, finding that in order to maintain the necessary pressure gradient, "an oceanic source of sensible and latent heat is required." (Malkus and Riehl, "On the Dynamics and Energy Transformations in Steady-State Hurricanes," *Tellus*, Vol. 12, No. 1 [February 1960].)

In retrospect it appears that Riehl and Malkus stood on the verge of determining, from a heat-engine framework, the correct limit on the maximum intensity of a hurricane. It is this central value that should shift in the direction of greater intensity because of global warming, according to Emanuel. Indeed, as Joanne Simpson put it in an interview with Herbert Riehl in 1989: "Within the last two or three years, Kerry Emanuel did a much more elegant mathematical model of the very thing that you and I did earlier, perhaps in a cruder way." (American Meteorological Society/ University Corporation for Atmospheric Research Tape Recorded Interview Project, Interview with Herbert Riehl, September 9, 1989; Joanne Simpson, interviewer.)

For further discussion of the continuities between the work of Riehl and Malkus and that of Emanuel, see Emanuel, "A Century of Scientific Progress," in Simpson, ed., *Hurricane!: Coping with Disaster*. For a more scientifically detailed account (i.e., full of equations!), see Emanuel, "Tropical Cyclone Energetics and Structure," available online at http://wind.mit.edu/~emanuel/tropical/Lilly_KE_ver2.pdf.

**40  "Atmospheric machines"**... *Tropical Meteorology*, p. 326.

**41  the basic mechanisms**...In addition to the writings of Riehl, this "how hurricanes work" section draws upon the writings of Emanuel, including the book *Divine Wind* as well as the article "Tropical Cyclones," *Annual Review of Earth and Planetary Sciences*, Vol. 31 (2003), pp. 75–104.

**42 sea-spray effects**...For a further discussion of the current understanding on this subject, see Emanuel, "Tropical Cyclones," pp. 75–104.

**43 Hurricane Wilma**...National Hurricane Center, Tropical Cyclone Report, Hurricane Wilma, updated September 28, 2006. Available online at http://www.nhc.noaa.gov/pdf/TCR-AL252005_Wilma.pdf.

**43 "sensitive to slight"**... *Tropical Meteorology,* p. 331.

**43 it ought to be possible**...As Riehl put it on pages 331–32 of *Tropical Meteorology:* "The temperature anomalies, especially when negative, correlate well with seasonal hurricane frequencies. It is certain that reliable synoptic charts of sea-surface-temperature deviations from the mean on a monthly or shorter time basis could provide a valuable aid for longer-term prognoses."

## CHAPTER 3:...and Computer Models
PAGE

**44 a very active Atlantic hurricane era**...For the definition of this era, see Stanley Goldenberg et al., "The Recent Increase in Atlantic Hurricane Activity: Causes and Implications," *Science,* Vol. 293 (July 20, 2001), pp. 474–79.

**44 San Felipe/Okeechobee Hurricane of 1928**...For the story of the disaster, see Emanuel, *Divine Wind,* Chapter 17.

**44 Great New England Hurricane of 1938**...See Emanuel, *Divine Wind,* Chapter 21.

**44 1969's Camille**...For more on Camille, see Emanuel, *Divine Wind,* Chapter 26, and Roger A. Pielke, Jr., et al., "Thirty Years After Hurricane Camille: Lessons Learned, Lessons Lost," July 12, 1999. Available online at http://sciencepolicy.colorado.edu/about_us/meet_us/roger_pielke/camille/report.html.

**44 "The old antebellum residences"**...R. H. Simpson et al., "The Atlantic Hurricane Season of 1969," *Monthly Weather Review,* Vol. 98, No. 4 (April 1970), pp. 293–306.

**45 outside the meteorological mainstream**...Indeed, in a historical overview of the development of knowledge of hurricanes in the modern era, Kerry Emanuel would later write, "A review of the literature on hurricanes published during the first two-thirds of the twentieth century reveals a striking separation between tropical meteorologists and the rest of the meteorological community." Emanuel, "A Century of Scientific Progress," in Simpson, ed., *Hurricane!: Coping with Disaster.*

**45 "It was not that popular"**...Interview with T. N. Krishnamurti, May 31, 2006.

**46 posthumous stature**...When Charney died of cancer at the age of sixty-four, in 1981, the *New York Times* ran a lengthy obituary. See "Dr. Jule G. Charney is Dead at 64; Worldwide Leader in Meteorology," *New York Times,* June 18, 1981. By comparison, a Lexis-Nexis database search shows that when Herbert Riehl died in 1997 at the age of eighty-two, only the *Rocky Mountain News* ran a brief obituary—and that, presumably, is because it was a local paper. In 1960, Riehl had relocated from the University of Chicago to Colorado State University in Fort Collins, where he founded its atmospheric science department. See Joseph B. Verrengia, "Herbert Riehl, Pioneer in Tropical Storm Research, at 82," *Rocky Mountain News,* June 10, 1997.

**46 Charney's early career**...For Charney's biography, see Morton G. Wurtele, "Charney Remembered," in Richard Lindzen, Edward Lorenz, and George Platzman, eds., *The Atmosphere—A Challenge: The Science of Jule Gregory Charney* (Boston, Mass.: American Meteorological Society, 1990). See also Norman A. Phillips, "Jule Gregory Charney, January 1, 1917–June 16, 1981," available online at http://www.nap.edu/readingroom/books/biomems/jcharney.pdf.

**46 a "chore"**...Quoted in Lindzen et al., eds., *The Atmosphere—A Challenge,* p. 20.

**46 Weather map analysis**...As noted in Wurtele, "Charney Remembered."

**46 far too subjective**...Indeed, Norman Phillips noted: "Much of the change in meteorology from an art to a science is due to [Charney's] scientific vision...." Phillips, "Jule Gregory Charney."

**46 "*haute problème*"**...Quoted in Lindzen et al., eds., *The Atmosphere—A Challenge,* p. 49.

**46 the thesis**...J. G. Charney, "The Dynamics of Long Waves in a Baroclinic Westerly Current," *The Journal of Meteorology,* Vol. 4, No. 5, October 1947, pp. 135–62.

**46 "baroclinic instability"**...For more detail on this very influential meteorological theory, see "Baroclinic Instability," R. T. Pierrehumbert and K. L. Swanson, *Annual Review of Fluid Mechanics,* Vol. 27, 1995, pp. 419–67.

**46 origins of extra-tropical cyclones**...The Bergen School scientists had already described extra-tropical cyclones by invoking the clash of tropical and polar air masses along a front. But Charney had provided the much broader atmospheric context, as well as the equations to explain dynamically why such storms arise. Knowing what to look for, later scientists found analogous baroclinic eddies in the oceans and even on other planets, such as Mars and Jupiter.

**47 The bias was embedded**...On this point, see Emanuel, "A Century of Scientific Progress," in Simpson, ed., *Hurricane!: Coping with Disaster.*

**47 dominant paradigm**..."It is hard to imagine any phenomenon that, following its discovery, has formed the subject of more dissertations and papers," MIT meteorologist Edward Lorenz would later write of baroclinic instability. Edward N. Lorenz, "The Evolution of Dynamical Meteorology," in Fleming, ed., *Historical Essays in Meteorology.*

**47 different sections**...Meanwhile, important processes that take place at scales smaller than the smallest section of the model—the formation of clouds, for instance—must be "parameterized," or represented on the basis of approximations or assumptions. This inevitably requires judgment calls on the part of the scientists designing and running the model, as different parameterization schemes can yield very different results. The overarching aim remains the same: Apply the equations of physics to the atmosphere in a massive computational project that yields useful predictions.

**48 an "exact science"**...Quoted in Cox, *Storm Watchers*, p. 154.

**48 dramatically off base**...For more on Richardson, see Oliver M. Ashford, *Prophet—or Professor?: The Life and Work of Lewis Fry Richardson* (Bristol; Boston, Mass.: Adam Hilger, c. 1985). See also Peter Lynch, *The Emergence of Numerical Weather Prediction: Richardson's Dream* (Cambridge, UK, and New York: Cambridge University Press, 2006).

**48 calculating the weather**...I've borrowed this phrase from the title of Nebeker, *Calculating the Weather.*

**48 Princeton's Institute for Advanced Study**...For the history of the Princeton project, see the following sources: Nebeker, *Calculating the Weather,* Chapter 10, "John von Neumann's Meteorology Project"; Phillips, "Jule Gregory Charney"; and George W. Platzman, "The ENIAC Computations of 1950—Gateway to Numerical Weather Prediction," *Bulletin of the American Meteorological Society,* Vol. 60, No. 4 (April 1979), pp. 302–12.

**48 an "investigation of the theory"**...As Charney later wrote of von Neumann: "To him meteorology was *par excellence* the applied branch of mathematics and physics that stood the most to gain from high-speed computation." Quoted in Jule Charney, "Impact of Computers on Meteorology," *Computer Physics Communications,* Vol. 3, Suppl. (1972), pp. 117–26.

**48 Charney's participation**...After publishing his thesis and spending almost a year in the stimulating atmosphere of the University of Chicago, followed by a fellowship that took him to Oslo to visit with some of the leading Norwegian meteorologists, Charney was at the height of his scientific powers when he came to Princeton in 1948.

**48 the first numerical weather prediction**...The results were later published as Charney et al., "Numerical Integration of the Barotropic Vorticity Equation," *Tellus,* Vol. 2 (1950), pp. 237–54.

**48 Edward Lorenz**...For the influence of Lorenz, see Nebeker, *Calculating the Weather,* Chapter 13, "The Recognition of Limits to Weather Prediction."

**49 more accuracy when it came to projecting**...For progress in dynamical modeling of hurricane tracks, see Kurihara et al., "The GFDL Hurricane Prediction System and Its Performance in the 1995 Hurricane Season," *Monthly Weather Review,* Vol. 126 (May 1998), pp. 1307–22. See also Kerry Emanuel, "A Century of Scientific Progress," and Mark DeMaria and James M. Gross, "Evolution of Prediction Models," both in Simpson, ed., *Hurricane!: Coping with Disaster.* Finally, see Sheets and Williams, *Hurricane Watch,* Chapter 9, "Computer Modeling."

**49 a significant breakthrough**...For a comprehensive history of hurricane forecasting, see Mark DeMaria, "A History of Hurricane Forecasting for the Atlantic Basin, 1920–1995," in Fleming, ed., *Historical Essays on Meteorology,* pp. 263–306.

**49  a 1972 essay**... Charney, "Impact of Computers on Meteorology."

**50  The resultant clash**... See Katsuyuki V. Ooyama, "Footnotes to 'Conceptual Evolution,'" presented at the 22nd Conference on Hurricanes and Tropical Meteorology in Fort Collins, Colorado, 1997, on file with the author.

**50–51  "there have always been incidents"**... Quoted in Lindzen et al., eds., *The Atmosphere—A Challenge*, p. 69.

**51  Charney traveled**... Interview with Robert and Joanne Simpson, October 12, 2006.

**51  a 1964 paper**... Jule Charney and Arnt Eliassen, "On the Growth of the Hurricane Depression," *Journal of the Atmospheric Sciences,* Vol. 21 (January 1964), pp. 68–75.

**51  Vic Ooyama**... Katsuyuki Ooyama, "Numerical Simulation of the Life Cycle of Tropical Cyclones," *Journal of the Atmospheric Sciences,* Vol. 26, No. 1 (January 1969), pp. 3–39.

**51  criticized Charney's account**... See Ooyama, "Footnotes to 'Conceptual Evolution.'" As Ooyama notes: "I immediately saw disaster in the model, but Charney did not listen to my alarm... It was regrettable that Charney did not pursue his interest in tropical cyclones beyond CE64 [Charney and Eliassen's 1964 paper]. The name, *conditional instability of the second kind,* had the dogmatic ring of universality, and took on, later, the aura of an authoritative cover for abuse."

**51  CISK sought to solve**... My account of the growth of CISK relies on Anthes, Richard: "Hot Towers and Hurricanes," pp. 139–48. I also draw upon Emanuel, "A Century of Scientific Progress," in Simpson, ed., *Hurricane!: Coping with Disaster.*

**51  simple models produced**... See, for example, Douglas K. Lilly, "On the Theory of Disturbances in a Conditionally Unstable Atmosphere," *Monthly Weather Review,* Vol. 88, No. 1, January 1960, pp. 1–17, noting, "The conclusion that cloud-scale motions grow more rapidly than those of meso- or cyclone-scale obviously does not preclude the existence of the latter, but relegates their explanation to methods not used in this study. It appears, further, that the smaller-scale motions, because of their compensating dry downdraft regions, tend to discourage development of larger-scale disturbances unless or until an organized meso-scale or large-scale ascending core can be established by nonconvective processes."

**51  CISK sought to explain**... Interview with Richard Anthes, University Corporation for Atmospheric Research, June 14, 2006 (telephone).

**51  a positive-feedback relationship**... As Emanuel describes CISK: "A key concept that emerges in this work is the idea that organized latent heat release drives a circulation, which in turn feeds moisture into the system; the key feedback is between latent heating and moisture supply." In "A Century of Scientific Progress," in Simpson, ed., *Hurricane!: Coping with Disaster.*

**52  It has been observed**... Emanuel, "A Century of Scientific Progress."

**52  some arguably mislabeled**... It has even been suggested that "the confusion about the popular acronym CISK is so wide-spread that it has become a useless term in any sensible communication." See Katsuyuki V. Ooyama, "Conceptual Evolution of the Theory and Modeling of the Tropical Cyclone," *Journal of the Meteorological Society of Japan*, Vol. 60, No. 1 (February 1982), pp. 369–79.

**52 "There are fashions"**...Interview with Doug Lilly, June 5, 2006.

**52 in the tropics**...Interview with Greg Holland, August 7, 2006. See also Anthes, "Hot Towers and Hurricanes," noting, "in the real tropical environment, the effect of cumulus convection is to gradually modify the environmental lapse rate towards a moist adiabatic (neutral) state."

**53 CISK explicitly ignored**...As Charney and Eliassen put it: "We have implicitly assumed that the depression forms over the tropical oceans where there is always a source of near-saturated air in the surface boundary layer. However, we shall ignore any flux of sensible heat from the water surface."

**53 a "setback" for the field**...Emanuel, "A Century of Scientific Progress," noting, "In many ways, the advent of CISK was a setback for tropical meteorology and for the study of hurricanes in particular."

**53 "Don't bury me"**...See Ooyama, "Footnotes to 'Conceptual Evolution.'"

**53 Riehl also argued**...Interview with William Gray, October 12, 2006.

**54 the trajectory of research**...My account of the development of climate science in this section draws upon James Rodger Fleming, *Historical Perspectives on Climate Change* (New York: Oxford University Press, 1998), and Spencer R. Weart, *The Discovery of Global Warming* (Cambridge, Mass.: Harvard University Press, 2003).

**54 first discovered the greenhouse effect**..."The solar heat possesses...the power of crossing an atmosphere; but, when the heat is absorbed by the planet, it is so changed in quality that the rays emanating from the planet cannot get with the same freedom back into space," wrote Tyndall in 1859. "Thus the atmosphere admits of the entrance of the solar heat, but checks its exit; and the result is a tendency to accumulate heat at the surface of the planet." Quoted in Fleming, *Historical Perspectives on Climate Change*, Chapter 6, p. 66. For more on Tyndall, see also Weart, *The Discovery of Global Warming*.

**54 Svante Arrhenius**...On Arrhenius, again, see Fleming, *Historical Perspectives on Climate Change*, Chapter 6. Like Tyndall, Arrhenius was most interested in explaining how the ice ages of the past may have occurred (i.e., global cooling), and didn't seriously worry about the likelihood of dramatic global warming. He assumed it would take thousands of years to double the concentration of $CO_2$ in the atmosphere. When Arrhenius won the Nobel Prize in chemistry in 1903, it wasn't for anything involving greenhouse warming, but for his work on the role of electricity in chemical reactions.

**54 climate science developed unevenly**...During the Enlightenment and in early America, many theories linking climatic changes to the growth and prosperity of civilizations had flourished. See Fleming, *Historical Perspectives on Climate Change*, Chapters 1, 2, and 4. By the opening decades of the twentieth century, however, the view had taken hold that climate was "stable *by definition*," as historian Spencer Weart notes it in *The Discovery of Global Warming*. The notion that human beings could alter the climate through their own actions remained, at best, a little-heeded speculation, hardly powerful enough to counter the widespread assumption that our activities simply cannot rival the tremendous forces of nature. The study of climate, meanwhile, was a "sleepy backwater," writes Weart.

**54 the new concern about climate change**...The reawakening began in the late 1930s with Guy Stewart Callendar, a British engineer who dabbled in climate research. Temperatures had been steadily rising throughout the Northern Hemisphere, and Callendar, who tracked the growing concentrations of carbon dioxide in the atmosphere, thought humans were responsible. Not that he had much of a problem with that: Like previous scientists, Callendar thought global warming would be beneficial, that it would save us from the return of the "deadly glaciers" (quoted in Fleming, *Historical Perspectives on Climate Change*, p. 115). His publications, however, helped generate renewed discussion of the issue and set the stage for its reemergence. For more on Callendar, see James Rodger Fleming, *The Callendar Effect: The Life and Times of Guy Stewart Callendar, the Scientist who Established the Carbon Dioxide Theory of Climate Change* (Boston, Mass.: American Meteorological Society, 2006).

**55 several breakthrough papers**...See, for example, Syukuro Manabe and Robert F. Strickler, "Thermal Equilibrium of the Atmosphere with a Convective Adjustment," *Journal of the Atmospheric Sciences*, Vol. 21 (July 1964), pp. 361–85; and Syukuro Manabe and Richard T. Wetherald, "Thermal Equilibrium of the Atmosphere with a Given Distribution of Relative Humidity," *Journal of the Atmospheric Sciences*, Vol. 24, No. 3 (May 1967), pp. 241–59. Manabe's team had constructed a very simple one-dimensional model that simulated the vertical transfer of heat between the sun, the upper atmosphere, and the Earth's surface. It contained a role not only for radiation, but also for convection: Rising currents of warm air (often saturated with evaporated water) carried heat upward, cooling the surface and helping to offset heating from the sun or due to the greenhouse effect. The model was called a "radiative convective equilibrium" model, and its core elements would later get incorporated into the architecture of the more complex GCMs that several different groups of scientists were steadily improving.

**55 Hansen's group got 4 degrees**...This modeling history is related in Weart, *The Discovery of Global Warming*, Chapter 5, "Public Warnings."

**55 a 1970 paper**...Syukuro Manabe et al., "Tropical Circulation in a Time-Integration of a Global Model of the Atmosphere," *Journal of the Atmospheric Sciences*, Vol. 27 (July 1970), pp. 580–612.

**56 involved in climate science**...Charney's climate research also included very influential work on the formation of deserts. In a 1975 paper, he speculated about how changes in human land use—due, for instance, to overgrazing—might lead to a decline in vegetation, followed by greater reflectivity of the Earth's surface, followed by cooling and less rainfall, followed ultimately by desertification. Charney wasn't necessarily right on the specifics, but the larger point, undoubtedly correct, was that the way human beings change the landscapes they inhabit could in turn change the climate. See Louis Berkofsky, "Charney's Influence on Desert Research," in Lindzen et al., eds., *The Atmosphere—A Challenge*, pp. 139–41. See also Weart, *The Discovery of Global Warming*, pp. 101–102.

**56  the Charney Report**... *Carbon Dioxide and Climate: A Scientific Assessment*, Report of an Ad Hoc Study Group on Carbon Dioxide and Climate (Jule Charney, Chair). Washington, D.C.: National Academy of Sciences, 1979. Available online at http://www.atmos.ucla.edu/~brianpm/download/charney_report.pdf.

**56  Carter's science adviser**...Frank Press, "Science and Technology in the White House, 1977–1980: Part 2," *Science*, Vol. 211 (January 16, 1981).

## CHAPTER 4: "Lay That Matrix Down"

**PAGE**

**59  "Pistol Packin' Mama"**...For the song's rather storied history, see http://www.nashvillesongwritersfoundation.com/fame/dexter.html.

**60  another fan of Francis Bacon's inductive methods**...As Darwin put it in his *Autobiography:* "My first note-book was opened in July 1837. I worked on true Baconian principles, and without any theory collected facts on a wholesale scale...." *The Autobiography of Charles Darwin*, Nora Barlow, ed. (New York; Norton, 1958), p. 119 (1993 paperback edition).

**60  nearly interchangeable profiles**...For a sampling of newspaper profiles, see Jack Cox, "Eyeing the Storm: Nothing Calm these Days for Gray," *Denver Post*, September 16, 1995; Diane Lacey Allen, "Forecaster Lives to Study, Predict," *Lakeland (Florida) Ledger*, May 26, 1996; Michael Cabbage, "Hurricane Man," *Fort Lauderdale Sun-Sentinel*, May 31, 1998; Jeff Klinkenberg, "Hurricane Bill," *St. Petersburg Times*, May 30, 1999; and Kevin Lollar, "Renowned Forecaster Still Pitching His Predictions," *Fort Myers News-Press*, May 27, 2001.

**62  a front-page story**...Valerie Bauerlein, "Cold Front: Hurricane Debate Shatters Civility of Weather Science," *Wall Street Journal*, February 2, 2006.

**62  an interview on CNN**...CNN, "It's a new era of hurricanes," September 23, 2005.

**62  the period of warming**...For a discussion of twentieth-century global temperature trends, see http://www.grida.no/climate/ipcc_tar/wg1/005.htm.

**62  a seventh-grade paper**...William Gray press conference, National Hurricane Conference, April 13, 2006.

**63  Climate scientists today suspect**...Interview with Anthony Broccoli, August 21, 2006.

**63  some journalists**...One of the worst cases was Peter Gwynne, "The Cooling World," *Newsweek*, April 28, 1975. Available online at http://www.wmconnolley.org/sci/iceage/newsweek-coolingworld.pdf.

**63 A few alarmed scientists**...See Weart, *The Discovery of Global Warming,* pp. 80–83.

**63 something of a canard**...See RealClimate.org, "The global cooling myth," January 14, 2005, available online at http://www.realclimate.org/index.php?p=94.

**63 "Ice Age people"**...National Hurricane Conference, Closing General Session Part II, April 14, 2006, audio on file with the author.

**64 "the only thing I wanted"**...William M. Gray, "The Misuse of Science and Global Warming," November 15, 2005, essay on file with author.

**64 a college knee injury**...William M. Gray, Biographical Sketch in Patrick Fitzpatrick, *Hurricanes: A Reference Handbook* (Santa Barbara, Calif.: ABC-CLIO, 2006) (second edition), pp. 205–206.

**64 the very first course**...See William M. Gray, "A Personal View of the Progress in Tropical Meteorology Over the Last 50 Years," presentation at the American Meteorological Society's 26th Conference on Hurricanes and Tropical Meteorology (2004), available online at http://ams.confex.com/ams/pdfpapers/75447.pdf.

**64 "On the Scales of Motion and Internal Stress Characteristics of the Hurricane"**...The dissertation was published in the *Journal of the Atmospheric Sciences,* Vol. 23 (May 1966), pp. 278–88.

**65 compositing**...For a discussion of compositing methodology, see William M. Gray, "Hurricanes: Their Formation, Structure and Likely Role in the Tropical Circulation," in *Meteorology Over the Tropical Oceans,* ed. D. B. Shaw (London: Royal Meteorological Society, 1979), pp. 155–218.

Gray's use of compositing was a necessary move in a scientific sense. Due to the sparseness of rawinsonde stations and the rarity of hurricanes, there was never enough data from any single storm to support general conclusions. Similarly, while storm-flying provided great data, it brought with it a wide variety of logistical woes. Compositing, however, allowed for quantitative reasoning about storm characteristics by assembling and combining data from a large number of individual cases.

**65 one of his most famous papers**...William M. Gray, "Global View of the Origin of Tropical Disturbances and Storms," *Monthly Weather Review,* Vol. 96, No. 10 (October 1968), pp. 669–700. Ironically, the paper flirted with the idea of Conditional Instability of the Second Kind, although nowadays that's hardly its most important feature. Gray initially supported CISK but subsequently became skeptical of it. (Interview with William Gray, October 12, 2006.)

**65 six ocean basins**...Different names and different breakdowns are used by different authors for the global hurricane basins. In general, I have relied, for my own breakdown and naming, upon the U.S. National Hurricane Center—which, for instance, uses "Atlantic" rather than "North Atlantic"—and upon Chris Landsea's Hurricane FAQ, available online at http://www.aoml.noaa.gov/hrd/tcfaq/F1.html. The exception is the Southern Hemisphere, where unlike Landsea I have opted to treat the South Indian as one basin and the Southwest Pacific as the other. Here I am following the lead of Peter Webster and colleagues in their paper for *Science,* discussed in detail in Chapter 9.

**67 traveled the globe**...For further discussion of Gray's career, see Sheets and Williams, *Hurricane Watch*. See in particular pp. 193, 199–202, and 268–71.

**67 a 1979 paper**...Gray, "Hurricanes: Their Formation, Structure and Likely Role in the Tropical Circulation."

**68 theoretical and modeling insights**...Interview with Richard Anthes, February 14, 2006.

**68 hurricanes weren't a very hot topic**...As Gray himself complained in a coda to his 1979 paper: "It is [important] that more meteorologists take up seriously the study of tropical cyclones. To date, very few research meteorologists have devoted many years or a high percentage of their time to the study of these systems."

**68 The lull period**...See Goldenberg et al., "The Recent Increase in Atlantic Hurricane Activity: Causes and Implications."

**68 a backwater**...The 1970s and 1980s were "quiet in the Atlantic, and they were quiet for hurricane research," as Kerry Emanuel observed in an interview on May 22, 2006.

**68 "When I came through"**...Interview with William Frank, May 30, 2006.

**68 including Emanuel**...See Kerry Emanuel, "Nuclear Winter: Towards a Scientific Exercise," *Nature,* Vol. 319, No. 6051 (January 23, 1986), p. 259: "[The] recent literature on 'nuclear winter' research...has become notorious for its lack of scientific integrity."

**68 Sagan and a group of sympathetic scientists**...R. P. Turco et al., "Nuclear Winter: Global Consequences of Multiple Nuclear Explosions," *Science,* Vol. 222, No. 4630 (December 23, 1983).

**69 "He took an extremist view"**...Interview with Greg Holland, February 13, 2006.

**69 The El Niño phenomenon**...See J. Madeleine Nash, *El Niño: Unlocking the Secrets of the Master Weather-Maker* (New York: Warner Books, 2002). For an overview of the effect of El Niño on hurricanes, see Pao-Shin Chu, "ENSO and Tropical Cyclone Activity," in Murnane and Liu, eds., *Hurricanes and Typhoons: Past, Present, and Future.*

**69 the El Niño connection**...This discovery represented something of a departure from Gray's earlier insights on storm genesis. Rather than looking to universal environmental factors that influence hurricanes across the globe, it strongly linked a global climate phenomenon—El Niño—to a pronounced regional effect: the suppression of Atlantic hurricane activity. And unlike much of Gray's previous data crunching, the El Niño insight sprang from research that he did largely in seclusion. "He did a lot of work on his own late at night down in his basement, staying up to eleven or twelve at night," recalls William Frank. "And he came up with that one totally on his own, without any students involved originally."

**70 the endeavor that would make him most famous**...William M. Gray, "Atlantic Seasonal Hurricane Frequency. Part I: El Niño and 30 mb Quasi-Biennial Oscillation Influences," *Monthly Weather Review,* Vol. 112 (September 1984), pp.

1649–68; and "Atlantic Seasonal Hurricane Frequency. Part II: Forecasting Its Variability," *Monthly Weather Review,* Vol. 112 (September 1984), pp. 1669–83. The first study lingered on the strong correlation between El Niño years in the Pacific and less active hurricane seasons in the Atlantic. The second outlined the forecasting scheme.

70  **"He was doing all of these empirical things"**... Interview with Richard Anthes, February 14, 2006.

71  **Hugo**... For definitive details on Hugo, see Bob Case and Max Mayfield, "Atlantic Hurricane Season of 1989," *Monthly Weather Review,* Vol. 118 (May 1990), pp. 1165–77. Additional discussion of Hugo's meteorological and damage statistics can be found in the 1994 National Research Council report *Hurricane Hugo: Puerto Rico, the Virgin Islands, and Charleston, South Carolina, September 17–22, 1989,* prepared for the Commission on Engineering and Technical Systems.

72  **$7 billion**... For Hugo's contemporary and adjusted damage figures, and for a comparison of its intensity with that of other U.S. land-falling storms, see E. S. Blake, E. N. Rappaport, J. D. Jarrell, and C. W. Landsea, "The Deadliest, Costliest, and Most Intense United States Tropical Cyclones from 1851 to 2004 (and Other Frequently Requested Hurricane Facts)." *NOAA Technical Memorandum NWS TPC-4,* 2005.

72  **1989 led Gray to add another**... The 1989–90 changing of the forecasting scheme, and the reasons for it, are reported in two articles by Robert C. Cowen: "1990 Hurricane Alert," *Christian Science Monitor,* December 12, 1989, and "Hurricane Forecaster Predicts Active Season in N. Atlantic," *Christian Science Monitor,* June 14, 1990.

72  **Gilbert**... For the definitive details on this storm, see Miles B. Lawrence and James M. Gross, "Atlantic Hurricane Season of 1988," *Monthly Weather Review,* Vol. 117 (October 1989), pp. 2248–59.

72  **an Atlantic basin record**... Hugh Willoughby et al., "A Record Minimum Sea Level Pressure Observed in Hurricane Gilbert," *Monthly Weather Review,* Vol. 117 (December 1988), pp. 2824–28.

72  **three additional storms**... See Miles B. Lawrence and James M. Gross, "Atlantic Hurricane Season of 1988," *Monthly Weather Review,* Vol. 117 (October 1989), pp. 2248–59; Case and Mayfield, "Atlantic Hurricane Season of 1989."

72  **"In the next ten to twenty years"**... Quoted in Paula Dittrick, "More Hurricanes Likely in 1990s," United Press International, April 20, 1990.

72  **coastal population and property value**... See National Oceanic and Atmospheric Administration, "Population Trends Along the Coastal United States, 1980–2008," September 2004, available online at http://www.oceanservice.noaa.gov/programs/mb/pdfs/coastal_pop_trends_complete.pdf. See also Roger Pielke, Jr., and Daniel Sarewitz, "Bringing Society Back into the Climate Debate," *Population and Environment,* Vol. 26, No. 3 (January 2005).

72  **a 1990 study**... William M. Gray, "Strong Association between West African Rainfall and U.S. Landfall of Intense Hurricanes," *Science,* Vol. 249, No. 4974 (September 14, 1990), p. 1251.

73 **"Stock up on candles"** . . . Jim Puzzanghera, "When Senegal Sends a Squall: Hurricane watcher says rain in Africa means an E. Coast battering," *Newsday,* September 14, 1990.

73 **the Sahel predictor** . . . Interview with William Gray, May 12, 2006.

73 **Today scientists suspect** . . . Interview with Chris Landsea, November 8, 2006.

73 **a perspective on Gray** . . . Interview with Robert and Joanne Simpson, October 12, 2006.

74 **numerous studies on Atlantic hurricanes and the Sahel** . . . See, for example, C. W. Landsea, and W. M. Gray, "The strong association between Western Sahelian monsoon rainfall and intense Atlantic hurricanes," *J. Climate,* Vol. 5 (1992), pp. 435–53; C. W. Landsea, W. M. Gray, P. W. Mielke, Jr., and K. J. Berry, "Long-term variations of Western Sahelian monsoon rainfall and intense U.S. landfalling hurricanes," *J. Climate,* Vol. 5 (1992), pp. 1528–34; and W. M. Gray and C. W. Landsea, "Examples of the large modification in US East Coast hurricane spawned destruction by prior occurring West African rainfall conditions," ICSU/WMO International Symposium on Tropical Cyclone Disasters, J. Lighthill, Z. Zhemin, G. Holland, and K. Emanuel, eds. (Beijing: Peking University Press, 1993), pp. 182–89.

74 **successful doctoral students** . . . William Gray vitae, on file with author.

74 **a staggering nineteen storms** . . . For the official report on the 1995 Atlantic hurricane season, see Landsea et al., "The Extremely Active 1995 Hurricane Season: Environmental Conditions and Verification of Seasonal Forecasts," *Monthly Weather Review,* Vol. 126 (May 1998), pp. 1174–93.

74 **Person of the Week** . . . Bill Gray, *ABC World News Tonight,* September 8, 1995.

75 **"I have never seen anybody"** . . . Interview with Hugh Willoughby, May 16, 2006.

75 **modelers have even begun** . . . For a discussion of this technique, see Frédéric Vitart, "Dynamical Seasonal Forecasts of Tropical Storm Statistics," in Murnane and Liu, eds., *Hurricanes and Typhoons: Past, Present, and Future.*

75 **Crichton distrusts** . . . Michael Crichton, *State of Fear* (New York: Harper-Collins, 2004). As Crichton puts it (p. 570): "Before making expensive policy decisions on the basis of climate models, I think it is reasonable to require that those models predict future temperatures accurately for a period of ten years. Twenty would be better."

75 **"seething with disgust"** . . . William M. Gray, "The Misuse of Science and Global Warming," November 15, 2005, essay on file with the author.

76 **Gray charges** . . . William Gray, Answers to Follow Up Questions relating to September 28, 2005 Senate testimony, on file with the author.

76 **"innate sense"** . . . William M. Gray, Written Testimony, Hearing on the Role of Science in Environmental Public Policy, Senate Committee on Environment and Public Works, September 28, 2005. On file with the author.

76 **Different scientific commentators mean different things** . . . See Carl Wunsch,

"What Is the Thermohaline Circulation," *Science*, Vol. 298 (November 8, 2002), pp. 1179–80; and Stefan Rahmstorf, "Thermohaline Ocean Circulation," *Encyclopedia of Quaternary Sciences*, ed., S. A. Elias (Amsterdam: Elsevier, 2006).

**76 Gray and his fellow hurricane scientists**...Goldenberg et al., "The Recent Increase in Atlantic Hurricane Activity."

**76 Atlantic Multidecadal Oscillation**...The term "Atlantic Multidecadal Oscillation" was apparently first used in print in Richard Kerr, "A North Atlantic Climate Pacemaker for the Centuries," *Science*, Vol. 288 (June 16, 2000), p. 1984. As climate scientist Michael Mann recalls, the phrase came up in a conversation between himself and Kerr: "I still remember the question and answer, 'Dick: So what should we call this?' Me: 'Well, we have a Pacific Decadal Oscillation, so why not call this the "Atlantic Multidecadal Oscillation?"'"

**77 Gray himself goes farther still**...Gray's views are captured in William Gray, "Global Warming and Hurricanes," presentation at the 2006 American Meteorological Society 27th Conference on Hurricanes and Tropical Meteorology, Monday, April 24, 2006. Extended abstract available online at http://ams.confex.com/ams/pdfpapers/107533.pdf. A number of apparently unpublished papers on file with the author also summarize Gray's views, including "Forecast of Global Circulation Characteristics in the Next 25–30 Years" (1996) and "Climate Trends Associated with Multi-Decadal Variability of Atlantic Hurricane Activity" (1997), co-authored with John D. Sheaffer and Christopher W. Landsea.

**77 much published evidence**...See Tom Delworth and Michael Mann, "Observed and Simulated Multidecadal Variability in the Northern Hemisphere," *Climate Dynamics*, Vol. 16 (2000), pp. 661–76.

**77 climate models link it**...Jeff R. Knight et al., "A signature of persistent natural thermohaline circulation cycles in observed climate," *Geophysical Research Letters*, Vol. 32, L20708 (2005), noting, "The results imply the AMO is a genuine quasi-periodic cycle of internal climate variability persisting for many centuries, and is related to variability in the oceanic thermohaline circulation (THC)."

**77 A surprising 2005 study**...Harry L. Bryden, Hannah R. Longworth, and Stuart A. Cunningham, "Slowing of the Atlantic Meridional Overturning Circulation at 25° N," *Nature*, Vol. 438 (2005), pp. 655–57.

**77 hard to detect any trend**...See Real Climate, "Ocean Circulation: New Evidence (Yes), Slowdown (No)," October 31, 2006. Available online at http://www.realclimate.org/index.php/archives/2006/10/ocean-circulation-new-evidence-yes-slowdown-no/.

**77 "all seat-of-the-pants stuff"**...Real Climate, "Gray and Muddy Thinking About Global Warming," April 26, 2006. Available online at http://www.realclimate.org/index.php/archives/2006/04/gray-on-agw/.

**78 widely accepted today**...Interview with V. Ramaswamy, October 6, 2006.

**78 "brain fossilization"**...Bauerlein, "Cold Front."

### CHAPTER 5: From Hypercanes to Hurricane Andrew

**PAGE**

80  **"The equation was so simple"**...Quoted in Lindzen et al., *The Atmosphere—A Challenge*, pp. 25–26.

80  **"more fulfilling aesthetic"**...Kerry Emanuel, "Response of Tropical Cyclone Activity to Climate Change," in Murnane and Liu, eds., *Hurricanes and Typhoons*, quotation on p. 396.

80  **"Our philosophy"**...Quoted in Jack Cox, "Eyeing the Storm: Nothing Calm these Days for Gray," *Denver Post*, September 16, 1995.

81  **Hurricane Gloria**...For the definitive meteorological statistics on Hurricane Gloria, see Robert A. Case, "Atlantic Hurricane Season of 1985," *Monthly Weather Review*, Vol. 114 (July 1986), pp. 1390–1405.

81  **"she followed me home"**...Interview with Kerry Emanuel, October 19, 2006.

81  **a media conference call**...Clear the Air Teleconference on Hurricane Intensity and Global Warming, May 22, 2006. Transcript available online at http://www.cleartheair.org/hurricane_briefing.vtml.

81  **its first forecast**...NOAA News Online, "NOAA Predicts Very Active 2006 North Atlantic Hurricane Season," May 22, 2006. Available at http://www.noaanews.noaa.gov/stories2006/s2634.htm.

81  **Emanuel has another hypothesis**...The published form of this argument is Michael Mann and Kerry Emanuel, "Atlantic Hurricane Trends Linked to Climate Change," *Eos*, Vol. 87, No. 24 (June 13, 2006).

82  **his initial turn toward the subject**...Interview with Kerry Emanuel, May 22, 2006.

83  **back-to-back papers**...The second study was coauthored with meteorologist Richard Rotunno of the National Center for Atmospheric Research in Boulder, Colorado. The two studies are Kerry A. Emanuel, "An Air-Sea Interaction Theory for Tropical Cyclones. Part I: Steady-State Maintenance," *Journal of the Atmospheric Sciences*, Vol. 43, No. 6 (March 15, 1986), pp. 585–604; and Richard Rotunno and Kerry Emanuel, "An Air-Sea Interaction Theory for Tropical Cyclones, Part II: Evolutionary Study Using a Nonhydrostatic Axisymmetric Numerical Model," *Journal of the Atmospheric Sciences*, Vol. 44, No. 3 (February 1, 1987), pp. 542–60.

83  **merely the instrument**...As the second paper put it: "...the CISK mechanism overemphasizes...the role played by cumulus convection since the really important interaction is between the developing vortex and the exchanges at the sea surface, with cumulus clouds merely redistributing upward the extra latent heat acquired at the surface."

83  **"important but it's not causal"**...Interview with Kerry Emanuel, May 22, 2006.

84  **a strong corollary**...As Emanuel's 1986 paper put it: "in principle, hurricanes might be extremely intense were the sea-surface temperature significantly higher or the lower stratosphere significantly colder than at present."

**84 Emanuel's first paper on hurricanes and climate**...Kerry Emanuel, "The Dependence of Hurricane Intensity on Climate," *Nature,* Vol. 326, No. 6112 (April 2, 1987), pp. 483–85.

**84 by about 5 percent for every degree Celsius**...So Emanuel summarized these results in another paper of his: "Increasing Destructiveness of Tropical Cyclones over the Past 30 Years," *Nature,* Vol. 436 (August 4, 2005), pp. 686–88.

**84 a tropical cyclone of unknown intensity**...See Christopher Landsea et al., "Can We Detect Trends in Extreme Tropical Cyclones?" *Science,* Vol. 313 (July 28, 2006), noting: "Another major tropical cyclone, the 1970 Bangladesh cyclone—the world's worst tropical-cyclone disaster, with 300,000 to 500,000 people killed—does not even have an official intensity estimate, despite indications that it was extremely intense." For more on the Great East Pakistan Cyclone of 1970, see Emanuel, *Divine Wind,* pp. 221–25.

**85 an almost-as-awful repeat**...For the details on 02B, see the Joint Typhoon Warning Center, 1991 Summary of Western North Pacific and North Indian Ocean Tropical Cyclones, available online at http://metocph.nmci.navy.mil/jtwc/atcr/1991atcr/pdf/chapter3.pdf.

**87 modest media coverage**...See "More Violent Hurricanes?" *Time,* April 20, 1987, and "Science Watch: Are Stronger Hurricanes in Offing?" *New York Times,* April 7, 1987.

**87 journalists soon interpreted**...See, for example, Thomas H. Maugh II, "Global Warming Storm Link Probed; Predicted Rise in Ocean Temperature May Increase Winds," *Los Angeles Times,* September 20, 1989.

**87 especially those making landfall**...Matthew C. Nisbet and Chris Mooney (2007), "The Next Big Storm? Understanding news coverage of the hurricane–global warming debate." Working paper. School of Communication, American University, Washington, D.C.

**87 a 1988 paper**...Kerry Emanuel, "The Maximum Intensity of Hurricanes," *Journal of the Atmospheric Sciences,* Vol. 45, No. 7 (April 1, 1988), pp. 1143–55.

**87 conditions far exceeding**...As Emanuel's paper put it, "Holding the temperature of the lower stratosphere constant, sea surface temperatures would have to be 6 to 10 C warmer than present values to sustain hypercanes. It is very unlikely that this has happened in the recent geologic past or will happen in the near future."

**87 surface winds of 500 miles per hour**...For hypercane winds, see Kerry Emanuel et al., "Hypercanes: A Possible Link in Global Extinction Scenarios," *Journal of Geophysical Research,* Vol. 100, No. D7 (July 20, 1995), 13755–13766, noting maximum winds near the surface of 220 meters per second in a modeled hypercane, which converts to roughly 492 miles per hour.

**87 an "incredible tornado"**...For the Fujita Scale, see http://www.outlook.noaa.gov/tornadoes/fujita.htm. It has actually been replaced by an "Enhanced Fujita Scale," available at http://www.spc.noaa.gov/faq/tornado/ef-scale.html.

**88 extinction of the dinosaurs**...Emanuel et al., "Hypercanes," 13755–13766. See also Jeff Hecht, "Did storms land the dinosaurs in hot water?" *New Scientist,* February 4, 1995.

**88 The press loved it**...For a brief sampling, see Charles Petit, "Like a Hurricane, but Worse," *San Francisco Chronicle,* December 8, 1994; Kurt Loft, "Hypercanes May Have Blown Away Dinosaurs," *Tampa Tribune,* September 26, 1995; and Robert C. Cowen, "Could 'Superhurricanes' Have Done in Dinosaurs?" *Christian Science Monitor,* October 10, 1995.

**88 Gore sought to translate**...For Gore's early activism, see Weart, *The Discovery of Global Warming,* pp. 142–43.

**88 a blockbuster statement**...As Emanuel would later opine of Hansen's testimony, "I don't think it was good for scientific research. It was such an outlandish view that it sparked a counterrevolution. We found ourselves in the middle of the Chicken Littles on the one hand, and the reactionaries on the other." Quoted in Sharon Begley, "He's Not Full of Hot Air," *Newsweek,* January 22, 1996.

**88 "It is time to stop waffling"**...Quoted in Philip Shabecoff, "Global Warming Has Begun, Expert Tells Senate," *New York Times,* June 24, 1988.

**89 Hansen cautioned**...James Hansen, "Let's Not Count on the Earth to Heal Itself; Wolf in the Greenhouse," *New York Times,* August 1, 1989.

**89 "manufacturing uncertainty"**...See David Michaels, "Manufactured Uncertainty: Protecting Public Health in the Age of Contested Science and Product Defense," *Annals of the New York Academy of Sciences,* Vol. 1076 (2006), pp. 149–62.

**89 altered his testimony**...Philip Shabecoff, "Scientist Says Budget Office Altered His Testimony," *New York Times,* May 8, 1989.

**90 A group of global warming "skeptics"**...Chris Mooney, *The Republican War on Science* (New York: Basic Books, 2005), pp. 61–64.

**90 the "skeptics" attacked the models**...See Mooney, *The Republican War on Science,* pp. 62–64.

**90 anomalous satellite and radiosonde data sets**...See, for example, John Christy, Written Testimony, Senate Committee on Environment and Public Works, May 2, 2001. Available online at http://epw.senate.gov/107th/chr_0502.htm. Since then this debate has largely been resolved, as corrected tropospheric temperature data are now more consistent with the results provided by models. See *Temperature Trends in the Lower Atmosphere: Steps for Understanding and Reconciling Differences,* eds. Thomas R. Karl, Susan J. Hassol, Christopher D. Miller, and William L. Murray, 2006. A Report by the Climate Change Science Program and the Subcommittee on Global Change Research, Washington, D.C.

**90 These two questions**...For a formal discussion of "detection" and "attribution," see the Intergovernmental Panel on Climate Change, Third Assessment Report, Working Group I: The Scientific Basis, 12.1.1, "The Meaning of Detection and Attribution." Available online at http://www.grida.no/climate/ipcc_tar/wg1/443.htm#1211.

**90  "a higher frequency"**... American Meteorological Society Council and University Corporation for Atmospheric Research Board of Trustees, "The Changing Atmosphere—Challenges and Opportunities," *Bulletin of the American Meteorological Society,* Vol. 69, No. 12 (December 1988), pp. 1434–40.

**91  $26.5 billion**... See Jerry D. Jarrell et al., "The Deadliest, Costliest, and Most Intense United States Hurricanes From 1900 to 2000," available online at http://www.aoml.noaa.gov/hrd/Landsea/deadly/index.html. The unadjusted figures for costliest hurricanes during this time period are available at http://www.aoml.noaa.gov/hrd/Landsea/deadly/Table3.htm.

**91  and later told the tale**... For hurricane specialist Stanley Goldenberg's account of living through Andrew, see http://www.aoml.noaa.gov/hrd/Goldenberg/index.html.

**91  wind gusts over 160 miles per hour**... Interview with Richard Pasch, November 8, 2006. For a narrative account of the experience of Hurricane Andrew from the National Hurricane Center, see Sheets and Williams, *Hurricane Watch,* Chapter 10.

**91  a 2004 reanalysis**... Christopher Landsea et al., "A Reanalysis of Hurricane Andrew's Intensity," *Bulletin of the American Meteorological Society,* November 2004, pp. 1699–1712. Available online at http://ams.allenpress.com/archive/1520-0477/85/11/pdf/i1520-0477-85-11-1699.pdf.

**91  a prominent article in *Newsweek***... Sharon Begley and Daniel Glick, "Was Andrew a Freak—or a Preview of Things to Come?" *Newsweek,* September 7, 1992.

**91  "People who say"**... Quoted in Randolph E. Schmid, "Global Warming and Hurricanes: No Proven Connection Yet," Associated Press, August 25, 1992.

**91  personally wasn't linked**... Gray says he does not take energy industry funding. See, for example, Alan Prendergast, "The Skeptic," *Westword,* June 29, 2006, available online at http://www.westword.com/Issues/2006-06-29/news/feature_full.html.

**91  Patrick Michaels**... Michaels's industry ties were documented in Ross Gelbspan, *The Heat is On* (New York: Perseus Books, 1998 [updated version]), see pp. 40–44. See also Scott Allen, "Global warming debate joined; scientists at hearing doubt threat, activists cite industry ties," *Boston Globe,* November 17, 1995, noting, "Michaels contends that global warming is so minor that the media should 'go find some other issue.' But *Harper's* magazine this week suggests that Michaels has a financial motive to push that view: He has received grants of $115,000 from energy interests, and a coal industry group funds his newsletter... Michaels said he publicly disclosed the research funding from industry and denied that it affects his findings. He said he had testified before Congress about his doubts on global warming 'long before these industry guys knew we existed.'"

**92  "flies in the face"**... Patrick Michaels, "Andrew's Green Vapors," *Washington Times,* September 14, 1992.

**92  Michaels often criticized models**... See Mooney, *The Republican War on Science,* pp. 62–64.

**92 "merely an exercise"**...Patrick Michaels, "Mitch's Warming Afterglow," *Washington Times,* December 17, 1998.

**92 at their warmest**...Mark A. Saunders and Andrew R. Harris, "Statistical Evidence Links Exceptional 1995 Atlantic Hurricane Season to Record Sea Warming," *Geophysical Research Letters,* Vol. 24, No. 10 (May 15, 1997), pp. 1255–58.

**92 "I don't believe"**...Quoted in Bill Dawson, "Experts Debate Global Warming's Effect on Tropical Storm Climate," *Houston Chronicle,* October 22, 1995.

**92 Kevin Trenberth**...Also quoted in Dawson, "Experts Debate Global Warming's Effect."

**92 a recipient of considerable funding**...For example, according to company giving reports, ExxonMobil gave $270,000 to the Competitive Enterprise Institute in both 2004 and 2005. See http://www.exxonmobil.com/corporate/files/corporate/giving04_publicpolicy.pdf and http://www.exxonmobil.com/Corporate/Files/Corporate/giving05_policy.pdf. However, on November 3, 2006, the Competitive Enterprise Institute's Marlo Lewis wrote that "ExxonMobil stopped funding CEI months ago." Available online at http://www.cei.org/gencon/019,05587.cfm. ExxonMobil's 2006 giving report was not available as this book went to press.

**93 "Blaming hurricanes on recent warming"**...Robert C. Balling, Jr., "Calmer Weather: The Spin on Greenhouse Hurricanes," Competitive Enterprise Institute, May 1997. Available online at http://www.cei.org/pdf/1200.pdf.

**93 the Leipzig Declaration**..."TV Meteorologists Publicly Endorse Anti-Climate Treaty 'Leipzig Declaration'; Backlash Results After White House Prods Weathercasters to Promote Fears of Global Warming 'Catastrophe,'" *PR Newswire,* November 11, 1997.

**93 the 1998 National Hurricane Conference**...My account of the conference is based on the following press reports: Steve Stone, "Weather Expert Rains on Idea that Humans Cause Global Warming," *Virginia-Pilot,* April 11, 1998; Richard Stradling, "Hurricane Forecast: Rain or Shine, Cloudy or Sunny," *Daily Press,* April 11, 1998; Peter Bacque, "Climate Shifts Seen as Natural; Weather Experts Discount Human Effects on Warming," *Richmond Times Dispatch,* April 11, 1998; and Michael Cabbage, "Hurricane Meeting Spawns Hot Debate on Global Warming," *Austin American-Statesman,* April 11, 1998.

**94 "Tropical meteorologists"**...Interview with Hugh Willoughby, May 16, 2006.

**94 highly episodic in nature**...Nisbet and Mooney, "The Next Big Storm?"

**94 a journalist called up scientists**...See, for example, J. Madeleine Nash, "Wait Till Next Time; If a Little Heated Water in the Atlantic Can Create Floyd, What Storms Will Global Warming Bring?" *Time,* September 27, 1999.

**95 a 1994 paper**...J. Lighthill et al., "Global Climate Change and Tropical Cyclones," *Bulletin of the American Meteorological Society,* Vol. 75 (1994), pp. 2147–57.

**95 dismissed entirely the notion**...As the paper put it, "There are grave scientific objections to…directly applying climate models, even though at present these have to use coarse grids just because they must represent changes over many decades, to study the statistics of tropical 'disturbances.' (Such disturbances are then assumed, in spite of the grid coarseness, to be related to real TCs with very fine structure in their most energetic regions.) Comprehensive climate models are undoubtedly well suited to predicting climate changes, which they do with good consistency among themselves, but that consistency disappears completely when they are misapplied in an attempt to offer direct indications of TC statistics."

**95  a trajectory of research**…Manabe et al., "Tropical Circulation in a Time-Integration of a Global Model." For another early attempt to study tropical cyclones in a GCM, see Lennart Bengtsson et al., "Simulation of Hurricane-type Vortices in a General Circulation Model," *Tellus,* Vol. 34 (1982), pp. 440–57.

**96  "like mushrooms"**…Interview with Syukuro Manabe, August 21, 2006.

**96  either increases *or* decreases**…Anthony Broccoli and Syukuro Manabe, "Can Existing Climate Models Be Used to Study Anthropogenic Changes in Tropical Cyclone Climate?" *Geophysical Research Letters,* Vol. 17, No. 11 (October 1990), pp. 1917–20.

**96  more and stronger storms**…Reindert J. Haarsma et al., "Tropical Disturbances in a GCM," *Climate Dynamics,* Vol. 8 (1993), pp. 247–57.

**96  substantially fewer**…Lennart Bengtsson et al., "Will Greenhouse Gas-induced Warming over the Next 50 Years Lead to Higher Frequency and Greater Intensity of Hurricanes?" *Tellus,* Vol. 48A (1996), pp. 57–73. Other GCM studies of hurricanes under enhanced greenhouse conditions include T. N. Krishnamurti et al., "The Impact of Current and Possible Future Sea Surface Temperature Anomalies on the Frequency of Atlantic Hurricanes," *Tellus,* Vol. 50A (1998), pp. 186–210, and Ruth McDonald et al., "Tropical storms: representation and diagnosis in climate models and the impacts of climate change," *Climate Dynamics* (2005), pp. 19–36.

**96  their critical letters**…See, for example, Jenni L. Evans, "Comment on 'Can Existing Climate Models Be Used to Study Anthropogenic Changes in Tropical Cyclone Climate,'" *Geophysical Research Letters,* Vol. 19, No. 14 (July 24, 1992), pp. 1523–24, arguing, "Claims that current climate GCMs are appropriate tools for exploring the relationship between greenhouse warming and tropical storm activity certainly seem to be overly ambitious." Going back farther, see John L. McBride, "Comments on 'Simulation of Hurricane-type Vortices in a General Circulation Model,'" *Tellus,* Vol. 36A (1984), pp. 92–93, noting: "The picture that emerges is one whereby the model cyclones are dependent on certain parameters in common with real cyclones but are independent of others."

**96  "there is no a priori way"**…Anthony Broccoli et al., "Comment on 'Global Climate Change and Tropical Cyclones': Part II," *Bulletin of the American Meteorological Society,* Vol. 76, No. 11 (November 1995), pp. 2243–45. As the authors further noted, "We do not agree [that] empirical approaches are 'thoroughly sound and appropriate' while the use of current climate models is 'not a methodology from which useful information is available.' Each of these methods has strengths and weaknesses. If one is mindful of the limitations of *all* of the methods for studying this issue, the use of existing climate models appears to be no worse than the methods employed by [Gray and coauthors]." See also Anthony Broccoli and Syukuro Manabe, "Reply to Evans," *Geophysical Research Letters,* Vol. 19, No. 14 (July 24, 1992), pp. 1525–26. Emanuel, meanwhile, defended the capacity of global climate models "in principle" to study future numbers of tropical storms, if not their intensity (due to the low resolution). See Kerry Emanuel, "Comment on 'Global Climate Change and Tropical Cyclones': Part I," *Bulletin of the American Meteorological Society,* Vol. 76, No. 11 (November 1995), pp. 2241–43.

**97 1995 report**...John Houghton et al., *Climate Change 1995: The Science of Climate Change. Contribution of Working Group I to the Second Assessment of the Intergovernmental Panel on Climate Change* (Cambridge, UK: Cambridge University Press, 1996), p. 334.

**97 a group of experts**...Ann Henderson-Sellers et al., "Tropical Cyclones and Global Climate Change: A Post-IPCC Assessment," *Bulletin of the American Meteorological Society,* Vol. 79, No. 1 (January 1998), pp. 19–38.

**97 Gray's empirically derived set**...As the report put it, "Elementary applications of empirical relationships from the current climate to a future climate are fraught with danger and offer little useful insight."

**97 a similar theory**...Holland, "The Maximum Potential Intensity of Tropical Cyclones," *Journal of the Atmospheric Sciences,* Vol. 54 (November 1, 1997), pp. 2519–41.

**97 maximum wind speed increases**...See Thomas Knutson, "Possible Relationships Between Climate Change and Tropical Cyclone Activity," summary prepared for the Sixth International Workshop on Tropical Cyclones, 2006. Available online at http://severe.worldweather.org/iwtc/document/Topic_4_2_Tom_Knutson.pdf.

**98 employing since 1995**...See Yoshio Kurihara et al., "The GFDL Hurricane Prediction System and Its Performance in the 1995 Hurricane Season," *Monthly Weather Review,* Vol. 126 (May 1998), pp. 1306–22.

**98 an additional 7 to 20 millibars**...Thomas Knutson et al., "Simulated Increase of Hurricane Intensities in a $CO_2$ Warmed Climate," *Science,* Vol. 279 (February 13, 1998), pp. 1018–20.

**98 sole focus on storm intensity**...Interview with Thomas Knutson, August 21, 2006.

**99 and now it's too late.** This concern was expressed by Max Mayfield in his January 31, 2006, presentation at the American Meteorological Society meeting in Atlanta. Author's notes.

**99 Emanuel led the way**...See Kerry Emanuel, "Thermodynamic Control of Hurricane Intensity," *Nature,* Vol. 401 (October 14, 1999), pp. 665–69.

**99  Close to 600 miles**...For Floyd's size, see NASA Earth Observatory, "Hurricane Floyd's Lasting Legacy," March 1, 2000. Available online at http://earthobservatory.nasa.gov/Study/FloydIntro/.

**99  Category 5 strength**...See National Hurricane Center Preliminary Report, Hurricane Floyd, November 18, 1999. Available online at http://www.nhc.noaa.gov/1999floyd.html.

**99  achieving its full potential**...As Emanuel said of Floyd, "It's pretty much at its potential....Probably only 1 percent of storms reach what we call their potential intensity." Quoted by Seth Borenstein, "Conditions Are Perfect for Mighty Hurricane: Meteorologists Amazed by Combination of Factors that Breeds Huge Storm," Knight Ridder, September 15, 1999.

**99  "any given intensity"**...Kerry Emanuel, "A Statistical Analysis of Tropical Cyclone Intensity," *Monthly Weather Review*, Vol. 128 (April 2000), pp. 1139–52.

**99  "too simplified"**...Matthew Fordhal, "New Model May Help Forecasters Predict Hurricane Intensity," Associated Press, October 13, 1999.

**100  neither scientist**...Notes on Kerry Emanuel and Bill Gray debate at AMS Hurricane Conference, Fort Lauderdale, 2000, taken by Julian Heming. On file with the author.

**100  a circus**...The direct quotations from the debate arise from the reporting of Peter Whoriskey, "Secret Is Out: Hurricane Forecasters Just a Bunch of Blowhards," *Miami Herald*, May 30, 2000.

**100  "a Kerry Emanuel roast"**...Interview with Kerry Emanuel, October 19, 2006.

## PART II: Boiling Over

PAGE

**101  "Because it demands"**...Thomas S. Kuhn, *The Structure of Scientific Revolutions* (Chicago, Ill.: The University of Chicago Press, 1962).

## INTERLUDE: Among the Forecasters

PAGE

**103  the conference's final session**...National Hurricane Conference, Closing General Session Part II, April 14, 2006, audio on file with the author.

**104  during the previous active hurricane period**...William M. Gray and Philip J. Klotzbach, "Forecast of Atlantic Hurricane Activity for October 2004 and Seasonal Update Through September," October 1, 2004. Available online at http://typhoon.atmos.colostate.edu/Forecasts/2004/oct2004/.

**104  Hurricane Opal**...For meteorological statistics on Hurricane Opal, see Miles Lawrence et al., "Atlantic Hurricane Season of 1995," *Monthly Weather Review*, Vol. 126 (May 1998), pp. 1124–51. Note that at least according to Wikipedia, Opal's minimum central pressure of 916 millibars was the lowest pressure ever recorded in a storm that never officially reached Category 5 strength. I was unable to find any

other confirmation of this apparent record. Available online at http://en.wikipedia
.org/wiki/Hurricane_Opal.

**104 1998's Mitch**... For details on Hurricane Mitch, see a report from the National Climatic Data Center, "Mitch: The Deadliest Atlantic Hurricane Since 1780."
Available online at http://lwf.ncdc.noaa.gov/oa/reports/mitch/mitch.html. See also
the National Hurricane Center, Preliminary Report, Hurricane Mitch, Revised May
4, 2000, available online at http://www.nhc.noaa.gov/1998mitch.html.

**105 the *Fantome***... See Jim Carrier, *The Ship and the Storm: Hurricane Mitch and
the Loss of the Fantome* (Camden, Maine: International Marine, 2001).

**105 Hurricane Georges**... For information about how close Georges came to triggering a Katrina-type scenario, see the New Orleans *Times-Picayune*'s special graphic
illustration of the storm's progress, available online at http://www.nola.com/hurricane/
images/georgesflashback.pdf.

**105 Hurricane Isabel**... National Hurricane Center Tropical Cyclone Report, Hurricane Isabel, January 16, 2004, available online at http://www.nhc.noaa.gov/2003isabel
.shtml.

**105 239 miles per hour**... See Sim Aberson et al., "Hurricane Isabel (2003): New
Insights into the Physics of Intense Storms, Part II: Extreme Localized Wind," *Bulletin of the American Meteorological Society*, October 2006, pp. 1349–54.

**105 Tropical Storm Ana**... See National Hurricane Center Tropical Cyclone Report, Tropical Storm Anna, December 19, 2003. Available online at http://www.nhc
.noaa.gov/2003ana.shtml.

**106 a boilerplate section**... This section appeared in the forecasts as early as 1995.
Gray's December 1995 "Summary of 1995 Atlantic Tropical Cyclone Activity and
Verification of Author's Seasonal Prediction" stated, "there is no plausible way that increases in man-induced greenhouse gases can be even remotely related to this year's
extremely active Atlantic basin hurricane season."

**106 a witty story on climate skeptics**... Joel Achenbach, "The Tempest," *Washington Post Magazine*, May 28, 2006.

**106 TCSDaily.com**... "About TCS Daily," available online at http://www.tcsdaily
.com/about.aspx. The site states: "On September 19, 2006, DCI Group LLC announced the sale of TCS Daily to its editor, Nick Schulz. As part of this process,
our previous sponsorship agreements have expired. Updates about the transition in
ownership will be posted on this page as they are available." For more information, see
also http://www.dcigroup.com/tcsstatement/ and http://www.tcsdaily.com/article
.aspx?id=091906D.

**106 funding in the past**... ExxonMobil's 2003 giving report lists a donation of
$95,000 to the "Tech Central Science Foundation" for "Climate Change Support."
On file with the author.

**106 retained DCI's lobbying services**... Lobbying registration forms for 2005 and
2006 on file with the author.

106 **"Science Roundtable"**...The "Science Roundtable" can be found at http://www.tcsdaily.com/sections/science_roundtable.aspx#.

## CHAPTER 6: The Luck of Florida
PAGE

109 **how to interpret other storms**...For examples see W. C. Redfield, "Remarks on Mr. Espy's Theory of Centripetal Storms," *The Journal of the Franklin Institute,* 1839.

109 **a devastating tornado**...See James Rodger Fleming, *Meteorology in America, 1800–1870* (Baltimore, Md.: The Johns Hopkins University Press, 1990), pp. 31–35.

109 **Cyclone Gafilo**...My main source of meteorological information on Gafilo has been the Joint Typhoon Warning Center's report on the storm. Available online at: https://metocph.nmci.navy.mil/jtwc/atcr/2004atcr/SH/StormSH/SH16.html.

109 **minimum central pressure**...Gafilo's minimum central pressure estimate is provided by the Joint Typhoon Warning Center in its Annual Tropical Cyclone Report for 2004. Available online at http://metocph.nmci.navy.mil/jtwc/atcr/2004atcr/.

109 **left homeless**...International Federation of Red Cross and Red Crescent Societies, Final Report: Madagascar, Cyclone Gafilo, February 25, 2005. Available online at: http://www.reliefweb.int/library/documents/2005/IFRC/ifrc-madagascar-25feb.pdf.

110 **the ferry sank in the storm**...See news reports including Agence France Presse, "Survivor found in Madagascar ferry tragedy, 16 corpses recovered," March 13, 2004; Lloyd's List, "Survivors recount Samson sinking off Madagascar," March 12, 2004; Agence France Presse, "Ferry carrying 113 people in Madagascar probably sank: Comoran official," March 11, 2004; Agence France Presse, "Moroni officials disclose chronology of Comoran ferry disaster," March 11, 2004.

110 **"Genesis does not occur"**...Gray, "Hurricanes: Their Formation, Structure and Likely Role in the Tropical Circulation," in *Meteorology Over the Tropical Oceans,* pp. 155–218 (quotation on p. 181).

110 **a clockwise spiraling cyclone**...For NASA imagery of Catarina, see the following links: http://earthobservatory.nasa.gov/NaturalHazards/natural_hazards_v2.php3?img_id=12037 and http://earthobservatory.nasa.gov/NaturalHazards/natural_hazards_v2.php3?img_id=12036.

110 **peak sustained winds**...For official track and intensity information on Catarina, see Ron McTaggart-Cowan et al., "Analysis of Hurricane Catarina (2004)," *Monthly Weather Review,* Vol. 134 (November 2006), pp. 3029–53.

110 **more than 35,000 homes**...Marcelino et al., "Cyclone Catarina: Damage and Vulnerability Assessment." Available online at http://www.dsr.inpe.br/geu/Rel_projetos/Relatorio_IAI_Emerson_Marcelino.pdf.

110 **meteorologists sparred**...See Bernd Radowitz, "Spiraling Storm Hits Southern Brazil as Scientists Disagree Whether It Is South Atlantic's First Hurricane," Associated Press, March 27, 2004.

111 **called it a hurricane**...For another analysis that judges Catarina to have been a true hurricane in the full sense of the word, see McTaggart-Cowan et al., "Analysis of Hurricane Catarina (2004)."

111 **according to their model**...U.K. Met Office, "Catarina Hits Brazil," date unclear. Available online at http://www.metoffice.gov.uk/weather/tropicalcyclone/ catarina.html.

111 **storms occasionally turning up in the South Atlantic**...See for example Broccoli and Manabe, "Can Existing Climate Models Be Used to Study Anthropogenic Changes in Tropical Cyclone Climate?" *Geophysical Research Letters,* Vol. 17, No. 11 (October 1990), pp. 1917–20, noting: "Poor aspects of the simulations included the dearth of storms in the eastern North Pacific...and the formation of storms in the South Atlantic, where no tropical storms form in reality." By 2005, however, Ruth McDonald and her colleagues could say: "A tropical storm-like cyclone was observed in March 2004 off the coast of Brazil, in the region where this model produces tropical storms." R. E. McDonald et al., "Tropical Storms: Representation and Diagnosis in Climate Models and the Impacts of Climate Change," *Climate Dynamics,* Vol. 25 (2005), pp. 19–36.

111 **"a problem with the model"**...Interview with Ruth McDonald, July 28, 2006.

111 **two scientists at the University of Melbourne**...Alexandre Pezza and Ian Simmonds, "The First South Atlantic Hurricane: Unprecedented Blocking, Low Shear and Climate Change," *Geophysical Research Letters,* Vol. 32, L15712 (2005).

111 **24 to 25 degrees Celsius**...Not all scientists consider the 26.5 degree Celsius "threshold" to be universally required for the formation of storms that can be called hurricanes. In the case of Catarina, while sea-surface temperatures were anomalously cool, cold air aloft increased the potential intensity that the storm could achieve. See McTaggart-Cowan et al., "Analysis of Hurricane Catarina (2004)."

112 **in 1991**...See Chris Landsea, "Why doesn't the South Atlantic experience tropical cyclones?" Available online at http://www.aoml.noaa.gov/hrd/tcfaq/G7.html.

112 **in January of 2004**...See Jeff Halverson, "A South Atlantic rogue," *Weatherwise,* July 1, 2004.

112 **in the Northwest Pacific**...See Johnny Chan, "Variations in the Activity of Tropical Cyclones over the Western North Pacific: From Interdecadal to Intraseasonal," in Murnane and Liu, eds., *Hurricanes and Typhoons: Past, Present, and Future* (New York: Columbia University Press, 2004).

113 **"The potential for mass destruction"**...Joint Typhoon Warning Center annual report, 1979, p. 77. Available online at http://www.npmoc.navy.mil/jtwc/atcr/ 1979atcr/pdf/1979_complete.pdf.

113 **fully ten typhoons**...The Japanese storms were Conson, Dianmu, Namtheun, Malou, Megi, Chaba, Songda, Meari, Ma-On, and Tokage. Not all made landfall at full typhoon strength. For more information see the Joint Typhoon Warning Center's annual tropical cyclone report for 2004. Available online at: http://metocph.nmci .navy.mil/jtwc/atcr/2004atcr/.

113 **Supertyphoon Chaba**...For the Joint Typhoon Warning Center's report on Chaba, see http://metocph.nmci.navy.mil/jtwc/atcr/2004atcr/NWP_IO/StormNWP_ IO/WP19.html.

113 **Typhoon Tokage**...For the Joint Typhoon Warning Center's report on Tokage, see http://metocph.nmci.navy.mil/jtwc/atcr/2004atcr/NWP_IO/StormNWP_IO/ WP27.html.

114 **Hurricane Alex**...For details on Alex see James L. Franklin, "Tropical Cyclone Report: Hurricane Alex," October 26, 2004, National Hurricane Center. Available online at: http://www.nhc.noaa.gov/pdf/TCR-AL012004_Alex.pdf.

114 **Alex eclipsed Hurricane Ellen**...This record is noted in William M. Gray and Philip J. Klotzbach, "Summary of 2004 Atlantic Tropical Cyclone Activity and Verification of Author's Seasonal and Monthly Forecasts," November 19, 2004. Available online at: http://hurricane.atmos.colostate.edu/Forecasts/2004/nov2004/.

114 **"ONE FOR THE RECORD BOOKS"**...National Hurricane Center, Hurricane Alex Discussion Number 19, August 4, 2004. Available online at: http://www .nhc.noaa.gov/archive/2004/dis/al012004.discus.019.shtml?.

114 **Charley looked ominous**...For details on Charley see National Hurricane Center Tropical Cyclone Report: Hurricane Charley, October 18, 2004. Available online at: http://www.nhc.noaa.gov/pdf/TCR-AL032004_Charley.pdf.

114 **"NO OBVIOUS REASON"**...National Hurricane Center, Tropical Storm Charley Discussion Number 7, August 10, 2004. Available online at: http://www.nhc .noaa.gov/archive/2004/dis/al032004.discus.007.shtml.

114 **the low-lying Tampa Bay–St. Petersburg area**...See Kevin Duffy, "Could Tampa Bay Be the Next New Orleans," *Palm Beach Post*, Sunday, July 9, 2006. For a simulation of a strong hurricane storm surge hitting Tampa Bay, see http://www .tbo.com/weather/hurricane/worstcase/. Finally, for a scientific discussion of storm surge possibilities, see Robert H. Weisberg and Lianyuan Zheng, "Hurricane Storm Surge Simulations for Tampa Bay." Available online at http://ocgweb.marine.usf.edu/ Products/StormSurge/TB_stormsurge.pdf.

114 **the storm veered to the right**...In the wake of the destruction—made all the more severe by Charley's merciless last-minute intensification—came accusations that the experts had poorly forecast the hurricane's track. In fact, the ultimate site of landfall fell within the (wide) cone of uncertainty inherent in the official forecast. Because Charley's northward momentum paralleled the coast, however, its turn to the right (or northeast) translated into a great shift in point of landfall. In the arguments over the forecast, a more important message was lost: Tampa–St. Petersburg *will* be hit by a major hurricane someday, and when it happens, the destruction could be catastrophic.

115 **an estimated $15 billion**...See Blake et al., "The Deadliest, Costliest, and Most Intense United States Tropical Cyclones from 1851 to 2004," *NOAA Technical Memorandum NWS TPC-4*. Available online at http://www.aoml.noaa.gov/hrd/Land-sea/dcmifinal2.pdf.

**115 "THE HURRICANE IS NOT A POINT"**...National Hurricane Center, Hurricane Frances Discussion Number 24, August 30, 2004. Available online at http://www.nhc.noaa.gov/archive/2004/dis/al062004.discus.024.shtml?.

**115 Hurricanes vary so much in size**...Kerry Emanuel, "Anthropogenic Effects on Tropical Cyclone Activity." Available online at http://wind.mit.edu/~emanuel/anthro2.htm.

**115 in 1926**...See Emanuel, *Divine Wind,* Chapter 15, "Miami, 1926."

**115 exceeding $140 billion**...See R. A. Pielke, Jr., J. Gratz, C. W. Landsea, D. Collins, M. Saunders, and R. Musulin, 2007. "Normalized Hurricane Damages in the United States: 1900–2005," *Natural Hazards Review* (submitted). Available online at http://sciencepolicy.colorado.edu/publications/special/nhd_paper.pdf.

**115 1935 Labor Day Hurricane**...See Emanuel, *Divine Wind,* Chapter 19, "The Labor Day Hurricane of 1935."

**116 Frances developed several outer eye walls**...Such unpredictable developments—known as "concentric eye wall cycles"—are one reason that hurricane models have such a hard time getting storm intensity right.

**116 Ivan**...See National Hurricane Center Tropical Cyclone Report, Hurricane Ivan, updated May 27, 2005. Available online at http://www.nhc.noaa.gov/pdf/TCR-AL092004_Ivan.pdf.

**117 a city below sea level**...If for no other reason than Ivan, New Orleanians should not have been surprised by the destruction that befell them a year later. Had it maintained its course toward the city, Ivan could have been much worse than Katrina. After the storm, Shirley Laska, a professor at the University of New Orleans who studies hazard assessment, projected what might have happened from a direct landfall of an "extreme storm" like Ivan at Category 4 or 5 intensity. Among other impacts, she wrote, Ivan would have "caused the levees between the lake and the city to overtop and fill the city 'bowl' with water from lake levee to river levee, in some places as deep as 20 feet." "Hurricane Ivan had the potential to make the unthinkable a reality," Laska concluded. "Next time New Orleans may not be so fortunate." See Shirley Laska, "What if Hurricane Ivan Had Not Missed New Orleans?" *Natural Hazards Observer,* Vol. XXIX, No. 2 (November 2004). Available online at: http://www.colorado.edu/hazards/o/archives/2004/nov04/nov04.pdf.

**117 the biggest waves**...David Wang et al., "Extreme Waves Under Hurricane Ivan," *Science,* Vol. 309 (August 5, 2005).

**119 "AFTER CONSIDERABLE AND SOMETIMES ANIMATED"**...National Hurricane Center, Tropical Depression Ivan Special Discussion Number 67, September 22, 2004. Available online at http://www.nhc.noaa.gov/archive/2004/dis/al092004.discus.067.shtml?.

**119 $45 billion**...See Blake et al., "The Deadliest, Costliest, and Most Intense United States Tropical Cyclones from 1851 to 2004."

**119 tirelessly warning about**...For another example of such warnings, see Chris Landsea and William Gray, "Florida's Coming Hurricane Calamities," *Miami Herald,*

July 23, 2002. Available online at http://www.aoml.noaa.gov/hrd/Landsea/herald/index.html.

**119 because of its extreme winds**...Interview with Richard Pasch, November 8, 2006.

**119 a pretty good job**...William Gray and Philip J. Klotzbach, "Extended Range Forecast of Atlantic Seasonal Hurricane Activity and U.S. Landfall Strike Probability for 2004," December 5, 2003. Available online at http://hurricane.atmos.colostate.edu/Forecasts/2003/dec2003/.

**120 "This year did not behave"**...William M. Gray and Philip J. Klotzbach, "Forecast of Atlantic Hurricane Activity for October 2004 and Seasonal Update Through September," October 1, 2004. Available online at: http://typhoon.atmos.colostate.edu/Forecasts/2004/oct2004/.

**120 Gray's October 1, 2004, hurricane forecast**...Gray and Klotzbach, "Forecast of Atlantic Hurricane Activity for October 2004."

**120 a *Washington Post* report**...David Brown, "2 Storms in Florida Not Seen as Trend; Experts Don't Fault Global Warming," *Washington Post,* September 3, 2004.

**120 *Los Angeles Times***...Usha Lee McFarling, "Storm Activity Part of a Cycle; Ridges of high pressure are routing hurricanes onto a track across Florida, experts say," *Los Angeles Times,* September 11, 2004.

**121 many other factors**...My discussion of the climatic factors feeding into the 2004 Atlantic season draws upon Brian H. Bossak, "'X' Marks the Spot: Florida is the 2004 Hurricane Bull's Eye," *EOS,* Vol. 85, No. 50 (December 14, 2004), pp. 541–52; as well as Philip J. Klotzbach and William M. Gray, "Causes of the Unusually Destructive 2004 Atlantic Basin Hurricane Season," *Bulletin of the American Meteorological Society* (October 2006), pp. 1325–33.

**121 a telephone press conference**..."Hurricanes and Global Warming News Conference," Center for Health and Global Environment, Harvard Medical School, October 21, 2004. Transcript available online at: http://www.ucar.edu/news/record/transcripts/hurricanes102104.pdf.

## CHAPTER 7: Frictional Divergence
PAGE

**123 "I can get you guys onto a flight"**...Interview with Jim Kossin, November 22, 2006.

**123 "We just showed up in Miami"**...Interview with Chris Landsea, November 8, 2006.

**123 plenty of barf bags**...An account of the flight, written by Stephen Hodanish, appeared in *Twin Tower Topics,* a publication for Friends and Alumni of Lyndon State College, Vol. 3, No. 5, Winter 1988–89.

**123 the historic flight**...See Willoughby et al., "A Record Minimum Sea Level Pressure Observed in Hurricane Gilbert."

**124 HURDAT project**...See C. W. Landsea, et al., "The Atlantic Hurricane Database Reanalysis Project."

**124 the hurricane that affected San Diego**...Michael Chenoweth and Christopher Landsea, "The San Diego Hurricane of 2 October 1858," *Bulletin of the American Meteorological Society* (November 2004), pp. 1689–97.

**125 El Niño conditions**...During the powerful 1997 El Niño year, the Category 5 Hurricane Linda, the most intense storm ever recorded in the Northeast Pacific with maximum sustained winds of 185 miles per hour and a pressure drop down to 902 millibars (26.64 inches), also gave California a scare when some models predicted it might recurve and approach the coast (although those predictions turned out to be way off base). For the official meteorological statistics on Linda see National Hurricane Center, Preliminary Report, Hurricane Linda, October 25, 1997. Available online at http://www.nhc.noaa.gov/1997linda.html.

**125 San Diego and Los Angeles**...Interview with Greg Holland, February 13, 2006.

**126 one very widely cited 2001 paper**...Goldenberg et al., "The Recent Increase in Atlantic Hurricane Activity."

**126 in media interviews**...See, for example, Heather J. Carlson, "Global Warming Cited in Storms," *Washington Times,* October 22, 2004, and Usha Lee McFarling, "Storm Activity Part of a Cycle; Ridges of High Pressure are Routing Hurricanes onto a Track Across Florida, Experts Say," *Los Angeles Times,* September 11, 2004.

**126 a study in late September 2004**...The Knutson and Tuleya study was published online by the *Journal of Climate* on Tuesday, September 28, 2004. See Andrew Revkin, "Global Warming Is Expected to Raise Hurricane Intensity," *New York Times,* September 30, 2004.

**127 Any consistent results**...Thomas Knutson and Robert Tuleya, "Impact of $CO_2$-Induced Warming on Simulated Hurricane Intensity and Precipitation: Sensitivity to the Choice of Climate Model and Convective Parameterization," *Journal of Climate,* Vol. 17, No. 18 (September 15, 2004).

**128 to critique the Knutson study**...Patrick Michaels et al., "Comments on 'Impacts of $CO_2$-Induced Warming on Simulated Hurricane Intensity and Precipitation: Sensitivity to the Choice of Climate Model and Convective Scheme,'" *Journal of Climate,* Vol. 18 (December 1, 2005), pp. 5179–82.

**128 Knutson and his coauthor stood firmly**...Thomas Knutson and Robert Tuleya, "Reply," *Journal of Climate,* Vol. 18 (December 1, 2005), pp. 5183–87.

**128 "please don't do this"**...Interview with Chris Landsea, November 8, 2006.

**129 the character of precipitation**...See, for example, Kevin Trenberth et al., "The Changing Character of Precipitation," *Bulletin of the American Meteorological Society* (September 2003), pp. 1205–17.

**129 In a warmer world**...See Kevin Trenberth, "Changes in Climate and Hurricanes," *Preprint: AMS Meteorology and Oceanography of the Southern Hemisphere,* Brazil, April 2006.

**129  the Harvard conference call**...Harvard Medical School, Center for Health and Global Environment, Hurricanes and Global Warming News Conference, October 21, 2004. Available online at: http://www.ucar.edu/news/record/transcripts/hurricanes102104.shtml.

**129  a press release**...Harvard Medical School, Center for Health and the Global Environment press release, "Experts to Warn Global Warming Likely to Continue Spurring More Outbreaks of Intense Hurricane Activity," October 21, 2004. Available online at: http://chge.med.harvard.edu/media/releases/hurricanepress.html.

**130  Emanuel added in a 2004 article**...Kerry Emanuel, "Response of Tropical Cyclone Activity to Climate Change: Theoretical Basis," in Murnane and Liu, eds., *Hurricanes and Typhoons.*

**130  "I think it's extremely difficult"**...Quoted in Todd Neff, "Politics Fuel Climate Spat," *Scripps Howard News Service,* January 27, 2005.

**130  Trenberth suspected**...Interview with Kevin Trenberth, December 29, 2006.

**130  Paul Epstein**...As Epstein put it at the press conference, "Since 2001, we know a lot more about the system. We know more about the deep ocean warming throughout the world. We know that surface pressures and winds are affected and polar winds are affected so that gradients are set up and so that storms can become more intense and are seeing these swings back and forth from dry periods to wet, et cetera. For Americans in the Southeast—Florida, Texas—this can be devastating; for Haiti, we've seen the impacts already this year. In terms of the direct public health impact of the lives lost in the U.S. alone, these hurricanes killed 128 people. We know that throughout the Caribbean over thousands, particularly in Haiti. We know Granada has been devastated. Their [indiscernible] is a loss so this is about development and poverty and ripples through the economy back to health. It means that this year's unusually intense period of destructive weather activity of four hurricanes hitting the U.S. in a five-week period could be a harbinger of even more extremes to come."

**130  "They are all smart guys"**...Quoted in Bruce Ritchie, "Scientists Debate Global Warming," *Tallahassee Democrat,* October 22, 2004.

**131  billboards along the I-4 corridor**...U.S. Newswire, "Billboards Say Bush Ignores Threat of Worse Hurricanes from Global Warming; Panel Says Warmer, Higher Seas Make Damage Worse," October 25, 2004.

**132  a job that entailed**...Interview with Kevin Trenberth, January 3, 2006.

**132  a letter**...Juliet Eilperin, "Hurricane Scientist Leaves U.N. Team; U.S. Expert Cites Politics in a Letter," *Washington Post,* January 23, 2005.

**132  "I personally cannot in good faith"**..."Chris Landsea Leaves IPCC," *Prometheus,* January 17, 2005. Available online at http://sciencepolicy.colorado.edu/prometheus/archives/science_policy_general/000318chris_landsea_leaves.html.

**133  he'd sought internal reassurance**...Chris Landsea e-mail to IPCC leaders and Kevin Trenberth, November 5, 2004. Available online at http://sciencepolicy.colorado.edu/prometheus/archives/ipcc-correspondence.pdf.

**133** **"Individual scientists can do what they wish"**...R. K. Pachauri, e-mail to Chris Landsea, November 20, 2004. Available online at http://sciencepolicy.colorado.edu/prometheus/archives/ipcc-correspondence.pdf.

**133** **Landsea protested**...Chris Landsea, e-mail to IPCC leaders, December 8, 2004. Available online at http://sciencepolicy.colorado.edu/prometheus/archives/ipcc-correspondence.pdf.

**133** **in January 2005**..."Chris Landsea Leaves IPCC."

**133** **major media coverage**...Eilperin, "Hurricane Scientist Leaves U.N. Team."

**133** **"ridiculous"**...Quoted in Eilperin, "Hurricane Scientist Leaves U.N. Team."

**133** **Landsea said he would work**...Timothy Gardner, "UN Storm Brews over Hurricane-Global Warming Link," Reuters, January 21, 2005.

**133** **"The sad thing about this"**...Chris Landsea e-mail to IPCC leaders and Kevin Trenberth, November 5, 2004.

**134** **"stark example"**...James Inhofe, statement on "Bringing Integrity Back to the IPCC Process," November 15, 2005. Available online at http://epw.senate.gov/speechitem.cfm?party=rep&id=248811.

**134** **did not put out**...Interview with Kevin Trenberth, February 14, 2006.

**134** **The paper, which appeared in *Science***...Kevin Trenberth, "Uncertainty in Hurricanes and Global Warming," *Science*, Vol. 308 (June 17, 2005), pp. 1753–54.

**136** **reportedly damaged nearly all standing structures**...New Zealand Press Association, "Cyclone Percy Running Out of Puff," March 4, 2005.

**136** **Cyclone Zoe**...See World Meteorological Organization, RA V Tropical Cyclone Committee for the South Pacific and South-East Indian Ocean, Tenth Session, Final Report, noting: "Although Tropical Cyclone Zoe can be claimed to be the most intense tropical cyclone yet in the SW Pacific (with Dvorak Technique), this however, still needs to be verified." Available online at: http://www.wmo.int/web/www/TCP/Reports/RA5_TCC10.pdf. The 879 millibar pressure estimate comes from the Joint Typhoon Warning Center, South Pacific and South Indian Ocean Tropical Cyclones, 2003. Available online at https://metocph.nmci.navy.mil/jtwc/atcr/2003atcr/chapter2/chapter2.html.

**136** **yet another "record"**...Island Climate Update 56, May 2005. Available online at http://www.niwascience.co.nz/ncc/icu/2005-05/article.

## CHAPTER 8: Meet the Press
PAGE

**137** **"back-of-the-envelope calculation"**...Interview with Kerry Emanuel, October 19, 2006.

**138** **Emanuel first published**...Kerry Emanuel, "Contribution of Tropical Cyclones to Meridional Heat Transport by the Oceans," *Journal of Geophysical Research*, Vol. 106, No. D14 (July 27, 2001), pp. 14771–81.

138 "cool tropics paradox"...See Kerry Emanuel, "A Simple Model of Multiple Climate Regimes," *Journal of Geophysical Research,* Vol. 107, Issue D9, pp. ACL 4-1, 2002.

138 The early Eocene...For scientific papers discussing this past era's climate and attributes, especially in the Arctic, see Kathryn Moran et al., "The Cenozoic Palaeoenvironment of the Arctic Ocean," *Nature,* Vol. 441 (June 1, 2006), pp. 601–605; Appy Sluijs et al., "Subtropical Arctic Ocean Temperatures During the Palaeocene/Eocene Thermal Maximum," *Nature,* Vol. 441 (June 1, 2006), pp. 610–13; J. R. Obst et al., "Characterization of Canadian Arctic Fossil Woods," in *Tertiary Fossil Forests of the Geodetic Hills, Axel Heiberg Island, Arctic Archipelago,* eds. R. L. Christie and N. J. McMillan, *Geological Survey of Canada,* Bulletin 403 (1991), pp. 123–46. More generally, see James Zachos et al., "Trends, Rhythms, and Aberrations in Global Climate 65 Ma to Present," *Science,* Vol. 292 (April 27, 2001), pp. 686–93.

139 helped transport large amounts of heat...For a much fuller exploration of this idea, see the thesis of Emanuel's student Robert Korty, "On the Maintenance of Weak Meridional Temperature Gradients During Warm Climates," June 2005. Available online at http://www.mit.edu/~korty/thesis.pdf.

139 Hurricane/Typhoon John...For information on Hurricane/Typhoon John, see the Central Pacific Hurricane Center's Tropical Cyclone Records page, available online at http://www.prh.noaa.gov/cphc/pages/FAQ/Tropical_Cyclone_Records.php. John's 8,000-mile travel distance is noted by NOAA's Hurricane Research Division, http://www.aoml.noaa.gov/hrd/tcfaq/E7.html.

139 John strengthened and weakened...For the best track data on Hurricane John, see the National Hurricane Center's preliminary tropical cyclone report, available at the following links: http://www.nhc.noaa.gov/archive/storm_wallets/epacific/ep1994-prelim/john/prelim03.gif; http://www.nhc.noaa.gov/archive/storm_wallets/epacific/ep1994-prelim/john/prelim04.gif; http://www.nhc.noaa.gov/archive/storm_wallets/epacific/ep1994-prelim/john/prelim05.gif.

140 "power dissipation index"...Kerry Emanuel, "Increasing Destructiveness of Tropical Cyclones Over the Past 30 Years," *Nature,* Vol. 436 (August 4, 2005), pp. 686–88.

140 a doubling of the amount of power...Emanuel, "Increasing Destructiveness of Tropical Cyclones."

140 "The trend sort of jumped"...Interview with Kerry Emanuel, January 4, 2006.

141 an interview with *Discover*..."Year in Science: Hurricanes Intensify Global Warming Debate," *Discover,* Vol. 27, No. 1 (January 2006). Available online at http://www.discover.com/issues/jan-06/cover/.

142 "I changed my mind in a big way"...Author's notes, Monterey meeting on Hurricanes and Tropical Meteorology, April 25, 2006.

142 they weren't convinced. Interview with Kerry Emanuel, January 4, 2006.

**142** **"the problem for me"**... Quoted in Peter Whoriskey, "The Gathering Winds: Since 1995, the U.S. has seen a rise in deadly storms. Unknown is what future hurricane seasons will bring," *Washington Post,* November 27, 2005.

**142** **a rebuttal**... See Richard Monastersky, "Future Forecast: Stronger Hurricanes?" *Chronicle of Higher Education,* September 16, 2005.

**142** **It ultimately appeared**... Roger A. Pielke, Jr., et al., "Hurricanes and Global Warming," *Bulletin of the American Meteorological Society,* November 2005, pp. 1571–75. Available online at http://sciencepolicy.colorado.edu/admin/publication_files/resource-1766-2005.36.pdf.

**142** **chief cause of our vulnerability**... Roger A. Pielke, Jr., and Daniel Sarewitz, "Bringing Society Back into the Climate Debate," *Population and Environment,* Vol. 26, No. 3 (January 2005), pp. 255–68.

**142** **Emanuel doesn't necessarily disagree**... See "Emanuel Replies," *Nature,* Vol. 438 (December 22–29, 2005), p. E13.

**143** **Dennis**... National Hurricane Center Tropical Cyclone Report, Hurricane Dennis, updated March 17, 2006. Available online at http://www.nhc.noaa.gov/pdf/TCR-AL042005_Dennis.pdf.

**143** **Hurricane Audrey**... For more on Hurricane Audrey, see Robert B. Ross and Maurice D. Blum, "Hurricane Audrey, 1957," *Monthly Weather Review,* June 1957, pp. 221–27.

**143** **"The bayou folk swam"**... "Audrey's Day of Horror," *Time,* July 8, 1957. Available online at http://www.time.com/time/magazine/article/0,9171,825085,00.html.

**143** **Emily**... For the official history of Hurricane Emily, see National Hurricane Center, Tropical Cyclone Report, Hurricane Emily, March 10, 2006. Available online at http://www.nhc.noaa.gov/pdf/TCR-AL052005_Emily.pdf.

**144** **a postseason reanalysis**... See Robert P. King, "New Member Added to Cat 5 Class of '05," *Palm Beach Post,* March 16, 2006.

**144** **"a terrible paper"**... Quoted in Scott Allen, "Hurricanes More Powerful, Study Says: Researcher at MIT Sees Larger Storms with Stronger Winds," *Boston Globe,* August 1, 2005.

**144** **"the people who have a bias"**... Quoted in Miguel Bustillo, "Katrina Hits the Gulf Coast; Storm Turns Focus to Global Warming; Though some scientists connect the growing severity of hurricanes to climate change, most insist that there's not enough proof," *Los Angeles Times,* August 30, 2005.

**144** **"People are jumping"**... Quoted in Tom Meersman, "Hurricane Katrina; Big storms open up big climate debate; As some scientists back a theory that global warming is behind more intense hurricanes, others call it a part of the natural cycle," *Minneapolis Star-Tribune,* September 11, 2005.

**145** **"If I'm proven wrong"**... Quoted in Dan Vergano, "In the Eye of the Storms," *USA Today,* September 25, 2005. Available online at http://www.usatoday.com/tech/science/2005-09-25-hurricane-science_x.htm.

145 "all these medicine men"...CNN, "It's a New Era of Hurricanes," September 23, 2005.

145 "The idea is to frighten the public"...Quoted in Kathy A. Svitil, "Discover Dialogue: Meteorologist William Gray," *Discover*, Vol. 26, No. 09 (September 2005). Available online at http://www.discover.com/issues/sep-05/departments/discover-dialogue.

145 a slightly above-average year...William Gray and Philip Klotzbach, "Extended Range Forecast of Atlantic Seasonal Hurricane Activity and U.S. Landfall Strike Probability for 2005," December 3, 2004. Available online at http://typhoon.atmos.colostate.edu/Forecasts/2004/dec2004/.

145 Gray had upped the forecast...Gray and Klotzbach, "Extended Range Forecast of Atlantic Seasonal Hurricane Activity and U.S. Landfall Strike Probability for 2005," May 31, 2005. Available online at http://typhoon.atmos.colostate.edu/Forecasts/2005/june2005/.

145 NOAA...had similarly predicted...NOAA 2005 Atlantic hurricane outlook, issued May 16, 2005. Available online at http://www.cpc.ncep.noaa.gov/products/outlooks/hurricane2005/May/hurricane.html.

145 2005 ultimately shattered all records...For the complete tracks of the twenty-eight storms, see http://www.nhc.noaa.gov/tracks/2005atl.pdf. The major hurricanes were Dennis, Emily, Katrina, Maria, Rita, Wilma, and Beta.

146 dynamical seasonal hurricane forecasting...For a discussion of this technique, see Frédéric Vitart, "Dynamical Seasonal Forecasts of Tropical Storm Statistics," in *Hurricanes and Typhoons: Past, Present, and Future.* See also Vitart and Stockdale, "Seasonal Forecasting of Tropical Storms Using Coupled GCM Integrations," *Monthly Weather Review*, Vol. 129 (October 2001), pp. 2521–37.

146 the glint of an ability...See Frédéric Vitart et al., "Dynamically-Based Seasonal Forecasts of Atlantic Tropical-Storm Activity," 2006, in press.

146 Meteo-France...As noted in American Geophysical Union, "Hurricanes and the U.S. Gulf Coast: Science and Sustainable Rebuilding," June 2006. Available online at http://www.agu.org/report/hurricanes/. E-mail correspondence with Frédéric Vitart, January 8, 2007.

146 16.2 storms...Frédéric Vitart et al., "Dynamically-Based Seasonal Forecasts of Atlantic Tropical-Storm Activity," 2006, in press.

146 the probability, across many model runs...As Frédéric Vitart describes the reasoning: "By creating a large number of forecasts, it is possible to sample the probability distribution function of the atmospheric variable of interest. An analogy would be playing cards with a deck where some red cards have been removed. If someone draws randomly a card from the deck, it would be impossible to conclude that the deck is not a regular deck. But if the person puts the card back inside the deck and repeats the same operation a very large number of times, it will become clear that black cards are drawn more often than red cards. If the operation

is repeated a sufficient number of times, then the person will be able to assess that statistically there is very little chance that the deck is a regular deck. The size of the ensemble for seasonal forecasting usually ranges between 5 and 50 operations and is limited by the cost of computer time. The obligation to create an ensemble of forecasts makes dynamical seasonal forecasting very expensive." (Vitart, "Dynamical Seasonal Forecasts of Tropical Storm Statistics.")

**147 And then came Katrina**...For the definitive meteorological history of Katrina, see the National Hurricane Center, Tropical Cyclone Report: Hurricane Katrina, updated August 10, 2006. Available online at http://www.nhc.noaa.gov/pdf/TCR-AL122005_Katrina.pdf.

**147 the infamous Loop Current**...See Benjamin Jaimes et al., "Influence of Loop Current Ocean Heat Content on Hurricanes Katrina, Rita, and Wilma," paper given Monday, April 24, 2006, at the 27th Conference on Hurricanes and Tropical Meteorology. Extended abstract available at http://ams.confex.com/ams/pdfpapers/108249.pdf.

**147 Corps of Engineers**...For a powerful and devastating indictment of the failures of the Corps, see Michael Grunwald, "Progmation," *The New Republic,* August 14–21, 2006.

**147 Mississippi River Gulf Outlet**...Of the "Mr. Go," Douglas Brinkley writes, "The result was the same as if a team of top-flight engineers had been assigned to build an instrument for the quick and effective flooding of New Orleans." *The Great Deluge: Hurricane Katrina, New Orleans, and the Mississippi Gulf Coast* (New York: William Morrow, 2006), p. 219.

**147 track and landfall predictions**...Department of Commerce, Service Assessment: Hurricane Katrina, August 23–31. Available online at http://www.weather.gov/om/assessments/pdfs/Katrina.pdf. Note page 12: "NHC's official track forecasts for Katrina issued within about two and a half days of landfall in Louisiana were exceptionally accurate and consistent. The forecast errors were considerably less than the average official Atlantic track errors for the 10-year period 1995–2004. Every official forecast that was issued beginning at 5 p.m. EDT on August 26 showed a track crossing the coast of Mississippi and/or southeastern Louisiana."

**148 invoked natural cycles.** Gerry Bell et al., "The 2005 North Atlantic Hurricane Season: A Climate Perspective," Climate Prediction Center, The National Weather Service. Available online at http://www.cpc.noaa.gov/products/expert_assessment/hurrsummary_2005.pdf.

**148 easterly trade winds**...See Jyotika Virmani and Robert Weisberg, "The 2005 Hurricane Season: An Echo of the Past or Harbinger of the Future?" *Geophysical Research Letters,* Vol. 33, L05707 (2006).

**149 June-to-October temperature anomaly**...Kevin Trenberth and Dennis Shea, "Atlantic Hurricanes and Natural Variability in 2005," *Geophysical Research Letters,* Vol. 33, L12704 (2006).

**149 Ross Gelbspan**...Ross Gelbspan, "Katrina's Real Name," *Boston Globe*, op-ed, August 30, 2005.

**149 "The American president closes his eyes"**...Quoted in Craig Whitlock, "Environment Minister Criticizes U.S. Policy; 'Neglected Climate Protection' to Blame," *Washington Post*, September 2, 2006.

**150 "It's just unadulterated garbage"**...Interview with Greg Holland, February 13, 2006.

**150 "absurd"**...Kerry Emanuel, "Anthropogenic Effects on Tropical Cyclone Activity," Revised January 2006, available online at http://wind.mit.edu/~emanuel/anthro2.htm.

**150 articles over the years discussing**...This media-coverage data was compiled using Lexis-Nexis Guided Search. A search was performed, in the "general news" category, for the *New York Times* and *Washington Post*, for the words "hurricane" or "tropical storm" or "tropical depression" and "global warming" or "climate change" or "greenhouse gas" or "greenhouse effect." The "and not" feature was used to eliminate "news summary" or "information bank abstract" or "wall street journal." All of the categories were set on full text.

Each article was read, which involved both scanning for the search terms and analyzing the relationship between them. Articles that related a change in the regularity or strength of hurricanes to global warming were included in the count; other articles were removed. Article types included op-ed pieces, editorials, and letters to the editor, as well as more standard news stories.

**151 Some forty articles**...Matthew C. Nisbet and Chris Mooney (2007). "The Next Big Storm? Understanding news coverage of the hurricane–global warming debate." Working paper. School of Communication, American University, Washington, D.C.

**151 "Are We Making Hurricanes Worse?"**...*Time*, October 3, 2005.

**152 "filter"**...Interview with Kerry Emanuel, May 22, 2006.

**152 a survey by the Pew Research Center**...Pew Research Center, "Two-In-Three Critical of Bush's Relief Efforts; Huge Racial Divide Over Katrina and Its Consequences," September 8, 2005. Poll data available online at http://people-press.org/reports/display.php3?ReportID=255.

**152 "There is no relationship"**...Charles Krauthammer, "Where to Point the Fingers," *Washington Post*, September 9, 2005.

**152 partly funded by ExxonMobil**...The George C. Marshall Institute received $115,000 from ExxonMobil in 2005, according to the company's 2005 giving report available at http://www.exxonmobil.com/Corporate/Files/Corporate/giving05_policy.pdf.

**152 a news release**...George C. Marshall Institute, "Linkage Between Hurricanes and Global Warming Tenuous," September 6, 2005, available online at http://www.marshall.org/pdf/materials/319.pdf.

**153 Tech Central Station**...See a September 9, 2005, interview that Tech Central Station published with James J. O'Brien. Available online at http://www.tcsdaily.com/article.aspx?id=041106I.

**153 Competitive Enterprise Institute**...See Alex Kormendi and Charles C. W. Cooke, "Turning Science into Hot Air," *Washington Times,* September 4, 2005.

**153 an event**...George C. Marshall Institute, "Atlantic Hurricanes: The True Story," October 12, 2005. Full transcript available at http://www.marshall.org/pdf/materials/364.pdf.

**153 the most narrow metric conceivable**...See Judith Curry et al., "Mixing Politics and Science in Testing the Hypothesis That Greenhouse Warming Is Causing a Global Increase in Hurricane Intensity," *Bulletin of the American Meteorological Society,* August 2006. As the authors note, "regional datasets cannot, by their very nature, be used to reject the hypothesis that the frequency of the most intense hurricanes is increasing globally."

**153 a major study**...Barnett et al., "Penetration of Human-Induced Warming Into the World's Oceans," *Science,* Vol. 309 (July 8, 2005).

### CHAPTER 9: "The #$%^& Hit the Fan"

**PAGE**

**155 "Only 11 percent"**...Interview with Peter Webster, March 10, 2006.

**156 the Aerosonde**...For more information, see Greg Holland, Peter Webster, Judith Curry, et al., "The Aerosonde Robotic Aircraft: A New Paradigm for Environmental Observations," *Bulletin of the American Meteorological Society,* Vol. 82 (May 2001), pp. 889–901.

**156 the leading rival to Emanuel's account**...Holland, "The Maximum Potential Intensity of Tropical Cyclones."

**156 Cyclone Tracy**...See Emanuel, *Divine Wind,* Chapter 30, "Cyclone Tracy."

**156–7 "jumping around"**...Interview with Greg Holland, August 7, 2006.

**157 No one on the Webster team**...Curry et al., "Mixing Politics and Science."

**157 "bloody hermit on a mountaintop"**...Interview with Greg Holland, February 13, 2006.

**158 "the #$%^& hit the fan"**...Judith Curry, comment to ClimateAudit.org, September 7, 2006, available online at http://www.climateaudit.org/?p=803#comment-44757.

**158 Seeking to cut budgets**...See William M. Gray et al., "Assessment of the Role of Aircraft Reconnaissance on Tropical Cyclone Analysis and Forecasting," *Bulletin of the American Meteorological Society,* Vol. 72, No. 12 (December 1991), pp. 1867–83.

**158 the Dvorak technique**...For more information, see Christopher Velden et al., "The Dvorak Tropical Cyclone Intensity Estimation Technique: A Satellite-Based Methodology That Has Endured for Over Thirty Years," *Bulletin of the American Meteorological Society,* September 2006, pp. 1195–1210.

159 **"not inconsistent with recent climate model simulations"** ... Peter Webster et al., "Changes in Tropical Cyclone Number, Duration, and Intensity in a Warming Environment," *Science*, Vol. 309 (September 16, 2005), pp. 1844–46.

160 **"a tar baby"** ... Interview with Judith Curry, March 10, 2006.

160 **"all coastal cities"** ... Curry et al., "Mixing Politics and Science."

160 **"Even senior scientists"** ... Curry et al., "Mixing Politics and Science."

161 **"an electric chair"** ... Interview with Judith Curry, March 10, 2006.

161 **Hurricane Rita** ... For the official meteorological statistics, see National Hurricane Center, Tropical Cyclone Report, Hurricane Rita, updated August 14, 2006. Available online at http://www.nhc.noaa.gov/pdf/TCR-AL182005_Rita.pdf.

162 **"Unless the storm turns south or north"** ... Eric Berger (Sci-Guy Blog), "From Bad to Worse, I Am Afraid," September 21, 2005. Available online at http://blogs.chron.com/sciguy/archives/2005/09/from_bad_to_wor.html.

163 **"Within an hour or two"** ... Eric Berger, "Seeking the Truth in a Fictional Storm: Computers Model Area's Perfect Storm," *Houston Chronicle*, February 20, 2005.

163 **At one point in Congress** ... Dan Vergano, "In the Eye of the Storms," *USA Today*, September 25, 2005. Available online at http://www.usatoday.com/tech/science/2005-09-25-hurricane-science_x.htm.

164 **"not a cause"** ... *USA Today*/CNN Gallup Poll, conducted October 21–23, 2005. Available online at http://www.usatoday.com/news/polls/2005-10-21-poll.htm.

164 **"I question"** ... *The Diane Rehm Show*, "The 2005 Hurricane Season," Wednesday, September 21, 2005. Audio available online at http://www.wamu.org/programs/dr/05/09/21.php.

164 **one GCM study** ... Kazuyoshi Oouchi et al., "Tropical Cyclone Climatology in a Global-Warming Climate as Simulated in a 20km-Mesh Global Atmospheric Model: Frequency and Wind Intensity Analysis," *Journal of the Meteorological Society of Japan*, Vol. 84, No. 2 (2006), pp. 259–76.

165 **storm surge** ... See Emanuel, *Divine Wind*, Chapter 20, "The Storm Surge," pp. 147–52.

165 **a rise in sea level** ... See, for example, Gerald Meehl et al., "How Much More Global Warming and Sea Level Rise?" *Science*, Vol. 308 (March 18, 2005), pp. 1769–72, finding, "Even if we could stabilize concentrations of [greenhouse gases], we are already committed to significant warming and sea level rise no matter what scenario we follow." The study applied two separate models to three separate greenhouse gas emissions scenarios, finding the following resulting ranges in sea level rise by 2100: 13 to 18 centimeters for the low-end emissions scenario, 18 to 25 centimeters for the mid-range scenario, and 19 to 30 centimeters for the high-end scenario. But these were deemed "minimum values" because the models did not include any ice-sheet or glacier melting.

166 **hurricane-spawned tornadoes** ... David J. Novlan and William M. Gray, "Hurricane-Spawned Tornadoes," *Monthly Weather Review*, Vol. 102 (July 1974), pp. 476–88.

166 **the number of hurricane-spawned tornadoes**...J. A. Belanger, B. Miller, J. A. Curry, P. J. Webster, "Recent Increase in Tornadoes Spawned by U.S. Landfalling Tropical Cyclones." *Journal of Applied Meteorology and Climatology* (submitted).

167 **does not show any trend**...See Roger A. Pielke, Jr., "Are There Trends in Hurricane Destruction?" *Nature,* Vol. 438 (December 22–29, 2005), p. E11.

167 **The 1926 Miami hurricane**...R. A. Pielke, Jr., J. Gratz, C. W. Landsea, D. Collins, M. Saunders, and R. Musulin, 2007. "Normalized Hurricane Damages in the United States: 1900–2005." *Natural Hazards Review* (submitted). Available online at http://sciencepolicy.colorado.edu/publications/special/nhd_paper.pdf.

167 **countless factors besides storm strength itself**...Interview with Richard Anthes, February 14, 2006.

167 **It stands to reason**...See Tom Knutson, "Perspectives on Focused Workshop Questions Regarding Past Economic Impacts of Storms or Floods," presentation at the Munich Re/University of Colorado Workshop on "Climate Change and Disaster Losses: Understanding and Attributing Trends and Projections," May 25–26, 2006. Available online at http://sciencepolicy.colorado.edu/sparc/research/projects/extreme_events/munich_workshop/knutson.pdf.

167 **Risk Management Solutions**...See Risk Management Solutions, "The 2006 RMS Expert Elicitation and Atlantic Hurricane Activity Rates Update," November 2006, available online at http://www.rms.com/Publications/2006_Expert_Elicitation.pdf. Controversy over the outcome is reported in Kevin Begos, "Insurance risk forecast called faulty," *Tampa Tribune,* January 7, 2007.

168 **"marginal" basin**...Interview with Thomas Knutson, August 21, 2006.

## CHAPTER 10: Resistance

PAGE

169 **Thomas Kuhn's famous 1962 book**...Thomas S. Kuhn, *The Structure of Scientific Revolutions* (Chicago, Ill.: University of Chicago Press, 1962).

169 **"novelty emerges only with difficulty"**...Quoted in Kuhn, *The Structure of Scientific Revolutions* (Third Edition, 1996), p. 64.

169 **"By ensuring that the paradigm"**...Kuhn, p. 65.

170 **"we did the work."** Interview with Judith Curry, March 10, 2006.

170 **"Because it demands"**...Kuhn, pp. 67–68.

171 **well aware.** As Kuhn noted, "except in occasional brief asides, I have said nothing about the role of technological advance or external social, economic, and intellectual conditions in the development of the sciences. One need, however, look no further than Copernicus and the calendar to discover that external conditions may help to transform a mere anomaly into a source of acute crisis" (pp. xi–xii).

171 **"I just can't have people"**...Interview with William Gray, February 12, 2006.

171 **"not valid"**...William M. Gray, comments on "Increasing Destructiveness of Tropical Cyclones Over the Past 30 Years" by Kerry Emanuel in *Nature,* Vol. 436 (July 31, 2005), pp. 686–88, submitted to *Nature* (October 19, 2005). Available online at

http://tropical.atmos.colostate.edu/Includes/Documents/Responses/emanuel_comments.pdf.

**172 Gray even argued**...William M. Gray, comments on "Changes in Tropical Cyclone Number, Duration, and Intensity in a Warming Environment" by Webster et al., *Science,* Vol. 309 (September 2005), pp. 1844–46. On file with the author.

**172 "sound science"**...See Mooney, *The Republican War on Science,* Chapter 7, "The Greatest Hoax."

**172 the hearing itself**...Senate Environment and Public Works Committee, Hearing on Science in Environmental Policy-Making, September 28, 2005. Video available online at http://epw.senate.gov/epwmultimedia/epw092805.ram.

**172 eco-terrorists conspiring**...Crichton, *State of Fear* (New York: Harper-Collins, 2004).

**174 inflammatory analogy**...Crichton, *State of Fear.* See Appendix I, "Why Politicized Science is Dangerous," in which Crichton draws an analogy between the eugenics movement and global warming. In his own words: "I am not arguing that global warming is the same as eugenics. But the similarities are not superficial" (p. 579).

**175 Hurricane Vince**...See National Hurricane Center Tropical Cyclone Report, Hurricane Vince, February 22, 2006. Available online at http://www.nhc.noaa.gov/pdf/TCR-AL242005_Vince.pdf.

**175 "more records being broken"**...Interview with Judith Curry, October 6, 2006.

**176 Hurricane Wilma**...For the definitive meteorological history, see National Hurricane Center Tropical Cyclone Report, Hurricane Wilma, updated September 28, 2006. Available online at http://www.nhc.noaa.gov/pdf/TCR-AL252005_Wilma.pdf.

**176 "THE DREADED PINHOLE EYE"**...National Hurricane Center, Hurricane Wilma Discussion Number 14, October 18, 2005, 11 pm EDT. Available online at http://www.nhc.noaa.gov/archive/2005/dis/al242005.discus.014.shtml.

**176 "smallest eye known"**...Quoted in National Hurricane Center Tropical Cyclone Report, Hurricane Wilma, updated September 28, 2006. Available online at http://www.nhc.noaa.gov/pdf/TCR-AL252005_Wilma.pdf.

**176 "LOWEST MINIMUM PRESSURE"**...National Hurricane Center, Hurricane Wilma Discussion Number 16, October 19, 2005, 5 A.M. EDT. Available online at http://www.nhc.noaa.gov/archive/2005/dis/al242005.discus.016.shtml.

**177 Dade, Broward, and Palm Beach counties**...Interview with Richard Pasch, November 8, 2006.

**177 "this enormous eye"**...Interview with Richard Pasch, November 8, 2006.

**179 lengthening the average tropical cyclone season**...This argument was presented at the American Geophysical Union 2006 meeting by Peter Webster, "Expanding Tropical Warm Pool: Increased Tropical Cyclone Season Length and Storm Duration," Tropical Cyclone-Climate Interactions on All Timescales I, December 15, 2006.

179 **"after fraternities"**...Author's notes, Monterey meeting on Hurricanes and Tropical Meteorology, April 25, 2006.

## CHAPTER 11: Consensus

PAGE

181 **a series of high-resolution experiments**...For an overview, see Thomas Knutson et al., "Impact of Climate Change on Hurricane Intensities as Simulated Using Regional Nested High-Resolution Models," in Murnane and Liu, eds., *Hurricanes and Typhoons.*

182 **Knutson didn't see**...See David Brown, "2 Storms In Florida Not Seen As Trend; Experts Don't Fault Global Warming," *Washington Post,* September 3, 2004. The story quotes Knutson saying, "I wouldn't read too much into a couple of individual events like this."

182 **apparently traveled up to Princeton**...Kent Laborde e-mail to Tom Knutson, September 30, 2004 ("I'll be there tomorrow also. I should arrive around 10:30 or 11"). Document obtained by Greenpeace through a Freedom of Information Act Request, 2006. All FOIA documents on file with the author. In addition, some are available online at http://www.greenpeace.org/usa/news/katrina-raises-heat-on-bush-gl.

182 **a series of talking points**...David P. Miller e-mail to Tom Knutson, October 21, 2004. Document obtained by Greenpeace through a Freedom of Information Act Request, 2006. All other internal NOAA e-mails cited in this chapter are from the same source unless otherwise noted.

183 **"I find the implications to be rather alarming"**...Quoted in Ronald Brownstein, "Hard Choices Blow in the Winds of Katrina, and Now Rita," *Los Angeles Times,* September 26, 2005.

183 **"That seemed to trip some wires somewhere"**...Interview with Thomas Knutson, August 21, 2006.

183 **"incomplete"**...Letter from President Bush to Senators Hagel, Helms, Craig, and Roberts, March 13, 2001. Available online at http://www.whitehouse.gov/news/releases/2001/03/20010314.html.

183 **a rapid independent evaluation**...Committee on the Science of Climate Change, National Research Council, *Climate Change Science: An Analysis of Some Key Questions* (Washington, D.C.: National Academies Press, 2001). Available online at http://fermat.nap.edu/books/0309075742/html.

184 **mouth an apparent endorsement**...Remarks by President Bush on Global Climate Change, June 11, 2001. Available online at http://www.state.gov/g/oes/rls/rm/4149.htm.

184 **brazenly mislead the public**...Bush press conference, March 29, 2006, transcript available online at http://www.whitehouse.gov/news/releases/2006/03/20060329-6.html.

184 **Bush himself was revealed**...Michael Janofsky, "Bush's Chat with Novelist Alarms Environmentalists," *New York Times,* February 19, 2006.

**184** **"a few noncommittal paragraphs"**...Andrew C. Revkin and Katharine Q. Seelye, "Report by EPA Leaves Out Data on Climate Change," *New York Times,* June 19, 2003.

**184** **In a leaked memo**...For the actual complaint memo itself, see http://www .nwf.org/nwfwebadmin/binaryVault/EPA%20Climate%20Section%20Memo.pdf.

**184** **had repeatedly sought to edit**...Andrew C. Revkin, "Bush Aide Edited Climate Reports," *New York Times,* June 8, 2005.

**185** **the lawyer resigned**...Andrew C. Revkin, "Former Bush Aide Who Edited Reports is Hired by Exxon," *New York Times,* June 15, 2005.

**185** **Piltz went further in his accusations.** See Rick S. Piltz, "On Issues of Concern About the Governance and Direction of the Climate Change Science Program," June 1, 2005. Available online at http://www.whistleblower.org/doc/ Memo%20to%20Superiors.pdf.

**185** **The National Assessment**...U.S. Global Change Research Program, "Climate Change Impacts on the United States: The Potential Consequences of Climate Variability and Change" (New York: Cambridge University Press, 2001). Available online at http://www.usgcrp.gov/usgcrp/nacc/default.htm.

**185** **U.S. National Assessment had also been endorsed**...Committee on the Science of Climate Change, National Research Council, *Climate Change Science: An Analysis of Some Key Questions* (Washington, D.C.: National Academies Press, 2001). See pp. 19–20: "The U.S. National Assessment of Climate Change Impacts, augmented by a recent NRC report on climate and health, provides a basis for summarizing the potential consequences of climate change." Available online at http:// fermat.nap.edu/books/0309075742/html.

**185** **sent into a "black hole"**...In a 2005 interview with *Environmental Science & Technology,* James R. Mahoney, then director of the Climate Change Science Program, confirmed that his program had been restricted "on our use of information" from the National Assessment. See Paul Thacker, "Blowing the Whistle on Climate Change: Interview with Rick Piltz," June 22, 2005, available online at http://pubs.acs.org/ subscribe/journals/esthag-w/2005/jun/policy/pt_piltz.html.

**185** **It hardly seems a coincidence**...For a more thorough discussion and documentation, see Mooney, *The Republican War on Science,* Chapter 7, "The Greatest Hoax." For additional information, see updates to the paperback edition (2006).

**186** **"If you get *any* press requests"**...Jana Goldman e-mail to Ron Stouffer, January 24, 2001.

**186** **"Can I ask why this is the policy?"**...E-mail exchange between Ron Stouffer and Jana Goldman, January 24–25, 2001.

**186** **"in the loop"**...Jana Goldman e-mail to Ants Leetmaa, June 11, 2001 ("Ideally I'd like to know before the interview takes place, but I realize that that cannot always happen...").

**186** **regular e-mails**...E-mail from Ron Stouffer to Jana Goldman discussing an interview with *Science* magazine, October 18, 2001.

**187  an article for *Science* magazine**...Thomas Karl et al., "Modern Global Climate Change," *Science,* Vol. 302 (December 5, 2003), pp. 1719–23.

**187  a senior NOAA official who debunked and criticized the article**...See, for example, David Perlman, "Climate Change Laid to Humans: Report warns there's 'no doubt' industry is primary cause," *San Francisco Chronicle,* December 4, 2003; and Theo Stein, "Unstable Climate Linked to Pollution," *Denver Post,* December 5, 2003.

**187  "unconscionable"**...This episode is reported in Earl Lane, "Marburger Defends Administration; Rebutting charges from top scientists," *Newsday,* March 28, 2004.

**187  a written NOAA policy**...NOAA Media Policy, issued June 28, 2004, and listed as "effective" June 22, 2004. Available online at http://www.corporateservices .noaa.gov/~ames/NAOs/Chap_219/naos_219_6.html.

**187  Scientists like Stouffer**...Interview with Ron Stouffer, October 6, 2006.

**187  Goldman asked to know**...Jana Goldman e-mail to Brian Gross, July 6, 2004.

**188  "You betcha"**...E-mail exchange between Jana Goldman and Brian Gross, about July 6, 2004 (precise date unclear).

**188  "My experience prior to that time"**...Interview with Anthony Broccoli, August 21, 2006.

**188  a study published in February 2006 in *Science***...V. Ramaswamy et al., "Anthropogenic and Natural Influences in the Evolution of Lower Stratospheric Cooling," *Science,* Vol. 311, No. 5764 (February 24, 2006), pp. 1138–41.

**188  the NOAA press release**...Maria Setzer e-mail to V. Ramaswamy, March 6, 2006.

**188  Ramaswamy had to liberate**...V. Ramaswamy e-mail to NOAA and other scientists, February 22, 2006.

**189  a Byzantine thirteen-step review process**...Maria Setzer e-mail to V. Ramaswamy, March 6, 2006.

**189  "Any updates on the 'clearance'?"**...V. Ramaswamy e-mail to Jana Goldman, date unclear, 2006.

**190  "those kinds of things should not really happen"**...Interview with V. Ramaswamy, October 6, 2006.

**190  "no problems from above"**...Ron Stouffer e-mail to Stefan Lovgren, April 15, 2004.

**190  Kent Laborde listened in**...Ron Stouffer e-mail to Brian Gross, April 16, 2004.

**190  "internal noaa talking points"**...Scott Smullen e-mail to Ron Stouffer, about May 24, 2004 (precise date unclear).

**190  "How close to the talking points"**...Ron Stouffer e-mail to Scott Smullen, May 24, 2004.

**190  "breaking the rules"**...Ron Stouffer e-mail to Andrew Revkin, September 13, 2004.

**190  a parody of the *Times* article**...John Lanzante e-mail to Ron Stouffer, around September 1, 2004 (precise date unclear).

191 **"you are still stuck with me"**...Ron Stouffer e-mail to John Lanzante, September 1, 2004.

191 **"a whole wide range of disciplinary things"**...Interview with Ron Stouffer, October 6, 2006.

191 **playing by the rules**...Ron Stouffer e-mail to Jana Goldman, March 16, 2005 ("Can I get back to her? I will say that sea level changes have very long time scales...").

191 **"The reporter got quite upset"**...Ron Stouffer e-mail to Brian Gross and Jana Goldman, November 29, 2005.

191 **Stouffer's own experience**...As summarized in an e-mail to Jana Goldman and Maria Setzer, March 1, 2006.

192 **the Commerce Department wanted to "coordinate"**...Jana Goldman e-mail to Erica Rule and Brian Gross, September 13, 2005.

192 **"the restrictions being placed on government scientists"**...Morris Bender e-mail to Brian Gross, September 13, 2005.

192 **another e-mail had gone out**...Richard Spinrad e-mail to NOAA officials, October 4, 2005.

192 **"jana needs to approve"**...Ants Leetmaa e-mail to Isaac Held, November 28, 2005.

192 **a major editorial in *USA Today***..."Global Warming Activists Turn Storms into Spin," September 26, 2005.

193 **Mayfield did not even cite**...Max Mayfield, testimony before the Senate Committee on Commerce, Science, and Transportation, Subcommittee on Disaster Prevention and Prediction, September 20, 2005. Available online at http://www.legislative .noaa.gov/Testimony/mayfieldfinal092005.pdf.

193 **"Without invoking global warming"**...Max Mayfield, comment before the Senate Committee on Commerce, Science, and Transportation, Subcommittee on Disaster Prevention and Prediction, September 20, 2005. Audio available at http:// commerce.senate.gov/archive.hurricaneprediction092005.ram (see approximately minutes 1:28–1:30).

193 **Mayfield dodged any mention**...House Committee on Science, full committee hearing, NOAA Hurricane Forecasting, October 7, 2005. Video available online at http://www.house.gov/science/hearings/full05/oct%207/index.htm (exchange between Ehlers and Mayfield begins at 1:52:45).

194 **"not related to greenhouse warming"**...NOAA press conference, "End of the 2005 Hurricane Season," National Press Club, Washington, D.C., November 29, 2005.

194 **"There is consensus"**...*NOAA Magazine,* "NOAA Attributes Recent Increase in Hurricane Activity to Naturally Occurring Multi-Decadal Climate Variability," November 29, 2005. Available online at http://www.magazine.noaa.gov/stories/ mag184.htm.

194 **a February 12, 1998, press release**...National Oceanic and Atmospheric Administration, "Hurricanes May Be Intensified by Global Warming" (press release),

February 12, 1998. Available online at http://www.publicaffairs.noaa.gov/pr98/feb98/noaa98-9.html.

**194–95 "scientists cannot say"**...Earth Day Remarks on Global Climate Change, Dr. D. James Baker, April 18, 2000, available online at http://www.noaanews.noaa.gov/stories/s412b.htm.

**195 "The honest answer"**...Quoted by Reuters, "Climate, Storms Hit Extremes in 2005—U.N. Weather Body," Robert Evans, December 15, 2005. Available online at http://www.planetark.com/dailynewsstory.cfm/newsid/34070/newsDate/16-Dec-2005/story.htm.

**195 *New York Times* page-one story**...Andrew C. Revkin, "Climate Expert Says NASA Tried to Silence Him," *New York Times,* January 29, 2006.

**195 George Deutsch**...Andrew C. Revkin, "A Young Bush Appointee Resigns His Post at NASA," *New York Times,* February 8, 2006.

**196 "The Hansen piece uncorked a bottle"**...Quoted in Nisbet and Mooney, "The Next Big Storm."

**196 Hansen continued to stir the pot**...Juliet Eilperin, "Censorship Is Alleged at NOAA; Scientists Afraid to Speak Out, NASA Climate Expert Reports," *Washington Post,* February 11, 2006.

**196 this one in the *New Republic***...John Judis, "NOAA's Flood," *The New Republic,* February 20, 2006.

**196 "This is an embarrassment"**...Ants Leetmaa, e-mail to James R. Mahoney, Ph.D., and other NOAA officials, February 12, 2006.

**197 an internal critique**...Tom Delworth, e-mail to Tom Knutson and other GFDL scientists, February 13, 2006.

**198 "freely and openly"**...Conrad C. Lautenbacher, Jr., "Message from the Under Secretary," February 14, 2006.

**198 "You will find near the bottom"**...Tom Delworth, e-mail to Tom Knutson and other NOAA-GFDL scientists, February 15, 2006.

**198 the first on-the-record allegations**...Antonio Regalado and Jim Carlton, "Statement Acknowledges Some Government Scientists See a Link to Global Warming," *Wall Street Journal,* February 16, 2006.

**198 public-affairs officials**...For further elaboration of Knutson's experiences with the NOAA public affairs process see his February 7, 2007, testimony before a Senate Commerce Committee hearing on "Climate Change Research and Scientific Integrity," available online at http://commerce.senate.gov/public/index.cfm?FuseAction=Hearings.Testimony&Hearing_ID=1812&Witness_ID=6489.

**199 "Tom, about that interview'"**...Interview with Thomas Knutson, August 21, 2006.

**199 "what is Knutson's position"**...Chuck Fuqua e-mail to Kent Laborde, October 19, 2005. E-mails from this exchange are available online at http://www.democrats.reform.house.gov/Documents/20060919101130-14873.pdf.

**199 "Why can't we have one of the other guys"**...Paul Thacker, "Climate-controlled White House," *Salon.com,* September 19, 2006, available online at http://www.salon.com/news/feature/2006/09/19/noaa/.

**199 Landsea...was outraged**...Interview with Chris Landsea, November 8, 2006.

**200 trying to shift debate**...In fact, another reporter documented precisely this phenomenon at work in early 2006. Writing for the *Providence Journal,* Peter B. Lord described his experience trying to get an interview with Knutson:

> Calls to NOAA's public-affairs office led to Kent Laborde, who was described as the public-affairs person who focuses on climate-change issues.
>
> Laborde made it clear that the NOAA has discounted the research tying global warming to worsening hurricanes.
>
> "What we've found is, if you look at a couple segments of science, observational or modeling, there is no illustrated link between climate change and hurricane intensity," Laborde said. "We actually have periods of intensity followed by periods of lower intensity. We have evidence of periods going back to the 1930s. It follows a clear pattern."
>
> Laborde was asked if he would approve an interview with Knutson.
>
> What is the topic? he asked.
>
> Emanuel's theories linking climate change to worsening hurricanes.
>
> "Chris Landsea would be better. He's an observational scientist," Laborde said.

(Peter B. Lord, "NOAA hiding truth about hurricanes, scientists say," *Providence Journal,* March 26, 2006.)

**200 "Very courageous of Tom"**...James Hansen e-mail to Ron Stouffer, February 16, 2006.

**201 this most obvious of lessons**...Due to its general focus on the hurricane–climate issue, this chapter by design does not give a full account of all of the science-related scandals and controversies that have plagued NOAA during the Bush administration. That would have been a larger project. However, for a sampling of other case studies, see Jim Erikson, "Climate Scientist Says 'Kyoto' Barred: Investigators Eye Censorship Claims About White House," *Rocky Mountain News,* December 11, 2006; and Kitta MacPherson, "Tempest Brews in Weather Think Tank," *Newark Star-Ledger,* October 1, 2006.

## CHAPTER 12: Preseason Warm-Ups

PAGE

**205 a panel**...The event was part of the 18th Conference on Climate Variability and Change, Session Four, "Observed Climate Change in the Atmosphere and Oceans, Part II," January 31, 2006. Author's notes.

**205 a planned debate**...Bauerlein, "Cold Front."

**205 "tongue-lashing"**...Interview with William Gray, February 16, 2006.

**206** "**it's become personal entirely on one side.**" Interview with Greg Holland, February 13, 2006.

**206 had invited**...E-mail from Elizabeth Ritchie to Max Mayfield, William Gray, Kerry Emanuel, Peter Webster, and Chris Landsea (from now on referred to as "group"), November 3, 2005. The e-mails cited and quoted here were later circulated beyond this group of individuals.

**206 Webster and Emanuel quickly expressed concerns.** E-mails by Kerry Emanuel and Peter Webster quoted in e-mail by William Gray to group, November 14, 2005.

**206** "**will behave themselves**"...E-mail by William Gray to group, November 14, 2005.

**207 justification for further grant support**...E-mail from William Gray to group, December 16, 2005; e-mail copy provided by its author.

**207 Ritchie quickly swooped in**...E-mail from Elizabeth Ritchie to group, November 14, 2005.

**207** "**To disagree with science**"...E-mail from Peter Webster to group (now including Greg Holland and Russell Elsberry), November 15, 2005.

**207 Ritchie wasn't giving up.** Elizabeth Ritchie, e-mail to Peter Webster and Kerry Emanuel, November 16, 2005.

**207 a skeptic**...See Johnny Chan, "Comment on 'Changes in Tropical Cyclone Number, Duration, and Intensity in a Warming Environment,'" *Science*, Vol. 331 (March 24, 2006), p. 1713.

**207** "**still time to backtrack**"...William Gray, e-mail to group, November 29, 2005.

**207 a joking message**...Chris Landsea e-mail to Ritchie, Gray, Emanuel, and Webster, November 4, 2005.

**207** "**Bill, please, stop**"...Chris Landsea e-mail to group, November 29, 2005.

**208 Landsea launched into his presentation**...For another firsthand account of the substance of Landsea's presentation, see Jeff Masters, "Are Category 4 and 5 hurricanes increasing in number?" *WunderBlog*, March 27, 2006. Available online at http://www.wunderground.com/blog/JeffMasters/comment.html?entrynum=327 &tstamp=200603.

**208 The Dvorak method**...For more information, see Velden et al., "The Dvorak Tropical Cyclone Intensity Estimation Technique."

**208 a few North Indian basin cyclones**...Later in an article in *Science,* Landsea and a group of coauthors further noted that the infamous 1970 Bangladesh cyclone, which killed hundreds of thousands of people, "does not even have an official intensity estimate, despite indications that it was extremely intense." Landsea et al., "Can We Detect Trends in Extreme Tropical Cyclones?"

**209 a subject Knutson would discuss**...Thomas Knutson, "Assessment of Twentieth-Century Regional Surface Temperature Trends Using the GFDL CM2 Coupled Models," American Meteorological Society, February 1, 2006. Author's notes.

**209 contrast hurricane intensity measurements**...Chris Landsea presentation, March 29, 2006, Lamont Campus, Earth Institute of Columbia University. Author's notes.

**209 Carol...isn't even officially classified as a hurricane**...Interview with Chris Landsea, November 8, 2006.

**209 overestimated or underestimated**...Author's notes, Monterey meeting on Hurricanes and Tropical Meteorology, April 25, 2006.

**209 "There is no evidence"**...J. A. Curry et al., "Mixing Politics and Science."

**210 the same two American Meteorological Society awards**...Both scientists won the Max Eaton Prize, awarded for the best student paper in hurricane research and tropical meteorology: Holland in 1982 for a study concerning hurricane intensity, and Landsea in 1992 for work on the relationship between African rainfall and hurricane activity in the Atlantic. For the Max Eaton prizewinners, see http://www .aoml.noaa.gov/hrd/Landsea/EatonPrize.htm. Reprising another decadal cycle, Holland and Landsea both also won the Banner I. Miller Award for "an outstanding contribution to the science of hurricane and tropical weather forecasting." Holland won in 1985 for two studies on tropical cyclone motion; Landsea was a co-recipient in 1994, for a paper with Gray and coauthors on the prediction of Atlantic hurricane activity six to eleven months into the future. For the Banner I. Miller prizewinners, see http://www.aoml.noaa.gov/hrd/Landsea/banner.html.

**211 "doing their own thing"**...Interview with Kerry Emanuel, May 22, 2006.

**211 they began haunting scientific conferences**...See Nisbet and Mooney, "The Next Big Storm."

**211 The trend was epitomized**...Bauerlein, "Cold Front."

**212 Jeff Masters**...In one of the most harrowing stories of modern hurricane science, Masters nearly perished during a disastrous low-level research flight into Hurricane Hugo in 1989, and never flew another storm. For the story of the near-crash that almost killed a large number of the nation's top hurricane scientists, see http:// www.wunderground.com/hurricane/hugo1.asp.

**212 a naming system**...Dr. Jeff Masters' WunderBlog, "South Atlantic Tropical Depression Dissipates," February 24, 2006. Available online at http://www.wunderground .com/blog/JeffMasters/comment.html?entrynum=309&tstamp=200602&page=2.

**212 tropical-looking disturbance**...Dr. Jeff Masters' WunderBlog, "Brazilian Tropical Disturbance, and Tornado Damage Surveys," March 15, 2006. Available online at http://www.wunderground.com/blog/JeffMasters/comment.html?entrynum=320 &tstamp=200603.

**212 translated into Saffir-Simpson categories**...For a conversion of these 2005–2006 storm intensities into more familiar terms, see the National Climatic Data Center: http://www.ncdc.noaa.gov/oa/climate/research/2006/2006-aussie-trop-cyclones.html.

**212 Larry**...Severe Tropical Cyclone Larry Report, Bureau of Meteorology, Queensland Regional Office, updated December 2006. Available online at http://www.bom .gov.au/weather/qld/cyclone/tc_larry/.

**213 "That something is global warming."** Jeffrey Kluger, "Polar Ice Caps Are Melting Faster Than Ever...More And More Land Is Being Devastated By Drought...

Rising Waters Are Drowning Low-Lying Communities... By Any Measure, Earth Is At... The Tipping Point," *Time,* April 3, 2006.

**213 possibly a Category 4**... Best track data on Larry, provided by Unisys Weather, rates the storm as a Category 3. See http://weather.unisys.com/hurricane/s_pacific/2006/LARRY/track.dat. Wikipedia (not necessarily reliable) puts the storm at Category 4: http://en.wikipedia.org/wiki/Tropical_Cyclone_Larry.

**213 closer to 115 miles per hour**... Again, see the National Climatic Data Center: http://www.ncdc.noaa.gov/oa/climate/research/2006/2006-aussie-trop-cyclones.html.

**213 Severe Tropical Cyclone Glenda**... For best track data on Glenda, see http://weather.unisys.com/hurricane/s_indian/2006/GLENDA/track.dat. For Glenda's track itself, see Severe Tropical Cyclone Glenda report, Western Australia Regional Office, Bureau of Meteorology, available at http://www.bom.gov.au/announcements/sevwx/wa/watc20060315.shtml.

**213 898 millibars**... See Dr. Jeff Masters' WunderBlog, "An Extraordinary Cat 5 in Australian Waters," March 28, 2006, available online at http://www.wunderground.com/blog/JeffMasters/comment.html?entrynum=328&tstamp=200603. For the Bureau of Meteorology's estimate, see http://www.bom.gov.au/announcements/sevwx/wa/watc20060315.shtml.

**214 Severe Tropical Cyclone Monica**... For the official report on Monica, see the Australian Bureau of Meteorology, Northern Territory Regional Office. Available online at http://www.bom.gov.au/announcements/sevwx/nt/nttc20060417.shtml. Best track data for Monica available at http://weather.unisys.com/hurricane/s_pacific/2006/MONICA/track.dat.

**214 one of the two strongest**... According to meteorologist Jeff Masters, "Monica ranks as the 14th most intense tropical cyclone in world history, and is tied with Cyclone Zoe of 2003 as the strongest Southern Hemisphere cyclone on record." See http://www.wunderground.com/blog/JeffMasters/comment.html?entrynum=344&tstamp=200604.

**214 879 millibars**... See Dr. Jeff Masters' WunderBlog, "How Strong Was Monica?" April 24, 2006. Available online at http://www.wunderground.com/blog/JeffMasters/comment.html?entrynum=345&tstamp=200604.

**214 868.5 millibars**... See http://cimss.ssec.wisc.edu/tropic/adt/archive2006/23P-list.txt.

**214 isn't necessarily reliable**... E-mail from Jim Kossin, December 6, 2006.

**214 If we can't get dependable measurements**... For a further discussion, see Dr. Jeff Masters' WunderBlog, "How strong was Monica?" April 24, 2006. Available online at http://www.wunderground.com/blog/JeffMasters/comment.html?entrynum=345&tstamp=200604.

**215 The online write-up**... William Gray, "Global Warming and Hurricanes," presentation at the 2006 American Meteorological Society 27th Conference on Hurricanes and Tropical Meteorology, Monday, April 24, 2006. Extended abstract available online at http://ams.confex.com/ams/pdfpapers/107533.pdf.

**215  the scariest idea yet**...David S. Nolan, E. D. Rappin, and K. A. Emanuel, "Could Hurricanes Form from Random Convection in a Warmer World?" Presentation at the 2006 American Meteorological Society 27th Conference on Hurricanes and Tropical Meteorology, Monday, April 24, 2006. Extended abstract available online at http://ams.confex.com/ams/pdfpapers/107936.pdf. Recorded presentation available online at http://ams.confex.com/ams/27Hurricanes/wrfredirect.cgi?id=5323.

**216  "All six or seven of them."** Interview with Hugh Willoughby, May 16, 2006.

**216  more than 550**...Stephanie Kenitzer, American Meteorological Society, e-mail communication, December 1, 2006.

**216  Gray didn't disappoint.** Recorded presentation available online at http://ams.confex.com/ams/27Hurricanes/wrfredirect.cgi?id=5470.

**218  a recent study**...The work referenced was Harry Bryden et al., "Slowing of the Atlantic Meridional Overturning Circulation at 25° N," *Nature,* Vol. 438 (2005), pp. 655–57.

**219  an impassioned defense**...This exchange was also reported by Richard Kerr, "A Tempestuous Birth for Hurricane Climatology," *Science,* Vol. 312 (May 5, 2006), pp. 676–78.

**219  an equation-intensive talk**...Kerry Emanuel, "Environmental Influences on Tropical Cyclone Variability and Trends," Presentation at the 2006 American Meteorological Society 27th Conference on Hurricanes and Tropical Meteorology, Monday, April 24, 2006. Extended abstract available online at http://ams.confex.com/ams/pdfpapers/107575.pdf. Recorded presentation available online at http://ams.confex.com/ams/27Hurricanes/wrfredirect.cgi?id=5413.

**220  "no personal comments"**...Author's notes, April 25, 2006, Monterey, California.

**221  seasonal typhoon activity**...See Johnny Chan, "Variations in the Activity of Tropical Cyclones over the Western North Pacific: From Interdecadal to Intraseasonal," in Murnane and Liu, eds., *Hurricanes and Typhoons.*

**221  I sought out Gray**...Author's notes, April 26, 2006, Monterey, California.

**222  Florida Governor's Hurricane Conference**...Author's notes at the Florida Governor's Hurricane Conference, Fort Lauderdale, May 12, 2006.

## CHAPTER 13: Where Are the Storms?

**PAGE**

**224  The protesters were in a chanting mood**...The description of this event is based upon the author's firsthand experience and notes.

**225  ABC News ran a story**...ABC News, "Ignoring Science? Protesters Call for Resignations, Say Government Ignoring Global Warming Effect on Hurricanes," May 31, 2006. Available online at http://abcnews.go.com/Technology/story?id= 2025372&page=1.

**225  "natural disaster made worse by global warming"**...Statement on file with the author.

225 **he claimed not to have been convinced**...Again, see ABC News, "Ignoring Science?" Mayfield is quoted in the story as follows: "I'm always looking forward to looking at new data. If I get convinced, so be it. But I'm not convinced yet."

226 **burned out**...Ken Kaye and Sally Kestin, "After 34-year Career, Hurricane Center's Chief to Leave in January," *South Florida Sun-Sentinel*, August 26, 2006.

226 **"no U.S. taxpayer funded website"**...Mike Tidwell, "Hurricanes and Global Warming: The NOAA Cover Up," on file with the author.

227 **"ALBERTO COULD BECOME A HURRICANE"**...National Hurricane Center, Tropical Storm Alberto Discussion Number 10, June 12, 2006. Available online at http://www.nhc.noaa.gov/archive/2006/al01/al012006.discus.010.shtml?.

227 **the earliest to strike Florida in forty years**...This factoid is attributed to National Hurricane Center forecaster Eric Blake by the *Washington Post*. See Peter Whoriskey, "Florida Braces for Early-Arriving Alberto," June 13, 2006. Available online at http://www.washingtonpost.com/wp-dyn/content/article/2006/06/12/AR2006061200531.html.

227 **a four-foot storm surge**...See National Hurricane Center Tropical Cyclone Report, Tropical Storm Alberto, August 11, 2006. Available online at http://www.nhc.noaa.gov/pdf/TCR-AL012006_Alberto.pdf.

227 **"It is now generally recognized"**...Quoted in Brendan Farrington, "President Clinton urges state Democrats to be party of values," Associated Press, June 12, 2006.

228 **the first year since 1997**...Philip J. Klotzbach and William M. Gray, "Summary of 2006 Atlantic Tropical Cyclone Activity and Verification of Author's Seasonal and Monthly Forecasts," November 17, 2006. Available online at http://hurricane.atmos.colostate.edu/Forecasts/2006/nov2006/nov2006.pdf.

228 **four new forecasters**...Interview with Chris Landsea, November 8, 2006.

228 **"MILTON BERLE."** National Hurricane Center, Tropical Storm Beryl Discussion Number 5, July 19, 2006. Available online at http://www.nhc.noaa.gov/archive/2006/al02/al022006.discus.005.shtml.

228 **"REGARDING THE PRONUNCIATION OF BERYL"**...National Hurricane Center, Tropical Storm Beryl Discussion Number 7, July 19, 2006. Available online at http://www.nhc.noaa.gov/archive/2006/al02/al022006.discus.007.shtml?.

228 **it's a good curse to have.** See Dr. Jeff Masters, "Chris Nears Hurricane Strength," August 2, 2006. Available online at http://www.wunderground.com/blog/JeffMasters/comment.html?entrynum=442&tstamp=200608.

228–29 **"a quiet decade"**...Interview with Kerry Emanuel, October 19, 2006.

229 **In downgrading their forecast**...Philip J. Klotzbach and William M. Gray, "Forecast of Atlantic Hurricane Activity for September and October 2006 and Seasonal Update Through August," September 1, 2006. Available online at http://typhoon.atmos.colostate.edu/Forecasts/2006/sep2006/.

229 **a 12.1 storm season**...See Frédéric Vitart et al., "Dynamically-Based Seasonal Forecasts of Atlantic Tropical-Storm Activity," 2006, in press.

**229 Hurricane John**...See the National Hurricane Center Tropical Cyclone Report, Hurricane John, November 16, 2006. Available online at http://www.nhc.noaa.gov/pdf/TCR-EP112006_John.pdf.

**229 the unnamed 1858 San Diego storm**...Chenoweth and Landsea, "The San Diego Hurricane of 2 October 1858." Granted, the scenario described here would be uncommon behavior for any hurricane in the Northeast Pacific basin, most of which travel westward out to sea. Some make it as far as Hawaii, but rarely do they manage to travel north to California because of quickly cooling sea temperatures off the U.S. West Coast. El Niño years warm those temperatures, and 1858 may have been such a year. During the record-breaking 1997 El Niño, the Category 5 Hurricane Linda, the most intense storm ever recorded in the Northeast Pacific, with maximum sustained winds approaching 185 miles per hour and a pressure fall down to 902 millibars (26.64 inches), also gave California a scare when some models predicted it might curve northeastward and reach Southern California in a weakened state (although that turned out to be way off base). For more information on Linda, see the National Hurricane Center Preliminary Report, Hurricane Linda, October 25, 1997, available online at http://www.nhc.noaa.gov/1997linda.html.

That same year, Hurricane Nora struck the Baja California peninsula and traveled northward over land far enough to deliver tropical storm–force winds to the United States near the California/Arizona border. The storm caused flooding, power outages, and considerable agricultural losses. For more information, see the National Hurricane Center Preliminary Report, Hurricane Nora, October 30, 1997, available online at http://www.nhc.noaa.gov/1997nora.html.

**229 Hurricane Sergio**...National Hurricane Center, Tropical Cyclone Report, Hurricane Sergio, November 29, 2006. Available online at http://www.nhc.noaa.gov/pdf/TCR-EP212006_Sergio.pdf.

**230 "do not occur"**...Gray, "Global View of the Origin of Tropical Disturbances." On page 678 Gray writes: "In the SW Atlantic and central Pacific, where tropical storms do not occur, the observed climatological tropospheric wind shear is large (i.e., 20–40 kt.). This is believed to be the major inhibitor to development in these areas."

**230 Hurricane Iniki**...For the Central Pacific Hurricane Center's report on Iniki, see http://www.prh.noaa.gov/cphc/summaries/1992.php#Iniki.

**231 "THIS IS THE FIFTH CATEGORY 5"**...Central Pacific Hurricane Center, Hurricane Ioke Discussion Number 25, August 25, 2006. Available online at http://www.prh.noaa.gov/cphc/pages/prod.php?file=/cphc/tcpages/archive/2006/TCDCP2.CP012006.25.0608260248.

**231 920 millibars**...Best track data for Ioke available at http://weather.unisys.com/hurricane/e_pacific/2006/IOKE/track.dat.

**231 "IOKE COULD ENTER THE RECORD BOOKS"**...Central Pacific Hurricane Center, Hurricane Ioke Discussion Number 29, August 26, 2006. Available

online at http://www.prh.noaa.gov/cphc/pages/prod.php?file=/cphc/tcpages/archive/
2006/TCDCP2.CP012006.29.0608270240.

**231 "198 CONSECUTIVE HOURS"**...Central Pacific Hurricane Center, Tropical Weather Summary for the Central North Pacific, November 30, 2006. Available
online at http://www.prh.noaa.gov/cphc/pages/TWS.php.

**232 Hurricane Ivan had lasted**...See National Hurricane Center Tropical Cyclone
Report, Hurricane Ivan, updated May 27, 2005. Available online at http://www.nhc
.noaa.gov/pdf/TCR-AL092004_Ivan.pdf. The total of 192 hours is computed by
analyzing the best track data provided here. For thirty-two consecutive six-hourly reports (192 hours), Ivan was at or above an intensity of 115 knots, the cutoff for Category 4 designation. However, I could not find a definitive source stating that Ivan
actually held the record prior to Ioke.

**232 "It's unusual to see one storm"**...Jeff Masters WunderBlog, "Another Extreme Typhoon for the Philippines," November 10, 2006. Available online at http://
www.wunderground.com/blog/JeffMasters/comment.html?entrynum=575&tstamp
=200611.

**233 "not a consensus"**...Quoted in Reuters, "President Briefed on Storms, Warming; Weather experts tell Bush there's 'not a consensus' connecting the two," August
1, 2006.

**233 in the president's hands**...Interview with Chris Landsea, November 8, 2006.

**233 Landsea dressed sharply**...For the photo, see http://www.whitehouse.gov/
infocus/hurricane/.

**233 "you didn't typically see this kind of behavior from scientists"**...Judith
Curry notes on Jeb Bush meeting, on file with the author.

**234 two opposed positions**...For a more thorough discussion of the contrast between
"sound science" and the "precautionary principle," see Mooney, *The Republican War on
Science,* Chapter 6, "Junking 'Sound Science.'"

**235 "Alice falling down the rabbit hole"**...Judith Curry, post to RealClimate.org,
August 19, 2006, 8:33 A.M., available online at http://www.realclimate.org/index.php/
archives/2006/08/fact-fiction-and-friction/#comment-17948.

**235 "falling out of the Ivory Tower"**...Judith Curry presentation, "Falling Out of
the Ivory Tower," American Geophysical Union meeting, December 12, 2006, San
Francisco.

**235 Curry had been shocked**...Interview with Judith Curry, October 6, 2006;
Curry presentation, "Falling Out of the Ivory Tower."

**236 Doug Blackmon**...Interviewed on January 17, 2007.

**236 sprang from societal and demographic trends**...See, for example, Roger A.
Pielke, Jr., "Disasters, Death, and Destruction: Making Sense of Recent Calamities,"
Seventh Annual Roger Revelle Commemorative Lecture, *Oceanography,* Vol. 19, No. 2
(June 2006). Available online at http://sciencepolicy.colorado.edu/admin/publication_
files/resource-2449-2006.02.pdf. As Pielke notes, "To emphasize, humans have an ef-

fect on the global climate system and reducing greenhouse-gas emissions makes good sense. But reducing emissions will not discernibly affect the trend of escalating disaster losses because the cause of that increase lies in ever-growing societal vulnerability."

237 **a "lurker"**...Interview with Judith Curry, March 10, 2006.

237 **a kind of field experiment**...Climate Audit, "The Georgia Tech Report Card," October 4, 2006, available online at http://www.climateaudit.org/?p=846.

237 **"putting together a jigsaw puzzle"**...Peter Webster, "Gray's New Climate Science, Jigsaws and the Theory of Epicycles," comment posted to RealClimate.org, May 1, 2006. Available online at http://www.realclimate.org/index.php/archives/2006/04/gray-on-agw/#comment-12716.

237 **blog comments**...Judith Curry, post to RealClimate.org, August 19, 2006, 8:33 A.M. Available online at http://www.realclimate.org/index.php/archives/2006/08/fact-fiction-and-friction/#comment-17948.

239 **further work by the Webster group**...See Carlos Hoyos et al., "Deconvolution of the Factors Contributing to the Increase in Global Hurricane Intensity," *Science,* Vol. 312 (March 16, 2006), pp. 94–97. Other papers supportive of a significant global warming influence on hurricanes published in 2006 include James Elsner, "Evidence in Support of the Climate Change–Atlantic Hurricane Hypothesis," *Geophysical Research Letters,* Vol. 33, L16705 (2006); and Ryan Sriver and Matthew Huber, "Low Frequency Variability in Globally Integrated Tropical Cyclone Power Dissipation," *Geophysical Research Letters,* Vol. 33, L11705 (2006).

239 **Patrick Michaels**...Patrick Michaels et al., "Sea-surface Temperatures and Tropical Cyclones in the Atlantic Basin," *Geophysical Research Letters,* Vol. 33, L09708 (2006).

239 **Chris Landsea**...Landsea et al., "Can We Detect Trends in Extreme Tropical Cyclones?"

239 **Phil Klotzbach**...Philip J. Klotzbach, "Trends in Global Tropical Cyclone Activity Over the Past Twenty Years (1986–2005)," *Geophysical Research Letters,* Vol. 33, L10805 (2006).

239 **Gerry Bell**...Gerry Bell and Muthuvel Chelliah, "Leading Tropical Modes Associated with Interannual and Multidecadal Fluctuations in North Atlantic Hurricane Activity," *Journal of Climate,* Vol. 19 (2006), pp. 590–612.

239 **"the card-carrying tropical cyclone people"**...Interview with Judith Curry, March 10, 2006.

239 **an increase in atmospheric water vapor**...Kevin Trenberth et al., "Trends and Variability in Column-integrated Atmospheric Water Vapor," *Climate Dynamics,* Vol. 24 (2005), pp. 741–58.

239 **downplaying...the Atlantic Multidecadal Oscillation**...Trenberth and Shea, "Atlantic Hurricanes and Natural Variability in 2005."

239 **Mann and Emanuel**...Mann and Emanuel, "Atlantic Hurricane Trends Linked to Climate Change," *EOS,* Vol. 87 (June 13, 2006), pp. 233–41.

**240 twenty-two different climate models**...Benjamin Santer et al., "Forced and Unforced Ocean Temperature Changes in Atlantic and Pacific Tropical Cyclogenesis Regions," *Proceedings of the National Academy of Sciences,* Vol. 103, No. 38 (September 19, 2006), pp. 13905–10.

**240 hurricane breeding grounds**...In another modeling study by Thomas Knutson and his colleagues, the warming of the main hurricane development region in the Atlantic was again attributed to human factors. See Thomas Knutson et al., "Assessment of Twentieth-Century Regional Surface Temperature Trends Using the GFDL CM2 Coupled Models," *Journal of Climate,* Vol. 19, No. 9 (2006), pp. 1624–51. The study suggested that "the warming late in the 20th century in this region represents the emergence of a long-term anthropogenically forced warming signal from the background of substantial multidecadal variability."

**240 an environmentalist public relations firm**...Resource Media describes itself as "dedicated to making the environment matter. We provide media strategy and services to non-profits, foundations and other partners who are working on the front lines of environmental protection." See http://www.resource-media.org/.

**240 "provides the final link"**...Resource Media press release, "New Wave of Hurricane Science: Research Since Katrina Establishes Link Between Global Warming, Hurricanes," September 7, 2006, on file with the author.

**240 "kind of closes the loop here"**...Resource Media conference call, August 31, 2006, author's notes.

**240 "increased federal funding for tropical cyclone research"**...William Gray, comment on "Forced and Unforced Ocean Temperature Changes in Atlantic and Pacific Tropical Cyclogenesis Regions," on file with the author.

**240 "that's not a big issue"**...Interview with Chris Landsea, November 8, 2006.

**241 some misleadingly framed the findings**...See, for example, Randolph E. Schmid, "New Study Ties Global Warming to Stronger Hurricanes," Associated Press, September 11, 2006, noting in its first sentence, "Most of the increase in ocean temperature that feeds more intense hurricanes is a result of human-induced global warming, says a study that one researcher says 'closes the loop' between climate change and powerful storms like Katrina"; Katy Human, "Report Blames Humans for Storms' Ferocity: The new study points to greenhouse gases as the cause of warmer ocean waters where hurricanes form. Other scientists argue that the methodology is flawed," *Denver Post,* September 12, 2006, whose opening begins: "Human beings are warming the oceans where hurricanes are born, scientists said Monday, and the storms are getting fiercer as a result"; and an editorial in the *Charlotte Observer,* September 13, 2006, which began: "Researchers in a new study of global warming and rising sea surface temperatures have drawn some conclusions that ought to compel the attention of policymakers, public officials and taxpayers in the Carolinas: Increased hurricane intensity, they concluded, is almost certainly related to manmade pollution." For a counter-example, see Martin Merzer, "Report

Points to Link Between Global Warming and Hurricanes," *Miami Herald,* September 11, 2006.

**241 "windshield wiper" effect**...Andrew Revkin comment made in a public debate at the 2006 Society of Environmental Journalists conference. Audio available online at http://www.desmogblog.com/podcasts-from-the-sej-2006-conference.

**241 strategic communication**...This distinction between different strategies for communicating about climate change has been highlighted by American University communication professor Matthew Nisbet. Matthew C. Nisbet, "Framing as a Tool for Engaging the Public," Environmental Science Seminar Series, American Meteorological Society, Washington D.C., November 28, 2006. Summary available online at http://www.ametsoc.org/atmospolicy/EnvironmentalScienceSeminarSeries.html.

**241 *Nature***...Jim Giles, "Is U.S. Hurricane Report Being Quashed?" *Nature,* Vol. 443 (September 28, 2006), p. 378.

**242 an internal group of government experts**...Interview with Ants Leetmaa, October 18, 2006.

**242 not particularly controversial**...The document can be read online at http://hurricanes.noaa.gov/pdf/hurricanes-and-climate-change-09-2006.pdf.

**242 Leetmaa got an e-mail**...Giles, "Is U.S. Hurricane Report Being Quashed?"

**242 "war on science"**...Quoted in Randolph E. Schmid, "Journal Says Agency Blocked Report on Hurricanes, Warming," Associated Press, September 27, 2006.

**242–43 promptly contradicted**...Giles, "Is U.S. Hurricane Report Being Quashed?" p. 378.

**243 a statement**..."Message from the Under Secretary—Scientific Debate and Transparency Within NOAA," October 3, 2006, on file with the author.

**244 "perched on a ledge"**...David A. Fahrenthold, "2 Men Arrested on a Ledge at NOAA Building; Silver Spring Demonstration Staged Over Global Warming," *Washington Post,* October 24, 2006.

**244 a press release**...U.S. Newswire, "Protesters Occupy Ledge Above Federal Agency To Demand Action on Global Warming; Standoff with Police Occurs at NOAA Headquarters in D.C. Area; Six Protesters Blockade Main Entrance Denouncing Bush Climate Policies," October 23, 2006.

## CHAPTER 14: Hurricane Climatology

PAGE

**245 Frank Lautenberg**...J. Scott Orr, "Global-warming Factions Agree: Let Data Flow; Senate Panel Hears Plea Against Censorship," *Newark Star-Ledger,* December 7, 2006.

**246 The resulting study**...Jim Kossin et al., "A Globally Consistent Reanalysis of Hurricane Variability and Trends," *Geophysical Research Letters,* Vol. 34, 2007, L04815, doi:10.1029/2006GL028836.

**246 Kossin had presented the results publicly.** Jim Kossin, "What Can We Say

About Hurricanes and Climate Change With Our Present Data?" Presentation to the American Meteorological Society Environmental Science Seminar Series, October 20, 2006. Available online at http://www.ametsoc.org/atmospolicy/documents/Kossin102006.pdf.

**246 "primate change"**...Bruce A. Harper, "On the Importance of Reviewing Historic Tropical Cyclone Intensities." Presentation at the 2006 American Meteorological Society 27th Conference on Hurricanes and Tropical Meteorology, April 24, 2006. Extended abstract available online at http://ams.confex.com/ams/pdfpapers/107768.pdf. Recorded presentation available online at http://ams.confex.com/ams/27Hurricanes/wrfredirect.cgi?id=5477. (Quotation is from the recorded presentation.)

**247 "I'd have to step back"**...Interview with Kerry Emanuel, October 19, 2006. Similarly, during a January 15, 2007, presentation at the annual American Meteorological Meeting in San Antonio, Emanuel was asked about the Kossin study and replied, "I do agree with Jim's results, I think they've done very, very nice work on that." (Author's notes from the event.)

**247 Storm numbers in the Atlantic**...See Greg Holland and Peter Webster, "Heightened Tropical Cyclone Activity in the North Atlantic: Natural Variability or Climate Trend?" *Proceedings of the Royal Society A: Mathematical, Physical Engineering Sciences,* 2006 (accepted).

**247 "no rational reason"**...Greg Holland, "On the Changing Characteristics of Atlantic Hurricanes," Presentation to the American Meteorological Society Environmental Science Seminar Series, October 20, 2006. Available online at http://www.ametsoc.org/atmospolicy/documents/Holland102006.pdf. Holland also made this point while presenting at the American Geophysical Union meeting in San Francisco on December 15, 2006 (author's notes).

**247 a new data-centric argument**...As this book went to press in early 2007, the hurricane–climate debate was just fully shifting into this new phase. For more details, see the author's report on a debate between Holland and Landsea at the January 2007 American Meteorological Society meeting in San Antonio, entitled "AMS Dispatch: Numbers Game." Available online at http://www.scienceblogs.com/intersection/2007/01/ams_dispatch_numbers_game.php.

**248 Earth Simulator**...Kazuyoshi Oouchi et al., "Tropical Cyclone Climatology in a Global-Warming Climate as Simulated in a 20km-Mesh Global Atmospheric Model: Frequency and Wind Intensity Analysis," *Journal of the Meteorological Society of Japan,* Vol. 84, No. 2 (2006), pp. 259–76.

**248 14,000**...E-mail communication from Harvey Leifert, January 4, 2007.

**251 "The tropical cyclones' contribution"**...William M. Gray, "Hurricanes: Their Formation, Structure and Likely Role in the Tropical Circulation."

**251 ocean heat transport**...Emanuel, "Contribution of Tropical Cyclones to Meridional Heat Transport by the Oceans."

**251 "tropical cyclones running around all the time"**...Interview with Matthew Huber, September 5, 2006.

**251 complementary account**...See Kevin Trenberth, "Changes in Climate and Hurricanes," *Preprint: AMS Meteorology and Oceanography of the Southern Hemisphere,* Brazil, April 2006, noting, "It is thus suggested that tropical storms, and hurricanes in particular, play a unique role in the overall heat budget by cooling the ocean...Hence they should also play this role as the climate changes."

**252 hurricanes do a far more efficient job**...This description of hurricanes transporting heat from the tropics is based on an interview with Kevin Trenberth, February 14, 2006.

**252 redistributing heat**...The atmospheric redistribution of heat in hurricanes occurs in the vertical; heat also gets transported pole-ward in the storm's outflow jets and by atmospheric winds. In addition, when tropical cyclones undergo extra tropical transition, that also has the effect of transporting heat pole-ward. These forms of pole-ward heat transport presumably complement the pole-ward heat transport that Emanuel has described tropical cyclones as producing through ocean mixing. (Interview with Greg Holland, January 2, 2007.)

**252 80 or 90 tropical cyclones per year**...Others question whether the 80-storms-per-year number signifies anything special—after all, the number had to be something. See, for example, William M. Frank and George S. Young, "The 80 Cyclones Myth," presentation at the 27th Conference on Hurricanes and Tropical Meteorology, Monterey, California, April 2006.

**252 "cart horses"**...Interview with Peter Webster, March 10, 2006.

**253 paleotempestology**...For an introduction to the subject, see Kam-biu Liu, "Paleotempestology: Principles, Methods, and Examples from Gulf Coast Lake Sediments," and Jeffrey P. Donnelly and Thompson Webb III, "Back-barrier Sedimentary Records of Intense Hurricane Landfalls in the Northeastern United States," both in Murnane and Liu, eds., *Hurricanes and Typhoons: Past, Present, and Future.*

**253 Jeff Donnelly**...J. Donnelly, "Climate Forcing of North Atlantic Tropical Cyclone Activity over the last 6000 years," presentation at the "Tropical Cyclone-Climate Interactions on All Timescales" panel, American Geophysical Union Fall Meeting, San Francisco, December 15, 2006.

**254 "hurricane climatology"**...This phrase is not uncommon, but my use of it was influenced by Richard Kerr, "A Tempestuous Birth for Hurricane Climatology," *Science,* Vol. 312 (May 5, 2006), pp. 676–78.

**254 "merely statistical extrapolation"**...Peter Webster and Greg Holland, "Hurricanes in a Warming World: From Genesis to Revelation," PowerPoint presentation on file with the author.

**255 for over a decade**...For the early history of the Marshall Institute's global warming "skepticism," see Weart, *The Discovery of Global Warming.*

**255 partly funded**...The George C. Marshall Institute received $115,000 from ExxonMobil in 2005, according to the company's 2005 giving report available at http://www.exxonmobil.com/Corporate/Files/Corporate/giving05_policy.pdf. The 2006 giving report was not available as this book went to press.

**255 independence from fossil fuel interests**...William Gray, "The Global Warming Fuss," undated, on file with the author. Gray states in this article: "Most of the meteorological skeptics I know (including me) do not have any association with the fossil-fuel industry or right-wing organizations. We just don't believe humans are now or will in the next century be able to significantly alter the globe's temperature."

**255 evening out the ledger**...Interview with William Gray, October 12, 2006. For Gray's insistence that he doesn't accept industry payments, see also Alan Prendergast, "The Skeptic," *Denver Westword,* June 29, 2006.

**255 the Marshall Institute talk**...William Gray, "Hurricanes and Climate Change," George C. Marshall Institute Washington Roundtable on Science and Public Policy, October 11, 2006. Slides available online at http://www.marshall.org/pdf/materials/461.pdf.

**256 "Not any more"**...Quoted in Jim Erikson, "Tempest Erupts Over Hurricanes; Global warming debate at conference spawns name calling," *Rocky Mountain News,* October 26, 2006.

**256 "look it up in the book of Genesis"**...Senate Floor Statement of James Inhofe, "Peace in the Middle East," March 4, 2002.

**256 "economy-killing carbon caps"**...Environment and Public Works Committee, "Senator Inhofe Reacts to U.N. Climate Conference in Kenya and Comments on Upcoming 110th Congress," November 16, 2006. Available online at http://epw.senate.gov/pressitem.cfm?party=rep&id=265956.

**257 "natural cycles at work"**...For the joint PowerPoint presentations of D'Aleo and Gray, see http://epw.senate.gov/repwhitepapers/DCMeetingNov16.pdf.

**258 "...absolutely revolutionize human life."** Bertrand Russell, *Sceptical Essays* (London: Unwin Books, 1961), p. 10 (original edition 1928).

## CONCLUSION

**PAGE**

**260 "the wonderful world of projections"**...Interview with Greg Holland, February 13, 2006.

**261 El Niño tends**...For an overview of the effect of El Niño on hurricanes see Pao Shin Chu, "ENSO and Tropical Cyclone Activity," in *Hurricanes and Typhoons: Past, Present, and Future.* Note that the effect of El Niño in the Pacific varies: For the Northwest Pacific, storms shift eastward, equator-ward, and last longer; for the Northeast Pacific, storms shift westward, get more intense, and last longer, in the process also traveling farther westward; and for the Central Pacific (north of the equator), more storms form and more also arrive in the basin from the Northeast Pacific.

**261 some type of change ought to occur**...Interview with Kevin Trenberth, December 29, 2006.

**261 a new consensus**...For another useful overview of the state of the debate as this book went to press, see J. Marshall Shepherd and Thomas Knutson, "The Current

Debate on the Linkage Between Global Warming and Hurricanes," *Geography Compass*, Vol. 1 (2006): 10.1111/j.1749-8198.2006.00002.x.

**262  summary statement**...World Meteorological Organization, 6th International Workshop on Tropical Cyclones, "Summary Statement on Tropical Cyclones and Climate Change," 2006. Available online at http://www.wmo.ch/web/arep/press_releases/2006/iwtc_summary.pdf. In addition to the summary statement, a longer statement was released after being developed at the workshop, available online at http://www.wmo.ch/web/arep/press_releases/2006/iwtc_statement.pdf/.

**262  "Summary for Policymakers"**...Intergovernmental Panel on Climate Change, "Climate Change 2007: The Physical Science Basis, Summary for Policymakers," available online at http://www.ipcc.ch/SPM2feb07.pdf.

**262  more than justify worry**...For a debate among hurricane experts over the extent to which we should take a precautionary outlook on the question of hurricane intensification due to global warming, see Pielke, Jr., et al., "Hurricanes and Global Warming"; Anthes et al., "Hurricanes and Global Warming—Potential Linkages and Consequences," *Bulletin of the American Meteorological Society*, May 2006, pp. 623–28; and Roger A. Pielke, Jr., et al., "Reply to 'Hurricanes and Global Warming—Potential Linkages and Consequences,'" *Bulletin of the American Meteorological Society*, May 2006, pp. 628–31.

**263  half of the U.S. population**...National Science Board, "Hurricane Warning: The Critical Need for a National Hurricane Research Initiative," Draft, September 29, 2006.

**263  "we're not prepared for hurricanes as they are today."** Interview with Chris Landsea, November 8, 2006. See also R. A. Pielke, Jr., and R. A. Pielke, Sr., *Hurricanes: Their Nature and Impacts on Society* (London: John Wiley & Sons Press, 1997), p. 187, noting: "Before asking if we are prepared for the future, we ought to ask if we are prepared even for past known events and climate fluctuations. The future is uncertain—the recent past, however, is certain. Once we consider ourselves 'prepared for the past,' so to speak, we can seek additional proactive improvements for the future."

**263  top-ten list of places**...International Hurricane Research Center, "10 Most Hurricane Vulnerable Areas." Available online at http://www.ihc.fiu.edu/media/docs/10_Most_Hurricane_Vulnerable_Areas.pdf.

**264  "it should in no event detract"**...Statement on the U.S. Hurricane Problem, July 25, 2006. Available online at http://wind.mit.edu/~emanuel/Hurricane_threat.htm.

**265  "You just have to adapt."** Interview with Roger Pielke, Jr., January 5, 2007.

**266  mandatory caps**...See Roger A. Pielke, Jr., "Turning the Big Knob: An Evaluation of the Use of Energy Policy to Modulate Future Climate Impacts," *Energy and Environment*, Vol. 11 (May 22, 2000), pp. 255–76.

**269  "conservative estimate"**...Interview with Hugh Willoughby, May 16, 2006.

**269  "a cultural distinction that's unnecessary."** Interview with Kerry Emanuel, May 22, 2006.

**270** "a considerable debating disadvantage"...Curry et al., "Mixing Politics and Science."

**271** honed in on scientific disagreements...Nisbet and Mooney, "The Next Big Storm."

**273** "Katrina is the standard"...Press Briefing by Scott McClellan and Senior Officials on Levee Reconstruction, December 15, 2005. Available online at http://www.whitehouse.gov/news/releases/2005/12/20051215-4.html.

**273** The protections ignored worst-case scenarios...My analysis of Hurricane Betsy and its aftermath relies upon John McQuaid and Mark Schleifstein's *Path of Destruction: The Devastation of New Orleans and the Coming Age of Superstorms* (New York: Little, Brown, 2006), centrally Chapters 3 and 4. See also U.S. Government Accountability Office, Testimony before the Subcommittee on Energy and Water Development, Committee on Appropriations, House of Representatives, "Army Corps of Engineers: Lake Pontchartrain and Vicinity Hurricane Protection Project," September 28, 2005. Available online at http://www.gao.gov/new.items/d051050t.pdf.

**273** "Are the levees protecting them"...Interview with Mark Schleifstein, November 24, 2006.

**274** the agency had promised to comply...Mark Schleifstein, "Flood Protection Plans Lacking; Changed Standards Mean New Strategies," *New Orleans Times-Picayune,* August 28, 2006.

**274** "the 100-year storm is the 86-year storm"...Schleifstein, "Flood Protection Plans Lacking."

**275** $32 billion or more...See John Schwartz, "Category 5: Levees are Piece of a $32 Billion Pie," *New York Times,* November 29, 2005.

**275** Category 5 defenses...Peter Whoriskey and Spencer S. Hsu, "Levee Repair Costs Triple: New Orleans May Lack Full Protection," *Washington Post,* March 31, 2006.

**275** press release...See Curry et al., "Mixing Politics and Science."

**276** lower Manhattan...NASA Press Release, "NASA Looks at Sea Level Rise, Hurricane Risks to New York City," October 25, 2006.

**276** "fundamental rethinking"...Munich Re, "Hurricanes: More Intense, More Frequent, More Expensive," 2006.

## APPENDICES
PAGE

**285** "classifications of cyclones"...Quoted by Dr. Jeff Masters in "Thingamabobbercane Revisited," November 8, 2006, available online at http://www.wunderground.com/blog/JeffMasters/comment.html?entrynum=574&tstamp=200611.

**285** eyelike structure...For an illuminating discussion of "blizzicanes," see another posting by Dr. Jeff Masters from February 14, 2006, available online at http://www.wunderground.com/blog/JeffMasters/comment.html?entrynum=303&tstamp=200602.

285 **"Halloween Storm" of 1991**...For a full meteorological account of the 1991 Halloween Storm, see this useful page from the National Climatic Data Center: http://www.ncdc.noaa.gov/oa/satellite/satelliteseye/hurricanes/unnamed91/unnamed91.html.

286 **"the subtropical cyclone"**...Interview with Richard Pasch, November 8, 2006.

286 **"Polar Low"**...See Masters, "Thingamabobbercane Forms off the Coast of Oregon," November 2, 2006. Available online at http://www.wunderground.com/blog/JeffMasters/comment.html?entrynum=569&tstamp=200611.

287 **Alfred Russel Wallace**...Wallace's famous essay, mailed from the island of Ternate in the Malay Archipelago and describing an idea that had come to him during a feverish malaria dream, was entitled "On the Tendency of Varieties to Depart Indefinitely from the Original Type." Receiving it by mail forced Darwin's hand. After consulting his scientist friends, Darwin had his own unpublished work presented jointly with Wallace's essay before the Linnean Society, a scientific club in London. Then Darwin rushed to press with *The Origin of Species*. By the time Wallace got back to England from the Malay Archipelago several years later, having collected over 100,000 specimens and named more than a thousand new species, all of Victorian society had been shaken by Darwin's (and his own) discovery. For more on the Wallace-Darwin episode, see Michael Shermer, *In Darwin's Shadow: The Life and Science of Alfred Russel Wallace* (New York: Oxford University Press, 2002), pp. 118–21.

288 **"these tempests might be so increased"**...Alfred Russel Wallace, *Man's Place in the Universe* (New York: McClure, Phillips & Co., 1903), pp. 242–43.

288 **the weight of air molecules**...For scientific critiques of Wallace's thoughts on hurricanes I am indebted to Richard Anthes, Greg Holland, and Kevin Trenberth.

288 **not uncommon at the time**...For details on early speculation about the relationship between solar changes and climate, see Spencer Weart, "Changing Sun, Changing Climate." Available online at http://www.aip.org/history/climate/solar.htm#L_0279.

288 **Tor Bergeron**...For an account of Bergeron's life, see Cox, *Storm Watchers*, Chapter 21.

289 **"Another problem, of much more far-reaching consequences"**...Tor Bergeron, "The Problem of Tropical Hurricanes," *Quarterly Journal of the Royal Meteorological Society*, Vol. 80 (1954), pp. 131–64.

290 **"Back then it was surprising"**...Interview with T. N. Krishnamurti, May 31, 2006.

290 **"more intense hurricanes"**...Interview with Joanne and Robert Simpson, October 12, 2006.

# BIBLIOGRAPHY AND RECOMMENDED READING

Anthes, Richard. "Hot Towers and Hurricanes: Early Observations, Theories and Models" in "Cloud Systems, Hurricanes, and the Tropical Rainfall Measuring Mission (TRMM)—A Tribute to Dr. Joanne Simpson." *AMS Meteorological Monograph,* Vol. 29 (January 2003), edited by Tao and Adler: 139–48.

Anthes, Richard, et al. "Hurricanes and Global Warming—Potential Linkages and Consequences." *Bulletin of the American Meteorological Society* (May 2006): 623–28.

Barnett, Tim, et al. "Penetration of Human-Induced Warming Into the World's Oceans." *Science,* Vol. 309 (July 8, 2005).

Bauerlein, Valerie. "Cold Front: Hurricane Debate Shatters Civility of Weather Science." *The Wall Street Journal,* February 2, 2006.

Bergeron, Tor. "The Problem of Tropical Hurricanes." *Quarterly Journal of the Royal Meteorological Society* 80 (1954): 131–64.

———. "Methods in Scientific Weather Analysis and Forecasting: An Outline in the History of Ideas and Hints at a Program." *The Atmosphere and the Sea Motion: Scientific Contributions to the Rossby Memorial Volume,* edited by Bert Bolin. New York: The Rockefeller Institute Press, 1959: 440–74.

Broccoli, Anthony, and Syukuro Manabe. "Can Existing Climate Models Be Used to Study Anthropogenic Changes in Tropical Cyclone Climate?" *Geophysical Research Letters* 17, no. 11 (October 1990): 1917–20.

Carrier, Jim. *The Ship and the Storm: Hurricane Mitch and the Loss of the Fantome.* Camden, Maine: International Marine, 2001.

Charney, Jule. "Impact of Computers on Meteorology." *Computer Physics Communications* 3, Suppl. (1972): 117–26.

Charney, Jule, and Arnt Eliassen. "On the Growth of the Hurricane Depression." *Journal of the Atmospheric Sciences* 21 (January 1964): 68–75.

Chenoweth, Michael, and Christopher Landsea. "The San Diego Hurricane of 2 October 1858." *Bulletin of the American Meteorological Society* (November 2004): 1689–97.

Cox, John D. *Storm Watchers: The Turbulent History of Weather Prediction from Franklin's Kite to El Niño.* Hoboken, N.J.: John Wiley & Sons, 2002.

Crichton, Michael. *State of Fear.* New York: HarperCollins, 2004.

Curry, J. A., P. J. Webster, and G. J. Holland. "Mixing Politics and Science in Testing the Hypothesis that Greenhouse Warming Is Causing a Global Increase in Hurricane Intensity." *Bulletin of the American Meteorological Society* (August 2006): 1025–37.

Delworth, Tom, and Michael Mann. "Observed and Simulated Multidecadal Variability in the Northern Hemisphere." *Climate Dynamics* 16 (2000): 661–76.

Emanuel, Kerry. "An Air-Sea Interaction Theory for Tropical Cyclones. Part I: Steady State Maintenance." *Journal of the Atmospheric Sciences* 43, no. 6 (March 15, 1986): 585–604.

———. "The Dependence of Hurricane Intensity on Climate." *Nature* 326, no. 6112 (April 2, 1987): 483–85.

———. "The Maximum Intensity of Hurricanes." *Journal of the Atmospheric Sciences* 45, no. 7 (April 1, 1988): 1143–55.

———. "Toward a General Theory of Hurricanes." *American Scientist* 76 (July–August 1988): 371–79.

———. "The Contribution of Tropical Cyclones to the Oceans' Meridional Heat Transport." *Journal of Geophysical Research* 106, no. 14 (2001): 771–81.

———. "Tropical Cyclones." *Annual Review of Earth and Planetary Sciences* 31 (2003): 75–104.

———. *Divine Wind: The History and Science of Hurricanes.* New York: Oxford University Press, 2005.

———. "Increasing Destructiveness of Tropical Cyclones over the Past 30 Years." *Nature* 436 (August 4, 2005): 686–88.

Espy, James P. *The Philosophy of Storms.* Boston, Mass.: C. C. Little and J. Brown, 1841.

Fitzpatrick, Patrick. *Hurricanes: A Reference Handbook.* Santa Barbara, Calif.: ABC-CLIO, 2006 (second edition).

Fleming, James Rodger. *Meteorology in America, 1800–1870.* Baltimore, Md.: The Johns Hopkins University Press, 1990.

———. *Historical Essays on Meteorology, 1919–1995.* Editor. Boston, Mass.: The American Meteorological Society, 1996.

———. *Historical Perspectives on Climate Change.* New York: Oxford University Press, 1998.

Goldenberg, Stanley, et al. "The Recent Increase in Atlantic Hurricane Activity: Causes and Implications." *Science* 293 (July 20, 2001): 474–79.

Gray, William M. "Global View of the Origin of Tropical Disturbances and Storms." *Monthly Weather Review* 96, no. 10 (October 1968): 669–700.

———. "Hurricanes: Their Formation, Structure and Likely Role in the Tropical Circulation." *Meteorology Over the Tropical Oceans,* edited by D. B. Shaw. London: Royal Meteorological Society, 1979: 155–218.

———. "Atlantic Seasonal Hurricane Frequency. Part I: El Niño and 30 mb Quasi-Biennial Oscillation Influences." *Monthly Weather Review* 112 (September 1984): 1649–68.

———. "Atlantic Seasonal Hurricane Frequency. Part II: Forecasting Its Variability." *Monthly Weather Review* 112 (September 1984): 1669–83.

———. "Strong Association between West African Rainfall and U.S. Landfall of Intense Hurricanes." *Science* 249, no. 4974 (September 14, 1990): 1251.

Henderson-Sellers, Ann, et al. "Tropical Cyclones and Global Climate Change: A Post-IPCC Assessment." *Bulletin of the American Meteorological Society* 79, no. 1 (January 1998): 19–38.

Holland, Greg. "The Maximum Potential Intensity of Tropical Cyclones." *Journal of the Atmospheric Sciences* 54 (November 1, 1997): 2519–41.

Holland, Greg, and Peter Webster. "Heightened Tropical Cyclone Activity in the North Atlantic: Natural Variability or Climate Trend?" *Proceedings of the Royal Society A: Mathematical, Physical Engineering Sciences* (2006).

Kerr, Richard. "A Tempestuous Birth for Hurricane Climatology," *Science* 312 (May 5, 2006): 676–78.

Kossin, James, et al. "A Globally Consistent Reanalysis of Hurricane Variability and Trends." *Geophysical Research Letters* 34 (2007), L04815, doi:10.1029/2006GL028836.

Knutson, Thomas, and Robert Tuleya. "Impact of $CO_2$-Induced Warming on Simulated Hurricane Intensity and Precipitation: Sensitivity to the Choice of Climate Model and Convective Parameterization." *Journal of Climate* 17, no. 18 (September 15, 2004).

Knutson, Thomas, et al. "Simulated Increase of Hurricane Intensities in a $CO_2$ Warmed Climate." *Science* 279 (February 13, 1998): 1018–20.

Kuhn, Thomas S. *The Structure of Scientific Revolutions.* Chicago, Ill.: University of Chicago Press, 1962.

Kutzbach, Gisela. *The Thermal Theory of Cyclones: A History of Meteorological Thought in the Nineteenth Century.* Boston, Mass.: American Meteorological Society Historical Monograph Series, 1979.

Landsea, Christopher, et al. "The Extremely Active 1995 Hurricane Season: Environmental Conditions and Verification of Seasonal Forecasts." *Monthly Weather Review* 126 (May 1998): 1174–93.

———. "A Reanalysis of Hurricane Andrew's Intensity." *Bulletin of the American Meteorological Society* (November 2004): 1699–1712.

———. "The Atlantic Hurricane Database Reanalysis Project: Documentation for 1851–1910 Alterations and Additions to the HURDAT Database." *Hurricanes and Typhoons: Past, Present and Future,* edited by R. J. Murnane and K. B. Liu. New York: Columbia University Press, 2004: 177–221.

———. "Can We Detect Trends in Extreme Tropical Cyclones?" *Science* 313 (July 28, 2006): 452–54.

Larson, Erik. *Isaac's Storm: A Man, a Time, and the Deadliest Hurricane in History.* New York: Vintage, 1999.

Lighthill, J., et al. "Global Climate Change and Tropical Cyclones." *Bulletin of the American Meteorological Society* 75 (1994): 2147–57.

Lindzen, Richard; Edward Lorenz; and George Platzman, editors, *The Atmosphere— A Challenge: The Science of Jule Gregory Charney.* Boston, Mass.: American Meteorological Society, 1990.

Manabe, Syukuro, et al. "Tropical Circulation in a Time-Integration of a Global Model of the Atmosphere." *Journal of the Atmospheric Sciences* 27 (July 1970): 580–612.

Mann, Michael, and Kerry Emanuel. "Atlantic Hurricane Trends Linked to Climate Change." *EOS* 87 (June 13, 2006): 233–41.

McQuaid, John, and Mark Schleifstein. *Path of Destruction: The Devastation of New Orleans and the Coming Age of Superstorms.* New York: Little, Brown, 2006.

McTaggart-Cowan, Ron, et al. "Analysis of Hurricane Catarina (2004)." *Monthly Weather Review* 134 (November 2006): 3029–53.

Monmonier, Mark. *Air Apparent: How Meteorologists Learned to Map, Predict, and Dramatize Weather.* Chicago, Ill.: University of Chicago Press, 1999.

Mooney, Chris. *The Republican War on Science.* New York: Basic Books, 2005.

Murnane, Richard J., and Kam-Biu Liu, editors, *Hurricanes and Typhoons: Past, Present, and Future.* New York: Columbia University Press, 2004.

Nash, J. Madeleine. *El Niño: Unlocking the Secrets of the Master Weather-Maker.* New York: Warner Books, 2002.

Nebeker, Frederik. *Calculating the Weather: Meteorology in the 20th Century.* San Diego, Calif.: Academic Press, 1995.

Nisbet, Matthew C., and Chris Mooney. "The Next Big Storm: Can Scientists and Journalists Work Together to Improve Coverage of the Hurricane–Global Warming Controversy?" *Skeptical Inquirer Online* (August 3, 2006). http://www.csicop .org/scienceandmedia/hurricanes/.

Palmén, Erik. "On the Formation and Structure of Tropical Hurricanes." *Geophysica* 3 (1948): 26–38.

Piddington, Henry. *The Sailor's Horn-Book for the Law of Storms.* London: Smith, Elder, & Co., 1848.

Pielke, Jr., Roger A. "Turning the Big Knob: An Evaluation of the Use of Energy Policy to Modulate Future Climate Impacts." *Energy and Environment* 11 (May 22, 2000): 255–76.

Pielke, Jr., Roger A., et al. "Hurricanes and Global Warming." *Bulletin of the American Meteorological Society* (November 2005): 1571–75.

Pielke, Jr., R. A., and R. A. Pielke, Sr. *Hurricanes: Their Nature and Impacts on Society.* London: John Wiley & Sons Press, 1997.

Rahmstorf, Stefan. "Thermohaline Ocean Circulation." *Encyclopedia of Quaternary Sciences*, edited by S. A. Elias. Amsterdam: Elsevier, 2006.

Redfield, William C. "Remarks on the Prevailing Storms of the Atlantic Coast, of the North American States." *American Journal of Science and Arts* XX (July 1831): 17–51.

Riehl, Herbert. "Waves in the Easterlies and the Polar Front in the Tropics." *Misc. Rep.*, No. 17, Department of Meteorology, University of Chicago, 1945, 79 pp.

———. "On the Formation of Typhoons." *Journal of Meteorology* 5, no. 6 (December 1948).

———. "A Model of Hurricane Formation." *Journal of Applied Physics* 21 (September 1950): 917–25.

———. *Tropical Meteorology.* New York: McGraw-Hill Book Company, 1954.

Rosenfeld, Jeffrey. *Eye of the Storm: Inside the World's Deadliest Hurricanes, Tornadoes, and Blizzards.* New York: Basic Books, 1999.

Santer, Benjamin, et al. "Forced and Unforced Ocean Temperature Changes in Atlantic and Pacific Tropical Cyclogenesis Regions." *Proceedings of the National Academy of Sciences* 103, no. 38 (September 19, 2006): 13905–10.

Sheets, Bob, and Jack Williams. *Hurricane Watch: Forecasting the Deadliest Storms on Earth.* New York: Vintage, 2001.

Simpson, Robert, editor, *Hurricane!: Coping With Disaster.* Washington, D.C.: American Geophysical Union, 2003.

Tidwell, Mike. *The Ravaging Tide: Strange Weather, Future Katrinas, and the Coming Death of America's Coastal Cities.* New York: Free Press, 2006.

Trenberth, Kevin. "Uncertainty in Hurricanes and Global Warming." *Science* 308 (June 17, 2005): 1753–54.

Trenberth, Kevin, and Dennis Shea. "Atlantic Hurricanes and Natural Variability in 2005." *Geophysical Research Letters* 33 (2006): L12704.

Velden, Christopher, et al. "The Dvorak Tropical Cyclone Intensity Estimation Technique: A Satellite-Based Methodology That Has Endured for Over Thirty Years." *Bulletin of the American Meteorological Society* (September 2006): 1195–1210.

Vitart, Frédéric. "Dynamical Seasonal Forecasts of Tropical Storm Statistics." *Hurricanes and Typhoons: Past, Present, and Future,* edited by Richard J. Murnane and Kam-Biu Liu. New York: Columbia University Press, 2004.

Weart, Spencer R. *The Discovery of Global Warming.* Cambridge, Mass.: Harvard University Press, 2003.

Webster, Peter, et al. "Changes in Tropical Cyclone Number, Duration, and Intensity in a Warming Environment." *Science* 309 (September 16, 2005): 1844–46.

Willoughby, Hugh, et al. "A Record Minimum Sea Level Pressure Observed in Hurricane Gilbert." *Monthly Weather Review* 117 (December 1989): 2824–28.

# LIST OF INTERVIEWS

**INTRODUCTION: "The Party Line":** Judith Curry, Georgia Institute of Technology, February 21, 2006 (telephone); Kerry Emanuel, Massachusetts Institute of Technology, January 4, 2006 (telephone), April 26, 2006 (in person); Greg Holland, National Center for Atmospheric Research, February 13, 2006 (in person); Chris Landsea, Science and Operations Officer, National Hurricane Center, November 8, 2006 (in person); Harvey Leifert, Public Information Manager, American Geophysical Union, March 3, 2006 (e-mail); Richard Pasch, Senior Hurricane Specialist, National Hurricane Center, November 8, 2006 (in person); Richard Somerville, Scripps Institution of Oceanography, February 21, 2006 (telephone).

**Chimneys and Whirlpools:** Richard Anthes, University Corporation for Atmospheric Research, June 14, 2006 (telephone); Kerry Emanuel, Massachusetts Institute of Technology, May 22, 2006 (in person), October 19, 2006 (telephone); James Rodger Fleming, Colby College, June 2006 (in person); Ruth McDonald, Hadley Centre for Climate Prediction and Research, UK Met Office, July 28, 2006 (in person).

**Of Heat Engines...:** Richard Anthes, University Corporation for Atmospheric Research, June 14, 2006 (telephone); Ferdinand Baer, University of Maryland, June 5, 2006 (telephone); Kerry Emanuel, Massachusetts Institute of Technology, May 22, 2006 (in person); William M. Frank, Pennsylvania State University, May 30, 2006 (telephone); William Gray, Colorado State University, February 16, 2006 (in person), May 12, 2006 (in person), October 12, 2006 (in person); T. N. Krishnamurti, Florida State University, May 31, 2006 (telephone); Charlie Neumann, National Hurricane Center (former), November 8, 2006 (in person); Robert and Joanne Simpson, October 12, 2006 (in person); Hugh Willoughby, Florida International University, May 16, 2006 (telephone).

**...and Computer Models:** Richard Anthes, University Corporation for Atmospheric Research, June 14, 2006 (telephone); Ferdinand Baer, University of Maryland, June 5, 2006 (telephone); Kerry Emanuel, Massachusetts Institute of Technology, May 22, 2006 (in person); William M. Frank, Pennsylvania State University, May 30,

2006 (telephone); William Gray, Colorado State University, October 12, 2006 (in person); Greg Holland, National Center for Atmospheric Research, August 7, 2006 (telephone); T. N. Krishnamurti, Florida State University, May 31, 2006 (telephone); Doug Lilly, University of Oklahoma (professor emeritus), June 5, 2006 (telephone); Vic Ooyama, June 5 and July 10, 2006 (e-mails received); Robert and Joanne Simpson, October 12, 2006 (in person).

**"Lay That Matrix Down":** Richard Anthes, University Corporation for Atmospheric Research, February 14, 2006 (in person); Anthony Broccoli, Rutgers University, August 21, 2006 (in person); Tom Delworth, Geophysical Fluid Dynamics Laboratory, National Oceanic and Atmospheric Administration, August 25, 2006 (telephone); William M. Frank, Pennsylvania State University, May 30, 2006 (telephone); William Gray, Colorado State University, February 16, 2006 (in person), May 12, 2006 (in person), October 12, 2006 (in person); Greg Holland, National Center for Atmospheric Research, February 13, 2006 (in person); Chris Landsea, Science and Operations Officer, National Hurricane Center, November 8, 2006 (in person); Michael Mann, Penn State University, November 28, 2006 (telephone); V. Ramaswamy, Geophysical Fluid Dynamics Laboratory, National Oceanic and Atmospheric Administration, October 6, 2006 (telephone); Robert and Joanne Simpson, October 12, 2006 (in person); Frédéric Vitart, European Centre for Medium-Range Weather Forecasts, July 27, 2006 (in person); Hugh Willoughby, Florida International University, May 16, 2006 (telephone).

**From Hypercanes to Hurricane Andrew:** Anthony Broccoli, Rutgers University, August 21, 2006 (in person); Kerry Emanuel, Massachusetts Institute of Technology, May 22, 2006 (in person), October 19, 2006 (telephone); Julian Heming, UK Met Office, July 28, 2006 (in person); Greg Holland, National Center for Atmospheric Research, February 13, 2006 (in person), August 7, 2006 (telephone); Thomas Karl, National Climatic Data Center, National Oceanic and Atmospheric Administration, January 31, 2006 (in person); Thomas Knutson, Geophysical Fluid Dynamics Laboratory, National Oceanic and Atmospheric Administration, August 21, 2006 (in person); Jerry Mahlman, National Center for Atmospheric Research, May 30, 2006 (telephone); Syukuro Manabe, Princeton University, August 21, 2006 (in person); Michael Mann, Penn State University, November 28, 2006 (telephone); Ruth McDonald, Hadley Centre for Climate Prediction and Research, UK Met Office, July 28, 2006 (in person); Richard Pasch, Senior Hurricane Specialist, National Hurricane Center, November 8, 2006 (in person); Robert and Joanne Simpson, October 12, 2006 (in person); Frédéric Vitart, European Centre for Medium-Range Weather Forecasts, July 27, 2006 (in person).

**INTERLUDE: Among the Forecasters:** None.

**The Luck of Florida:** Julian Heming, UK Met Office, July 28, 2006 (in person); Greg Holland, National Center for Atmospheric Research, August 7, 2006 (telephone); Ruth McDonald, Hadley Centre for Climate Prediction and Research, UK Met Office, July 28, 2006 (in person); Richard Pasch, Senior Hurricane Specialist, National Hurricane Center, November 8, 2006 (in person).

**Frictional Divergence:** Thomas Knutson, Geophysical Fluid Dynamics Laboratory, National Oceanic and Atmospheric Administration, August 21, 2006 (in person); Jim Kossin, University of Wisconsin, November 22, 2006 (telephone); Chris Landsea, Science and Operations Officer, National Hurricane Center, November 8, 2006 (in person); James McCarthy, Harvard University, December 12, 2005 (telephone); Kevin Trenberth, National Center for Atmospheric Research, January 3, 2006 (telephone), February 14, 2006 (in person), December 29, 2006 (telephone).

**Meet the Press:** Tom Delworth, Geophysical Fluid Dynamics Laboratory, National Oceanic and Atmospheric Administration, August 25, 2006 (telephone); Kerry Emanuel, Massachusetts Institute of Technology, January 4, 2006 (telephone), May 22, 2006 (in person), October 19, 2006 (telephone); Matthew Huber, Purdue University, September 5, 2006 (telephone); Frédéric Vitart, European Centre for Medium-Range Weather Forecasts, July 27, 2006 (in person).

**"The #$%^& Hit the Fan":** Richard Anthes, University Corporation for Atmospheric Research, February 14, 2006 (in person); Judith Curry, Georgia Institute of Technology, March 10, 2006 (in person), October 6, 2006 (telephone); Greg Holland, National Center for Atmospheric Research, February 13, 2006 (in person), August 7, 2006 (telephone); Evan Mills, Lawrence Berkeley National Laboratory, January 29, 2007 (telephone); Richard Pasch, Senior Hurricane Specialist, National Hurricane Center, November 8, 2006 (in person); Peter Webster, Georgia Institute of Technology, March 10, 2006 (in person), October 6, 2006 (telephone); Hugh Willoughby, Florida International University, May 16, 2006 (telephone).

**Resistance:** Judith Curry, Georgia Institute of Technology, March 10, 2006 (in person), October 6, 2006 (telephone); Richard Pasch, Senior Hurricane Specialist, National Hurricane Center, November 8, 2006 (in person); Hugh Willoughby, Florida International University, May 16, 2006 (telephone).

**"Consensus":** Anthony Broccoli, Rutgers University, August 21, 2006 (in person); Tom Delworth, Geophysical Fluid Dynamics Laboratory, National Oceanic and Atmospheric Administration, August 25, 2006 (telephone); Jana Goldman, National Oceanic and Atmospheric Administration, Public Affairs, January 13, 2007 (in person); Thomas Knutson, Geophysical Fluid Dynamics Laboratory, National Oceanic and Atmospheric Administration, August 21, 2006 (in person); Chris Landsea, Science and Operations Officer, National Hurricane Center, November 8, 2006 (in person); Ants Leetmaa, director, Geophysical Fluid Dynamics Laboratory, National Oceanic and Atmospheric Administration, October 18, 2006 (telephone); Jerry Mahlman, National Center for Atmospheric Research, May 30, 2006 (telephone); V. Ramaswamy, Geophysical Fluid Dynamics Laboratory, National Oceanic and Atmospheric Administration, October 6, 2006 (telephone); Ronald Stouffer, Geophysical Fluid Dynamics Laboratory, National Oceanic and Atmospheric Administration, October 6, 2006 (telephone).

**Preseason Warm-Ups:** Kerry Emanuel, Massachusetts Institute of Technology, May 22, 2006 (in person), October 19, 2006 (telephone); William Gray, Colorado State University, February 16, 2006 (in person); Greg Holland, National Center for Atmospheric Research, February 13, 2006 (in person), August 7, 2006 (telephone); Hugh Willoughby, Florida International University, May 16, 2006 (telephone).

**Where Are The Storms?** Doug Blackmon, *The Wall Street Journal,* January 17, 2007 (telephone); Judith Curry, Georgia Institute of Technology, March 10, 2006 (in person); Kerry Emanuel, Massachusetts Institute of Technology, October 19, 2006 (telephone); Chris Landsea, Science and Operations Officer, National Hurricane Center, November 8, 2006 (in person); Ants Leetmaa, director, Geophysical Fluid Dynamics Laboratory, National Oceanic and Atmospheric Administration, October 18, 2006 (telephone); Michael Mann, Pennsylvania State University, November 28, 2006 (telephone).

**Hurricane Climatology:** Tom Delworth, Geophysical Fluid Dynamics Laboratory, National Oceanic and Atmospheric Administration, August 25, 2006 (telephone); Kerry Emanuel, Massachusetts Institute of Technology, October 19, 2006 (telephone); Matthew Huber, Purdue University, September 5, 2006 (telephone); Jim Kossin, Cooperative Institute for Meteorological Satellite Studies, University of Wisconsin-Madison, November 22, 2006 (telephone); Kevin Trenberth, National Center for Atmospheric Research, January 3, 2006 (telephone), February 14, 2006 (in person), December 29, 2006 (telephone); Peter Webster, Georgia Institute of Technology, March 10, 2006 (in person).

**CONCLUSION: Home Again:** Kerry Emanuel, Massachusetts Institute of Technology, May 22, 2006 (in person); Greg Holland, National Center for Atmospheric Research, February 13, 2006 (in person), January 2, 2007 (telephone); Chris Landsea, Science and Operations Officer, National Hurricane Center, November 8, 2006 (in person); Roger Pielke, Jr., University of Colorado, January 5, 2007 (telephone); Evan Mills, Lawrence Berkeley National Laboratory, January 29, 2007 (telephone); Mark Schleifstein, New Orleans *Times Picayune,* November 24, 2006 (telephone); Joseph Suhayda, Louisiana State University (retired), August 29, 2006 (telephone); Robert Reece Twilley, Louisiana State University, August 24, 2006 (telephone); Hugh Willoughby, Florida International University, May 16, 2006 (telephone).

# INDEX